LOSING CONTROL

"Tom Warner maps out the moral conservative right wing that queer liberation activists, feminists, and human rights activists have been up against. His meticulous tracing out of the networks of social conservatism from individual religious activists to those currently in positions of power in the Harper government allows us to see both the strengths and weaknesses of our enemies. This book provides critical analysis of the right-wing but also powerful ammunition that we need in our struggles today and in the future if we are to prevent the social conservatives from seizing the agenda."

   —Gary Kinsman, Professor, Sociology, Laurentian University, and co-author of *The Canadian War on Queers: National Security as Sexual Regulation*

"*Losing Control* is a real contribution to our understanding of Canadian politics. We have precious little serious writing about evangelical Christian involvement in Canadian public life. This wide-ranging chronicle brings together a huge amount of material produced by religious conservatives across the country, covers an impressive array of issues, and presents the material accessibly in its historical and political context."

   —David Rayside, Professor, Political Science and Sexual Diversity Politics, University of Toronto

LOSING CONTROL

Canada's Social Conservatives
in the Age of Rights

TOM WARNER

BETWEEN THE LINES

Toronto

Losing Control: Canada's Social Conservatives in the Age of Rights

First published in 2010 by
Between the Lines
720 Bathurst Street, Suite #404
Toronto, Ontario   M5S 2R4
Canada
1-800-718-7201
www.btlbooks.com

LIBRARY AND ARCHIVES CANADA CATALOGUING IN PUBLICATION

Warner, Tom
     Losing control : Canada's social conservatives in the age of rights / Tom Warner.

Includes index.
ISBN 978-1-897071-41-0 (pbk.)

     1. Religious right–Canada. 2. Christianity and politics–
Canada. 3. Conservatism–Canada. 4. Canada–Politics and government–2006–. I. Title.

FC640.W37 2010   322'.10971   C2010-901026-4

Cover design and page design and preparation by
David Vereschagin, Quadrat Communications
Printed in Canada

Mixed Sources
Product group from well-managed forests, controlled sources and recycled wood or fiber
www.fsc.org Cert no. SW-COC-000952
© 1996 Forest Stewardship Council
FSC

Between the Lines gratefully acknowledges assistance for its publishing activities from the Canada Council for the Arts, the Ontario Arts Council, the Government of Ontario through the Ontario Book Publishers Tax Credit program and through the Ontario Book Initiative, and the Government of Canada through the Book Publishing Industry Development Program.

THE CANADA COUNCIL | LE CONSEIL DES ARTS
FOR THE ARTS | DU CANADA
SINCE 1957 | DEPUIS 1957

Canada

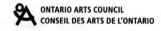

ONTARIO ARTS COUNCIL
CONSEIL DES ARTS DE L'ONTARIO

CONTENTS

PREFACE

Losing Control tells the story of a formidable Canadian countermovement, its leading organizations and spokespersons, and its advocacy. It does so by examining social conservatism as an angry and defiant insurgency, an anti-reform manifestation of evangelical Christians, both Protestant and Roman Catholic. It recounts their engagement in a religious counter-revolution to defeat the godless secularists, advocates of sexual immorality and moral relativism, politicians who promote immorality and anti-family policies, and unaccountable activist judges armed with the Charter. It explores how those insurgents dedicated themselves to organizing to regain control of the moral agenda.

I have opted to describe the members of this movement of evangelical Protestants and Roman Catholics as "social conservatives" rather than use the pejorative "fundamentalists" or "fundamentalist Christians." Evangelicalism, rather than fundamentalism, more accurately describes their religiosity, and most of the activists in the movement reject the "fundamentalist" label. I include "religious right" within "social conservative." Predominantly associated with and active in conservative political parties, social conservatives do not all fall within the right wing of the political spectrum. Many are purportedly otherwise liberal or progressive in their political views.

As a gay activist for nearly forty years, I have come to respect the social conservative movement as an impressively organized and dynamic opponent. At the same time I concede that I am not an impartial or dispassionate chronicler of the movement. The perspective I bring is that of a protagonist in most of the areas of advocacy and public policy that I examine here. The narrative in the following pages, I must also add, represents an unfinished history. Social conservatives remain active on a number of fronts, and they are determined to "take back Canada," to have the laws of God, as they interpret them, restored as the laws of the state. My chronicling of social conservatism in Canada is thus merely a snapshot of a particular point in time, and the events that have led up to it. The final chapter cannot yet be written.

Acknowledgements

I am grateful for the support that Between the Lines has shown for *Losing Control*, and in particular for the support of the editorial co-ordinators—Paul Eprile, Anjula Gogia, Amanda Crocker—who have helped to ensure its publication. I am especially grateful to Robert Clarke, whose skilful editing, insight, and thoughtful suggestions resulted in an immeasurably improved final manuscript. I also want to thank Ivan Dorsey, my partner of more than thirty years, for his cheerful support, long-suffering patience, and constant encouragement.

INTRODUCTION

Christianity is now under serious attack in
order to push it out of the public square so that
religious beliefs will cease to play a significant
role in determining public policy. . . . The final
struggle we are now undergoing is between
the believers and the non-believers. . . .
In the end, it will either be a Christian or an
anti-Christian victory.

– REAL Women of Canada, 2006

There was a time not so long ago when Judeo-Christian values were indisputably "Canadian values," when it was generally and willingly accepted that the role of the state was to promote and protect such values. This tendency was especially true in regard to the regulation of public morals. The state enacted and enforced criminal and other laws regarding contraception and abortion, sexual conduct, sexual expression, and family and spousal relationships. The public schools were mandated with indoctrinating children with Judeo-Christian moral values. The state's role was to nurture, strengthen, and resolutely protect marriage and family in accordance with Judeo-Christian beliefs and morality.

This role was a manifestation of the belief, expressed in the memorable words of the eighteenth-century conservative philosopher Edmund Burke, in the "indissoluble union" of church and state. That union, it was contended, was necessary to the preservation of a moral civil society founded on the supremacy of God and strict adherence to the natural or divine (God-given) law. The moral agenda of the state was to do everything in its power—within the sphere of laws, public policy and public institutions—to sustain the "universal moral order, ordained by God."

The staunchly Christian state that Canada once was began to change in the 1960s as the ties between church and state began to loosen and a new age of rights was born. That transformation was accelerated in the 1970s, with the advent of human rights legislation, and in the 1980s with the Canadian Charter of Rights and Freedoms. Secularism (the separation of church and state) and the assertion of the primacy of civil liberties and human rights became central to discourses within the public, political, and judicial realms. But the transformation was also propelled in no small way by the emergence of radical new social formations advocating for fundamental social and legal change, including the feminist, gay liberation, and same-sex equality rights movements. The result was the rise to dominance of new secular values that first challenged and then gradually replaced the old religious values and morality: respect for and tolerance of diversity, freedom from discrimination, reduction of harm to individuals and identifiable groups, and the moral imperative of human rights and equality of treatment for all persons. In the emergent age of rights, social conservatives found themselves losing control of the moral agenda.

The age of rights and these new movements pressing for fundamental change were deeply resented and fiercely resisted by a still substantial portion of Canadians, who formed their own countermovement of social conservatism—which would become one of the most prolific and visible movements of the last four decades in Canada.

ONE

Social Conservatism and the Canadian State

It is time to take Canada back. Back to
common law. Back to respecting the statutes
and laws written by democratically elected
representatives of the people. It is time to say
no to the tyranny of judges and demand that
traditional values of Canadians be respected. It
is time to demand freedom of religion and stop
the eradication of religious thought from our
land. It is time to demand equal treatment for
religious thinking people. It is time to demand a
return to decency, civility and morality.

– Charles McVety, 2001

In 2003, as leader of the Opposition—not yet prime minis-
ter—an earnest Stephen Harper delivered a glowing tribute to the modern social
conservative vision and its promise for Canadians. In "Rediscovering the Right
Agenda," an essay published in *Citizens' Centre Report*, Harper condemned "the
social agenda of the modern Left." He had no time for the left's "system of moral
relativism, moral neutrality and moral equivalence," which, he said, was "beginning to dominate its intellectual debate and public-policy objectives." The modern
left, Harper contended, stood for "moral nihilism—the rejection of any tradition
or convention of morality, a post-Marxism with deep resentments, even hatreds,

of the norms of free and democratic western civilization." In contrast, Harper argued, social conservatism stood for social order. It "stresses respect for custom and traditions (religious traditions above all), voluntary association, and personal self-restraint reinforced by moral and legal sanctions on behaviour."[1]

Harper, of course, does not stand alone in this expression of solidarity with the aspirations of social conservatism and harsh admonishment of the "modern Left." A few years earlier Brian Stiller, the former president of the Evangelical Fellowship of Canada (EFC), similarly complained, "After hundreds of years in which religious values have shaped our culture, all the way from the Supreme Court through the House of Commons to the writings of public education, Judeo-Christian beliefs are now systematically pushed to the side." For Stiller, this lamentable trend began in the 1960s when "life radically changed" because of, among other things, scientific discoveries, "an anti-establishment mood," and the protests by "gay liberation activists" and "radical students" who clamoured for their rights.[2]

Some two decades earlier another spokesperson Ken Campbell, a renowned fundamentalist Baptist minister, had weighed in on much the same theme. Instead of watching the world around them go to rack and ruin, Campbell suggested, modern evangelical Christians should work to become a "dominant minority." They could be a "prayer-meeting crowd ... whose radical Christian discipleship could bring our nations back from the brink and give us an extension of freedom and relative quietness and peace."[3]

The words of Harper, Stiller, and Campbell represent only a small sampling of the voices of a large aggregation of churches, advocacy groups, high-profile polemicists, think tanks, institutes, and politicians—the grassroots movement that is social conservatism. For decades this movement has tenaciously struggled against the entrenchment of secularism (the separation of church and state) and the godless "moral relativism" in Canada's laws, public policies, and social institutions. At the same time the adherents of the movement have sought, and continue to seek, to impose or reimpose their religious beliefs and moral values on the state and state institutions. In doing so they have delivered an angry, reactionary, and intolerant response to the revolution in social and sexual attitudes that has swept North American culture since the late 1960s. The foot soldiers of the movement have been millions of evangelical Protestants and conservative Roman Catholics. They have fought mightily in a concerted holy war, a righteous counter-revolution dedicated to protecting and in some instances restoring Judeo-Christian morality and values as the foundation of Canada's laws and public policy.

As a movement, social conservatism conjures up many different images. The Christian right, the religious right, fundamentalists, or God's warriors: these are a few of the terms that outsiders apply to the movement activists. Opponents denounce them as anti-gay and homophobic, as anti-feminist, anti-woman, and misogynist, as patriarchal, paternalistic, and authoritarian. They are condemned for being intolerant or, worse, as bigots and hate-mongers. Many more liberal-minded Canadians dismiss them as a fringe element of extreme holy-roller Christians not representative of mainstream or modern Canadian values, a force no longer worth worrying about. Other Canadians have a tendency to simply dismiss them as a loony and reactionary band of religious zealots. The members of the movement tend to portray themselves as pro-family and pro-life, as crusaders for family values, traditional marriage, and "Canadian values."

But beyond this plethora of terms, what really is social conservatism in Canada today? What motivates the leaders and the legions of devout followers who, in the memorable lyrics of that venerable Christian hymn, "Onward Christian Soldiers," are, with the cross of Jesus, marching as to war?

In Canada the shape of modern social conservatism has deep roots in the country's history of evolution from colony to nation-state and the fostering of a national identity. Canada, after all, was founded as a socially conservative country devoted to preserving British traditions and Christian values and morality. Those traditions and values were vigorously promoted by the state and state institutions in colonial times and for nearly one hundred years following Confederation in 1867. Until the mid-twentieth century, if not longer, Christianity and most particularly Christian values and morality were central to the national identity. As historian George Egerton observed, "Canadian Christendom" had developed by the time of the Second World War "to where the Christian religion exercised a privileged constitutional, legal and cultural role."[4]

A respect for tradition and authority and the preservation of social order had become explicit mandates of the state and state institutions. In the English-speaking parts of Canada, tradition and authority included maintaining and celebrating a British heritage, represented by the monarch as head of state, the enthusiastic embracing of British culture and customs, adoption of a form of parliamentary democracy based on the Westminster model, and, until well into the twentieth century, stalwart allegiance to the imperial British state and its vast colonial empire. But respect for tradition and authority also necessitated the assertion by the state and its citizens of a resolutely Christian identity and ethos as proud members of the "civilized" countries of the world that constituted Christendom.

In Quebec, tradition and authority, as well as national aspirations, were associated with orthodox Roman Catholicism and the preservation of the French language and culture. The sense of nationhood fostered within Quebec was not that of "Britishness" or fealty to the imperial state. It was the fostering and asserting of a resolutely Catholic and French identity that would ensure Quebec's survival within a predominantly English and increasingly Protestant North America.

The Roman Catholic Church also became a major force in the economic and social life of Quebec. It controlled the education system at all levels. It founded and operated countless social service agencies, including shelters and homes for orphans, the homeless and destitute, unwed mothers, prostitutes, and many others. The Church and its leaders promoted the economic interests and self-sufficiency of Quebec through such means as Catholic trade unions, farmers associations, and credit unions. In the 1930s and 1940s this project included the promotion of corporatism, a form of collaboration among various elites including the hierarchy of the Roman Catholic Church and the members of various other strata (employers, workers, farmers) for the betterment of themselves and the nation as a whole. The hope was that through corporatism a new social order could be established as an alternative to a host of perceived evils: liberalism, socialism, communism, secularism, and the general moral corruption of an increasingly godless society.[5]

Outside Quebec the state supported and encouraged a Protestant Christianity that, for most of the first one hundred years or so of the nation, gained a particular expression in evangelicalism. By the first years of the twentieth century the predominant manifestation of that evangelicalism was premised on Christianity as a social religion concerned fundamentally with the equality of human relations. Evangelical reformers preached social democracy based on co-operative action to achieve social and economic justice. They advocated for the introduction of social programs—welfare, unemployment insurance, old-age pensions, and labour laws supporting the formation and rights of trade unions. They were also instrumental in fostering what would become modern sociology and social work and in the establishment of the social welfare state. Many of these evangelical Protestant activists saw no contradiction between Christianity and socialism and were involved with socialist political groups. In contrast with the modern social conservative movement, these Christian activists were generally regarded in their day as progressive social reformers dedicated to preserving and promoting Christian values and ensuring the well-being and morality of the nation and its people.[6]

In Quebec orthodox Catholic activism remained a dominant force until the 1960s. But elsewhere in Canada Protestant evangelicalism suffered early on from splits and divisions. The reformers faced increasing dissension from more conservative elements that did not equate evangelism or Christianity with socialism, with the conservatives embracing a new fundamentalism that had been growing in popularity since the late nineteenth century. The tendency represented a turning back to the "old-time" religion based on traditional Protestant theology, with old-time values. In particular, it rested on the belief that the Bible is inerrant and that "the end of times" as prophesized in the book of Revelations was close at hand. Individuals, through conversion (being saved by Jesus) and by leading lives of holiness, and the world as a whole, through godly and moral government and public policy, must be prepared for the Judgment Day in order to receive eternal life in heaven after physical death.

By the 1920s fundamentalism had gained influence within the Baptist, Presbyterian, and other established churches. It had also prompted the growth of new denominations that included the Christian and Missionary Alliance, established in 1890, and the Pentecostal Assemblies of Canada, founded in 1919. The new evangelical groups and denominations built an evangelical infrastructure of Bible institutes and colleges that trained the ministers, missionaries, and activists of fundamentalism and ministries dedicated to the new evangelicalism (including the use of radio programming by charismatic and purportedly prophetic preachers). The rise of fundamentalism and the emergence of this evangelical infrastructure provided a solid foundation for building a modern social conservative movement that focused predominantly on moral issues and values—but was not much interested in social democracy and the equality of human beings or human relations.

The modern social conservative movement was, then, a grassroots reaction to revolutionary changes in moral and social values and the increasing secularism of the state—and especially to the weakening of the traditional Canadian identity rooted in Judeo-Christian morality. The activists of the movement became particularly concerned with perceived sexual immorality, especially homosexuality, and sexual activity outside of marriage. They became preoccupied with the effect that these conditions would have on the family and family values. They also decried what they considered the diminishing of the sanctity of life that would result from the decriminalization of abortion and the broader (although still not universal) access to abortion services. They were particularly alarmed at the rise of the movement to promote choice for women regarding abortion, the new women's movement more broadly, and the lesbian and gay liberation movement.

Roman Catholic evangelicalism

For a brief period during the 1960s, the worldwide Roman Catholic Church went through a period of modernization and liberalization ushered in by the Second Vatican Council. Convened in 1962 by Pope John XXIII and ending in 1965 during the papacy of Paul VI, Vatican II was conceived as a modernizing response to the challenges faced by the church in contemporary society: increasing secularism; the advances of science and technology; the need to hold mass in the vernacular of the congregation rather than always in Latin; and more pluralist communities and an increasing ecumenism emphasizing the community of Christian faiths of which the Catholic Church was the most prominent member. Vatican II issued a series of pronouncements that through subsequent interpretation challenged and changed much of what had been traditional Catholicism. In Canada the bishops of the Church embraced the decrees emanating from Vatican II, and the new spirit that they evidenced, with zeal. One result was the initiation of a program of modernization within the Roman Catholic Church similar to the push for change already underway in a number of the mainline Protestant churches.

Yet on matters of morality, especially in the realm of marriage, sexuality, and reproduction, the Roman Catholic Church changed very little. It continued to adhere to the traditional views on marriage and condemned contraception, abortion, and homosexuality as grave sins. Most notable of these was a 1968 encyclical issued by Paul VI. *Humanae Vitae* reasserted an orthodox, rigid, and dogmatic theological position on sexuality and reproduction. It upheld the institution of a God-ordained, lifelong monogamous marriage that had procreation as its fundamental purpose. It condemned "artificial" contraception and pronounced that "all direct abortion, even for therapeutic reasons," was to be "absolutely excluded" as a lawful (under the natural law of God) means of regulating the number of children to be conceived by a married couple. Contraception was permissible only when a married couple took "advantage of the natural cycles immanent in the reproductive system"—in other words, by engaging in marital intercourse only during the periods of infertility: the infamous and unreliable "rhythm method" of birth control that requires a couple to abstain from sex during a time determined by counting backwards a specific number of days from the anticipated start of menstruation. The encyclical also contained a call to "rulers of nations" to contribute to the "preservation of morals." Leaders were instructed: "Do not tolerate any legislation which would introduce into the family those practices which are opposed to the natural law of God."[7] *Humanae Vitae* provided papal authority for Roman Catholic lay activists and priests to take up their pro-life crusade against abortion. Roman Catholic women in particular responded to the cause by forming a series of organizations across the country in the following decades.

By the 1980s the term "evangelical Catholic" had entered the lexicon to describe the champions of a movement aimed at asserting Catholic orthodoxy and responding to modern society's emphasis on pluralism and religious freedom of choice. The evangelical Catholics emphatically rejected the belief that the Catholic Church was only one among many more or less equal Christian denominations. Evangelical Catholics, notes historian William L. Portier, "embrace Catholic identity voluntarily" in a pluralistic society. Unlike their parents or grandparents, they are Catholics by conscious choice and not simply as a consequence of family ties or ethnic origin. Some have converted to Catholicism. Like evangelical Protestants, they embrace the "evangelical ethos" that involves "shar[ing] the faith not only through preaching in church or faith-sharing groups in one's congregation but also through active forms of witness in 'public' spaces."[8]

With the enthusiastic support of the institutional church and Pope John Paul II, the movement of evangelical Catholicism had by the 1990s altered much of the face of the Catholic faithful. In style and form, they were more like evangelical Protestants than like their majority Catholic contemporaries or predecessors. They shared with their Protestant cohort the fundamentalist nature of the biblical doctrines of death, judgment, and heaven and hell and the belief that the Bible is inerrant. Evangelical Catholic youth thronged to the massive World Youth Day events initiated so successfully by Pope John Paul II, a pope who was "a hero to the 'new faithful.'" This new breed of young Catholics did not separate belief in and commitment to Catholic orthodoxy from the pursuit of social justice. They were interested in "Catholic-specific issues" and loved the pope. They were pro-life and believed that premarital sex was always wrong. They responded to the siren calls of John Paul II for "evangelizing culture" and for asserting the supremacy of the Church and its relationship to the secular state. Indeed, Portier contends, John Paul II "embodie[d] an evangelical Catholic ethos" and was "the premier Christian evangelist of our time."[9]

Yet not all within the Roman Catholic Church shared that view of John Paul II or celebrated the propagandizing role of World Youth Day events. Despite the growing movement of evangelical Catholics, there remained within the Church a vocal and persistent group of liberal or progressive Catholics who fought against the efforts to reassert orthodoxy and papal supremacy. Groups such as the Catholic Network for Women's Equality, founded in 1981, agitated for the ordination of women as priests and the inclusion of women in leadership and decision-making roles within the church. That organization also aimed to "raise consciousness about the nature and consequences of patriarchy in the church." Another dissident group, Catholics for Choice–Canada, founded in 1987, has advocated for access to family planning and reproductive choice, including, significantly, access to abortion services. It also proclaims to "support a person's right to dissent from institutional Church teaching, yet still remain a Catholic. The teaching of the institutional Church should assist us to inform our consciences, not dictate our moral decisions." Catholics for Choice–Canada was a signatory to a 2009 letter protesting *Humanae Vitae*. Published on the fortieth anniversary of the papal encyclical, the letter, notes Catholics for Choice, "prompted a swift reprimand from the Vatican."[10]

Then too, during the World Youth Day held in Toronto in 2002 a small group of Catholic youth and other dissidents within the church organized alternative youth day events. Challenge the Church criticized the "Pope-mania" surrounding World Youth Day, a prominent feature of which has been adulation of the pope in a manner reminiscent of the treatment of rock stars. Challenge the Church member Milton Chan stated that the group wanted to provide an alternative for Catholic youth to the "week-long Sunday school extravaganza," with its "top-down teaching style and the avoidance of substantial issues." As Challenge the Church noted in its message issued to the youthful attendees of World Youth Day, the Vatican and Toronto organizers of the event "won't tolerate any dissent … neither will they acquaint youth with the diversity of thought and spirituality within Catholic tradition."[11]

The more progressive Catholic groups, however, remained ostracized from and in confrontation with the Roman Catholic Church's archly conservative hierarchy committed to ruthlessly imposing orthodoxy and rigid conformity within worldwide Catholicism. Not surprisingly, Canada's Catholic Bishops took more dogmatic positions on social and moral issues, adhering strictly to official Vatican pronouncements. They also became more politically engaged on issues that they believed threatened traditional Christian morality or the state of the family. The Canadian Conference of Catholic Bishops and a provincial counterpart, Ontario Conference of Catholic Bishops, emerged in the 1980s as leading participants in the social conservative movement.

At the same time evangelical Catholic lay people expanded their activism beyond the opposition to abortion to encompass a broader range of issues. One of the most prominent of the new Catholic activist groups, the Catholic Civil Rights League (CCRL), was formed in 1985. It dedicated itself "to the faithful expression of the Magisterium [the authority of the church to teach religious doctrine] of the Catholic Church in public affairs for the renewal of Canada, and the benefit of the common good." The CCRL affirmed "the traditional family to be the only secure basis on which society can be built."[12] It actively opposed the gay rights and pro-choice movements and generally supported other social conservative causes, being especially active in fending off what it considered attacks on the Catholic Church's rights of religious freedom and expression.

Another leading social conservative group with roots in Catholic pro-life advocacy, REAL Women of Canada, was founded in 1983. The "REAL" stands for Realistic, Equal, Active for Life. The organization asserted itself as "Canada's alternative women's movement," promoting "women's rights, but not at the expense of human rights."[13] According to REAL Women founder Gwendolyn Landolt, the group was a response to the pro-life belief that the feminist groups leading the new women's movement did not speak for all women and especially did not speak for them. REAL Women was thus established as "another voice for women" who saw themselves as the "REAL women" of Canada.[14]

Since its inception, REAL Women has been particularly active in opposing legislation to prohibit sexual-orientation discrimination and to grant legal recognition to same-sex relationships. It has also been virulently pro-life, proudly proclaiming its reaffirmation of the family as "society's most important unit: we value equally every family member, born or unborn. Reproductive choice is exercised prior to conception, because conception and birth are consequences of choice; not choices in themselves." Along with other social conservative groups, REAL Women has also asserted pro-life positions on reproductive technologies, or assisted human reproduction, and supported a total ban on embryonic stem cell research.[15]

Protestant evangelicalism

By the 1970s evangelical Protestant denominations were soaring as their members took comfort in the clarity and certainty of their orthodox theology and religious fundamentalism. But as religion scholar John Stackhouse states, while these groups could "rejoice in their newly won status, they confronted a society that had become only more secular as they had become relatively more powerful." Still, they could take heart in a recognition that the various evangelical Protestant denominations had significant areas of agreement, and "shared beliefs and concerns."[16] Among other things, they were steadfastly opposed to abortion and opposed to human rights protections for gays and lesbians as well as to the legal recognition of same-sex relationships. While rooted in the traditional beliefs of orthodox Christianity, the modern social conservative movement was taking the righteous battle against sin and secularism to a whole new range of issues that simply would not have been imaginable in earlier times.

Pentecostal ministers, in particular, rose to prominence as leaders of the new social conservative advocacy groups that sprang up in North America during the 1970s and 1980s. One of those early leaders was Pentecostal minister David Mainse, who, for over four decades on his television program *100 Huntley Street*, would serve up a poisonous menu of evangelical commentary on a host of social issues, including, especially, opposition to the spread of homosexuality and the advancement of rights for gays and lesbians. In the early twenty-first century, Mainse also became a crusader in the war to preserve special legal status and privilege for traditional, heterosexual marriage and lobbied against the legal recognition of same-sex marriage.

Another Pentecostal minister, Hudson T. Hilsden, similarly emerged as a high-profile social conservative advocate in the 1970s. Pastor of the Scarborough Gospel Temple in Toronto, Hilsden later became chair of the Pentecostal Assemblies of Canada and president of the Evangelical Fellowship of Canada. He ultimately became a standard-bearer for the newly named "family values" movement, launching the Coalition for Family Values (CFV) in Ontario in the mid-1980s. Through that organization he led the opposition to extending legislated human rights protections to gays and lesbians. The CFV and another group that Hilsden chaired, the Interchurch Committee on Pornography, were active in the 1980s in attempts to have more stringent pornography laws enacted.

But by far the most prolific social conservative advocate emerging in the 1970s was Ken Campbell, originally from Milton, Ontario. Angered by the presence of gay and lesbian activists in the school attended by his children, Campbell, in 1974, formed the Halton Renaissance Association, which later became Renaissance International and then Renaissance Canada. The movement to establish legislated human rights for gays and lesbians and the decriminalization of abortion were, for Campbell, symbolic of the disastrous decline of the moral values of the nation. Resolved to save the nation's morals and indeed the nation itself, Renaissance International was devoted to "propagating the values and philosophy of our Judeo-Christian heritage, the foundation of a free and responsible society."[17] Campbell used his groups to wage battles against the establishment of legal rights for lesbians and gays and to oppose abortion through what he described as a "dynamic, pro-family liberation movement."[18] In doing so he cited the biblical proscriptions on homosexual behaviour and liberally conjured dark and threatening images of homosexuals as proselytizers and corrupters of children. Among his other activist pursuits were the founding of the anti-abortion group Choose Life Canada in 1985 and the presumptuously named Canada's Civilized Majority, renowned in the 1990s for its intemperate anti-gay advocacy.

During the 1980s other social conservatives also came to the realization that increased advocacy was needed to influence the moral agenda of the state and stem the tides of sin and secularism. The Evangelical Fellowship of Canada, founded in 1964, broadened its mission to include bringing a united voice of Christians to government at all levels with the intent to foster "moral direction in government decisions." Over the course of the next two decades, Stackhouse notes, the EFC came to represent the "mainstream" of Canadian evangelicalism.[19] Focus on the Family (Canada), was established in 1983 as the Canadian chapter of the U.S. organization Focus on the Family (founded in 1977 by Dr. James C. Dobson), arguably the most influential Christian advocacy group in that country today. Its advocacy was motivated by a "growing concern that the traditional family, founded on Judeo-Christian moral values, is coming under increasing pressure in modern society."[20]

In 1997 the Canada Family Action Coalition (CFAC) was established as a "grassroots citizens action group with a vision to see Judeo-Christian moral principles restored in Canada." Formed and led by Pentecostals, CFAC is committed to pursuing a range of issues: more stringent criminal laws against child pornography;

opposing legal abortions funded by government medical care plans; reform of the tax system to remove discrimination against parents who choose to stay at home to care for their children; increasing the age of consent for consensual sex; and elimination of waste and corruption in government. But CFAC has most actively opposed rights for lesbians and gays, railed against the Charter of Rights and Freedoms and "judge-made law," and exhorted the devout to "take back Canada." Like other social conservative groups, it takes a stridently pro-life position on abortion: "We believe in the inherent dignity of human life, from conception to natural death."[21]

The clash of social movements

The rise of the modern social conservative movement was a response—a counter-revolution—to other social and political forces that since the 1960s have been reshaping the nature of the state, society, and culture. The movement is the manifestation of collective actors who, in the words of Miriam Smith, "participate in the mobilization of bias through the ways in which they make choices about values, ideologies, and strategies."[22] As a movement it seeks to "reinforce dominant ideologies and beliefs": that is, that Judeo-Christian values are "Canadian values" and that the role of the state is to promote and protect such values, including those related to the regulation of morality, to sexuality and relationships, and to the strengthening and nurturing of the traditional marriage and traditional family in accordance with Judeo-Christian beliefs.

The counter-revolutionary nature of modern social conservatism distinguishes it from its predecessors, such as Catholic Action and social gospel, which were, in their time, viewed as reformist and progressive. In the past, bringing one's religious faith and moral values to crusades to strengthen and preserve Canadian values, marriage, and the family was saluted as positively advancing the welfare of individuals and of society as a whole. Doing so in today's social milieu is perceived—rightfully—as a manifestation of a reactionary, anti-reform movement. Modern social conservatism, in contrast with its predecessor movement, is the militant and angry reaction to the true reform movements of our era: secularism, feminism, and the women's movement, lesbian and gay liberation and the movement for gay rights, and the movement to assert the primacy of human rights and equality of treatment. These modern reform movements have sought, among other objectives, to smash the alliance of church and state on matters of gender relationships, sexuality, morality, family, and social structures. They have challenged the historic relationships between church and state, between private religious belief and religious moral values and the moral agenda of the state. The advocates of the reform movements joined in collective action to overthrow what had been the entrenched status quo. They organized against the sexism, misogyny, homophobia, and heterosexism that were foundational to both Judeo-Christianity and Canada as a Christian state. They protested inequality and discrimination and fought against social and sexual oppression and repression.

These new social movements also challenged the distinction between public and private. They brought issues that were once defined as private into the public realm—issues such as gender-based domestic abuse and sexual assault, and sexuality and sexual expression. They asserted that the private realm was permeated with inequality and a lack of power on the part of women and of gays and lesbians. They promoted and celebrated a sense of identity and purpose that was radically different from and deliberately in confrontation with the old Canadian notions of citizenship and identity founded on Judeo-Christian morality and values. They were movements of cultural and sexual revolution that sought to reform and reshape the state and state institutions. They were quite unlike any reform movements that had appeared in the past, and many Canadians, particularly evangelical Christians, reacted to their arrival with shock, resentment, and considerable alarm.

The new women's movement in particular was not cast in the rather staid and conservative mould of the first wave of women's advocates, the suffragists of the early twentieth century. Indeed, the suffrage movement, like its other contemporaries, the temperance movement, social purity crusade, and social gospel, had not sought the radical social change so militantly advanced by the second-wave feminists. Suffragists had fought for and succeeded in winning the right of women to vote but did not advocate for the equality of women with men socially and economically. They did not object to the state regulating sexuality and morality in accordance with Judeo-Christian beliefs. It was, as Smith notes, a movement based on "maternal feminism" that emphasized the family responsibilities of women that were deemed to be essential for the development and maintenance of the Canadian nation. They supported the view that the family was the foundation of society and believed that giving women the right to vote would enhance the impact of traditional family values on politics and public policy. They did not favour women entering the workforce.[23]

The roots of the new feminist movement were planted with the formation of groups such as the Women's Peace Movement, Congress of Canadian Women, and Voice of Women. But the new women's movement truly blossomed in the late 1960s with the formation of a number of groups, including the Vancouver Women's Caucus, founded in 1968, and, over the next couple of years, the Montreal Women's Liberation Movement, Front de libération des femmes du Québec, Toronto Women's Liberation Movement, and Toronto New Feminists.

In 1970 the cross-country Abortion Caravan brought massive attention to women's issues, and especially the fight over the limited decriminalization of abortion resulting from Criminal Code amendments in 1969. By 1974 the Canadian Association for Repeal of the Abortion Law (CARAL) was formed as Canada's national abortion rights advocacy group. These actions, together with the trials and defence of Dr. Henry Morgentaler arising from criminal charges for performing safe abortions outside of hospitals, made a woman's right to choose a safe abortion a fiercely contested political and social issue.

By the mid-1970s women's advocacy groups and women's centres had sprung up in most major communities in Canada. The National Action Committee on the Status of Women (NAC), formed in 1971, emerged as an effective national advocacy group dedicated to improving the legal and social status of women. Its members worked massively in support of legal and social equality for women and fought for access to birth control and abortion services and for child-care services, and organized around many other issues. The feminists sought the elimination of sexism within the laws and the legal system, in the organization of society, in the perception and status of women within and across all facets of social, professional, and labour organizations, and within educational and cultural institutions. They sought legal equality in areas such as family law (pension rights for women, rights to matrimonial assets, financial support following the breakup of a common-law spousal relationship) and employment (removal of laws and policies that prevented women from being employed or entering professions, pay equity with men, maternity leave provisions).

Drawing on a feminist analysis and agenda, women organized to overthrow the patriarchy and liberate themselves from the oppression of male supremacy and misogyny promoted and perpetuated by the church and the state. They rejected the view that women's principal roles were as mothers and wives, subservient and obedient to and dependent upon the men (fathers, husbands, ministers and priests, doctors, and other so-called authority figures) who dominated and controlled their lives. Feminists celebrated their sexuality and the right to freely express it. They boldly proclaimed the right of women to control their own bodies, their sexuality and fertility, their sexual relationships. They mounted campaigns against domestic abuse and sexual violence against and exploitation of women. They established rape crisis centres, shelters for battered women, women's centres, and day-care services.

Lesbian and gay liberation also burst onto the scene as another movement challenging the old Christian Canada. It began in Canada in 1965 with the formation in Vancouver of the Association for Social Knowledge, a group that advocated for reform of the Criminal Code. It gained strength in 1969 with the founding of the University of Toronto Homophile Association—with its declaration that "Gay is Good" and its call on gays to fight back publicly against bigotry and discrimination. Other groups followed, such as the Front de libération du Québec in Montreal

(1970), Vancouver Gay Liberation Front (1971), Saskatoon Gay Action, Toronto Gay Action, and the Gay Alliance Toward Equality (GATE) in Vancouver (all in 1971). In August 1971, twelve lesbian and gay groups from across Canada gathered on Parliament Hill to stage the first-ever gay rights demonstration. They demanded an end to discrimination in employment and housing and the repeal or reform of various sections of the Criminal Code that, reflecting Christian moral values, criminalized consenting sexual activity. By 1975 a full-fledged national movement with a well-defined advocacy agenda of legislative and social change was launched with the formation of the National Gay Rights Coalition. Similar coalitions or campaigns were organized in several provinces to challenge provincial laws and policies that discriminated or permitted discrimination against gay and lesbians.[24]

Nothing like the lesbian and gay liberation movement had ever existed before. It rejected the historic and mainstream views that homosexuality was sinful, sick, or criminal. Gay liberationists asserted and exuberantly celebrated homosexuality as a natural and healthy alternative sexual orientation. They called on gays and lesbians to come out of the closet, to live their lives proudly and publicly, and to engage in their sexuality without loathing, fear, or guilt. Gay rights groups advanced an agenda to change laws, attitudes, and policies, developing an analysis of homophobia—the fear and hatred of homosexuality—that included a strong condemnation of anti-homosexual religious beliefs as a root cause of harassment, discrimination, and social oppression. They asserted that gays and lesbians were an identifiable minority that had historically experienced unjust discrimination and repression. Like modern feminism, the attainment of the movement's goals required a transformation of Christian Canada at the legal and social levels. The movement pitted lesbian and gay liberationists and the promotion of gay rights against the powerful and increasingly agitated forces of social conservatism.

Indeed, while social conservatives were awakening to the need to organize to counteract the specific threats that they saw being presented by feminism and gay liberation, they were also seeing these new movements as alarming manifestations of a broader and more pervasive anti-religiosity expressed in the form of secular humanism. They fretted about the evils of secular humanism and the threat it posed to religious freedom, the old social order, and the Christian state. Brian Stiller emphatically expressed modern social conservatism's pathological antipathy towards secular humanism and all that it stands for:

> The old assumption that Canada is centred around a biblical view of life no longer reflects today's realities. Secularism, the ruling ideology, attempts to remove the influence of belief in a personal God from public life. Religion becomes only that which is believed and practiced in the

private cloisters of churches or in personal life.[25]

Similarly, Campbell condemned secularism as satanic and equated "our secular society" with "our 'Sodom society'" that is "ripe for God's judgment." Just as God had destroyed the sinful city of Sodom and Gomorrah in ancient times, He was poised to do the same to the modern era's atheistic secular society because of its wickedness and moral decay. The Christian church, Campbell asserted, must work towards rescuing the secular state by saving the souls of thousands of individuals who believe and obey the gospel; this was declared a "soulwinning strategy."[26]

The abhorrence and condemnation of secular humanism are hardly surprising. Secular humanism is a philosophy—a way of thinking and living—engendered in response and opposition to the religious humanism that historically dominated worldwide Christendom. According to the Council for Secular Humanism, North America's leading organization for non-religious people, secular humanism rejects supernatural and authoritarian beliefs and affirms that people must take responsibility for their own lives and the communities in which they live. Secular humanism, the Council states, emphasizes reason and scientific inquiry, individual freedom and responsibility, human values and compassion, and the need for tolerance and co-operation.[27] Few of these attributes or qualities are readily found within social conservatism's ethos, cemented as it is by the supremacy of God and the inerrancy of the Bible.

Secular humanism criticizes and confronts many fundamental beliefs propagated by social conservatives. It subscribes to the separation of church and state. "Clerical authorities should not be permitted to legislate their own parochial views—whether moral, philosophical, political, educational, or social—for the rest of society," states the "Secular Humanist Declaration."[28] Compulsory religious oaths and prayers in public institutions, secular humanists believe, violate the principle of separation of church and state. Secular humanists also oppose the imposition of religious creed on young people before they are able to give consent. They contend that it is the duty of public education to provide "moral education in the schools that is designed to develop an appreciation for moral virtues, intelligence, and the building of character" rather than religious values and beliefs. Secular humanists emphatically support evolution of the species and deplore efforts requiring that "creationist theory be taught to students and requiring that it be included in biology textbooks." They reject the idea that God can save or redeem sinners and the literal interpretation of the Bible or other sacred texts.

The rise of these other social movements and the entrenchment of secular humanism occurred symbiotically with the enactment and expansion of human rights laws in the last decades of the twentieth century, leading to the crafting and advancing of a new moral agenda. That agenda was based on ensuring the human rights and equality of treatment of all persons, rather than on coerced conformity with religious morality. It represented an epochal altering of the relationship between church and state. It began with the United Nations Universal Declaration of Human Rights in 1948, to which Canada was a signatory. But the embracing of individual human rights and the articulation of them in Canada's laws accelerated from the 1960s onwards, beginning with the enactment of the Canadian Bill of Rights in 1960. Introduced by the Progressive Conservative government of John Diefenbaker, the Bill of Rights was the first effort by the Parliament of Canada to set out in law basic rights of equality and freedom.

Even more so than the Bill of Rights, the establishment of human rights laws, first by provincial legislatures and then at the federal level of government throughout the 1960s and 1970s, prohibited discrimination in such areas as employment, housing, and access to services. These laws had a profound impact, providing the means by which complaints of discrimination could be investigated and adjudicated by agencies of the state. While the grounds on which discrimination was unlawful were initially quite limited, such as religion or race, by the 1980s they were being expanded as a result of the advocacy of women's organizations and gay rights groups to include first sex and then sexual orientation.

As early as 1975 the Gay Alliance Toward Equality, Toronto, had expressed the human rights objective in a leaflet setting out its program of political action:

> The Gay Alliance Toward Equality seeks equality and liberation for gay people. We demand the extension to gays of all the rights now enjoyed by the straight world. To reach this goal, we must first concentrate on political change, for this alone will give gays a secure base from which to struggle for their liberation....
>
> In addition to the repeal of discriminatory laws, we demand the enactment of protective measures to assure civil rights for gays. The first step is to press for the inclusion of the term 'sexual orientation' among the general categories enumerated in the Ontario Human Rights Code and the Canadian Bill of Rights.[29]

By that means, firing or refusing to hire or promote a gay or lesbian person would be illegal, as would be refusing to rent an apartment to gays and lesbians or evicting them from one. So too would be refusing service to them in restaurants, stores, bars, and other commercial establishments, simply because they were homosexual. All of these discriminatory actions and many more were still everyday occurrences for gays and lesbians in the Canada of the 1970s. The activists in the gay liberation groups were determined to put an end to that unacceptable state by forcing the legislatures to amend their human rights laws.

To do so, they asserted that gays and lesbians were a legitimate minority group that like other minorities faced discrimination and harassment in myriad ways. They declared that having a homosexual sexual orientation was a human right. They demanded the right of gays and lesbians to fully express their sexual orientation, to be visible and public in all aspects of their lives, and to openly and proudly proclaim their sexual orientation without fear and reprisal.

The advancement of human rights culminated with the patriation of the Canadian Constitution in 1982, which included the Canadian Charter of Rights and Freedoms. Section 15 of the Charter—the equality rights section—came into effect in April 1985. As a result, equality rights—the right to be free from discrimination and harassment as well as from oppression by the state and state institutions—became both constitutionally enshrined and determinants of a new morality that characterized the Canadian identity, eventually eclipsing the old biblically dictated Judeo-Christian morality.

The adoption of the new human laws and the Charter with constitutional status represented a significant departure from the traditions and values inherited from Great Britain and that had been embraced and cherished by Canada since its inception. The notion of constitutional rights establishing the equality of all persons—an idea imported from France and the United States—was foreign to the British tradition. Indeed, the adoption of the human rights laws and the Charter marked one of the more visible ways in which Canada became not only less British but also demonstrably more socially liberal and more secular. The concern expressed by social conservatives was that enactment of these laws would shatter the consensus that had held for most of Canada's history, more or less without question: that Canada was a Christian nation founded on Christian values.

The Charter in particular had a colossal impact on the nature of Canada's jurisprudence and political culture in ways that both angered and disappointed social conservatives. The Charter was the constitutional embodiment of a new morality based on equality and the just treatment of all persons—rather than a morality predicated on religious dogma and dictates. It was also symbolic of a new national identity that was emerging for Canadians, an identity inextricably linked with the ringing principles enunciated in it, such as a person's right to life, liberty, and security. More and more, an increasing majority of Canadians and the country's judicial and political institutions would embrace, and expect the laws and public policy to reflect, the new moral dictate of the Charter: "Every individual is equal before and under the law and has the right to the equal protection and equal benefit of the law without discrimination."

Once the equality guarantees set out in section 15 of the Charter came into force in 1985, as Egerton states:

> The dominant themes entail[ed] the privatization of religion and its per-ipheralization in public life, with its former status, privileges and rights being diminished or removed, as Canadian jurisprudence came to incor-porate many features of American constitutional theories of "strict sep-aration" of church and state and which marked US jurisprudence in the 1960s and 1970s, while Canadian society increasingly resembled the secularized cultures of Europe.[30]

As the Chief Justice of the Supreme Court of Canada, Beverly McLachlin, also noted, the post–Second World War period in Canada can be properly called the "age of rights." As well as the specific enactment of laws and constitutional provi-sions, the age of rights was notable for what McLachlin describes as the evolu-tion of

> the idea that there exist fundamental norms of justice so basic that they form part of the legal structure of governance and must be upheld by the courts, whether or not they find expression in constitutional texts. And the idea is an important one, going to the core of just governance and how we define the respective roles of Parliament, the executive and the judiciary.

The question of whether judges "have the right to invoke fundamental norms to trump written laws," as a result, has become a Canadian preoccupation. Critics of such evolution, of course, as McLachlin notes, have "argued that the invocation of unwritten norms cloaks unelected and unaccountable judges with illegitimate power and runs afoul of the theory of parliamentary supremacy." But, as she also points out, "The idea of unwritten constitutional principles is *not* new and should not be seen as a rejection of the constitutional heritage" of Canada.[31]

The use by unaccountable or "activist" judges of fundamental but unwritten principles to strike down or change laws has been one of the loud and persistent complaints of social conservatives. They have argued that such principles and their exercise are contrary to natural law, the divine or eternal law of God. For McLachlin, however, there is no conflict between natural law, as understood in the modern legal and judicial contexts, and these unwritten principles. Rather, she contends:

The contemporary concept of unwritten constitutional principles can be seen as a modern reincarnation of the ancient doctrines of natural law. Like those conceptions of justice, the identification of these principles seems to presuppose the existence of some kind of natural order. Unlike them, however, it does not fasten on theology as the source of the unwritten principles that transcend the exercise of state power. It is derived from the history, values and culture of the nation, viewed in its constitutional context.[32]

Social conservatives have as a result targeted McLachlin as one of the most egregious of the unaccountable and activist judges whom they charge with imposing secularism and moral relativism as the public policy on a nation originally founded on the supremacy of God and Judeo-Christian values.

Social conservative fundamentals: church, faith, family, government

By the end of the twentieth century, social conservatives increasingly saw themselves as threatened and dispossessed. They lamented a loss of power, influence, and status, especially within the political and judicial realms, as their protagonists appeared to gain the ascendancy. They faced the grim reality that the issues that constituted the old moral agenda were radically changing. Social reformers were no longer the proudly devout Christians who brought their religious faith and moral values to crusades designed to strengthen and preserve Canadian values, marriage, and family. The evangelical Christians who had formed such an activist and influential cadre of the earlier reform movements now had to adjust to being thrust into a very different and quite unfamiliar role. Rather than being in the vanguard of reform, they were increasingly cast as an anti-reform movement, the counter-revolution to the social and sexual revolution that was sweeping through Canada and other countries. Even worse, they would be more and more dismissed as bigots and homophobes, as the purveyors of intolerance and hatred.

Still, in the new Canada, with its new moral agenda of rights and equality of treatment, Canada's social conservative advocacy groups clung with determination to the belief that the state is divinely constituted and must be godly. They continued to champion the notion that the state must reflect and uphold traditional values, including most particularly their religious and moral values, in laws and in public policy. They argued that the secular state must not reject or question divine law. In the words of Bruce Clemenger, president of the Evangelical Fellowship of

Canada: "In a society that understands institutions like the State and family to be human constructions, it is crucial to reflect on the divine intent for the State." As Clemenger asserted, the state is "created and designed by God to serve God in the fulfillment of its given task."[33]

An even more radical and disturbing blueprint for Canada was an August 2002 declaration signed by the leaders of Canada's Civilized Majority, Prayer Canada, and the Christian Heritage Party of Canada. Grandiosely called a "New Magna Carta for Canada," it proclaimed that the nation "watches with alarm as a militant Secularist minority (about 12 per cent) blatantly and unconstitutionally abuses the powers of our courts, media, public education and government to force its atheistic world-view upon us and our children—and even compels us to bear the heavy financial burden of this subversion of our nation and its culture!" It declared: "Any law or enactment from any legislature or council, and any judgement or ruling from any court or tribunal, if not in conformity to the principles laid down by God in Scripture, is *ipso facto* Unconstitutional." It contended, with breathtaking certainty, "any public official whose acts are contrary to that [Christian] faith acts *ultra vires* and in violation of their oath of fealty to the Crown [as Defender of the Faith], and must be removed from office."[34]

Modern social conservatives are thus left striving desperately to turn back the clock to times when the teachings of the churches were unapologetically reflected in public policy and public places. They are angry and resentful over the declining influence of the Christian religion on laws and state policies, and about their concomitant loss of both status and recognition as primary influencers of the moral agenda and public policy. A 2007 article by Kyle Janzten in a social conservative on-line publication, *C2C: Canada's Journal of Ideas*, clearly expressed that sentiment: "Church and church leaders in our country have lost political power, social status, moral authority, legal privileges, financial support, and (in general) the ear of the state. It is in this sense that Canada and other western countries are no longer Christian nations." In a 2003 column in the *Globe and Mail* Bishop Frederick B. Henry of the Roman Catholic Archdiocese of Calgary conveyed the same line of thought: "The mantra of 'separation of church and state' in our Canadian context is simply a crass secularist attempt to discount and marginalize persons with religious faith."[35] A year earlier Darrel Reid, president of Focus on the Family (Canada), had lamented:

I'm left asking myself if there is still room in Canada's public square for people of faith? True democracy cannot function without a vigorous debate about morality and first principles. But what we have seen is an increasingly nasty disregard for people of faith by those who view transcendence as an embarrassment—and maybe even dangerous....

Canadians of faith sense something essential is being drained from our national psyche.... I think it would be great to see social conservatives from all of our parties and traditions begin to reinsert their most deeply held convictions into our nation's political discourse.[36]

For Brian Rushfeldt, executive director of the Canada Family Action Coalition, a key problem was how governments were promoting the "negative moral and financial consequences of social liberalism." Rushfeldt deplored how "the family—God's fundamental institution for society—is labelled destructive by feminists, discriminatory by homosexuals, outdated and unnecessary by liberals." He encouraged people of faith to defend "the biblical view of humanity" and to become "an elected official or other public servant in your community and influence decision-making."[37]

For its part, the Roman Catholic Church commanded Catholics involved in the political process not to espouse "ethical pluralism." In a Doctrinal Note issued by the Congregation for the Doctrine of the Faith in 2002, the Church declared, "A well-formed Christian conscience does not permit one to vote for a political program or an individual law which contradicts the fundamental contents of faith and morals."[38] True to its mandate to faithfully uphold the teachings of the church, the Catholic Civil Rights League espoused similar views. "It is quite wrong to claim, as many now do, that religious conviction cannot form the basis for sound public policy, that religious beliefs cannot be permitted to influence political activity or shape legislation, or that principles of pluralism or democracy preclude the public expression of religious beliefs," CCRL declared in its publication "The Church and Politics."[39] In another position paper CCRL expounded on the obligation of the faithful to follow the laws of God when those conflict with the laws of the state:

Even when public authority becomes oppressive, Catholics are bound to obey the laws of the state *insofar as they do not conflict with divine law*. But no parliament, no legislature and no court has the authority to set aside the commandments of God, nor to command obedience to laws and regulations that are contrary to the natural moral law. When this abuse of authority occurs in a democracy, Catholics must take all legal and political steps necessary to defend ourselves and our fellow citizens, and may, in addition, resort to conscientious objection, civil disobedience, non-co-operation and other forms of non-violent resistance in accordance with the natural moral law and the Gospel.[40]

The principal mission of Canada's leading social conservative groups, then, is the commitment to restore traditional ideals and basic Christian moral principles, as well as to influence the role of government, all for the sake of ensuring social order and the welfare of the country. For social conservatives, social order, stability, and cohesion are predicated on respect for and preservation of traditional values and beliefs—which means, simply, asserting in laws and public policy the paramount importance of traditional Judeo-Christian constructs of family, marriage, morality, and sexuality and the shared role and responsibility of both the church and the state in promoting and protecting these approaches to life. They see ever-increasing secularism, the continuing liberalization of social attitudes, especially in regard to moral issues, and the seemingly unbridled expansion of human rights to embrace protections for moral transgressors as evidence of the need to wage with vigour and resolve their godly campaign to restore Canada as a resolutely Christian nation—and in doing so, to regain control of the moral agenda.

Through the lens of twenty-first-century Canadian values and identity we might be tempted to dismiss today's social conservatives as peculiarities, as devotees of an extreme religiosity more in tune with a large and powerful segment of the more deeply religious and politically conservative United States. Indeed, social conservatives are seemingly out of step with the values of tolerance, equality, and respect for and accommodation of difference and diversity that have come to characterize modern Canada. That perception derives in no small measure from the prevailing tendency of social conservatism to be influenced and informed by the centuries-old doctrines of orthodox or evangelical Christianity. This condition includes the particular interpretations of the Bible as the actual word of God—and of God as an omnipotent and omnipresent supernatural "Father" who is unchangeable, vengeful, autocratic, and patriarchal and to whom all observers must be obsequiously and unquestioningly obedient, if not downright servile.

But social conservatives also believe fervently in tradition and in Canada's "heritage"—ethnic and religious—which includes most especially the traditional family and traditional values and morality rooted unwaveringly in the precepts of Judeo-Christianity. They possess a strong desire to preserve and strengthen that tradition in modern society through civil and criminal law, state regulation, public policies, and stern and repressive social and cultural mores. The movement they created would become one of the most prolific and resilient pressure groups of the last four decades in Canada.

TWO

The Right to Life and the Right to Choice

Canadians, including politicians, go about
their business while the genocide of the past
four decades continues unabated. It is time for
politicians to make the protection of human life
from the moment of conception part of their
parliamentary business.

– Editorial, *The Interim*, April 21, 2009

Over forty years after the decriminalization of "therapeutic abortions" performed in Canadian hospitals, the opposition to abortion remains volatile. This in itself is somewhat astonishing given that opinion polls show that the majority of Canadians support the right of a woman to have an abortion, either in all circumstances or under certain circumstances. Support for legally prohibiting abortions in all circumstances—the radical position of the social conservative "pro-life" movement—remains at extremely low levels in the polls (only 5 five per cent, according to a 2008 survey).[1]

Yet despite the overwhelmingly pro-choice attitude of Canadians—with most Canadians' minds firmly made up about abortion and showing no signs of change—the debate continues to rage. Confrontations flare up periodically in the streets, the courtrooms, and the legislatures of the nation. Indeed, the pro-life movement today shows no signs of diminishment or atrophy, and in some ways it is being revitalized and renewed. As the Evangelical Fellowship of Canada reminded its followers, "Abortion remains a critical and controversial moral issue that must be addressed by Canadian lawmakers and citizens alike."[2]

Since the early 1970s, evangelical Protestants and Roman Catholics have been the dominant forces in the "pro-life movement." For them, life begins at conception and abortion is always wrong. They view the fetus, from the point of conception, as being an "unborn person." They condemn "abortionists" as murderers of babies and children; they refer to abortion clinics as "abortuaries." They label all those who support abortion as being "anti-life" or "pro-death."

The arguments against abortion have been as unequivocal as they have been provocative and apocalyptic. The social conservatives of this ilk accuse Canada of not valuing life. They denounce as the purveyors of death and despair the movement that seeks to ensure choice for women and those who provide abortion services. They portray a woman who becomes pregnant as no longer having any rights, as in effect being without choice. She no longer has any say over decisions made about her body, her health, or her life. According to the pro-life position, a pregnant woman, from the point of conception, becomes a mere vessel for the incubation and nurturing of the fetus. Her only obligation from that point on is to ensure that she gives birth to her child.

This social conservative advocacy, executed with a missionary zeal that brooks no opposition, has ensured that abortion remains on the country's political agenda. Such advocacy, it seems, has a shockingly disproportionate support among Canada's legislators, and it has made hotly contested issues out of the performance of abortions in clinics outside of hospitals, access to abortion services, and medicare coverage for abortions. The unrelenting, moralistic social conservative assault on abortion has aroused intense passions on both sides of the issue.

Abortion in Canada: from the early years to Trudeau

As with most other issues championed by social conservatism, the movement presents its opposition to abortion and defence of the right to life of the fetus as being rooted in fundamental and historic Canadian moral values. There is some truth to that claim. Canada's former law on abortion was based on the law in Great Britain and was intricately intertwined with Judeo-Christian religious beliefs. In its earliest forms, the British law captured the concept of "quickening," derived from the Christian church's concern about the earliest point at which a fetus could be considered to be human in the sense that it could demonstrate that it had life. But in this formulation the sanctity of life did not arise at the moment of conception, as the modern pro-life groups would have us believe; it appeared at some point after conception. The consensus down through many centuries was that life began, and the sanctity of life took hold, at the first time the infant in the womb moved, when it "quickened." Only at that moment was the fetus infused with a soul. Early on, abortion was also a concern of the church and not the state; performing an abortion on a fetus past the point of quickening was a grave sin, a moral offence, but not a crime.

This long-held concept of life beginning at the point of "quickening" is starkly at odds with the contemporary social conservative belief that life begins at conception, when a sperm fertilizes an egg cell, thus creating a new cell, a zygote that evolves to then form an embryo. Even the fetus, which evolves from the embryo at about eight weeks following fertilization, is not viable—cannot survive outside the womb—until after about twenty weeks of gestation. Nor is the contemporary articulation of the pro-life advocates consistent with what the Bible has to say about abortion or the fetus. For the Bible does not address either of those subjects directly. It makes no mention of abortion or the fetus. Many passages speak variously of "baby," "infant," or "child," but whether such terms are used in ways that extend to the "unborn" and imply humanity or personhood to the "unborn" is open to interpretation. This subject has been extensively debated—inconclusively—by theologians around the world.

The contention of some Christians that the Bible prohibits abortion under any circumstances is also based on the general prohibition against killing another person, promulgated most memorably in the Commandment "Thou shalt not kill." To apply that Commandment to the "unborn" requires that not only the fetus but also the cellular zygote and embryo be granted life as equated with humanity and personhood and, thereby, also a right to life. But as for God's and the Bible's prohibition on killing, anyone who reads the Bible will soon discover that it is replete with instances in which God either ordered or permitted the killing of people, often en masse, and including children. A good example of divine homicide—recounted without the slightest hint of irony by fervent evangelicals—is the destruction of Sodom and Gomorrah, allegedly because of the homosexual acts of residents of the two cities. God, in blazing, righteous anger and with fearsome retribution, purportedly destroyed everything in sight—men, women, and children. The same Christian ideologues who so ardently assert and defend the right of the "unborn child" to life from the point of conception, in speaking of the tale of Sodom and Gomorrah, express no remorse for or condemnation of God's murder of the born there. As with many other matters, the professed divine and biblical proscriptions against killing are highly selective and open to considerable interpretation.

As for the state's interest in the matter, only relatively recent in history did abortion become a criminal offence, something requiring regulation by criminal law. The first law criminalizing abortion was enacted in Great Britain in 1803. It not only made performing abortions after quickening punishable by death, but also, significantly, for the first time criminalized an abortion performed prior to quickening. A new law in 1837 mercifully eliminated the death penalty for performing an abortion. But the law also no longer distinguished between pre- and post-quickening abortions—all were treated in the same way. In 1861 British law was relaxed somewhat when the punishment for performing an abortion was reduced to three years' imprisonment. Yet, disturbingly because of the dire consequences for women, the new law also explicitly criminalized a pregnant woman who attempted to obtain or induce a miscarriage.[3]

In Canada colonial legislatures enacted abortion laws based on the 1803 British statute. Following Confederation, a new national law adopted in 1869, An Act Respecting Offences Against the Person, stipulated that women convicted of attempting to abort themselves could be sentenced to seven years' imprisonment. The new law also provided for a sentence of life in prison for procuring an abortion, making it even more repressive than Britain's abortion law of the time.

Significantly, in view of the pro-life movement's assertions about the fetus's historic right to life enshrined in Canada's laws, the new criminal law contained a provision that defined the point at which a child becomes a human being. That section remains in the Criminal Code today (section 223) and states unequivocally: "A child becomes a human being within the meaning of this Act when it has completely proceeded, in a living state, from the body of its mother whether or not (a) it has breathed, (b) it has an independent circulation, or (c) the navel string is severed." The law further stipulates, "A person commits homicide when he causes injury to a child before or during birth as a result of which the child dies after becoming a human being." Thus, while the Criminal Code did refer to a fetus as a child prior to birth, it did not ever confer on the child the legal status of a human being. This distinction in the law between a child/fetus prior to birth and a human being after birth is at odds with the notion that a fetus is a human being and has a right to life. Indeed, the legislators of the nineteenth century who enacted the Criminal Code would most likely not have seen any difference between a fetus and a child. In that case, section 223 of the Criminal Code could be argued as establishing that a fetus is not a human being. Indeed, as the Supreme Court of Canada noted in its 1989 judgment on abortion, *Tremblay v. Daigle,* the law in Britain and Canada had always protected the fetus to some extent. At the same time the Court observed that abortion was not generally considered equivalent to murder in law, and therefore the fetus was not viewed as having the rights of a person in the full sense.

For over one hundred years following Confederation, an abortion was extremely hard to obtain in Canada, even in cases in which the life or health of the mother was endangered as a result of pregnancy. To terminate unwanted pregnancies, desperate women resorted to various drastic and often deadly means of inducing miscarriages. Horrifically, they threw themselves down stairs, douched with disinfectants, or inserted coat hangers or knitting needles into their vaginas. Such ghastly measures often caused maiming, infection, shock, or even death. Other women who wanted abortions and could afford to pay for them sought out clandestine, illegal abortions. The backroom or "butcher" abortionists often lacked the requisite medical training or skill in the performance of the procedure and performed abortions furtively, often under unhygienic and dangerous conditions. Many women died as a result of botched abortions. Many women experienced irreparable medical consequences such as sterility, or received life-threatening injuries.[4] Doctors who performed abortions risked being charged and imprisoned.

It was not until 1929 that some relaxation on the prohibition was introduced through Parliament's enactment of the Infant Life Preservation Act, which decriminalized abortions that were necessary to preserve the life of the mother. A few years later a defence of "medical necessity" was established in common law, as a result of a 1938 British court decision known as *Rex v. Bourne*, which served as a precedent for Canadian courts. In that case, a gynecologist, Aleck Bourne, was acquitted of criminal charges of having performed an abortion on a fourteen-year-old who had been raped by five soldiers. As a result, doctors who formed a good faith opinion that a miscarriage was medically necessary had some assurance that they would not be convicted. Still, the legal situation remained murky, with doctors continuing to be at risk of criminal prosecution in cases in which the judgment of "medical necessity" might be disputed. To address that situation, physicians at some hospitals in larger cities formed committees of doctors to approve abortions performed in their hospitals. This tactic made it harder for the state to prosecute an individual doctor who performed an abortion.[5]

Although statistics on the number of illegal abortions performed in Canada prior to 1970 are scarce, the available data nonetheless present a horrendous state of premature and preventable female mortality. In the years from 1926 to 1947, between 4,000 and 6,000 women died as a result of botched, illegal abortions. Abortions were also hardly uncommon: estimates on the number of abortions performed in Canada during the 1960s range from 35,000 to 120,000—an astounding number given that abortions were both illegal and generally not available in hospitals.[6] In addition, between 1900 and 1972, 1,793 people were charged with procuring or attempting to procure an abortion, with 64 per cent of them being convicted. Between 1962 and 1966, abortion was a leading cause of death, accounting for nearly 20 per cent of deaths for women in Ontario. By 1962, 57,617 hospitalizations in Canada were attributed to abortion-related complications.[7]

Fortunately, by the mid-twentieth century attitudes towards abortion had become more liberal because of changing views about the role of religious beliefs and social mores on public policy as well as about the role of women and the family. Increased medical knowledge about fetal development and medical and technological advances had made the abortion procedure, when performed in a hospital, much safer for women.[8] In the 1960s a social consensus emerged that Canada's abortion laws were unclear and too restrictive, especially in respect of determining when a doctor would not be subject to criminal prosecution for performing the procedure. Significantly, Great Britain had amended its abortion law in 1967, and there was a push for Canada to do so as well.

In the late 1950s and the 1960s some Canadian media began calling for liberalization of the laws. *Chatelaine*, the popular national women's magazine, published an editorial in 1959 calling for such action. The *Globe and Mail*, articulating the necessity of separating morality from criminal law, began calling as early as 1961 for legislative amendments to permit legal abortions. Increasing demands for the legalization of abortion came from prominent mainstream organizations such as the Canadian Medical Association and the socially liberal United Church of Canada, which gave impetus to an amendment of Canada's Criminal Code.[9] Another key group advocating for reform was the Humanist Fellowship of Montreal under its president, Dr. Henry Morgentaler, who would later become the most prosecuted pro-choice advocate in the country.

Women's groups and others also advocated for the right of a pregnant woman to determine whether she wanted to continue with a pregnancy. The National Council of Women (dating from 1893) adopted resolutions urging that abortions be made more available. Its members argued their case based on a concern over the injustice of unequal access to doctors willing to perform abortions rather than from the perspective of a woman's right to choice. Tellingly, however, women's groups at this time had neither recognition nor status as influential stakeholders in a political process dominated by men. They were also relatively weak and non-confrontational in their advocacy. The many public meetings and forums held to debate abortion rarely included representatives of women.[10]

In the midst of these broad social developments, the federal Department of Justice began considering how to modernize the federal laws dealing with divorce, contraception, consenting sexual acts between adults, and abortion. The need for such reform was seen, among liberals and progressives, as an important element in the transformation of Canada from a colonial and Christian state. It was one of the manifestations of the ways in which, as Albert J. Menendez noted in *Church and State in Canada*, "Canada's relatively conservative and church-oriented society began to change dramatically in the 1960s."[11] Younger Canadians in particular were rejecting the old morality dictated by the churches as well as the authority of the old, colonially based state. The social and cultural makeup of the country was in a state of flux. Canada was metamorphosing from a socially conservative to a socially liberal society.

Responding to these changes in public opinion, the Liberal government of Prime Minister Pierre Elliott Trudeau introduced, and Parliament enacted, an omnibus bill in 1969 to reform various sections of the Criminal Code. It included the decriminalization of abortions performed for "therapeutic" reasons when the life or health of the mother was endangered—but only in accredited hospitals after approval by therapeutic abortion committees. The amendments primarily addressed the concerns of the medical profession by giving legal sanction to abortion review committees formed by doctors in hospitals. Notably, the rationale supporting the need for the amendments was completely devoid of the concerns of women and of the radical notion of a woman's right to choose whether or not to have an abortion.

Nor did the debate over decriminalization of abortions proceed with the articulation of "pro-life" and "pro-choice" positions, although some members of Parliament who opposed the legislation did make reference to the right to life of the fetus. The opponents most typically argued that abortion was morally wrong, was contrary to traditional Judeo-Christian teachings, and therefore should continue to be criminalized. The supporters of reform typically argued that termination of a pregnancy was the right thing to do when the medical circumstances warranted. In the profoundly sexist and male-dominated climate of the times, the right of women to determine for themselves their reproductive choices and to have control over their bodies and their sexuality was simply not seen as being an important consideration. Although new feminist groups such as the Canadian Committee on the Status of Women and the Toronto Women's Liberation Group did make submissions to the parliamentary committee that reviewed the amendments, they were essentially marginalized. They were not seen as major players in the debate.

Instead, reproductive issues were viewed as essentially medical decisions to be made by medical professionals, who were preponderantly male. As was the case in other professions, women doctors were few in numbers, did not hold positions of leadership, and were largely without influence. The debate over decriminalizing abortion thus became one principally involving men, whether doctors or politicians; and medical and professional concerns were the main drivers for the Criminal Code amendments. Those involved recognized only the need to clarify the criminal liabilities of doctors who performed abortions and to define the state's interest in regulating the abortion procedure. The solution was to give (male) doctors control over women's reproductive decisions, rather than to give that control to women themselves. Access to abortion was not seen as a right that women should or would have. Abortion was in essence a medical procedure that should be performed only when absolutely necessary. To the extent that pregnant women were considered, it was as the victims of backstreet abortionists—as victims who needed to be provided with a greater degree of protection by means of access in still very limited circumstances to abortions performed in hospitals.[12]

The adoption of the Criminal Code amendments in 1969, rather than putting an end to the abortion debate in Canada, ushered in an era of intense and protracted advocacy on both sides of the issue. Anti-abortion advocates condemned the new provisions as being overly broad and giving carte blanche to therapeutic abortion clinics. They accused the clinics of approving routinely and without proper scrutiny virtually every abortion application. Pro-choice advocates attacked the legislation for not going far enough, for creating a burdensome bureaucracy that impeded a woman's right to choose. They also questioned the legislation's failure to compel hospitals to perform abortions: women in certain parts of the country had no access to abortions because their local hospitals, many them run by religious (and frequently Roman Catholic) orders, refused to seek accreditation. For women in these communities—which were the vast majority of communities in Canada—the practical effect was that the law had not changed at all. They had no more access to safe and legal abortions than they had ever had. These concerns, together with demands to provide unfettered access to abortion services as a right of choice and self-determination for women, would become central elements of the burgeoning pro-choice movement in the early 1970s.

The birth of the pro-life movement: 1970s

Social conservative groups have mobilized massively to seek the recriminalization of abortion and to curtail access to abortion services using the emotionally charged "right-to-life" argument. Throughout the 1970s, the pro-life movement gained strength and an army of new supporters across the country. In a study of anti-abortion protest in Toronto, Michael W. Cuneo points out that the early pro-life movement was supported primarily by middle-class Catholic women—often the wives of professionals, often mothers and university-educated. Joining with the first national pro-life group, the Alliance for Life, was a network of devoutly conservative Christians who had formed increasingly militant pro-life groups across the country. The organizations included Toronto Right to Life (founded in 1971) and Alliance Against Abortion in Winnipeg and New Brunswick Right to Life Association (both founded in 1973). The political action arm of the pro-life movement was bolstered in 1973 with the formation of the Coalition for Life as a national advocacy group. After 1977, Campaign Life Coalition became the leading national pro-life organization working towards a repeal of the abortion law and the curtailment of access to abortion services. According to Cuneo, Campaign Life Coalition was "confrontational, politically absolutist, and unrepentantly hostile to post-1950s Canadian culture."[13] The new group's activists were a mix of conservative Catholic and conservative Protestant women committed to preserving the traditional role of women as wives and mothers.

In general, according to Cuneo, the pro-life movement activists linked the fight against abortion to a "defence of cherished yet beleaguered norms of sexual and family life." For them, "anti-abortionism was intrinsically a crusade against feminism, secularism and the rise of moral permissiveness in Canadian society," including the increasing tolerance of homosexuality.[14] The conservative "family values" crusade thus targeted not only abortion but also homosexuality and rights for gays and lesbians as well as feminist calls for employment equity for women, universal day care, and contraceptive and reproductive choice more generally.

The pro-life groups engaged in traditional forms of lobbying and used public demonstrations, public forums, and political rallies to secure political and public support for their position. They scored early and impressive gains. A 1975 petition bearing one million names and demanding legislation to protect the life of the "unborn" was delivered to the Trudeau government. Pro-life groups lobbied provincial governments to not fund or to cease funding of abortion services through the medicare system. In 1977 Toronto Right to Life and other groups organized an effective campaign of letters and telegrams sent to Trudeau and the federal health minister, Marc Lalonde; they voiced their objection to the government's efforts, by way of a federal-provincial agreement, to require hospitals to establish therapeutic abortion clinics. The campaign succeeded in forcing the less than resolute Trudeau government to back down from its proposal—which if put into effect would simply have facilitated the realization of the access to abortion that its own 1969 legislation decreed was no longer illegal.

The Trudeau government's retreat was evidence both of the disproportionate influence the pro-life zealots exerted on the country's political leadership, and of how sensitive governments were—and still are—to clamorous expressions of dissatisfaction by well-organized and highly visible groups seen as representing significant blocs of voters. It also callously confirmed that, for government, the decriminalization of abortion did not impel a public policy of proactively providing access to abortions in hospitals. Hospitals that did not wish to perform abortions, for whatever reasons, would not be compelled to do so, and the women in their geographic vicinities were simply out of luck. They could attempt to find a hospital elsewhere, at great expense and inconvenience. They could obtain an illegal abortion, if that was even possible where they lived. They could attempt to induce a miscarriage or continue with an unwanted pregnancy.

More generally, the Trudeau government took the position that it had legislatively dealt with the abortion issue in 1969. It would do nothing more on the issue. At best this do-nothing-more approach was testament to a lack of appetite for reopening the political debate on what was seen to be an emotional and divisive issue with entrenched positions held on either side. But it was also a dispiriting indication that Trudeau's much vaunted "Just Society"—a catch phrase he used prodigiously to signify the arrival of a new era of liberalization, reform, and justice in Canada—apparently did not extend so far as ensuring justice for women in the form of providing universal access to safe and legal abortions.

The birth of the pro-choice movement: 1970s

For women's groups and many women seeking access to abortions in the 1970s, the new abortion law had serious flaws and resulted in new ways of impeding access to abortion. Approval for an abortion in a hospital was a time-consuming and complicated procedure, and pregnant women had no control over the process. An application for an abortion had to be supported by three doctors. This step involved an interview to determine the physical and mental health risks associated with continuing the pregnancy, but it did not consider social and economic factors. If the application was referred to a therapeutic abortion clinic, approval for an abortion required a majority vote of the members of the committee. Some hospitals placed time limits on when an abortion could be performed—and the limits could be as low as ten to twelve weeks of gestation. Some hospitals saw delays of two or three weeks from the time a woman contacted the hospital until the application was considered. Many hospitals did not perform abortions at all; by 1982 only 261 of 861 public hospitals in Canada had therapeutic abortion clinics and could therefore perform legal abortions. Just forty-three hospitals performed fully 70 per cent of all abortions in the country. In only two provinces (Ontario and Quebec) were abortions reliably available, and in some instances even there abortions were available only through illegal clinics operated outside and independently of hospitals.[15]

The deplorable situation in which women could still not get access to safe, legal abortions led to the formation of a radical new pro-choice movement that grew out of the first national feminist protest against the abortion law, the Abortion Caravan of 1970. Organized by the Vancouver Women's Caucus, the Abortion Caravan started out in Vancouver and stopped in towns and cities along the way to Ottawa. Its activists gathered the stories and experiences of women and vowed to bring those voices to the government in Ottawa. Calling for "Free Abortions on Demand" and carrying placards with messages such as "Every Child a Wanted Child," the Caravan not only generated significant public attention, but also, and more importantly, helped to change the boundaries of the debate on abortion.[16]

In Ottawa, 150 Abortion Caravan women demonstrated at the prime minister's official residence to protest the shocking fact that not one member of the Trudeau government would meet with them. In a powerfully emotive demonstration of inspired political theatre, they brought with them a coffin symbolizing all the women who had died from illegal abortions. In a second demonstration, several hundred women rallied in front of the Parliament buildings, unfurling a huge banner proclaiming "Babies by Choice." Afterwards, demonstrators stormed into a parliamentary committee room to hear a presentation of a brief calling for an end to all legal restrictions on abortion.[17] In a daring act of civil disobedience, thirty-five women heroically chained themselves to the public gallery in the House of Commons, forcing the closure of Parliament for the first time in Canadian history. Outside, about eighty other women in black headscarves circled the Centennial flame, carrying their symbolic coffin and a banner that read, "Twelve thousand women die."[18]

By these actions, the new, more militant activists signalled the birth of an entirely different form of advocacy by women in pursuit of the right to determine for themselves what would be done with their bodies and their lives. These women were not the genteel ladies of old making polite requests of their male superiors. Many were socialists, members of the new left, active in the new feminist movement and practised in other forms of protest. For this new generation of activists, the fight for abortion and for women's liberation more generally was articulated most clearly and succinctly by a chant heard often in the 1970s and 1980s, shouted with throaty vigour by thousands of defiantly uppity women at countless demonstrations and public rallies: "Women must control their fate! Not the Church and Not the State!"

Not surprisingly, the Abortion Caravan rally prompted a counter-demonstration by the pro-life group Alliance for Life. It featured gaudy placards with provocative messages such as "Every Abortion Kills a Child" and "Population Control Yes, Abortion, No." In an ironic twist, one of the pro-life demonstrators was a high-school student from the Bishop Ryan (Catholic) High School in Hamilton.[19] Her name was Sheila Copps—she was the daughter of Hamilton's mayor—and years later, as a Liberal member of Parliament and cabinet minister, she would bear the enmity of the pro-life movement after becoming a staunch pro-choice advocate and supporter of legislated human rights protections for gays and lesbians. Her presence at the 1970 pro-life demonstration typified the tactics of the pro-life groups who sought to enlist the support of Catholic youth in their crusade against abortion. But Copps's later championing of women's choice on abortion was also evidence that people can and do change their views on such issues. More fundamentally, the Alliance for Life counter-demonstration was a foretaste of what the next three decades would hold in store—intense and raucous public confrontations between pro-choice and pro-life forces, each hoping to sway public opinion and persuade legislators to act on their diametrically opposed demands.

Following the Abortion Caravan, a number of feminist organizations focused their organizing on repeal of the abortion law and access to safe, accessible abortions in free-standing clinics (clinics not associated with or situated in hospitals).[20] The Canadian Association for Repeal of the Abortion Law, formed in 1974, would later become the Canadian Abortion Rights Action League (CARAL) and would serve as Canada's national pro-choice organization for three decades. Women's liberation groups set up a network to assist women seeking abortions to travel to U.S. clinics where the procedure was readily available. According to Judy Rebick, a former president of the National Action Committee on the Status of Women (NAC), abortion was the first issue to unite the new women's movement. It was the issue that put the greatest numbers of women into the streets in protest.[21]

These developments represented a radical departure from the prevailing discourse of previous years—of abortion as a medical procedure entailing control, by doctors and male politicians, and not women themselves, over women's bodies and reproductive decisions. The pro-choice groups were militantly asserting access to abortion as a fundamental right, as a matter of choice for women as the only ones who should have control over their sexuality and reproduction. It was no longer a debate about the rights of doctors and the interests of the state in regulating a medical procedure. The primary voices being heard were no longer those of the doctors, lawyers, judges, and state officials. The voices now being heard were those of the loud, angry, and articulate feminist activists who were putting the rights of women at the centre of the issue. These women sought not the reform of the abortion laws but their outright repeal. They sought not just abortions available in hospitals, but in free-standing clinics, independent of hospitals, that would be available across the country with the cost of the procedures covered by the publicly funded health-care system.[22]

The pro-choice movement articulated a new morality based on the equality and self-determination of women. It was a campaign embodied by the phrase "a woman's right to choose." In this sense, denying women the right to terminate a pregnancy and criminalizing them and those who assisted them in carrying out the abortion procedure were profoundly immoral acts and could no longer be justified. Forcing women to surreptitiously seek out illegally performed abortions and to risk serious injury, complications, sterility, or even death was not morally defensible. This new morality challenged and rejected the old, oppressive religious morality that imbued the laws and shaped public policy. The pro-choice activists methodically organized to wrest control of the moral agenda from the social conservative absolutists and demagogues and engaged the state and the broader community in a new discourse of rights for women. Inevitably, it put them in conflict with both their religious protagonists and a Canadian state initially hostile to their aspirations.

The state strikes back

Another important event in the history of the pro-choice movement was the formation, in 1972, of the Morgentaler Defence Committee in Montreal. Along with Henry Morgentaler, after whom it was named, the Committee became the focal point for defending the operation of free-standing, but still illegal, abortion clinics. The Committee was a broad-based coalition of doctors, members of family-planning associations, CARAL (after 1973), Trotskyists, feminists, and the women's commission of the Quebec teachers' union.[23] It provided support for Morgentaler, the Montreal physician who defied the Criminal Code provisions on abortion by operating a free-standing clinic. After a police raid in 1970, Morgentaler was criminally charged with conspiracy to commit an abortion. It marked the commencement of a gruelling eighteen-year journey through the courts on several criminal charges, and the multiple trials would make Morgentaler the public face of the pro-choice movement. For pro-life activists it also cast him in the role of the devil incarnate, a mass murderer of numberless unborn children whose deaths must be righteously avenged both by God and by the state as regulator of morality.

In 1973, to the utter shock and disbelief of the pro-life forces and judicial authorities, a Montreal jury acquitted Morgentaler, even though it was abundantly clear that he had violated the provisions of the Criminal Code dealing with abortion. Even more astounding, the jury's acquittal served as a testament that a substantial and ever-increasing segment of the Canadian populace, despite the loud and outraged protestations of the pro-life advocates, believed that the law was unjust.[24] The decision represented a breathtaking and historic repudiation of a law by a group of ordinary citizens.

The Quebec Liberal government of Robert Bourassa appealed the jury's decision—an action that generated outrage and anger among pro-choice advocates and much of the broader public. A year later the Quebec Court of Appeal issued a highly controversial judgment overturning the acquittal. Rather than ordering a retrial, which was normally the action taken by an appellate court in such instances, the Court of Appeal substituted its own decision. The judges found Morgentaler guilty and sentenced him to serve eighteen months in prison.

Morgentaler then appealed to the Supreme Court of Canada, which in 1975 upheld the conviction. In its judgment, *Morgentaler v. the Queen,* the Supreme Court acknowledged that the Court of Appeal decision "presents the highly unusual, if not the singularly exceptional, situation of an appellate court itself entering a conviction after setting aside a jury verdict of acquittal." Nonetheless, the Court held in essence that Morgentaler had not succeeded in his defence of "necessity" in the performance of the abortion that gave rise to his being charged. The Supreme Court justices contended that there was no evidence that the life or health of the woman on whom the procedure was performed would have been in the state of imminent risk that would necessitate performing the abortion outside of a therapeutic abortion clinic.

This first Morgentaler case featured interventions by advocacy groups both in support of and in opposition to Morgentaler. On one side, the Canadian Civil Liberties Association and Foundation for Women in Crisis made submissions arguing that the particular sections of the Criminal Code used to convict Morgentaler violated various provisions of the Canadian Bill of Rights—arguments that the Court emphatically rejected. On the other side, submissions from the Alliance for Life and Quebec pro-life groups—the Fondation de la vie, the Front commun pour le respect de la vie, and the Association des médecins du Québec pour le respect de la vie—opposed those arguments. The duel of legal arguments by opposing intervenor groups would become a regular feature of subsequent course cases involving the abortion law and access to abortions.

While Morgentaler was serving his prison term, a Quebec Superior Court jury, once more ignoring the provisions of the Criminal Code, acquitted him on a second set of charges. They did so even though, as the presiding judge, Claude Bisson, remarked, "I practically told the jury to find him guilty."[25] Then, following a prolonged national uproar by civil libertarians and pro-choice advocates over the Quebec appeal court's overturning of the first jury verdict, the Trudeau government introduced and Parliament enacted an amendment to the Criminal Code that prevented judges from being able to overturn jury decisions. It became known as the Morgentaler Amendment. As a result, Morgentaler's conviction was overturned. He was released from prison after serving ten months—but not before he had suffered a heart attack after being placed in solitary confinement. Despite Morgentaler himself being released from prison, the abortion law remained intact and his clinic was still illegal.

Incredibly, in a move that seemed simply vindictive and politically motivated, federal Justice Minister Ron Basford ordered a new trial for Morgentaler in 1976. The ostensibly liberal Trudeau government was continuing to take a disappointingly conservative stance on abortion. Remarkably, the retrial resulted in another resounding rejection of the law when still another jury acquitted Morgentaler. This acquittal in turn brought a refreshingly different response from government. The newly elected Parti Québécois government of René Lévesque responded by dropping all outstanding charges against Morgentaler. Reflecting its commitment to securing Quebec's independence from Canada, the PQ also audaciously rejected the disputed sections of the federally enacted Criminal Code, announcing that it would no longer enforce the abortion law in Quebec. It was a welcome response that represented a huge victory for Morgentaler and the pro-choice movement.

Borowski and the "right to life"

Anti-abortion activists also took up the fight in the courts, although in this case by choice and not because of prosecution by the state. Their counterpart to Morgentaler was pro-life activist Joe Borowski, a devout Roman Catholic.

Borowski was an enormously popular cabinet minister in Manitoba's New Democratic Party government. He was renowned and celebrated for his many years of activism for the rights of Northern Manitoba and of working people. Among his other claims to fame, Borowski founded the Alliance Against Abortion in 1973 and was one of the leaders of the movement to recriminalize abortion. He became incensed upon learning that the Mount Carmel Clinic in Winnipeg provided contraception services and abortion referrals. The clinic was sending women to the United States for abortions because of prohibitive time delays in the approval process at the therapeutic abortion clinic in the only Winnipeg hospital that had such a clinic. The provincial health insurance plan paid only a small fraction of the costs of the referrals, but, outraged nonetheless, Borowski called for an investigation into the legality of the Mount Carmel Clinic's actions. He charged that the clinic violated the Criminal Code by referring women to clinics for abortions that were not approved by a hospital's therapeutic abortion clinic.

Mounting a massive media campaign and declaring "Abortion is murder," Borowski attracted significant public support. He succeeded in having the NDP government of Edward Schreyer establish a policy of funding out-of-province abortions only if they complied with the provisions of the Criminal Code. This meant that the service had to be approved by a therapeutic abortion clinic.[26]

At the same time, the Manitoba government announced that abortions would be provided at two more hospitals in Winnipeg (they were not offered at any other hospitals in the province). Borowski responded with a crudely sexist and moralistic condemnation of any funding for abortions and the women who sought them: "When these immoral, secondary tramps get pregnant and go to New York for an abortion of convenience, it's bloody awful."[27] Based on his tenacity and such intemperate remarks, Borowski attracted considerable media and public attention and was celebrated by social conservatives as a staunch pro-life advocate. He became, in the admiring words of Campaign Life Coalition president Jim Hughes, "a catalyst, a disturber" who offered leadership "which grassroots Canadians saw as a beacon of hope, [and without which] the daily press would all but have ignored pro-life activities."[28]

As Borowski continued to fight on the front lines as an uncompromising pro-life advocate, he became convinced that there would be no political solution to the abortion issue. It was a view shared by Morris Schumiatcher, a prominent Saskatchewan lawyer, leading human rights advocate, and committed pro-life activist. Among Schumiatcher's credentials were drafting the Canadian Bill of Rights and serving as executive assistant to the Co-operative Commonwealth Federation (CCF) premier of Saskatchewan, Tommy Douglas. The lawyer approached Borowski about using the Bill of Rights, which contained a provision guaranteeing the right to life of every individual, to mount a challenge to the abortion law. Schumiatchter hoped to obtain a declaration from a court that the 1969 Criminal Code amendment violated that right to life. It would mean establishing that a child in the womb was an individual who had a right to life, a right that would take precedence over the right of a woman to have an abortion. He also hoped to obtain an injunction to prevent public funding for abortion services. Borowski agreed to be the figurehead for a legal challenge, which was launched in 1978. The case was supported by Campaign Life Coalition, the Alliance Against Abortion, and other pro-life groups.[29]

After being bogged down for several years over issues of legal jurisdiction, Borowski's case was finally heard by a Saskatchewan court in 1983. As the Canadian Charter of Rights and Freedoms had by that time come into effect, replacing the Bill of Rights, Borowski's claim was amended to assert that the abortion sections of the Criminal Code denied the child in the womb the right to life and the right not to be deprived of life: rights to which the Charter claimed everyone was entitled. To the dismay of Borowski and his supporters, the court ruled that a child in the womb was not a person under the law and therefore did not fall within the scope of the term "everyone" in the Charter. The decision was a reconfirmation that the law in Canada had never ascribed to the fetus in the womb the legal status of personhood.

Undeterred, Borowski appealed, arguing before the Saskatchewan Court of Appeal in 1985 that the rights of the "unborn" were violated "in the most devastating way possible" under the abortion provisions of the Criminal Code. There was nothing "therapeutic" about an abortion, he contended. "The unborn are systematically put to death," he declared. Only the unborn still faced capital punishment in Canada.[30] The appeal court resoundingly disagreed, holding that a fetus was not included within the legal definition of a person. Parliament, the court determined, had not specifically provided for fetal rights in law.

Borowski appealed to the Supreme Court of Canada. But before the case could be heard, in a stunning and historic decision involving Morgentaler the Supreme Court struck down the abortion law as unconstitutional. When the Borowski case was finally heard by the Supreme Court in 1989, the justices determined it to be moot in light of the *Morgentaler* decision. Yet, disturbingly, they opened up the possibility that the right to life of a fetus could be determined by the courts in a future case. They conceded that a case could conceivably be brought to challenge a specific new law or action by government on abortion because of its impact on Charter rights. They refused to take a position on the issue, they contended, out of reluctance to make an "abstract pronouncement" on fetal rights in a case that was now moot. Setting the stage for a possible future challenge to a law, the justices noted that in a legislative context any rights of the fetus could be considered or at least balanced against the rights of women guaranteed under the Charter.[31]

Although generally seen as representing a defeat for Borowski and the pro-life cause, the Supreme Court decision in *Borowski v. Canada (Attorney General)* moved the judicial yardstick in a way that offered as much encouragement to the pro-life cause as it did for pro-choice activists. Simply acknowledging that the fetus may have rights and that those rights could be balanced against the rights of women opened up the prospect that a pregnant woman's right to have an abortion could be significantly constrained in future. That balancing of rights would most likely find little disagreement in regard to a late-term abortion unless the life, or health of the mother was at risk. But what other scenarios might arise in which the right of the fetus to life would be seen as overriding the right of a woman to terminate a pregnancy? In that regard, Borowski and his cohorts in the pro-life movement should have viewed the Supreme Court's decision optimistically.

Instead, Borowski reacted petulantly. According to his biographer, Lianne Laurence, he vowed that had the Supreme Court justices been in the same place as he was, he would have punched them. He denounced the judges as "gutless" and the decision as "the ultimate cop out" and "political sleaze of the worst kind."[32] His anger and disappointment were no doubt intensified because of his vigorous but failed efforts at pressuring politicians to enshrine the right to life in the new Canadian Constitution during the period of political and public debate on that issue in the early 1980s. Infuriated by the Trudeau government's insistence that the

Constitution's new Charter of Rights remain neutral on the question of abortion, he embarked in May 1981 on a ninety-day fast to protest its lack of protection for the "unborn child." Borowski believed that if a charter was adopted without providing such protection, the result would be unrestricted abortion and "a death sentence for hundreds of thousands of unborn children."[33]

The fight for free-standing abortion clinics

By the early 1980s activists within the pro-choice movement had also decided that challenging the abortion law in the courts might ultimately have more impact than endless and fruitless political lobbying. Women involved during the 1970s with coalitions to try to expand access to abortion were not getting anywhere politically. In response, in 1982 Carolyn Egan and other women in the pro-choice movement formed the Committee for the Establishment of Abortion Clinics. Although their immediate objective was to find a doctor willing to open free-standing abortion clinics and to challenge the laws, they envisaged a broad-based movement mobilized to force change in the abortion law. Under the slogan, "A woman's right to choose," the issue would clearly be one of reproductive rights for women. They approached Morgentaler, who agreed to open clinics in Toronto and Winnipeg to test the laws. In September 1982, the activists formed the Ontario Coalition for Abortion Clinics (OCAC) with a mission to fight for free-standing abortion clinics (providing medically insured abortions) and the repeal of the abortion law.[34]

In OCAC's view, Egan noted, the only way of shifting the balance of power on the abortion issue was to view it as a power struggle with both the state and a highly organized right-wing, pro-life movement. OCAC, with the support of CARAL and other groups, conducted public education and did outreach to attract support from beyond women's groups. They secured the support of the Ontario Federation of Labour and Women Working with Immigrant Women, among others. Importantly, they were prepared for police raids on the Morgentaler Clinics and for protracted court cases to fight the charges. "Our feeling," Egan recalled, "was that Supreme Court justices do not function in a vacuum. They would want to uphold the law, but if the country was alive with people saying that this law was anachronistic, they would have to look at that. When there is no respect for a law, how can you uphold it?"[35]

The opening of the Morgentaler Clinic in Toronto on June 15, 1983, ignited pro-life counter-advocacy in that city and across Ontario. An All-Ontario Pro-Life Rally organized by Toronto Right to Life and held at the Ontario Legislature attracted 35,000 fervent supporters—the largest such rally in Canada to that time.

Toronto Right to Life also hosted an "all-Ontario pro-life meeting" to set strategy for opposing the operation of the abortion clinic.[36] A similarly determined reaction followed the announcement of the intention to open the Morgentaler Clinic in Winnipeg. Borowski and the Alliance Against Abortion, along with Alliance for Life, Manitoba League for Life, and Coalition for Life, vowed to use every available legal avenue to obstruct and delay the clinic opening. When the clinic finally did open in May 1983, Borowski organized picketing and demonstrations outside it. He also set up a "rescue" initiative of "families willing to help the distressed mothers by taking them in. And when the child is born, we will take the child off her hands." Borowski and other pro-life activists also prayed outside the clinic, prompting their arrest.[37]

Within a few short weeks of the opening of the clinics in Toronto and Winnipeg, police in each city conducted raids and charged Morgentaler and other doctors, including Leslie Smoling and Robert Scott, with "conspiracy to procure a miscarriage." But, in a repeat of the experiences in Quebec, Morgentaler and his colleagues were acquitted by a jury in the Toronto trial in 1984. The acquittal followed a December 1983 decision by Manitoba's NDP government to withdraw the conspiracy charge against Morgentaler and substitute the lesser offence of performing illegal abortions. It also decided to not proceed with prosecuting the charges arising from the raid on the Winnipeg clinic pending the outcome of the case in Toronto. Both of these actions angered Borowski and the pro-life groups, who sought the permanent closure of the Morgentaler Clinic.[38] Meanwhile, Ontario's Progressive Conservative government, led by Bill Davis, followed the lead of the Quebec government a decade earlier, appealing the acquittal on the Toronto charges. The Ontario Court of Appeal quashed the acquittal and ordered a new trial. Morgentaler once more appealed to the Supreme Court of Canada. This time, he hoped to receive a much different result.

Then, suddenly and surprisingly, the political climate in Ontario changed for the better after the 1985 provincial election. The Liberal Party under Premier David Peterson took power with a minority government supported through a formal political accord by the pro-choice New Democratic Party. The Liberals were much less willing than the Progressive Conservatives to support charging Morgentaler for operating his clinics. Abortion and abortion issues, and specifically the approach to be taken to the abortion clinics operated by Morgentaler and his associates, were among the big issues that confronted the new government. According to Attorney General Ian Scott in his memoir, *To Make a Difference*, "Abortion was clearly outlawed in the Criminal Code, which was a federal responsibility. Just as clearly, juries were refusing to convict Dr. Morgentaler, in spite of evidence that he was performing abortions."[39]

Following the first Morgentaler acquittal, both pro-choice and pro-life groups began picketing outside of Morgentaler's clinic. Pro-choice advocates also pressured Scott to bring an end to the prosecutions of Morgentaler. On the other side, pro-life activists began harassing women who attempted to enter the clinic. They absurdly claimed that such interventions were merely attempts at counselling in a loving and compassionate manner. Pro-life advocates, most notably Ken Campbell, accused Scott of not being vigorous enough in the prosecutions. Scott was also under pressure from Toronto's chief of police, Jack Marks, to have new charges brought against Morgentaler in an effort to stop him from practising abortions until the Supreme Court issued its decision. Scott stated that he "was alarmed at this request" and "did not want to give in to the pressure tactics of the anti-abortion groups." But he also did not want it to appear that he "endorsed the deliberate challenge to the law made by Morgentaler." Faced with the dilemma of what to do, Scott ultimately devised a controversial strategy of having charges laid against Morgentaler and then having the charges stayed (not acted upon) pending the Supreme Court's decision. Once this strategy was executed, new charges were laid against Morgentaler by the police and then stayed at the request of the Attorney General. One result of implementing this strategy, Scott recalled, was that "Anti-abortion groups then took out their anger on me by picketing my house."[40]

On January 28, 1988, the Supreme Court of Canada released its historic decision, *R. v. Morgentaler*, in which a majority of the justices ruled that the abortion law contravened section 7 of the Charter. Chief Justice Brian Dickson, who voted with the majority, noted: "Forcing a woman, by threat of criminal sanction, to carry a foetus to term unless she meets certain criteria unrelated to her own priorities and aspirations, is a profound interference with a woman's body and thus an infringement of security of the person."[41] The highest court in the country had adopted and validated the morality of a woman's right to choose. The abortion law was struck down and henceforth had no force or effect. Canada no longer had any abortion law. As a result, abortion on demand was now theoretically, although not actually, available to any woman in the country. The moral agenda in regard to abortion and the role of the state in its regulation had been dramatically changed.

The pro-life forces did have some consolation. The Supreme Court justices did not rule that the state could not enact a law to protect the fetus. In particular, the Court had not ruled that the state was prohibited from enacting a law that granted the right to life to a fetus. The justices had specifically noted that the state's interest in protecting the fetus was sufficiently important to justify limiting the Charter rights of a pregnant woman at some point. The decision thus raised an expectation that Parliament could enact a new law that complied with the Charter.

While an absolute prohibition on abortion would fail on Charter grounds, so too would unfettered access to abortion on demand at any stage of a pregnancy. This possibility gave the pro-life forces fodder they could use to renew their lobbying for the recriminalization of abortion. They had a new basis on which to lobby for legislative action—although admittedly much narrower in scope than they would have preferred—and which they have pursued ever since. Obtaining a new law criminalizing abortion at least in some circumstances would remain an active issue on their agenda for more than twenty years after *Morgentaler*.

On August 8, 1989, in the case of *Tremblay v. Daigle*, the Supreme Court of Canada rendered another significant judgment that had a dramatic impact on the politics of abortion. The case arose following the termination of a five-month cohabiting relationship between Chantal Daigle and her boyfriend, Jean-Guy Tremblay. Daigle was eighteen weeks pregnant at the time of their separation and decided to terminate the pregnancy. Tremblay responded by obtaining an injunction from the Quebec Superior Court preventing Daigle from having an abortion. The trial judge ruled that the fetus was not only a "human being" under the Quebec Charter of Human Rights and Freedoms and the province's human rights legislation, but also a "juridical person" as defined in Quebec's Civil Code. The fetus therefore enjoyed a "right to life," the judge concluded. He held that Tremblay had the necessary "interest" to request the injunction. The fetus's right to life was judged to prevail in the case. A majority decision of the Quebec Court of Appeal subsequently upheld the injunction.[42]

As doctors generally would not perform abortions after the twentieth week of pregnancy, Daigle defied the injunction by travelling to the United States and obtaining an abortion before it was too late to do so. In the meantime the case proceeded through the court system all the way to the Supreme Court of Canada, with both pro-life and pro-choice groups intervening on either side. The Campaign Life Coalition, Canadian Physicians for Life, and REAL Women of Canada intervened in support of Tremblay. The Canadian Abortion Rights Action League, Women's Legal Education and Action Fund (LEAF), and Canadian Civil Liberties Association were on the other side, in support of Daigle.

Ultimately the Supreme Court ruled that the injunction was to be set aside. The justices held that the rights accorded to the fetus by the lower court decisions and to Tremblay as the potential father did not exist in law. They held that a fetus was not included within the term of "human being" and did not enjoy the right to life conferred by the Quebec Charter. That Charter, the Court held, did not intend to give a fetus that status, did not contain any reference to a fetus or to fetal rights, and, in fact, did not include any definition of the terms "human being" or "person." Furthermore, the Canadian Charter of Rights and Freedoms could not be invoked, the Court ruled, because the case involved a civil action between two private parties; there was no state action that was being impugned. Finally, the justices held that there was nothing in the Quebec legislation or case law to support the argument that Tremblay's interest in a fetus that he helped to create gave him the right to veto Daigle's decisions in respect of the fetus she was carrying.[43] The judgment was significant for both repudiating the assertion that existing law supported a right-to-life position and affirming a woman's right to decide whether to continue with a pregnancy.

Attempting to recriminalize abortion

The *Morgentaler* decision infuriated the pro-life forces and was celebrated by the pro-choice movement. Certainly, the elimination of Canada's law on abortion was a great victory in the battle to ensure access to abortion services by women in Canada. Yet the decision did not resolve the issue. Instead, it elevated it to a new political level in which competing interests once more attempted to hold sway over elected decision-makers. CARAL vowed to fight to keep abortion out of the Criminal Code altogether. The Canadian Advisory Council on the Status of Women and the National Action Committee on the Status of Women passed resolutions stating that abortion should be a private matter between a woman and her doctor. The pro-life forces intensified their political advocacy, mounting a campaign to secure a new abortion law and renewing their commitment to fight against the establishment of free-standing abortion clinics.[44] In an impressive display of their ability to mobilize their ardent supporters, the office of Prime Minister Brian Mulroney was inundated with over 11,000 letters and telephone calls demanding that a law be passed providing full protection for pre-born children.[45]

The pro-life groups had reason to be optimistic about achieving a new law recriminalizing abortion. In 1984, a little over three years before the *Morgentaler* decision was issued, the federal Liberal government had been replaced by the Progressive Conservatives led by Mulroney. The new government was a coalition of economic and fiscal conservatives, social conservatives, and Quebec nationalists. Although the government had been elected with the largest majority in Canadian history, to stay in power it needed to ensure the continuing support of the various components of the coalition, which meant, in particular, dealing with a fractious but demanding and strategically important social conservative constituency.

Mulroney's successor as prime minister and his one-time justice minister, Kim Campbell, wrote in her memoirs that Mulroney had become convinced following the Morgentaler case that a new abortion law was necessary.[46] To that end, the government, in July 1988, sought guidance from MPs on how a new abortion law should be framed. Incredibly, the MPs voted down six different proposals, including one that would have permitted abortion in the early stages of a pregnancy if a licensed physician determined that continuation of the pregnancy was likely to threaten the woman's physical or mental well-being. Indicating the strong social conservative stance of an alarmingly large segment of parliamentarians, the proposal receiving the most support advocated narrowing the grounds on which an abortion could be performed to endangerment of a woman's life (but not her health).[47] The outcome of the vote raised the troubling prospect that if the government reflected the prevailing sentiment of MPs in a government bill, Canada would find itself with a new abortion law that was even more restrictive than the one struck down by the Supreme Court.

Eventually the Mulroney government managed to agree on the nature of a bill. It proposed a new provision of the Criminal Code stating that abortion was to be prohibited unless performed by or under the supervision of a doctor who had formed the opinion that failure to induce the abortion would threaten the life or health of the woman. "Health" was defined as mental, physical, or psychological. In Campbell's view, that approach was preferred over not having an abortion law at all. It would also return abortion to "the mainstream of medical practice for the purposes of funding." This remedicalization of abortion, Campbell contended, "would make it difficult for provinces to treat abortion as a non-essential procedure, and give them a rationale for resisting pressure to limit access to abortion."[48] Perhaps that was true, but as a measure to remedicalize abortion, the new bill was fatally flawed and problematic for doctors. The Canadian Medical Association argued that it failed to protect doctors from criminal liability for performing abortions in circumstances that did not meet the letter of the law. They expressed a concern that if the law were to be enacted, doctors would stop performing abortions out of fear of being prosecuted by pro-life advocates.[49]

For pro-choice advocates, Campbell's proposed new law simply confirmed a fear that any new law on abortion would in effect recriminalize the procedure. Abortions would be illegal unless performed in the still relatively restricted circumstances prescribed in the government's bill. Problematically, the proposal did not expand the circumstances in which abortion could be legally performed, to include, for example, women whose economic circumstances would not be conducive to providing a child with the necessities of life. But, fundamentally, Campbell's approach was an outright repudiation of a woman's right to reproductive choice, in effect granting no right at all for women to decide for themselves whether or not to terminate a pregnancy. By vesting that decision with medical practitioners, it would make women once more dependent on doctors and give them no say in or control over what would happen to their bodies and their lives.

Despite these shortcomings, the proposed new abortion law was introduced in November 1989 as Bill C-43. The pro-choice forces predictably organized a concerted campaign to have it defeated in Parliament. What was more surprising was that pro-life groups also took an uncompromisingly hardline approach to it, condemning the bill for being even more liberal than the old abortion law. Campaign Life Coalition denounced Bill C-43 for being "unremediably pro-abortion" and resulting in de facto abortion on demand[50]—a false and outrageous assertion that anyone who had studied the bill and was knowledgeable about the position of pro-choice groups would have recognized immediately. The Canadian Conference of Catholic Bishops called on MPs to amend the proposed bill so that the life of an unborn child would be protected. The Bishops too accused the bill of being so vague as to virtually give women the right of abortion on demand.[51]

In Parliament, Bill C-43 was also opposed by a large number of pro-life members of all parties, but especially those within the Progressive Conservative Party. Mulroney bowed to this dissent, allowing a free vote of MPs on the bill but insisting that cabinet ministers vote in support of it. Backbenchers remained free to vote as they saw fit. Among the opposition parties, pro-choice MPs could also not support Bill C-43. The Liberals and the New Democrats voted against the bill, with only two Liberals supporting it.[52] Nonetheless, the government retained enough support among MPs to ensure that its bill would pass. In May 1990 the House of Commons adopted Bill C-43 by a vote of 140 to 131.

The bill had to also pass through the Senate, which has the authority to amend or to refuse to adopt any legislation passed by the House of Commons. The appointed Senators as a rule acquiesce to the will of the elected government and MPs and grant fairly swift approval of bills referred to them. In this case, remarkably, the Senate vote, held in January 1991, resulted in a tie, which meant that the bill was not approved and therefore did not become law. The recriminalization of abortion and the denial of a woman's right to choice were defeated by what amounted to a parliamentary miracle—something that a Christian more magnanimous than most of the fervent right-to-lifers might describe as divine intervention, perhaps as representing God's will. Whatever the reason, and despite the determined efforts of the Mulroney government, Canada did not get a new abortion law.

In Bill C-43 the Mulroney government had not addressed the new dynamics of conflicting rights and opposing articulations of a moral response to abortion: the notion of the right to life of the fetus from the moment of conception pitted against the assertion of the right of women to determine for themselves their reproductive choices. The middle ground of medicalizing abortion was no longer politically feasible. Following the defeat of Bill C-43, successive federal governments took the path of least resistance, refusing to take any action whatsoever on abortion. The result was to leave Canada without any abortion law. This has undoubtedly been a good thing for the women of Canada, but it has also meant that so long as there is no abortion law, the possibility remains that one might some day be adopted by a government ideologically committed to the pro-life position.

Pro-life radicalism in the aftermath of "Morgentaler"

Shocked and outraged by the pronouncements of the courts and the state's failure to close down abortion clinics, some pro-life activists turned to more extreme forms of political action—embarking on a fanatical assault on the secular and godless society that they blamed for permitting abortion to become rampant. They took aim in particular at the doctors who performed abortions and the allegedly gutless politicians, unaccountable courts, and liberal media that aided and abetted what they castigated as state-sanctioned fetal holocaust.

The new pro-life insurgency was led by Ken Campbell, who, in his own words, was "stunned and sickened" by Morgentaler's acquittal "on charges of crimes against humanity which he'd fully admitted." The acquittal hardened his resolve to fight back against "the elite of secular subversives" who were destroying the morals of Canadian society, fostering godlessness and malevolently subverting the Canadian state itself: "The domination of our society by these secular fundamentalists is most outrageously evident in the discrimination against the pre-born, blatantly propagated, practiced and protected in Canada."[53] Campbell excoriated Morgentaler's clinic as, variously, "Henry's house of horrors," "a stronghold of Satan," and the "gates of Hell."

Campbell had formed a new pro-life group, Choose Life Canada, four years before the Supreme Court judgment, on December 14, 1984, "the day illegal abortions were resumed at the Morgentaler abortuary" in Toronto. The new group had, he said, "an evangelistic strategy, as a witness and service in the name of Christ on behalf of His Church, to the issue of abortion, and all other dimensions of the moral crisis in our society." Choose Life Canada, both a ministry and a political action group, preached "a public consciousness for the loving, life-affirming, civilized Christian alternative for women with crisis pregnancies, as the Morgentaler abortuary had generated an awareness for the 'cheap and violent solution of abortion-on-demand.'"[54] Within a couple of months, with the support of an owner of the building directly beside the Morgentaler Clinic in Toronto, CLC established its national headquarters along with a Christian coffee house and a "counselling ministry" called "The Way" Inn. It would soon become ground zero for increasingly desperate efforts to close down abortion clinics and restore the performance of abortions as a serious criminal offence.

CLC and Campaign Life Coalition organized almost daily picketing in front of the Morgentaler Clinic. Picketers prayed, sang hymns, held Bible readings, and attempted to block persons from entering the clinic. "Counsellors" were dispatched to "intervene between these women [seeking an abortion] and the lure of the abortuary," producing aggressive and confrontational interventions that were neither welcomed nor invited by the women. Campbell argued that the counsellors benignly offered practical help to the women: "housing during the pregnancy, financial and medical help, or emotional support as required. Their sincere, last-minute reaching out seems to appeal to women who are uncertain about their decision to abort, but who feel coerced by a boyfriend, husband or family."[55] Tellingly, he made no mention of what kind of support was offered after the birth of a child to a woman who needed housing, financial assistance, or other support to look after that child.

The earnest picketing and praying and the provocative interventions by "counsellors" made gaining access to the clinic unsafe and even dangerous. In response, the doctors, clinic staff, and pro-choice activists mounted vigils and counter-demonstrations. They arranged for women to be escorted through the hostile hordes of picketers and counsellors. In vivid contrast to Campbell's deceptively benevolent characterization of the counsellors, the clinic supporters characterized the interventions as coercive, harassing, intrusive, threatening, and intimidating. The street in front and the alley behind the abortion clinic became sites of fierce warfare in which women who were seeking to end their pregnancies were caught in the crossfire.

Following the Supreme Court decision in *Morgentaler*, Campbell and his CLC activists escalated their interventions to become full-fledged "rescue missions" at the clinic. Borrowing rhetoric from Operation Rescue, a radical anti-abortion group in the United States, Campbell declared, "Rescue missions are heroic attempts by God-fearing people to save babies and mothers from abortion on a particular day, by peacefully but physically blockading abortion mills with their bodies, to intervene between abortionists and their innocent victims." Rescue missions were inspired, Campbell said, by obedience to God, and they were justified in scripture. "We are simply being good, moral citizens by preventing the evil of aborting children." In being rescued, Campbell stated, children would be saved from death and mothers would be saved from exploitation. Claiming to have personal knowledge of God's divine intent, he proclaimed with righteous grandiosity, "'Rescuing' is a strategy God has established and blessed as an affirmation, in the name of Christ, of the humanity of the pre-born and as a rebuke of the pro-abortion perversity dominating politics and the judiciary in Canada."[56]

Rescue missions also had a deliberately political dimension. Campbell proudly declared that rescues would create the social tension necessary to producing political change. Their use would convince lawmakers that pro-lifers were serious in their determination to protect all "unborn children." "Rescues," Campbell piously stated in his political memoir, *5 Years Rescuing at 'the Gates of Hell,'* "provide godly people a fresh platform for lobbying their politicians to end this holocaust. May God help us to create a righteous uprising of God-fearing people across the country that will make child-killing illegal again." For added measure, he equated his embracing of rescue missions with Canada's national identity and historic values: "It is to keep the faith with the Fathers of Confederation who founded this nation on the values and philosophy of our Judeo-Christian heritage."[57]

In January 1989 Campbell and seventy-six followers conducted their first rescue by kneeling in prayer in the middle of the street directly in front of the Morgentaler Clinic and blocking entrance to it. Arrested for this action, they were later found guilty of trespassing and mischief and given suspended sentences. Significantly, the court also ordered them in future to keep at least 500 feet away from the clinic. But while that order restricted the seventy-six rescuers who had been arrested, it did not apply to their pro-life cohorts, and the rescue operations continued. Choose Life Canada, undeterred, carried on its activities. Throughout 1989 rescue missions took place at other abortion clinic locations in Toronto, Vancouver, and Montreal. [58]

In retaliation Morgentaler applied for and received an injunction banning all protesters and rescuers from congregating or picketing within 500 feet of his Toronto clinic. The injunction also banned obstructing, disturbing, or interrupting the functioning of the clinic, counselling people to break their contract with the clinic, or encouraging or condoning the disturbance or restriction of the clinic's operations. It effectively established a "bubble zone"—a safe area—in front of the clinic.[59] Similarly, in Vancouver, Everywoman's Health Clinic obtained an injunction to restrain persistent rescue operations. Protesters were banned from entering a bubble zone in front of the clinic. Those who violated the injunction faced upon conviction a five-month jail term and a fine.[60]

Campbell and CLC activists defied the injunction at the Morgentaler Clinic, holding another rescue mission and once again being arrested and jailed. While incarcerated and awaiting a bail hearing, Campbell issued a celebratory statement in which he exulted at being "In the Don Jail for Jesus."[61] At their trial all of the rescuers were found guilty and given suspended sentences. Still, despite the convictions, Campbell and other rescuers continued for some time to attempt interventions at abortion clinics. They also gradually extended the locales for their picketing and demonstrations to include hospitals that performed abortions and the offices and residences of doctors who performed them. These persistent and threatening actions ultimately led to the first attempt by a provincial government to curtail pro-life agitation. In 1991 the New Democratic Party government of Bob Rae in Ontario obtained what was initially a temporary injunction against pro-life picketers gathering near certain hospitals, the homes and offices of doctors, and abortion clinics.

The unrelenting pro-life demonstrations and interventions at abortion clinics created heightened concerns among pro-choice groups and the broader public about the safety of women seeking access to abortions and that of the doctors and staff in clinics and hospitals. In 1992 an arson attack and a fire-bombing of the Morgentaler Clinic in Toronto alarmingly increased those concerns. Although there was never any evidence suggesting that pro-life groups were involved with these incidents, the events were seen as disturbing indicators of the extent to which acts of violence could be perpetrated by pro-life extremists.

At the same time the pro-life forces expanded their picketing and demonstrations to harass and intimidate doctors and hospitals where abortions were performed. They hoped to publicly expose and vilify the doctors who performed abortions and to close down abortion clinics in hospitals. Pro-life groups, such as the London Area Campaign Life Coalition, engaged in a strategy of targeting and incrementally harassing doctors. Their first step was to ask doctors to stop performing abortions. If the doctors refused to stop, they were subjected to persistent picketing that featured placards and leaflets bearing inflammatory messages that the named doctor "kills unborn children" or that the named hospital "killed" a specified number of "pre-born babies." Picketers at doctors' homes carried garish and grotesque placards with pictures of aborted fetuses. They chanted and prayed as they marched, and they attempted to engage in "debate" with members of the families, neighbours, and passersby.[62] Sadly, a number of the targeted physicians, fearful for their safety and loss of privacy and concerned for their families, stopped providing abortion services. Through harassment, intimidation, and fear-mongering, the pro-life movement was achieving the reduction in access to abortion services that its members had been unable to accomplish through decisions of the courts or legislation. It was a new kind of tyranny manifested by hateful mob rule fuelled by religious conviction and zealotry.

Amid this poisonous and increasingly dangerous climate, the Task Group of Abortion Service Providers established by the Rae government came into play. Set up to provide advice on improving access to abortion services, it called upon the government to seek an expanded injunction to control harassment activity at abortion service facilities and at the homes of abortion providers.[63] In 1994 the Ontario government finally did secure an expanded injunction against demonstrations, picketing, or "counselling" within 500 feet at twenty-three named locations throughout Ontario: hospitals, free-standing abortion clinics, and offices and homes of doctors. The injunction infuriated pro-life activists, who now bitterly and loudly declared that their rights of free speech and free assembly were being infringed.

To the shock and dismay of pro-lifers, the injunction remained in force even after the 1995 Ontario election that brought to power the Progressive Conservatives led by staunch right-winger Mike Harris. Despite having previously denounced the injunction as an unwarranted suppression of free speech and promising that they would review it if elected to government, the Harris Tories now defended it as necessary for public safety. That decision prompted Campaign Life Coalition, in the fall of 1998, to hold pickets at the constituency offices of about ninety members of the legislature.[64]

Still hoping to bring the Tory government back into the pro-life fold, Jim Hughes of Campaign Life Coalition put the blame for the failure to remove the injunction on the sinister and entrenched socialist bureaucracy left over from the days of the despised NDP government. "The social leftists in the attorney-general's office continue to be a real bugbear," he opined.[65] That same sentiment showed up years later in a 2008 statement by Tony Gosgnach, a pro-life journalist: "The injunction had been engineered by the virulently pro-abortion, socialist NDP government and its extreme feminist attorney general, Marion Boyd."[66] Perplexingly for pro-life activists, the injunction has continued in force in Ontario over the years since it was first issued. Although Campaign Life Coalition has continued to vehemently protest the measures, it has failed to persuade the successive governments to have it removed.

Ceaseless picketing and rescue operations in Vancouver also prompted British Columbia's NDP government led by Mike Harcourt to seek an injunction. Between November 1988 and January 1989, Operation Rescue organized massive demonstrations at the Everywoman's Health Centre, blocking access to the clinic. A January 1989 demonstration effectively prevented the clinic from operating. In response the clinic obtained an interim injunction establishing a bubble zone around abortion clinics that prohibited leafleting, sidewalk counselling, or any attempt to dissuade people from performing or having abortions. The injunction also prohibited demonstrations outside doctors' offices and homes. Vancouver's other clinic offering abortion services, the Elizabeth Bagshaw Clinic, also obtained an injunction.[67]

In 1995 British Columbia's NDP government adopted the Access to Abortion Services Act. The first legislation of its kind in Canada, it provided for the establishment of access (bubble) zones at facilities providing abortions, doctors' residences, and doctors' offices. The legislation responded to the 1994 shooting of Vancouver's Dr. Garson Romalis, a physician who performed abortions. The attempted murder of Romalis caused shock and fear throughout the medical and pro-choice communities. It raised the horrific spectre that some within the pro-life movement had taken their militancy to a new and deadly level. Those fears were heightened in 1996 when Dr. Hugh Short was shot in the arm by a sniper at his home in Ancaster, Ontario, and again in 1997 when Dr. Jack Fainman was shot in the shoulder through the back window of his home in Winnipeg. In 2000 Romalis became the victim of violence for a second time when he was stabbed outside his clinic. Despite intensive police investigations, no arrests were made in respect of any of the incidents.[68]

As in Ontario, the B.C. pro-life activists argued that the bubble zone law infringed freedom of religion and freedom of expression. Determined to have the Act struck down as unconstitutional, they mounted a number of court challenges involving belligerent pro-lifers deliberately intruding into the bubble zones carrying placards, handing out leaflets, or engaging in "counselling" of women seeking abortions.[69] The cases raised fundamental issues about a stark conflict of rights and the extent to which the Charter, and the courts through the interpretation and application of the Charter, must arbitrate a resolution. They presented the courts with the challenging task of determining whether freedom of religion and freedom of expression are absolute, even when the exercise of them invades the privacy and impinges on the safety and security of other people.

The stakes in the cases were high for both the pro-life and the pro-choice movements. If the pro-lifers were successful, not only might the particular act be struck down, but the injunction in Ontario might also not withstand a challenge for the same reasons. Canada would return to the days of virtually unfettered demonstrations and interventions. The harassment of abortion clinics, of their doctors and staff and the women who seek to enter them, and of hospitals, doctors' offices, and residences would be back full-scale. The change would unleash a virtual open season on abortion providers and the women who seek out their services; it would represent a huge victory for an unrelenting pro-life movement that would be emboldened to continue the crusade on behalf of the "unborn" with ever more vigour and extremism.

So far the courts have upheld the constitutionality of the B.C. legislation, determining that the actions of pro-life protesters create an unsafe environment and may have detrimental effects on the health and well-being of women who seek out legal abortions. In *R. v. Spratt*, a judgment released in September 2008, three justices of the B.C. Court of Appeal noted that the evidence disclosed in the case indicated that the actions of the protesters and "counsellors" outside the clinic:

> evoked a range of emotions in women attending the clinic. Those emotions extended from mild distress to absolute fear. Clinic employees testified that once women passed the protesters, they often presented as being extremely upset, crying, shaking or anxious. The women expressed fear not only about a violent or traumatic interaction with the protesters, but also about a loss of confidentiality.

Medical consultants had testified, "The confrontation experienced by the women outside the clinic was deleterious to their health." Accepting such evidence, the justices declared emphatically, "The obvious intent of the protests was to stop abortions, whether it was by persuasion or intimidation and fear."[70]

Pro-life activists predictably denounced the judgment. Misrepresenting the pro-life intrusions into the access zone as benign and benevolent, the Catholic Civil Rights League professed in a press release that the actions of the protesters were "peaceful in nature." The league lamented the law's provisions that "also ban handing out leaflets or praying on a public sidewalk that is within an access zone."[71] One of the protesters, Don Spratt, vowed to continue his fight against the access law, declaring on his web page: "My intention has always been to take this all the way to the Supreme Court of Canada, if necessary, win or lose. If justice is not found in Canadian courts, it will be found in the Court of Heaven."[72] Unhappily for him, the Supreme Court of Canada ruled in June 2009 that it would not hear the appeal, and the judgment of the B.C. appeal court remained in force.

A long-time, militant pro-life activist, Spratt doggedly pursued the case through the courts for ten years. It began after he was arrested in 1998 for deliberately invading the access zone in front of the Everywoman's Health Centre—he was carrying a nine-foot cross and a sign saying, "You Shall Not Murder." On his website, describing himself as a businessman, evangelist, and evangelical minister (he graduated from Full Gospel Bible College, affiliated with the Apostolic Church of Pentecost of Canada), Spratt says he "worked closely with his friend and fellow minister, the late Ken Campbell" during the late 1980s and early 1990s organizing and leading Rescue Canada (Operation Rescue). He has been repeatedly jailed for contempt of court for what he states in his biography as "obeying God rather than man." He has also "organized lobby efforts to Ottawa on behalf of the unborn and participated in many campaigns in support of moral and socially conservative issues."[73]

With a characteristic evangelical presumption and certainty, Spratt states in biblical terms: "I believe God called me to speak on behalf of those who have no voice and to be a witness to truth ... to prophetically speak truth to power." Like his old friend Campbell, Spratt is a religious fanatic who has denounced "secular humanist hypocrites who esteem the Charter above holy writ," the courts that "totally disregard our religious convictions and demand we disregard and disobey our Lord (ultimate authority)," and the "willing blindness and moral corruption of our legal system." In his holy mission to save the unborn, he declares: "There is something extremely wrong with a nation when it pays mass murderers like Henry Morgentaler millions to execute the innocent, then gives him the Order of Canada, while jailing people of conscience who dare speak of his thousands of victims."[74]

Spratt and other right-to-life militants remain defiant about the various rulings of the courts, continuing to demonstrate outside abortion clinics and to invade the access zones. Perhaps the most notorious—certainly the most persistent— is Linda Gibbons, an evangelical Christian who participated in rescue missions with Campbell. Gibbons has been arrested repeatedly for violating the injunction intended to buffer the Scott Clinic in Toronto, including an arrest in July 2008. In total Gibbons has spent more than five years in jail. Pro-life leaders have lionized her as a martyr, saint, heroine, and "political prisoner." In 1999, during one of Gibbons's periods of incarceration, Charles McVety of Canada Christian College commented, "That she's spending her days in prison as a forgotten political prisoner instead of being allowed to carry on her ministry is nothing less than a tragedy."[75] Generally Gibbons engages in prayer and attempts to "counsel" women entering the clinic. On occasion she has carried placards with messages such as "Abortion is Murder." Sometimes she has dumped headless baby dolls on the doorsteps of the clinic to symbolize the murder of "unborn children" at the clinic.

These actions are evidence of the continuing warfare being waged on the streets outside Canada's abortion clinics. Some twenty years after Campbell held his first rescue mission outside of the Morgentaler Clinic, his radical strategy remains a troubling but enduring feature of pro-life activism. It is a strategy that "God has established and blessed"—of picketing and protesting, of intrusively "counselling" women attempting to get access to abortion clinics, and "rescuing" the unborn from "murder" at the bloody hands of evil abortionists. While Campbell's prophetic "righteous uprising of God-fearing people" has not led to the hoped-for recriminalization of abortion, the pro-life movement has shown remarkable resilience and tenacity. Convinced of their holy mission on God's behalf, the pro-life warriors reject and defiantly challenge all injunctions, court decisions, and laws that stand in their way.

Access to and public funding of abortion services

Despite their setbacks, the pro-life movement has successfully curtailed both access to abortions and public funding of abortion services. Indeed, their uncompromising and sustained advocacy over the last four decades has to be seen as one of the principal reasons that shockingly few hospitals in Canada provide abortion services. Tragically, less than one in five hospitals in Canada today offers that help.[76] Appallingly, Prince Edward Island has never approved a hospital for abortions, and no abortions are available in that province. To further restrict access, virtually every hospital providing abortion services is located within 150 kilometres of the U.S. border. Ontario in 2008 had, according to one report, "not a single abortion provider north of the Trans-Canada Highway."[77] To make matters worse, hospital rules governing approval for abortion procedures are inconsistent and arbitrary, especially in respect of the gestation periods during which a pregnancy can be terminated.[78] Excessive waiting times for abortions in hospital clinics present a significant additional deterrent.

The scarcity of hospital abortion clinics and the difficulties faced by women seeking to get access to their services create a greater need for and reliance on private abortion clinics. Yet, few private clinics—less than two dozen—exist, and most of them are located in a handful of cities in British Columbia, Ontario, and Quebec. Prince Edward Island, Nova Scotia, Saskatchewan, Yukon, the Northwest Territories, and Nunavut have no private clinics. Problematically, access to abortion services in private or free-standing abortion clinics has been even more severely hindered in some provinces in which governments have attempted to prevent their establishment or to deny public funding for services provided in them. Lack of public funding through provincial health-care systems for abortions obtained outside of hospitals creates a significant impediment to women seeking to terminate their pregnancies.

Ensuring the denial or elimination of health-care funding for abortions, whether performed in hospitals or clinics, has been one of the other major objectives of the pro-life movement. As early as 1975, Toronto Right to Life lobbied the Ontario government to cease covering abortions under the health insurance plan.[79] In 1989 Choose Life Canada endorsed a national strategy developed by the Saskatchewan Pro-Life Association, calling on the Mulroney government to enact legislation extending universal health care to include the protection and care of the "unborn from the point of conception." In effect, this move would have prohibited any medicare funding of abortion services.[80] Campaign Life Coalition has unabashedly declared, "Free abortions mean more abortions" and—outrageously because it is simply untrue—"Public funding encourages the use of abortion as birth control." According to it, "Abortion is never medically necessary."[81] Campaign Life and other groups have demanded that abortion be classified as an elective procedure (not medically necessary) under the Canada Health Act, which would result in its ineligibility for coverage under government health plans.

The awful truth is that the pro-life campaign against public funding for abortion procedures has resonated with legislators over the years. Although provincial governments now provide varying degrees of public funding for abortions performed in hospitals, some have done so only reluctantly. In British Columbia, for instance, the Social Credit government of Premier Bill Vander Zalm, a devout Roman Catholic and staunch social conservative, attempted in 1988 to refuse to pay for abortions through the provincial medicare program. Vander Zalm supported that position with various incendiary comments, such as "Abortion diminishes society's respect for human life," and "The baby's body is cut up [during an abortion] . . . without so much as an anesthetic." Lives, he said, were "terminated at the slightest whim or notion of women."[82] The B.C. government reversed its stance and agreed to cover the costs of abortions only after a huge public outcry against Vander Zalm's remarks and a 1988 judgment of the B.C. Supreme Court.

In Alberta the Progressive Conservative government of Ralph Klein attempted to de-insure abortion services in 1996 after a vigorous lobby by a provincial pro-life group, the Committee to End Tax-Funded Abortions. The government backed down only after the College of Physicians and Surgeons, with which it was required to consult under the provisions of the Canada Health Act, refused to agree to a definition of "medically necessary" that would have excluded abortion services.[83] Next door in Saskatchewan, the staunchly pro-life Progressive Conservative government of Grant Devine held a non-binding plebiscite (referendum) during the 1991 provincial election on the question, unleashing a furious public debate. The pro-life campaign leading up to the vote raised the apparently horrific spectre of public funding being extended to free-standing abortion clinics, attempting to portray Morgentaler as an evil outsider determined to set up his killing clinic in the province. They claimed that less than 1 per cent of abortions performed in the province were "obtained for legitimate health reasons," and called on voters to tell the government to end "this offensive and irresponsible use of tax dollars."[84] When the vote was held, an astounding 62 per cent of Saskatchewan voters voted "no" to government funding of abortions.

Other provinces have been reluctant to extend medicare funding to cover abortion services provided by clinics operated by Morgentaler. Allegedly liberal

Quebec refused to cover the costs of abortions performed at the Morgentaler Clinic until it was forced to do so by a 2006 Quebec Superior Court ruling. In Manitoba the New Democratic Party government of Premier Gary Doer did not start paying for abortions performed at the Morgentaler Clinic in Winnipeg until 2004. Successive governments in New Brunswick have adamantly refused to provide funding for abortions performed in the Morgentaler Clinic in Fredericton. Morgentaler initiated a lawsuit in that province in hope of securing a court decision that will require the government to reverse its policy.[85]

The pursuit of right-to-life legislation

In continuing to work arduously to secure legislation that would recriminalize abortion, pro-life groups have enjoyed significant support from federal politicians. The efforts of the Mulroney government to reintroduce Criminal Code sections on abortion are just one example. Pro-life MPs are well represented and well organized within Parliament. Following the 2006 federal election, Campaign Life Coalition published a list of seventy-three MPs, based on its election survey, who were pro-life or "pro-life with exceptions." The list included fifty-nine Conservatives and fourteen Liberals,[86] but the actual number of pro-life MPs may be somewhat higher. The Abortion Rights Coalition of Canada (ARCC) found that 63 per cent of Conservative MPs and 21 per cent of Liberal MPs had either introduced or supported private member's bills that would restrict abortion or have otherwise indicated an anti-abortion position. By that estimate, the number of pro-life MPs would be closer to one hundred, or nearly one-third of all MPs.[87]

Since 1994, MPs from the various conservative parties—Progressive Conservative, Reform Party (1987–2000), Canadian Alliance (2000–2003), and Conservative Party of Canada (2003–present)—and a substantial number of Liberals have formed the Pro-Life Parliamentary Caucus. They work in common cause to secure pro-life legislation, mainly through the introduction of private member's bills intended to amend the Criminal Code. Despite their minority numbers, they remain optimistic that their efforts will succeed one day. As Pro-Life Caucus member Dean Del Mastro, the Conservative MP for Peterborough, Ontario, noted when speaking at the annual March for Life rally on Parliament Hill in 2007: "The laws will change in this country."[88]

Members of the Pro-Life Caucus have made a number of unsuccessful attempts to secure right-to-life legislation. In 2001 Garry Breitkreuz, then the Canadian Alliance MP for the Saskatchewan constituency of Yorkton-Melville, introduced a private member's motion calling for introduction of legislation "defining a 'human being' as a human fetus or embryo from the moment of conception, whether in the womb of the mother or not and whether conceived naturally or otherwise." The motion was never voted on by MPs.[89] In 2006 and 2007 Leon Benoit and Ken Epp, two members of the Pro-Life Caucus, attempted to have private member's bills enacted that would make it a crime to injure or kill a fetus in the course of an attack on a pregnant woman.[90] Public outcries against the bills stymied their chances of success, and neither of them proceeded to final votes. Deceptively labelled "victims of crime" or "fetal homicide" legislation, these bills had as their the principal objective to establish in law that a fetus has a right to life and to separate in law the fetus from a pregnant woman. They would thus have pitted the rights of the fetus against the rights of the pregnant woman, to the detriment of the woman. As the Abortion Rights Coalition of Canada noted: "If a fetus is a legal entity with the right not to be killed, how can abortion be exempt, and why should a pregnant woman's potentially harmful behaviours be exempt? The law opens the door to pregnant women being targeted for their behaviours or for self-abortions, as has happened in the U.S."[91]

ARCC has cited harrowing examples of the potential dangers of similar fetal homicide laws adopted by thirty-seven U.S. states. Pregnant women are more likely to be punished for behaviours and conditions that are not criminalized for other people. Women have been charged and convicted under the laws for drug or alcohol abuse or mental illness on the contention that their behaviour or condition harmed the fetus. Women with drug abuse problems have been arrested under fetal homicide laws although they had virtually no access to drug treatment programs. Horrendously, women have been charged with or jailed for murder in the United States, according to ARCC, for "experiencing a stillbirth after refusing a caesarean section, or just from suffering a stillbirth." ARCC also worried that a pregnant woman might be punished by use of a fetal homicide law as a result of being unable to leave an abusive relationship in which the fetus might be vulnerable because of an assault on the woman.[92]

The many possible dire consequences for pregnant women arising from the adoption of a fetal homicide law contrasts sharply with what is likely to be the relatively few convictions of perpetrators of actual violence against women that leads to the woman's death or injury or to the death or injury of the fetus. Yet the sponsors of such legislation and their vocal pro-life supporters have ignored or remained silent about such consequences. They remain singularly focused on obtaining legislation, in any form, that enshrines the right to life. Mary Ellen Douglas of Campaign Life Coalition, when urging support for such bills, has declared: "The Canadian criminal code must be revised to recognize the obvious fact that the child in the womb is worthy of recognition as a human being." Similarly, the

Catholic Civil Rights League lauded Epp's bill: "The League has always supported such legislation as a needed step in recognizing the personhood of the unborn child and the dignity of women."[93]

Benoit's bill was followed a week later by a private member's bill that proposed criminalizing the procurement of an abortion after twenty weeks of gestation. It was introduced by Paul Steckle, a Liberal MP and former co-chair of the Pro-Life Caucus who represented the rural Ontario riding of Huron-Bruce. The bill would have established only a limited exception from conviction in the case of a miscarriage that was necessary "to save the life of a woman whose life is endangered by a physical disorder, physical illness or injury, including a physical condition caused by or arising from the pregnancy itself" or "to prevent severe pathological physical morbidity of the woman."[94]

Steckle's bill was seemingly a reasonable attempt to criminalize abortions only in the third trimester of pregnancy, which based on available data constituted only 0.3 per cent of abortions performed in Canada. Almost all such abortions are performed because of serious health problems of the mother or the fetus. But what the bill would have achieved, if adopted, would be, as the ARCC noted, "a foot-in-the-door to enact even more restrictions against abortion."[95] The fear was that adoption of the bill would have opened the door to future legislation establishing the right to life of the fetus and curtailing abortions prior to the third trimester of pregnancy. Fortunately, the bill was never voted on due to the termination of the parliamentary session and the holding of the 2008 federal election.

In 2007 Conservative MP Maurice Vellacott, the co-chair of the Pro-Life Caucus, made a further attempt to secure right-to-life legislation. Vellacott introduced, for the third time, a private member's bill that would protect the conscience rights of health-care workers who refuse to participate in performing abortions. The bill sought to ensure the right to employment and job advancement of health-care practitioners unwilling to take part in medical procedures offensive to a tenet of the practitioner's religion, or the belief of the practitioner that human life is inviolable. The bill's purported intent was simply to "safeguard health care workers' fundamental human rights" (which is beyond the purview of the Criminal Code).[96] Yet, if adopted, the bill would have facilitated the curtailment of the performance of abortions by limiting the number of health professionals available to provide or assist in providing abortion procedures. Even more troubling was a provision that would have made a fetus a human being in law "at any stage of development, beginning at fertilization or creation." The proposal thus would have granted by statute the right to life to a fetus that would serve as a precedent that could be used to further expand that right in other sections of the Criminal Code in future.

If private member's bills like those introduced by the members of the Pro-Life Caucus were to be adopted, the circumstances that would be held to constitute the lawful termination of a pregnancy would be significantly narrowed. Problematically, a new section of the Criminal Code would be created that would be in conflict with the existing section 223(1), which states that a child is not a human being until it completely exits from the birth canal in a living state. The result would be confusion and contention over which section would have precedence in law. The issue would thus arise—and it would be up to the courts to decide—as to how to resolve the conflict in the Criminal Code provisions. With the right kind of judicial appointments made in future by a government committed to enshrining social conservative values as the values of the state, the conflict could well be resolved in favour of the provision deeming fetuses to be human beings with all of the rights of personhood.

What is truly alarming is that Epp's bill was adopted on first reading, which means that a majority of MPs present for the vote supported it, including, significantly, Stephen Harper. It was derailed only because of electoral considerations in the summer of 2008. Liberal opposition leader Stéphane Dion vowed to block it— but only after twenty-seven Liberal MPs had voted in favour, along with Conservative members. Dion's gesture put pressure on Harper to stake out a public position on the bill. In the end the Harper government's interest in winning re-election dictated that it would have to abandon support for the proposal. The bill had generated controversy in Quebec, becoming an issue in two by-elections then being held in that province. It had also been protested by Quebec women's groups and by the College of Physicians of Quebec. The Epp bill simply presented too great a political risk for it to proceed any further through the legislative process. Harper, gearing up for a general election in the fall of 2008, needed to increase support for the Conservative Party in Quebec in order to have any prospect of securing a majority mandate. Justice Minister Rob Nicholson was hastily dispatched to announce that the government was abandoning its support for Epp's bill.[97]

Harper's action temporarily removed the contentious abortion bills from the legislative agenda, but did not bring an end to the abortion issue. The frightening prospect that the Conservative Party's true agenda is to recriminalize abortion in the long run was revived when the party's membership, at its fall 2008 convention, approved a policy supporting the adoption of a fetal homicide law similar to Epp's. Armed with that position as party policy, and given that more than half of the Conservative Party MPs (according to ARCC data) are pro-life, there is genuine cause for concern that, should the party obtain a majority government, it will act upon its true intentions. That the fetal homicide bill came so perilously close to being adopted, with the support of Harper and other members of his government, creates profound concern about what might happen in future should another bill be introduced at a time when the government is less concerned about an immediate need to ensure its re-election.

An issue that won't go away

In 2002, when the advocacy group LifeCanada was formed, its president, Peter Ryan, pledged that the new organization was "standing on guard for life." "True to our moniker, we believe in two things: life and Canada!" Ryan boasted. "And stand on guard, for both life and Canada, we must. For a country that fails to respect human life—*all* human life—is no country at all."

Linking the pro-life message with the patriotism of standing on guard for Canada neatly connected the organization's objectives with the social conservative origins of Canada as a nation and the Judeo-Christian moral values that were the foundation of the national identity of Canadians. In this mind frame people who are not pro-life are unrepresentative of true Canadian values and the Canadian heritage. Moreover, LifeCanada explicitly associated the defence of the right to life with the principles of governance set out in the British North America Act of 1867. As Ryan pointed out:

> Social scientists sometimes characterize the Canadian identity by referring to our historical desire for "peace, order and good government." But for Canada to be true to its identity as a land that cherishes "peace, order and good government," it must be rock solid—like the Canadian Shield, like Newfoundland, like the Rockies—in respecting human life. Our Prime Minister [Chrétien] has said we have "social peace" on the issue of abortion. Yet what kind of *peace* can there be in a land where prenatal child-killing is the number one cause of death? What kind of *order* can there be when respect for life is so sorely lacking? As Mother Teresa said, if a mother can kill her own child what is to stop us all from killing one another? And how can we have *good government* when the last things politicians want to consider are issues like abortion and euthanasia?[98]

In the November 2007 issue of Campaign Life Coalition's on-line magazine, *The Interim*, Mary Ellen Douglas, the group's national organizer, looked ahead to "the days after abortion is finally re-criminalized." She stated emphatically, "We must not allow misdirected compassion for the mother to suggest that she and the person she hires to carry out the killing of her baby, the doctor, should be above the law and receive no jail time." She added, "Jail time for those who commit the crime of abortion is not only just, but absolutely necessary." Natalie Hudson, executive director of Right to Life Association of Toronto and Area, has similarly declared: "Those who carry out abortions or who counsel a woman to abort should be prosecuted to the full extent of the law for murder. ... Their act is the epitome of cold-blooded murder and, because it is often repeated numerous times, they can be considered the perpetrators of genocide."[99]

As these declarations attest, the pro-life movement remains steadfast—and frighteningly absolutist—in its pursuit of the right to life for the fetus. In its members' minds, they are engaged in a genuine holy war against immorality and evil. Nothing short of the restoration of an absolute ban on abortion, as testament to the old "Canadian values" and traditional morality, will truly satisfy them. Many of them are downright and dangerously delusional, righteously convinced that they have been commanded by God to carry on their campaign to save the unborn.

Dismissive of the majority of Canadians who support a woman's right to choose, the pro-life militants refuse to accept that they no longer have control of the moral agenda in regard to abortion. They refuse to accept that they do not have the right to impose their moral agenda on everyone else. As long as there is a pro-life movement, there must be a strong and active pro-choice movement to counter it. The stakes, especially for women, are simply too high to remain complacent, to cease being vigilant, or simply to acquiesce.

THREE

Regulating Sexuality and Social Order

Since homosexuality, adultery, prostitution and
pornography undermine the foundations of the
family, the basis of society, then the State must
use its coercive power to proscribe or curtail
them in the interests of the common good....
An evil act remains an evil act whether it is
performed in public or private.

– Bishop F. B. Henry, Calgary, 2005

For social conservatives, the sexual permissiveness and promiscuity of modern society are deeply troubling—so much so that their militancy
in opposing the decriminalization of abortion has been matched by the zeal of
their war against sex and sexual expression. In this regard too, for reinforcement
they tend to look back to the Judeo-Christian values and morality that once both
shaped and characterized the Canadian state and its culture. Social conservatives
champion the pervasive anti-sex nature of the old Christian Canada: the time typified by a national character of sexual repression and prudery as symbolized by
the many Victorian-era laws criminalizing consenting sexual activity and public
expressions of sexuality. They see modern trends as representing a historic and
dangerous shift away from these standards. Not surprisingly, then, they have
organized massively to resist the many changes they see happening around them
all too rapidly and consistently. Their objective, in the words of U.S. Moral Majority leader Jerry Falwell, is to "call the nation back to God."[1]

From this point of view, sexual activity outside of marriage or that is not essentially procreative in purpose is against God's design. It is immoral, anti-family, and socially destructive. A social order based on what is purported to be God's divine intent and the vulnerability and susceptibility of "man" to sin and temptation are fundamental pillars of evangelicalism and social conservatism. The beliefs about sex are firmly based on what they contend the Bible has to say, as the true word of God. According to the Bible, God commanded, "Thou shalt not commit adultery." That condemnation of sex outside of marriage is seen as absolute. Sexual intercourse is a necessary act between a man and a woman, but it is fundamentally intended for procreation. Only a heterosexual couple within a lifelong monogamous marriage can acceptably and morally engage in sex. Its exclusivity to marriage is essential to ensuring social order and regulation. "As marriage entails a covenantal commitment, it promotes social stability and good order," proclaims the Evangelical Fellowship of Canada. "It promotes a depth of relationship which cohabitation outside of marriage cannot provide. By emphasizing sexual fidelity, it operates as a force for the social regulation of sexuality."[2]

Otherwise for the social conservative, sex is a sin—dangerous and destructive. Like every other sin, sexual sin must be punished, viewed with disgust, shrouded in shame, and avoided. It must be restricted, constrained, and controlled. That is done first by the individual through a self-discipline and self-restraint informed and enforced by religious faith as expressed through rigid adherence to the dictates of the Bible. Chastity or sexual abstinence is the only morally appropriate condition for unmarried persons. Premarital and extramarital sex are immoral and harmful, and so too are any forms of expression or behaviour that might encourage individuals to succumb to the temptations of their sexuality. After all, as the *Catechism of the Catholic Church* proclaims, "Chastity is a moral virtue" and a "gift from God," and "Sexuality is ordered to the conjugal love of man and woman." Lust, masturbation, fornication, prostitution, and homosexuality are all sins gravely contrary to chastity.[3] Indeed, even thinking "sinful thoughts" of a sexual nature is a sin. It is a form of adultery that must be repressed. So too (for heterosexual men presumably) is looking lustfully at a woman, which for a man, according to one Bible passage, is committing adultery "in his heart."

The temptation to tolerate and engage in sinful sexual activity is particularly strong in today's "hyper-sexualized culture," the Evangelical Fellowship of Canada laments. "It is easy for both adults and children to become desensitized to sexual sin, and to accept our culture's guiding principle that choice determines whether sexual activity is acceptable." This distressing "postmodernism" is based on commonly held "assumptions" that "are characterized by a belief in autonomy, that we are a law to ourselves, rather than under God's creational law." The result is that "there are no God-given norms or absolutes" any longer, and "we are choosing to do what is right in our own eyes rather than looking to God for his revealed truth."[4]

Of course, the social regulation of sexuality cannot be achieved solely by the exercise of individual self-discipline and self-restraint. Because all persons, in the evangelical view of things, can be tempted and corrupted and the vulnerable (especially women and young persons) can be coerced and seduced into sexual behaviour, social regulation also demands the state's regulation of sexuality through the instrument of stringent criminal law. That is why social conservatives have always sought more state regulation of sexuality. In the late nineteenth and early twentieth centuries, the social purity movement championed by evangelical Protestants argued for stronger criminal laws dealing with bawdy houses, acts of indecency, and prostitution and advocated for increasing the age of consent for sexual activity.[5]

Today's social conservatives, like their forbearers in earlier decades, have advocated staunchly for the retention, and in some cases for the strengthening, of laws that deal with prostitution and other forms of illicit sexual activity, the age of consent for sexual activity, "acts of indecency," and "obscenity" in all of its forms. As the EFC's Bruce Clemenger declared, "The criminal code is a moral code and Evangelicals, as other Canadians and communities, seek to influence it."[6]

In this intense and determined campaign the forces of social conservatism clash with other interests and stakeholders who are also seeking to influence social mores, public policy, and the judicial and statutory regulation of sexuality and sexual expression. Civil libertarians, cultural activists (artists, writers, performers, polemicists), and sexual liberation activists, most notably gay and lesbian groups, have organized for reform or outright repeal of repressive sex laws, especially those that censor or constrain freedom of expression. The age of feminist advocacy also brought new interpretations and applications of the state regulation of sexuality and sexual expression based on ensuring the dignity and equality of women. This construct gradually replaced the anti-sex religious morality of the old Christian Canada as the rationale for the state's adoption and enforcement of sex laws. The result has been a new, secular morality that impels state regulation to prohibit and severely penalize forms of sexuality and sexual expression that are deemed harmful to women, children, and society as a whole, that exploit, degrade, and dehumanize women and encourage not just the unequal treatment of women but also violence against them.

For social conservatives, this opposition and new wave of forces create a new configuration. They have to strive to maintain relevance and influence and to avoid marginalization as stakeholders in the process of influencing public policy and legislation. In no small way, they have to augment their old religious morality arguments for regulating sexuality and sexual expression with the new secular morality of equality for women, protection of children, and reduction of harm.

The campaign for stronger pornography laws

During the 1970s, renewed activism among Roman Catholics and evangelical Protestants fostered a new crusade to stem what they deplored as the dangerous proliferation of filth and depravity in print and visual media. They condemned the growth of what they characterized as a horrific pornography industry. Along with the pro-life movement, the fight to secure stronger obscenity laws and more vigorous state action to eradicate pornography became a defining issue for social conservatism. It was the more political and visible manifestation of a campaign that had begun in the late 1940s and 1950s against printed materials, available at newsstands, that were deemed to be objectionable and were being sold to young people. The objectionable materials included comic books depicting scenes of violence and crimes and magazines having sexually explicit content.

As Dany Lacombe pointed out in *Blue Politics: Pornography and the Law in the Age of Feminism,* it was during those earlier decades that religious conservatives began to agitate vigorously around the increasing availability of sexually explicit magazines. Pornography, they argued, corrupted public morality. It was also associated with other harmful social consequences, such as crime, alcohol and drug use, prostitution, sexually transmitted diseases, adultery, the breakdown of marriages, illegitimate children, and divorce. Their view, states Lacombe, was that "pornography is dangerous to society because it undermines morality—that is to say, it constitutes a threat to the existence of the community. As an affront to morality, pornography must be legally proscribed."[7] The concern in the immediate postwar period was over so-called pulp novels, fiction with sexually suggestive or explicit content, and the burgeoning adult magazine trade. Especially shocking, for them, was the brashness and vulgarity, and popularity and widespread availability, of adult publications such as *Playboy.*

The concern about the proliferation of pornography led to the establishment in Parliament of the Senate Committee on Salacious and Indecent Literature in 1952. It held public hearings to determine how criminal law should deal with the prevailing material. In 1958 the Diefenbaker government established the first statutory definition of "obscene" in an effort to increase the prospects of conviction of those charged with selling or distributing materials considered to be harmful.[8] The result was a section of the Criminal Code that stated, "Any publication a dominant characteristic of which is the undue exploitation of sex, or of sex and any one or more of the following subjects, namely crime, horror, cruelty, and violence shall be deemed to be obscene." The section remains in the Criminal Code today, as section 163(8)—tellingly appearing under the condemnatory heading, "Offences Tending to Corrupt Morals." The new obscenity law left to the courts the interpretation of the vague and highly subjective terms "a dominant characteristic" and "undue exploitation." Their interpretation hinged on determining "community standards"—standards that until only recently had been resolutely based on Christian morality. The courts applied the definition with reference to a legal test of community standards of tolerance—what would the community tolerate?

Not surprisingly, Diefenbaker's law quickly came under attack, first from civil libertarians and the arts community and later from gay and lesbian activist groups and some feminists. In opposition to the stance adopted by the state, these groups sought the repeal of the obscenity laws through the articulation of an essentially anti-censorship, freedom of expression rationale. Some questioned the whole notion of a "common good." Others contended that the state should not criminalize what was labelled immoral because of religious beliefs. The 1970 report of the Commission on Obscenity and Pornography in the United States, in articulating what became the liberal view regarding state regulation, asserted that having an interest in sex was normal, good, and healthy. Based on its extensive research on the effects of pornography, the Commission concluded that the state should not interfere with the right of adults to read, view, or obtain sexually explicit materials. That view was adopted by civil libertarians in Canada, who argued that the Criminal Code section should either be amended (liberalized) or repealed.[9]

Religious and moral conservatives had their critique too, but they saw the obscenity law and its enforcement as ineffective in curtailing pornography and sexually explicit materials. These opposing views would clash with each other in the public and political realms over the subsequent decades, much in the same way that the pro-life and pro-choice forces did on abortion. The social conservative protagonists seeking tougher laws and more censorship generally were supported by conservative politicians eager to appease an important electoral constituency. More liberal politicians, in contrast, did not stake out clear or unequivocal anti-censorship positions. Instead, they were caught somewhere in the middle of the debate. As legislators, they futilely sought and ultimately failed to find a middle ground between essentially irreconcilable positions.

In the mid-1970s the momentum grew for toughening the obscenity law. A powerful alliance of the Roman Catholic Church and evangelical Protestant groups formed to pressure politicians on the issue. Their campaign accelerated in 1976 when Philip Pocock, the Roman Catholic Archbishop of Toronto, spearheaded a highly publicized effort to secure tougher laws. Pocock authored a "Pastoral Letter of Concern" about pornography that was read out during Catholic masses. That action led in turn to a series of meetings with politicians and community organizations and the creation of an anti-pornography bandwagon aimed at pressuring governments to act. One notable success was a public declaration from Ontario's attorney general, Roy McMurtry, a Progressive Conservative, who denounced the availability of "depraved filth" and the harmful effects it had on children exposed to it.[10]

In Parliament Progressive Conservative and Liberal MPs formed an inter-party committee to obtain support for the anti-pornography position. The committee worked closely with the Toronto police service's Morality Squad and representatives from the Canadian Council of Churches. Their efforts led in March 1978 to public hearings on the obscenity law by the Parliamentary Standing Committee on Justice and Legal Affairs. Churches, police representatives, and anti-pornography feminist groups made representations to the hearings, and the Committee duly recommended significantly tightening the prohibition on pornography by extending its definition to include exploitation of crime, horror, cruelty, violence, or the undue degradation of the human person.[11] This finding represented a continuing shift away from the articulation of pornography as essentially an offence against sexual morality and religious values and towards a more harms-based analysis. It was ostensibly a secular articulation of the need to criminalize pornography that nonetheless was still fundamentally moral, because it was predicated on the morality of protecting vulnerable people (essentially women and children) from the harm, exploitation, and degradation of pornography.

Organizing by the anti-pornography forces continued into the 1980s. The leading social conservative players were REAL Women of Canada, the Coalition for Family Values, and the Interchurch Committee on Pornography headed by Pentecostal minister Hudson T. Hilsden and Suzanne Scorsone of the Office of Family Life of the Catholic Archdiocese of Toronto.[12] Later these groups would be joined by others, including the Evangelical Fellowship of Canada, of which Hilsden was a leader. Unlike the police and feminist groups, they were primarily motivated by biblical principles and a fervent belief in the state's promotion and protection of Judeo-Christian morality and the Christian concepts of marriage and family. The participation of Roman Catholic activists in particular reflected the condemnation of pornography found in the *Catechism of the Catholic Church*: that pornography "offends against chastity because it perverts the conjugal act." For that reason, the *Catechism* declares, "Civil authorities should prevent the production and distribution of pornographic materials."[13]

The opposition of REAL Women to pornography strongly echoed that of the Catholic Church. In its policy position it expressed the view that "pornographic material separates sex from a loving, conjugal relationship. Thus, the men and women involved become objects to satisfy sexual desires." Similarly, the EFC asserted its belief "that as Christians, in accordance with the Scriptures, we are called to care for the vulnerable, uphold human dignity and maintain family integrity. These principles guide our response to pornography." Linking pornography with the undermining of marriage and family, the EFC contended: "Pornography, by depicting sexual experience outside of loving, mutually supportive marriage, reduces sexuality merely to the physical component. Instead of supporting healthy sexual relationships within marriage, pornography serves to stimulate sexual appetites divorced from all human relationships."[14]

At the same time these social conservative groups faced a dilemma: how to position their campaign to eradicate pornography within changing social and political climates in which secular rather than religious arguments were becoming increasingly influential. The more that social conservative anti-pornography advocates clung solely to their religion-based objections to pornography, the more marginalized they would become within the powerful coalition of forces mobilizing to demand stronger laws against pornography. The police and new anti-pornography feminist groups did not articulate their stances in terms of religious morality, and it was the arguments of those members of the anti-pornography coalition that were being heard by the courts and legislators. The opposition of civil liberties groups and representatives of artistic and cultural groups about the dangers to freedom of expression inherent in criminal laws against pornography were also being heard, serving as a counterweight to the calls for ever more stringent laws.

The secularization of the anti-pornography campaign was clearly reflected in a policy on pornography formulated by the Trudeau Liberals. Women's studies professor Lise Gotell notes that this policy had four components: the proliferation of sexually explicit materials was an urgent problem; the problem should continue to be addressed primarily through the criminal law; the law should be based on the principle of sexual equality and should introduce the concept of "undue degradation of the human person"; and child pornography was a central concern that required specific and harsh penalties. At the same time the government acknowledged a need to introduce considerations for freedom of expression as a concession to civil libertarians and the arts community.[15] But the policy statement was also notable for a complete absence of any reference to moral objections to pornography; and it emphatically acknowledged a new politics of anti-pornography that succeeded in presenting sexual representation as harmful, the expression of sexuality as potentially violent and dangerous, and pornography as an important contributing factor to the societal problem of violence against women. It accepted the premise that new forms of legal regulation of pornography were needed to address the great harm caused to women by pornography and sexually explicit materials.

The social conservative anti-pornography crusaders responded to the changing dynamics by appropriating feminist anti-pornography analysis as a means of bolstering their own religion-based positions. As Brenda Cossman and Sharon Bell put it, "Radical feminist anti-pornography discourse was incorporated into conservative religious discourse."[16] That tendency was dramatically revealed in a "Statement on Pornography" adopted by REAL Women. Without any apparent embarrassment over the inherent contradiction of doing so, the organization unabashedly borrowed from the feminist analysis of pornography: "Much of pornographic material would appear to be exploitative of women—viewing them as mere objects or possessions to be used as a man sees fit." Citing "recent studies" by the police and academics, REAL Women asserted that pornography "contributes to the escalating problem of rape and battered women in society."[17] For its members, the articulation of pornography as harmful to women was simply an augmentation of their principal concern that pornography posed a threat to marriage and the family. They condemned pornography because it promoted and endorsed extramarital sex, separated sexuality from monogamous heterosexual marriage, and undermined traditional gender roles within the family. For a cause that had until then been presented as anti-sex and repressive, the feminist analysis of the harm done to women by pornography provided an aura of respectability and modernity—banning pornography and sexually explicit materials as a means of advancing the equality of women and combating the sexual abuse and exploitation of women.

Working in common cause, the secularist feminist groups and social conservative anti-pornography forces exerted significant influence on politicians and the political process, most notably influencing the content of a report made by the Special Committee on Pornography and Prostitution (the Fraser Committee), established in 1983 by the Trudeau government. Ironically for the social conservatives, it was the argument that pornography degrades and exploits women, and causes violence towards women, rather than the need to uphold Judeo-Christian morality, that became the centrepiece of the Fraser Committee's recommendations. The Committee called for eliminating from the Criminal Code the use of the term "obscenity," with its connotations of moral outrage and indecency. It also called for deletion of the section dealing with "Offences Tending to Corrupt Public Morals."

The Fraser Committee accepted a key premise: that pornography is harmful because it leads to an increase in sexual assaults, causes harm to members of the public involuntarily subjected to it, and undermines the right to equality for women. This is in itself a dubious premise: scientific research on the subject remains inconclusive as to the link between pornography and increased sexual assaults. But promoting the link had the appearance of addressing substantively, at the root cause level, the issue of the sexual exploitation, degradation, and subordination of women and children, which made it both socially and politically attractive.

The Fraser Committee's approach to dealing with pornography was never implemented as amendments to the Criminal Code. By the time its report was released in 1985, the Progressive Conservatives under Mulroney had formed the government. Their approach to dealing with pornography more closely reflected the position that the social conservatives were advocating. In an early speech in the House of Commons, Mulroney accentuated the importance of family values and his government's commitment to deal with "threats to the fabric of our family life." He pledged to move swiftly against pornography, drug abuse, and child abuse.[18] In 1986, a statement from Barbara McDougall, the Minister for the Status of Women, reiterated the government's commitment to take action to deal more severely with pornography. She announced that legislation would be introduced to:

> support and strengthen the institution of the Canadian family, among them introduction of measures to end violent and degrading forms of pornography involving women and men, legislation to take effective action against child pornography and initiatives against the traffic in illicit drugs, which will help to improve the quality of life for Canadian families, for Canadian parents and, in particular, for Canadian young people.[19]

Shortly after McDougall's announcement, the government introduced Bill C-114, which went well beyond the recommendations made by the Fraser Committee by proposing to criminalize sexually explicit material that was neither violent nor degrading. It defined pornography in breathtakingly sweeping terms as "any visual matter showing vaginal, anal or oral intercourse, ejaculation, sexually violent behaviour, bestiality, incest, necrophilia, masturbation or other sexual activity."[20] The new law would have been more severely restrictive than the existing one, significantly expanding the nature of materials deemed to be pornography. Civil liberties groups and anti-censorship forces were outraged, fearing that the new definition would include far too much material that would be sexually explicit or that would at least contain depictions of sexual activity, including those of an educational nature. They condemned the legislation as imposing Victorian-era morality and being dangerously authoritarian. The Canadian Civil Liberties Association (CCLA) was concerned, in particular, that the definition might include depictions of "hugging, kissing or perhaps even holding hands."[21]

Still, even within the Mulroney government an influential Tory "family caucus," a robust group of social conservative MPs, contended that the proposed new

law did not go far enough. That hard-line stance was in concert with the sentiments of the Interchurch Committee on Pornography and REAL Women of Canada.
They appeared before a parliamentary committee reviewing Bill C-114 to urge that
it be amended to provide for a total prohibition on all sexually explicit material.
Their position reflected the view, articulated by REAL Women, that the "demean-
ing portrayal of women occurs also in 'soft core' porn or sexually explicit material.
Recent studies indicate that to view explicit sexual material or 'soft core' porn *is
not harmless*, as it results in an increased desire for stronger material and a less-
ening of concern for women and children, as well as discourages monogamous
family life."[22]

Feminist groups, for their part, were divided on the question of supporting
Bill C-114. NAC rejected the bill completely, denouncing it as "extremely puritan and
totally unacceptable." But other groups saw Bill C-114 as an opportunity to secure
amendments that would reflect the feminist anti-pornography position. The Canadian Coalition against Media Censorship, Canadian Advisory Council on the Status
of Women, Committee against Pornography, and Canadians Concerned about Violent Entertainment wanted the bill's provisions expanded to include material that
was harmful and degrading. They also wanted the bill changed to remove the ability of the courts to interpret what would fall within the meaning of harmful or violent material. They demanded that the provisions of the bill providing for defences
on the basis of artistic, educational, or scientific merit be removed.[23]

Fortunately, Bill C-114 generated a wave of condemnation that succeeded in
forcing the Mulroney government to retreat, and it was never enacted. But they
tried again in 1987 with new legislation in the form of Bill C-54, which contained
a narrower definition of what constituted pornography. The proposed bill provided for an exemption for and definition of "erotica" that would not be subject
to criminal charges, as distinct from pornography, which would be. Such material
would only be legally available to persons over the age of eighteen. But the bill also
required that erotica could be displayed for sale only if the product contained a
prominently displayed warning notice for members of the public or if the materials
were hidden behind a barrier or covered by an opaque wrapper.[24]

The public debate over Bill C-54 was largely a repeat of the storm that had
raged over Bill C-114. The new law was supported by a number of feminist groups,
including the Canadian Advisory Council on the Status of Women, Canadian
Coalition against Media Pornography, and Metro Committee on Violence Against
Women and Children (a Toronto group). But NAC rejected it as an ineffective and
inappropriate means of dealing with pornography. So too did some feminists who
had advocated for stronger pornography laws. One of the most prominent, Susan
G. Cole, denounced Bill C-54 for being

based more on the decency contingent's opinions about morality than on women's experience of harm. That all forms of sexual activity are included in the bill indicates that the bill is meant to target public displays of sexuality of all kinds. The bill does not focus on violent or degrading pornography, and instead collapses all sexual behaviours under one pornography category.... In the main, the drafters seem to have been more interested in removing images that offended moralists' sensibilities than in taking action against materials that hurt women.[25]

Civil liberties groups, the arts community, anti-censorship feminists, gay and lesbian groups, and the media also spoke out strongly against Bill C-54. Social conservative groups, in contrast, sought an even more stringent law. Their concern, expressed by the Interchurch Committee on Pornography, was that Bill C-54 might actually lead to significant liberalization of the pornography law. They also charged that the bill would be insufficient to control child pornography because it did not prohibit simulated sexual activity with children or the depiction of children as sexual objects.[26] Thus, once more faced with a contentious law that was opposed by as many groups and interests as supported it, the Mulroney government abandoned Bill C-54, and it too never became law. Having now twice failed to secure a new definition of pornography in the Criminal Code, the Conservatives did not make another attempt.

As for the social conservative anti-pornography crusaders, the failure of Bill C-54 meant that they had lost their best and ultimately their last chance to have the Criminal Code amended. They had failed in the quest to have pornography and sexually explicit materials officially and legally characterized as grave threats to marriage, the family, and moral society. In future they would make no headway in advancing those arguments on the legal front. Instead, they would have to vie with feminist groups, police forces, and, increasingly, child welfare advocates for positions of leadership and influence in the anti-pornography movement. They could—and did—add their cacophonous voices to the growing chorus calling for stronger laws to deal with the harm caused to women and children by pornography. But they would no longer do so as the leaders of that movement or even as the most influential of the players.

The judicial redefinition of pornography

In a pattern similar to the struggle with the law on abortion, the failure of the legislators to act to redefine pornography meant that the courts would be left to pronounce on the extent to which the state should rightfully criminalize materials containing sexual content. That opportunity came quickly. In 1987 police laid an astonishing 250 criminal charges against Donald Butler, the owner of a shop in Winnipeg that sold what was described as hard-core pornographic video-tapes, magazines, and sexual paraphernalia. The offences included selling obscene material, possessing obscene material for the purpose of distribution or sale, and exposing obscene material to public view. The ensuing court case dealt, for the first time, with the question of whether the obscenity section of the Criminal Code contravened the guarantee of freedom of expression provided by the Canadian Charter of Rights and Freedoms.

At trial, the trial judge ruled that while the obscenity law did infringe free-dom of expression, the infringement is justifiable in a free and democratic society. However, he also cited section 1 of the Charter as the basis for finding that the only materials that could be prohibited were those that contained violence or cruelty in conjunction with sexual activity, that depicted a lack of consent to sexual activity, or that could otherwise be said to dehumanize a person in a sexual context. Butler was convicted on eight counts and acquitted on all of the others. The government appealed, and the Manitoba Court of Appeal overturned the trial judge's decision, convicting Butler on all counts. That decision was in turn appealed to the Supreme Court of Canada.

In a momentous 1992 decision known as *R. v. Butler*, the Supreme Court exercised its power of judicial interpretation to radically change the commun-ity standards test for obscenity. The test now became a matter of exploitation of sex in a degrading and dehumanizing manner that is perceived by public opinion to be harmful to society and especially to women. The decision thus accepted as irrefutable and made into law the feminist analysis of pornography and the pur-ported harm that it does to women. It supported the arguments made by one of the intervenors in the case, Women's Legal Education and Action Fund. LEAF, Gotell observes, "sought to disrupt the dominant, moral conservative underpinnings of obscenity regulation in favour of an approach emphasizing sexual equality and the 'harmful' effects of pornography for women."[27] The Supreme Court had in effect articulated a new, secular moral standard for the regulation of pornography.

Curiously, given the intensity of their activism against pornography, the more prominent social conservative groups did not intervene in *Butler*. It was the government intervenors—the Manitoba attorney general and the federal attor-ney general—who argued that one of the roles of the criminal law was to be the guardian of public morality in the traditional anti-sex sense of Judeo-Christianity. That position was echoed by the Manitoba-based Group Against Pornography (GAP), the sole non-governmental intervenor supporting the interpretation of the obscenity law to ban sexually explicit materials. GAP asserted that pornography was a threat to the family and caused the devaluation and depreciation of the importance of monogamy, undermining marriage as an institution. At the same time these intervenors recognized the persuasiveness of the arguments presented by the anti-pornography feminists and also put forward the position that pornography harms women and leads to violence against women.[28]

The Supreme Court's judgment makes clear that the interventions based on the necessity to criminalize pornographic materials in order to preserve public morals ultimately did not sway the court. Indeed, the judgment staked out new judicial ground—articulating proscriptions against pornography that were far removed from the community standards of tolerance based principally on the Judeo-Christian precepts of sexual morality, and sidestepping the issue of the expression or representation of sexual behaviour as being offensive to the morals of the community. As the judgment stated: "There has been a growing recognition in recent cases that material which may be said to exploit sex in a 'degrading or dehumanizing' manner will necessarily fail the community standards test, *not because it offends against morals* but because it is perceived by public opinion to be harmful to society, particularly women."[29] Feminist analysis and not Judeo-Christian morality had emerged as the more persuasive influencer of the judiciary on the question of obscenity.

The social conservative forces found little in the *Butler* decision to cheer about. Their militant views were now more than ever in the minority. Nor could they have been pleased with the long-term societal impact of the *Butler* decision. Instead of broadening the ambit of the obscenity law to criminalize erotica or "soft porn," as REAL Women and other groups had advocated, the Court had significantly expanded the legal market for pornography to include full nudity and graphic, sexually explicit content. The only written or visual materials that would meet the legal test of being obscene were those that might be found by the courts to be degrading and dehumanizing, and thereby harmful to society, or those that constituted child pornography.

The *Butler* decision coincided with the advent of new forms of media such as videocassettes (and later DVDs) that allowed millions of pornography enthusiasts to view sexually explicit images in their homes at relatively low cost. The technology brought with it an even greater proliferation of pornography free from the threat or consequences of criminal charges. In the late 1990s, as the availability and use of the Internet exploded, the limitless nature and quantity of pornography that could be viewed online on personal computers led to a country (and a world) awash in sexually explicit content. Even if they so desired, the state and its agents would have been incapable of effectively combating the trend. Significantly for the legislators, the *Butler* decision obviated the need to take legislative action. It saved the

politicians from having to reopen the divisive and contentious issue of an amendment to the Criminal Code to deal with pornography and obscenity in general.

The child pornography law

More positively for the social conservative groups, the *Butler* decision provided an impetus for the Mulroney government to finally act on its commitment
to enact stronger child pornography legislation. *Butler* identified the portrayal of
explicit sex that "employs children in its production" as being clearly within the
definition of undue exploitation of sex. It gave judicial validation to perceptions
and concerns about child pornography that had been gaining currency among
both advocacy groups and legislators for several years.

Social conservative forces had also been marshalling support for new laws to
protect vulnerable children from sexual abuse and exploitation. REAL Women of
Canada, in typical fashion, articulated its concerns in stark and foreboding terms:

> There has been a sharp increase in child pornography, with almost
> one-quarter of all pornography using children. Accompanying this has
> been an alarming rise in the reports of direct sexual assault on chil-
> dren. Unfortunately, the psychological effects of sexual abuse and
> exploitation of children are felt long into adulthood, and even for a life-
> time, causing traumatic emotional damage. Then, too, the number of
> children disappearing annually is escalating, leading to growing fears
> that these children are abducted to participate in "kiddy porn" enter-
> prises. Some children do turn up later as murder victims, following sex-
> ual assaults.[30]

The EFC expressed its motivation for crusading to achieve more stringent
child pornography laws in more explicitly religious terms, citing rampant sexual
permissiveness and modern immorality. "One of the factors which contributes to
the growing crisis of child pornography is the spirit of the age of our time," it stated.
In the EFC's view this prevailing spirit was fostering an "approach to sexual activity
[that] allows people to act in any way they choose. There are no boundaries and
there is no authority which can deny one's choice." In such an environment, it
maintained, the consumption of child pornography and sex with children become
commonplace and even tolerated. As in its approach to pornography in general,
the EFC declared that it was compelled to oppose child pornography based on "biblical principles" to protect the vulnerable, protect human dignity, and uphold family integrity.[31]

The advocacy in support of stronger child pornography laws was rewarded in May 1993, when Justice Minister Pierre Blais introduced amendments to the Criminal Code that prohibited the possession, production, and distribution of material involving any person under the age of eighteen, or "depicted as being under the age of eighteen," engaged in "explicit sexual activity." Although the Criminal Code already prohibited the production of child pornography, for the first time the new law made the possession of it a crime. It also increased to ten years, from two, the maximum penalty for producing child pornography. As it proceeded through the legislative process, the definition of "child pornography" was broadened even further to include pictures of "a sexual organ or the anal region of a person under the age of eighteen years." The provisions were also expanded to criminalize possession both of written materials or visual representations advocating or counselling sex with children and possession of material depicting or advocating the sexual exploitation of children.[32] The child pornography bill received quick approval in the House of Commons and the Senate.

The only significant opposition came from outside Parliament, from groups that held little sway with the legislators. Civil libertarians and groups representing the arts, media, and culture feared the censorial impact of the new law on freedom of artistic expression in general and on the production of educational materials and documentaries dealing with youth sexuality in particular. Alan Borovoy of the Canadian Civil Liberties Association accused the government bill of going well beyond what was necessary to address the issue of real children being used in the production of pornography or of showing children in explicitly sexual activity. The CBC worried that sexual activity among adolescents in educational documentaries or dramas would be deemed to be child pornography. The Coalition for Lesbian and Gay Rights in Ontario (CLGRO) voiced alarm that homophobia and deeply entrenched anti-gay religious and moral beliefs would lead to the law being used disproportionately, or with more vigour, against the production of or possession of representations or depictions of same-sex consensual activity.[33]

As draconian as the new child pornography law was, it was not long before social conservative groups began lobbying for it to be made even stronger. The campaign took on new life especially after charges were laid in 1995 against John Robin Sharpe, who had been found in possession of fictional stories involving sadomasochistic sexual acts with boys under the legal age of consent. Sharpe had written the stories and also had photographs of nude boys displaying their genitals. In 1999 Justice Duncan Shaw of the B.C. Supreme Court struck down as unconstitutional the prohibition in the Criminal Code on possession of child pornography. In doing so, he dismissed as unfounded the basic premise on which the child pornography law was based, namely that it puts children at increased risk

of sexual assault by predators and pedophiles. "There is no evidence that demonstrates a significant increase in the danger to children caused by pornography,"
Justice Shaw stated. Further, "only assumptions" supported the contention that
child pornography incites persons to have sex with children. "A person who is
prone to act on his fantasies," the judge declared, "will likely do so irrespective of
the availability of pornography." It was debatable, he suggested, that laws against
possession of child pornography protect children. Rejecting outright the arguments put forward by the prosecutor that pornography puts children at risk from
pedophiles because it stimulates some child molesters to commit crimes, Justice
Shaw ruled that the charges against Sharpe presented a profound invasion of freedom of expression and personal privacy, thus violating the Charter. Noting that
other sections of the Criminal Code protected children from abuse and exploitation arising from pornography, he held that the possession prohibition went too
far by outlawing such personal belongings as books, diaries, and pictures.[34]

A cacophony of outrage and wild accusations about a miscarriage of justice
ensued following Sharpe's acquittal. Gwen Landolt of REAL Women condemned
the decision as a shocking indication of rampant sexual permissiveness: "If we're
allowed to do whatever we want to express our essential self, there would be anar-
chy and social upheaval." She also accused Justice Shaw of using the Charter to
"manipulate social values" and of engaging in "social engineering." More ominously, she accused him of thinking that child pornography was "okay." Ted Morton,
a political science professor at the University of Calgary and an activist in the social
conservative movement and its political wing, the Reform Party, put the blame on
the Supreme Court of Canada. He accused it of "relying on moral relativism" in the
decisions that had served as precedents in the Sharpe case. Radio talk shows and
newspaper opinion pieces condemned both the judgment and Justice Shaw. "The
bonehead should be removed from the bench," declared Peter Warren, a Vancouver
radio talk show host. Angry letters to the editor appeared in newspapers across the
country. The hysteria and vitriol were such that at one point Justice Shaw received
a death threat and special security arrangements had to be instituted to protect his
safety. A retired B. C. Supreme Court judge, Lloyd McKenzie, commented that in
forty years as a judge he had never seen anything like the outcry against Shaw. "The
level of hate that has been directed at him is remarkable."[35]

In Parliament, Reform and Liberal MPs alike denounced the decision. B.C.
Reform MP Reed Elly cited the judgment as "one more example of social engineering where the courts make laws rather than Parliament." Another B.C. Reform MP,
John Reynolds, outrageously declared, "This decision has given pedophiles the
right to abuse children." More than half of the Liberal MPs in the House of Commons signed a letter urging Prime Minister Jean Chrétien to introduce stronger

child pornography legislation to mitigate Justice Shaw's decision. They also suggested invoking the notwithstanding clause of the Charter, which would allow for the decision to be overridden. The government rejected these demands, but agreed to intervene in support of the B.C. NDP government's appeal of the decision.[36] Both Focus on the Family (Canada) and the EFC also intervened in the appeal to oppose Justice Shaw's decision.

When the B.C. Court of Appeal upheld Justice Shaw's judgment, agreeing that parts of the child pornography law were unconstitutional, the governments appealed to the Supreme Court of Canada, which heard the case in January 2000. A crucial issue to be determined was Sharpe's contention that the materials seized were "works of the imagination" and did not involve real children. Another was whether the "artistic merit" defence provided in the Criminal Code could be applied to sexually explicit materials like the ones produced by Sharpe. Continuing their interventions at the Supreme Court, Focus on the Family and the EFC argued that child pornography should not be protected under the Charter. They characterized its effects on children as "akin to violence." The EFC held an earnest prayer vigil outside the Supreme Court building attended by "busloads of pastors as well as 17 EFC member churches," with the participants fervently "praying for the Lord's intervention in the Supreme Court."[37]

The Supreme Court, in its January 28, 2001, judgment, upheld the constitutionality of the child pornography law but clarified its provisions by creating very limited exemptions from its application. Written materials and visual recordings that were self-authored or self-produced for personal or private use were ruled lawful so long as they did not describe or depict unlawful activity, such as the use of actual children in real sexual acts. Depictions of casual kissing and hugging would not be prohibited, and educational, scientific, or medical works were also ruled to be lawful. In addition the justices opined that the "artistic merit" defence contained in the law "must be established objectively and should be interpreted as including any expression that may reasonably be viewed as art."[38] This aspect of the judgment particularly infuriated social conservatives, who immediately turned their advocacy attention to pressuring the government to repeal the artistic merit defence—a dangerous loophole, in their view—in order to substantially increase the child pornography law's effectiveness.

Social conservatives endured a further judicial outrage when Justice Shaw, in March 2002, acquitted Sharpe on new child pornography charges of possessing fictional materials. Shaw cited what the activists viewed as the odious artistic merit defence. Darrel Reid of Focus on the Family condemned the decision, stating with absolutist zeal that when it comes to child pornography, "there is no such thing as artistic merit. All child pornography is child abuse." Focus on the

Family also launched a highly emotional but undeniably effective public advocacy campaign demanding the swift amendment of the Criminal Code to provide "full legal protection for our children—rightly, ultimately, and finally placing the rights of our children above the rights of child pornographers." Over the next several months, the organization took out full-page newspaper advertisements to support its demand and delivered a petition to Parliament. The document, carrying over 65,000 names, demanded that the government "close the loopholes" in the child pornography law.[39]

Focus on the Family, like the other social conservative groups, publicly professed the need to protect children from harm and exploitation, but its prime motivations were religious beliefs and moral values. Its advocacy manifested the belief that sex outside of marriage, especially when it involves young persons, is sinful and dangerous, that young persons involved in sexual activity, even of a consensual nature, are being exploited and harmed; and all pornography encourages immoral sexual activity, violating the sacred state of chastity to which unmarried persons should strive. A Focus on the Family issues paper condemning the court decisions in the Sharpe case contended: "Pornography is at a crisis point in today's society. Marriages are breaking up, young minds are being polluted, and adults as well as children are being exploited because of pornography." It vowed that "Focus on the Family will continue to help protect marriages, adults, and children from the destructive influence of pornography."[40]

Still, Focus on the Family and other social conservative groups were not alone in using the judicial decision in the Sharpe case to lobby for legislative action to eradicate child pornography. An all-party "Roundtable" of MPs convened by Liberal Dan McTeague sought consensus among legislators on amending the child pornography law to close the "loophole" opened by the Sharpe decision. The Roundtable heard submissions from police officers, investigators, and prosecutors who, like the social conservative groups, contended that fictional child pornography was just as harmful to children as the use of actual children in the production of pornography. Intervenors argued that pedophiles use the materials to "feed their own urges." Police officials told the MPs that legislation was needed because the existing provisions of the Criminal Code and the decisions of the courts in interpreting them had made it difficult to secure convictions.[41]

In the aftermath of the Sharpe case, both Liberal and Conservative governments were receptive to the outcry for stronger laws to deal with child pornography and sexual exploitation of youth. Between 2003 and 2005 the Liberals under Jean Chrétien and Paul Martin introduced three bills that sought to narrow the possible defences in child pornography cases. The first two bills were never enacted, but the third attempt, Bill C-2, was enacted in 2005. Through the protracted process of introducing and debating the bills, REAL Women, Focus on the Family, EFC, and Canada Family Action Coalition all lobbied for the elimination of the artistic merit defence and alternative exceptions that had been proposed by the government or that would give the courts discretion to interpret whether the subject matter giving rise to the laying of charges met the test of being child pornography. Typical was the scepticism expressed by Landolt about how the courts would interpret the law. She stated, "Anything is possible with our liberal courts today and it would have been preferable to simply remove all defenses for child pornography."[42]

Meanwhile, child pornography amendments became one of the hot-button issues injected by social conservative groups into the 2004 federal election campaign. The Canada Family Action Coalition called upon people of faith to elect a government that, among other virtues, "had the courage and will write the laws and overrule court dictatorship." Similarly, REAL Women urged its supporters to ask candidates in the election if they would "support legislation to outlaw the production, possession and distribution of all child pornography." The organization's election materials stated unequivocally, "There is NO public good in child pornography. Period. There is also NO artistic merit in child pornography. Period. Any and all child pornography must be illegal. Period."[43]

The newly formed Conservative Party enthusiastically embraced the crusade against child pornography, adopting the uncompromising language of the social conservative groups. It promised, if elected, to "pass legislation that will adopt a zero tolerance policy for child porn."[44] The Conservatives used the failure to enact a stronger child pornography law to bash the Liberals and smear Prime Minister Martin and the NDP MPs, accusing them of supporting or condoning child pornography.[45] These tactics exposed a malevolent and deeply disturbing characteristic of the new Conservative Party.

After the election Martin's Liberal minority government reintroduced child pornography amendments to the Criminal Code, replacing the artistic merit defence with a vague and difficult to prove defence of "legitimate purpose related to the administration of justice or to science, medicine or art." Additionally problematic was a provision that required a person accused of a child pornography offence to not just argue for a "legitimate purpose," but also to prove that an undue risk of harm was not posed to persons under the age of eighteen by the alleged act. Failure to establish to a court's satisfaction that there was no undue risk of harm would result in conviction, which would in turn make the new law inconsistent with the principle of innocent until proven guilty.

The new legislation was touted as providing protection to children. Yet government and the groups clamouring for a tougher law would certainly have known that criminal laws do not in fact protect children, or women, or anyone else. They are in essence statements made by the state about what is and is not acceptable behaviour. At best they serve as deterrents, although just how effect-ively they deter behaviour is debatable. People do not stop committing murder, acts of violence, or theft because they know these are criminal offences. Similarly, the enactment of criminal laws against child pornography will not protect the chil-dren who are participants in its production. What criminal laws do is provide for the arrest and prosecution of individuals and for the determination of the severity of the penalty for those who are convicted. But they do not "protect" those who are injured or victimized by the actions of other people.

The efficacy of the proposed new criminal code provisions could be further contested on the grounds that Canada already had a strong child pornography law. The courts are not likely to rule that there should be no such law. No one with any credibility would argue that using children in the production of pornog-raphy should be legally permitted. The real objective of those seeking a stronger child pornography law was to expand the prohibition well beyond the actual use of real children in making pornography and to provide significantly harsher penal-ties for transgressors. Disguising that objective in the garb of protecting children and the vulnerable was misleading and dishonest. It also helped to promote and sustain a more expansive moral panic about pornography in general—and about the dangers of rampant sexuality and the perceived threats to marriage and family ascribed to the permissiveness of modern society.

The government cited as justification for the legislation the need to honour Canada's commitment arising from its ratification of the 1989 United Nations Con-vention on the Rights of the Child and a related UN protocol that pledged to pro-tect children from all forms of sexual exploitation and sexual abuse. Significantly, however, the UN protocol defined child pornography more narrowly than Canada's Criminal Code did. For the UN it signified "any representation, by whatever means, of a *child engaged in real or simulated sexual activities or any representation of the sexual parts of a child for primarily sexual purposes.*"[46] The language of the protocol contemplated the use of actual children in pornography and "the growing avail-ability of child pornography on the Internet and other evolving technologies." It did not include the production or mere possession of fictional or imaginary expres-sions—that do not involve actual children or simulations—or educational materi-als. In going significantly beyond what was demanded by the UN agreement, the Liberal bill reflected, without explicitly acknowledging, the concerns expressed by the social conservative groups, which sought to have an already disturbingly broad and vague law against child pornography made even more so.

With good reason, organizations representing the arts community and civil liberties groups expressed opposition to the "legitimate purpose" provision because it would result in narrowing the available defences in such instances as fictionalized depictions of sexual acts among young persons under the age of eighteen years. The B.C. Civil Liberties Association (BCCLA) denounced the legislation as "obnoxious to democratic values and an infringement of the fundamental freedoms of thought and expression protected by the Charter." The inclusion of the "legitimate purpose" defence, it speculated, was "an invitation to the judiciary to make it [having a legitimate purpose] up as they go along, presumably drawing on their personal moral convictions."[47] The Writers' Union of Canada expressed alarm that the new law would place unnecessary and undesirable restraints on freedom of expression. In its brief the Union stated, "We do not believe that censorship laws address the problems created by sexual abuse and exploitation of children." The risk posed by the legislation was that "writers must be able to portray children in sexual situations in a variety of works, including autobiographies, coming-of-age stories on page or stage, accounts of crime in books, newspapers or magazines, and sex education materials without fear of being penalized for crossing subjective, arbitrary barriers."[48]

Social conservative groups attacked the bill as woefully inadequate. During the hearings of the standing committee, they lined up to press for amendments that would establish "zero tolerance" for child pornography by having any defences removed from the Criminal Code. Landolt accused the government of leaving the artistic merit defence intact: "The supposition that child pornography can be excused or defended because it is 'artistic' defies common sense and it can never have a legitimate purpose." The EFC also urged the elimination of a defence based on artistic grounds but did not object to otherwise leaving in place a defence based on "possession within a professional context for the pursuit or administration of justice, medicine, or science or education for the express end of preventing or fighting child pornography."[49]

The legislation was adopted without controversy by both the House of Commons and the Senate and became law in the summer of 2005. In the end it went much further than the civil libertarians, arts groups, and gay and lesbian groups had feared, but not as far as social conservative groups had sought, after their years of arduous and aggressive lobbying. Nonetheless, it was social conservative groups that could take credit for the very introduction of the amendments to the Criminal Code. Had they not organized so massively and effectively in outrage against the Sharpe decision, the politicians may well not have acted at all.

Saving children from sexual exploitation

While they were pressing for a stronger child pornography law, social conservatives were also channelling their belief that sex is both sinful and dangerous into other areas of advocacy. They undertook highly organized and ultimately successful efforts to strengthen the Criminal Code provisions dealing with sexual exploitation of children and the age of consent for sexual activity. They contended that the sexual exploitation of children and child pornography were interconnected—that Canada had a shockingly low age of consent for sexual activity, which was a direct cause of both child pornography and the sexual exploitation of children. The age of consent issue in particular was integral to their moralistic anti-sex crusades because, in their view, a low age of consent encouraged and condoned sexual activity among young people, who should remain chaste until married. For them youth sexuality was symptomatic of the general immorality and permissiveness of modern society. They spoke frequently about children and youth being lured into sexual behaviour and corrupted by pedophiles and sexual predators. Through sexual activity, they contended, young persons could be exploited and abused, recruited into prostitution and pornography, and led astray from God, biblical sexuality, family, and marriage.

Social conservative groups had been dismayed by the Mulroney government's agreement with a 1986 parliamentary committee's call for the age of consent to be made consistent at fourteen years. That meant eliminating a number of differing ages of consent for certain circumstances that took into account the nature of the relationship between the consenting (opposite sex) individuals. One of those was a "morals clause," which prohibited a male from engaging in sexual intercourse with a female between the ages of fourteen years and sixteen years to whom he was not married if the female was of "chaste character." In contrast, individuals as young as fourteen years of age were permitted to marry so long as there was parental consent; and the age of consent for same-sex sexual acts had remained at twenty-one since 1969. Such differences could no longer be sustained because of the equality rights provisions established by section 15 of the Charter.

To remove those inconsistencies, the government enacted Criminal Code amendments (which took effect in 1988) that established the age of consent generally as fourteen years (except for anal intercourse, for which the age was set at eighteen). At the same time, with the intention of protecting children and youth from sexual exploitation, the government also introduced new provisions dealing with adults engaging in sexual activity or sexual intercourse with persons under the age of eighteen. The underlying premise for such measures was not the state's traditional assumption of the role of protector and regulator of the morals of youth, or to promote chastity and marriage, but rather the perceived need to protect vulnerable children and youth from sexual abuse and exploitation. Despite the scope and severity of the new provisions, social conservative advocates argued strenuously in the ensuing years that establishing a consistent age of consent, generally at fourteen years, had horrific consequences for young people, purportedly witnessed by an increase in the sexual exploitation of children.

Beginning in the late 1990s, social conservative groups along with representatives of the police and child welfare advocates began to focus their attention on increasing the age of consent. In 1997 REAL Women adopted a position calling for the age to be increased to eighteen years, viewing this matter as a "grave issue." Launching an advocacy campaign for a criminal code amendment, the organization wrote to all federal and provincial ministers of justice urging them to support such action. REAL Women argued that it is "reasonable that the age of consent be *raised* to 18 years to match the child pornography law." That would also make the age of consent law consistent with other laws that established eighteen as the age of adulthood, such as those setting the legal age for consuming alcohol.[50]

Representatives of the police and child welfare advocates also called for increasing the age of consent. The Canadian Association of Police Boards urged adoption of sixteen years as the age to "assist in the prosecution of adults who buy sex from young people because it would permit a prosecution for sexual assault without the necessity of proof that there was payment of money or other consideration." Canadians Addressing Sexual Exploitation—known until 1997 as Canadians for Decency—lobbied for the age to be set at eighteen years. Another group, Beyond Borders, formed in 1996, advocated for the establishment of sixteen years, while supporting a "close in age" exemption under which young persons whose ages were within five years of each other would not be subject to conviction.[51] These various groups scored a success in 1999, when the thirteen federal and provincial justice ministers expressed support for raising the age of consent to sixteen years in response to public consultations that had been held on what laws should be introduced to protect children from abuse.

The efforts of those advocating for a higher age of consent also succeeded in gaining the support of a majority of Canadians. By 2002 a public opinion poll commissioned by Focus on the Family indicated that fully 72 per cent of Canadians polled supported an increase to sixteen years. An additional 8 per cent of poll respondents favoured increasing the age of consent to eighteen years.[52] In Parliament, Canadian Alliance and Progressive Conservative party members introduced a number of private member's bills calling for an increase in the age of consent. Although the bills failed to be adopted, they proved effective in keeping the age of consent issue on the legislative agenda.

In an attempt to respond to this sentiment, the Liberals included in their bills to strengthen the child pornography law other amendments to the Criminal Code that addressed the age of consent for sexual activity. They introduced a vaguely worded provision that criminalized sex between an adult and a young person (aged fourteen to seventeen) if the adult "is in a relationship with a young person that is exploitative of the young person." It extended the criminalization of adult-youth sexuality considerably beyond the existing provisions of the Criminal Code. The age of the young person, the age difference between the two persons, the evolution of the relationship, and the degree of control or influence by the older person over the younger person: these were all specified as grounds for a judge to "infer" that the relationship was exploitative.

Not surprisingly, social conservative groups opposed the "exploitative relationship" provision as an unacceptable alternative to the outright raising of the age of consent. In one of her presentations to the parliamentary committees that reviewed the bills, REAL Women's Landolt attacked the failure to raise the age of consent. She argued that the low age of fourteen for consensual sex in combination with Canada's position as the country with the highest number of Internet users in the world "has increased the number of cross-border pedophiles." Tellingly, in respect of her group's views on youth sexuality, she also declared: "Children of 14 do not have the maturity to make responsible decisions in regard to sexual activities with adults. Sex between young persons and adults leads to long-range problems: sexually transmitted disease, AIDS, unexpected pregnancies, the lowering of self-esteem, loss of education, and it goes on and on." She urged increasing the age of consent "to at least 16 years of age, but preferably to 18 years of age."[53] So too did the Evangelical Fellowship of Canada. Using almost exactly the same language as REAL Women, EFC spokesperson Janet Epp Buckingham stated: "The current low age of consent makes Canada more open to problems related to child prostitution and child abuse. Pedophiles continue to lure vulnerable children. Cross-border pedophile activity into Canada is rampant and is enhanced by the fact that Canada's age of consent for sex is only 14 years—one of the lowest of all western nations."[54]

A recurring argument was the claim that Canada was a haven for pedophiles and child molesters because of its low age of consent. The Canada Family Action Coalition made the assertion in news releases and other materials that it used in its lobbying efforts. "Internationally, Canada has now established a reputation as a sex tourism 'hot spot' and an attractive destination for pedophiles," CFAC's executive director Brian Rushfeldt stated in a 2001 press release announcing a petition campaign to support legislative change. In an outrageous and deliberately misleading assertion the release declared, "Adults can legally prey on and have sex with children in Canada." It went on to contend, without providing any substantiating data, "Since the age of consent was reduced to 14 in 1987, there have been increased incidents of vulnerable young boys and girls being exploited by adult sexual predators."[55]

The CFAC allegation was probably an extrapolation made from findings of various studies, reports, and news stories about child prostitution. A number of studies, including several conducted by the Canadian government, had identified a problem with child prostitution in various Canadian cities. Other government reports had focused on Canadians travelling to other countries that offered child prostitutes. Some media reports, however, had fuelled the perception that sex tourism targeting children in Canada was a pervasive problem. A news report in 2000 about underage prostitutes in Vancouver and a much-cited RCMP reference to a "kiddie stroll" posted on Internet websites heightened the alarm over the extent of child prostitution. The report, published in the *Toronto Star* and picked up by other media, also referred to a study conducted by the Canadian Council on Social Development (CCSD) that dealt with child prostitution. Yet a key focus of the CCSD report was that poverty and disadvantage, as well sexual abuse of children in the home by family members, were often contributing factors to children becoming involved in the sex trade.[56] CFAC and the other social conservative groups tended to avoid citing these contributing factors.

For groups seeking a higher age of consent, the issue of youth sexual exploit-ation was inseparably linked with the belief that any sexual relationship between an adult and a teenager should be outlawed. In a Beyond Borders fact sheet, provocatively entitled "Canada's Abuser-Friendly Age of Consent," the group asserted that although raising the age of consent to sixteen years "would not be a catch-all solution to ending all child sex abuse, it would send a strong message that children in this vulnerable age bracket are off-limits to adults. It is a clear, definable limit that is simple to prosecute and leaves the onus on the offender, not the victim."[57]

Proponents of increasing the age of consent also hoped to play upon the hor-ror and revulsion conjured by contemplating sexual relations between a youth and a much older person. Their advocacy materials invariably included this scenario, along with the assumption, whether stated or merely implied, that such relation-ships were by their very nature exploitative of and damaging to the younger person. According to their characterization, youth under the age of eighteen are particu-larly vulnerable to manipulation, abuse, and exploitation. Noted Beyond Borders, Canada's age of consent law "means that in many situations it is perfectly legal in Canada for a 50-year old to have sex with a 14-year old."[58] Similarly, the Catholic Civil Rights League, in lending its support to the CFAC petition campaign, declared: "In Canada, adults of any age are permitted to have sexual relations with children of just 14 years of age." Focus on the Family advised in a "Reality Check" on teen sexual-ity that a "myth" existed that, under Canada's age of consent laws, "It is illegal for a man in his fifties to engage in a sexual relationship with a child of 14 years."[59]

The premise was that although these consensual adult-youth relationships were not illegal, they should be criminalized and subjected to harsh penalties. It was an appeal to what might be called a visceral "stomach-churning" reaction as a means of winning broad community support for raising the age of consent. Inter-generational relations of that sort are repulsive for many people. In all likelihood not many parents would welcome their teenager having sex with a fifty-year-old. In addition, such relationships, the forces seeking a higher age of consent maintained, can be only superficially consensual. Not only were the relationships repulsive, the critics argued, but they were inherently and without exception exploitative or coercive. The relationships therefore must be criminalized, and the older person must be charged and convicted as a sex offender and child abuser.

Most social conservative groups actively seeking a higher age of consent also attempted to fortify their positions by asserting that youth are simply too immature and unready to engage in sexual relations. They maintained that the criminal law should act as a deterrent to rather than enabler of youth sexual activity. A higher age of consent, they submitted, would protect and benefit youth and children.

Always at the heart of their opposition to fourteen years as the age of consent was the fervent belief that sex outside of or prior to marriage was immoral and harmful, especially for young persons. Strenuous opposition to the age of consent law was consistent with, and supplementary to, the argument that abstinence education would discourage young people from engaging in sexual activity. Indeed, the EFC made such arguments in a submission to the federal Department of Justice:

> As well as physical effects, early sexual activity can have detrimental emotional effects. Sexual intimacy has emotional and social components. Biblically, sexual intimacy is reserved for marriage, in part because of the emotional and spiritual effects which are described as the woman and the man becoming "one flesh." Young teens may not have the foresight or maturity in judgment to choose a sexual partner wisely. The breakdown of the relationship or manipulation within the relationship are heavy burdens for ones so young to carry.

Observing that "law is a teacher" that reflects an understanding of right and wrong, the EFC brief concluded: "Raising the age of consent for sexual activity will not stop all sexual activity among adolescents.... However, it will deter some young Canadians and it will communicate to them a message about the dangers associated with early sexual activity."[60] Likewise, the Focus on the Family "Reality Check" on teen sexuality and the age of consent condemned "the message sent to adolescents by media and schools that there is no necessary harm from premarital sexual activity, and in fact sexual activity is part of a full and enjoyable adolescence." The organization contended that, to the contrary, "Many teens are coming to realize that this message is untrue and dangerous." Abstinence education and signing abstinence pledges, it asserted, could effectively prevent sexual activity among teenagers.[61]

By the time of the 2004 federal election, the groups seeking an increase in the age of consent had managed to make it an issue that could not be ignored. In their election materials, both the CFAC and REAL Women called for changes to the age of consent. CFAC regurgitated its arguments that as a direct result of the failure of the governing Liberals to increase the age of consent, "Canada has become a paradise for pedophiles." REAL Women called upon its supporters to ask candidates whether they supported raising the age of consent to at least sixteen years.[62]

The same issue was a priority in the election campaign platforms of the Conservative Party in both 2004 and 2006. Adopting the "protection of young people" mantra, the Conservatives pledged during the 2006 election to "Rename the Age of Consent to the Age of Protection and raise the age from 14 to 16 years of age to stop adults from sexually exploiting vulnerable children." The policy document declared that "families should be able to raise their children without fear of sexual predators in our communities" and accused the Liberals of refusing "to raise the age of consent to prevent adults from exploiting young teens." Like their social conservative constituents, the Conservative Party characterized all sexual relations between adults and teens as exploitative and peddled the notion that depriving teens under the age of sixteen of their legal capacity to give consent would "stop adults from exploiting vulnerable young people."[63]

Once elected to government, the Conservatives moved quickly to honour their commitment. In June 2006, in Bill C-22, they introduced "age of protection" legislation that increased the age of consent to sixteen years, while maintaining the age of eighteen for exploitative sexual activity. In an attempt to address concerns about criminalizing consensual sexual relations between teenagers, the legislation also provided for a "close-in-age" exemption that would permit fourteen- and fifteen-year-olds to legally engage in sexual activity with a partner less than five years older. It was a victory in particular for Beyond Borders. The bill reflected both the increase in the age of consent and the close-in-age exemption that the organization had been advocating for several years. The new law was also a victory for the representatives of Canada's police forces. It removed the problematic issue, for them, of having to determine whether a younger person had given consent to a sexual act or relationship. It would cast all such youth as "vulnerable" and "victims," and all of the older persons (five or more years older) as "sexual predators."[64]

EFC commended the law as "a strong commitment to protect Canadian children from those who would view and abuse them as sexual prey—both foreign and Canadian predators." Urging that society avoid "the early sexualization of our children," the EFC also, significantly, expressed its support for the increase in the age of consent in religious terms. "We will continue to promote the role of parents and their spiritual communities in sharing the values that shape youth, including understanding of their sexual identity from a Christian perspective."[65]

Few groups spoke out against the new law. One that did was the B.C. Civil Liberties Association, whose president, Jason Grati, expressed concern that it "represents a fundamental shift in policy and attitude toward sexuality." The existing protections for young people in the Criminal Code were adequate, he maintained. Grati disputed whether evidence of "a rampant social problem in relation to a differential age" had been presented to the justice committee, arguing that not a lot of relationships existed between older people and minors. "Our concern is that in the absence of some evidence of harm, the rush on the part of the current government to enact Bill C-22 is an unconsidered response to a moral objection, rather than a legislative response to harms that have been shown to exist."[66]

Other groups opposed to Bill C-22 included the national gay and lesbian lobby group Egale Canada, which characterized the legislation as "an unnecessary invasion into the sex lives of young Canadians." Kaj Hasselriis, Egale's executive director, noted that some teenagers of fourteen or fifteen years of age were having consensual sex with adults. "Egale believes very strongly that it is possible, even common, for 14- and 15-year-olds to consent to sex, even with people over the age of 20." The Canadian AIDS Society (CAS) voiced concern that raising the age of consent could result in youths being more secretive about their sexual practices, that they would not seek out information about sexuality, thus increasing their risk of contracting HIV or sexually transmitted diseases. As CAS spokesperson Nicole Downer noted, "The bill places unnecessary restrictions on youth, while not addressing the reality of sexual abuse." Downer contended, "Criminalizing the sexual behaviour of youths will do nothing to stop exploitative activity."[67]

The "age of protection" law, although adopted by the House of Commons in May 2007 with the support of all parties, was never passed by the Senate and therefore did not become law. It died when Prime Minister Harper prorogued Parliament to begin a new session of Parliament, and was then resurrected in fall 2007 as part of an omnibus bill amending various sections of the Criminal Code. The new bill promptly received approval in both the House of Commons and the Senate. The age for consensual sexual activity was increased to sixteen years.

The successful enactment of a new age of consent was an indicator of the enduring power and influence of the social conservative constituency on the political process and on politicians of all political stripes. Regulating sexuality and morality by severely restricting the ambit of consensual sexual activity available to young people was a powerful political issue that few politicians were inclined or dared to oppose. Supporting an increase in the age of consent while professing to protect vulnerable and immature youth from exploitation by older "predators" was quite simply an irresistible proposition. It was also a gesture that could attract the electoral support of the numerically significant social conservative voters.

The articulation of the need to protect children and youth effectively avoided the more problematic question of whether religious and moral beliefs that uphold the wrongness and harm of sexual activity by young people should dictate what the criminal law proscribes. It mattered not at all that the most public and persistent advocates of increasing the age of consent were the religious proponents of sexual abstinence for youth.

Criminalizing prostitution and other forms of sexual sin

In keeping with their belief that the state should criminalize and regulate sexual sin, social conservative groups have also campaigned to ensure that prostitution and the sex trade remain subject to criminal sanction and state censure. They have organized in opposition to removal of restrictions on prostitution and on consensual sexual activity occurring outside of the conjugal bedroom, in any venue still quaintly and moralistically referred to in the Criminal Code as "a common bawdy-house." To their dismay the laws have been gradually and incrementally liberalized, principally as a result of interpretations by the courts citing the Charter of Rights and Freedoms. As with other aspects of the regulation of sexuality, the courts have increasingly rejected the historic arguments that prostitution and bawdy house laws are needed to protect and preserve public morals. The justice system has instead adopted an analysis of whether the sexual activity causes harm to any persons or to the community.

Although prostitution per se has never been a criminal offence, soliciting and importuning sexual encounters for remuneration, as well as procuring for the purposes of prostitution and "living off the avails" of prostitution, are all criminal offences. Indirect criminalization of prostitution has remained a feature of Canadian law through the existence of Criminal Code sections making it an offence to operate, be an employee of, or be an "inmate" of a "common bawdy house"—which is defined as a place that is kept or occupied, or resorted to by one or more persons, for the purpose of prostitution or the "practice of acts of indecency."

Since the 1970s various government commissions and advocacy groups have issued calls for the decriminalization of prostitution and repeal of the bawdy house laws. There has been a recognition that the moral values of the old Christian Canada, as reflected in the regulation of sexual morality sections of the Criminal Code, are no longer appropriate for a modern, secular society with a more open and liberal view of sexuality. The Law Reform Commission (1978) and the Special Committee on Pornography and Prostitution (Fraser Committee, 1985) both long ago called for the repeal or reform of the bawdy house laws. In 1998 a Federal-Provincial Working Group on Prostitution, after conducting public consultations on what should be the appropriate response to street prostitution, youth involved in prostitution, and violence associated with prostitution, was unable to reach a consensus in its report to government on whether the bawdy house laws should be repealed.[68]

Over the last three decades, groups such as the B.C. Civil Liberties Association and National Action Committee on the Status of Women, and organizations advocating for gay and lesbian rights, such as the Coalition for Lesbian and Gay Rights in Ontario and Egale Canada, have advocated for reform of the Criminal Code. As well, sex workers' rights organizations began to spring up in the late 1970s to press for law reform and measures to deal with violence against sex workers. Those efforts began with radical, grassroots organizations such as BEAVER (Better End All Vicious Erotic Repression) in Toronto (1977–79), CASH (Coalition Against Street Harassment, 1979–80), and Canadian Organization for the Rights of Prostitutes (1983–92). More recently, the Sex Workers' Alliance of Toronto (SWAT), formed in 1992, Maggie's—the Toronto Prostitutes' Community Service Project—founded in 1986, and the Sex Professionals of Canada (SPOC), based in Toronto, have taken up the issue.[69]

But a number of court decisions since the 1970s have had the most significant impact on the Criminal Code sections dealing with prostitution and common bawdy houses. A landmark 1978 Supreme Court of Canada decision known as *R. v. Hutt* held that solicitation for the purpose of prostitution in a public place is a criminal offence only if the solicitation can be characterized as "pressing and persistent importuning." The effect of the decision was to significantly narrow the circumstances under which charges of street prostitution could be successfully prosecuted.

Another Supreme Court of Canada decision, *Re Prostitution 1990*, upheld the constitutionality of the sections of the Criminal Code dealing with communicating (solicitation) and common bawdy houses. The issues in the case were whether or not those sections infringed the right of freedom of expression and the right to liberty and security of the person. The morality of prostitution was not at issue. Rather, part of the judgment's rationale was that street prostitution was a social nuisance and that prostitution generally was degrading to prostitutes (with the vast majority of them being women), and that they were the real victims of prostitution. Chief Justice Antonio Lamer, in his written reasons, cited the 1984 report of the Ontario Advisory Council on the Status of Women, which characterized prostitution as a form of violence against women, a blatant form of exploitation and abuse of women by men who dominate, victimize, and subordinate women. As was the case with pornography, the justification for the Criminal Code sections relating to prostitution was no longer the need to regulate sexual morality (the original purpose of the laws). The reasoning had evolved to reflect the feminist analysis of degradation of and harm caused to women.[70]

In contrast with and most likely in response to these developments, social conservative groups began calling for more stringent laws and stronger law enforcement measures to eradicate prostitution altogether. REAL Women seeks the amendment of the Criminal Code to prohibit prostitution and all activities surrounding prostitution. On its website the organization argues that prostitution "has many harmful effects on prostitutes themselves, clients and their families, the business milieu in which this occurs, and society as a whole." Prostitutes, it contends, are "extremely vulnerable members of society" who should be protected from exploitation, degradation, and violence by the criminal law. But REAL Women also predicates its advocacy for stronger laws on an imperative rooted in Judeo-Christian morality. It voices concern about "the effect of prostitution on young children and teenagers, giving them the impression that sexuality is merely recreation and sport, not a responsible, loving expression best obtained within the desirable and permanent context of a conjugal relationship."[71] Similarly, on its website the EFC condemns prostitution as both dehumanizing and contrary to sexual morality: "Like pornography, prostitution focuses only on the sexual dimension of human nature to the exclusion of all else, creating a distorted perspective of people, their worth and their proper place in society." It adds, "Prostitution makes something very intimate, intended for a life-long relationship between a man and wife, into a commercial transaction between strangers."[72]

Until quite recently, little of significance was happening to stir social conservative activism within the political realm on the question of prostitution. It was simply not an issue that the politicians felt compelled to deal with. There had not been any serious intention or effort made to amend the Criminal Code sections dealing with prostitution. But during 2004 and 2005 social conservative groups became alarmed at the establishment of a parliamentary subcommittee with a mandate "to review the solicitation laws in order to improve the safety of sex-trade workers and communities overall." The subcommittee, struck in response to the horrific slaughter of at least twenty-six sex trade workers, allegedly by Robert Pickton, in British Columbia, was tasked with recommending changes that would "reduce the exploitation of and violence against sex-trade workers." The Pickton case engendered shock and disgust among Canadians and also served to highlight the ever-increasing number of homicides, acts of violence, and disappearances of sex trade workers every year.[73]

Many groups and individuals making submissions to the subcommittee called for the decriminalization of prostitution and, in some instances, repeal of the bawdy house laws as the appropriate legislative response. They contended that by decriminalizing prostitution and repealing the laws that make the business of prostitution illegal, the circumstances of sex trade workers would be dramatically changed for the better. The idea was that doing away with the fear of being arrested and prosecuted, and creating the ability to operate out of premises and establishments that, as legal businesses, would ensure the health and safety of sex trade workers, would remove the necessity of working on the streets and the dangers arising from street prostitution. Street prostitution exposes sex trade workers to greater incidences of violence from "bad dates" and to a greater probability of exploitation by pimps.

Social conservative groups mounted a campaign aimed at pressuring the subcommittee to avoid that kind of action. The EFC told the subcommittee, "We do not recommend decriminalizing solicitation as the current laws allow for police interventions that remove prostitutes from the streets and, if approached appropriately, can serve as the first step to an exit strategy." It added, "Prostitution violates human dignity by distorting and commodifying human intimacy, which we believe are ordained by God for marriage, and treats them as services to be bought or sold, turning acts of sexual intimacy into commercial transactions."[74] Instead of decriminalization, EFC called for increased penalties for johns and pimps and more funding for safe houses and programs offering exit strategies for street sex trade workers.

More radically, REAL Women called for the outright criminalization of prostitution and stronger laws to prohibit bawdy houses. "Since the act of prostitution itself is not an offence under the Criminal Code," it argued, "the latter should be amended to prohibit prostitution itself, as well as prohibit the activities surrounding prostitution; i.e. keeping a common bawdy house, living off the avails of prostitution, etc." Focus on the Family appealed to its supporters to "Contact your Member of Parliament and let him or her know why you believe that decriminalization is the wrong approach to deal with the problems associated with the sex trade."[75]

On the political level, some members of the subcommittee, such as NDP MP Libby Davies, publicly expressed support for decriminalization of solicitation and for repeal of the bawdy house laws. But another member, Conservative MP Art Hanger, spouted the view put forward by social conservative groups. He opposed decriminalization and accused the subcommittee of being out of control by not restricting itself to pursuing means by which the streets could be made safer. Like the EFC, he sought greater law enforcement targeting pimps and johns, coupled with an "exit strategy" to help sex trade workers get out of the business and into rehabilitation programs.[76]

The subcommittee issued an inconclusive report reflecting the differences of opinion among the members of the Conservative Party and the opposition parties (Liberal, NDP, and Bloc Québécois). They managed to reach unanimous agreement on recommendations that the Government of Canada ensure that the commercial sexual exploitation of minors (under eighteen years of age) remain a serious crime subject to severe penalties, that trafficking in persons remain a priority, and that traffickers be brought to justice. They also agreed on the need to conduct education programs to prevent people from entering prostitution because of a lack of choice or coercion, and that the government fund research into prostitution to obtain a clearer picture of the activities. A majority of subcommittee members also called for "concrete efforts" to "improve the safety of individuals selling sexual services and assist them in exiting prostitution if they are not there by choice." This recommendation suggests that the position put forward by the EFC had influenced these MPs more than the calls either to decriminalize prostitution or for the outright criminalization.

There was no consensus on the larger question of reform of the prostitution laws. While all members of the subcommittee urged the government to "recognize that the status quo with respect to Canada's laws dealing with prostitution is unacceptable, and that the laws that exist are unequally applied," they were unable to reach agreement on a solution to the problem. The Conservative Party members adamantly maintained that decriminalizing prostitution was not the answer. Instead, they favoured both more stringent laws and more stringent enforcement of the laws. They called for "a new approach to criminal justice in which the perpetrators of crime would fund, through heavy fines, the rehabilitation and support of the victims they create. These fines would act as a significant deterrent." The Conservative MPs also contended that "law enforcement must deal equally and consistently with all forms of prostitution, whether it be found on the street, in escort services, massage parlours, bawdy houses or other businesses."[77]

By late 2009 the minority Conservative government had not acted on the recommendations of the Conservative MPs, but it appeared likely that the question of decriminalizing solicitation would remain on the political agenda for the fore-seeable future. The social conservative groups are not likely to abandon their campaign to secure more forceful and effective regulation of what they consider to be immoral and socially harmful sexual behaviour. At the same time, groups advocating for decriminalization and for the rights of sex trade workers are determined to press for changes in the law. They denounced the outcome of the parliamentary subcommittee and vowed to challenge the prostitution laws in the courts. "The subcommittee had a unique opportunity to truly improve the lives and well being of thousands of women, men and trans people working in the sex trade," commented Kara Gillies on behalf of Maggie's. "Instead, their new report offers platitudes, moralism and band-aid solutions." Gillies dismissed the report as "disappointing, and very sex-negative." Valerie Scott of SPOC also criticized the report, pointedly noting, "What adult sex professionals who chose to be in this business need, and there are many of us, is the removal of the communicating, bawdy house and procuring laws—and fewer cowardly politicians to achieve this."[78]

Following the release of the subcommittee report, SPOC members initiated a Charter of Rights challenge to the sections of the Criminal Code dealing with communicating for the purposes of prostitution, keeping a common bawdy house, and living on the avails of prostitution. Valerie Scott, Amy Leibovitch, and Terri Jean Bedford made an application in the Ontario Superior Court claiming that these laws contravene the rights of freedom of thought, belief, opinion, and expression and of life, liberty, and security of the person guaranteed by the Charter. They intended to pursue the case to the Supreme Court of Canada in hope that the sections of the Criminal Code would ultimately be struck down.[79]

REAL Women, Catholic Civil Rights League, and Christian Legal Fellowship responded to the challenge by applying to the court to be granted intervenor status to argue against the striking down of the laws. REAL Women professed the need to intervene in typically apocryphal terms, arguing:

> If successful, [the legal challenge] will result in very detrimental effects—practical, social, legal and health, that will undermine the social fabric of Canada. More specifically, it will have the tragic effect of damaging the health and well being of the vulnerable in our society, including young people and prostitutes and those in communities in which they operate.[80]

The lawyer representing the groups in the proceeding argued more explicitly for the need to protect moral values through criminal laws against prostitution—the real motivation for the social conservatives' intervention. Ranjan Agarwal, in his submissions to the court, remarked, "It is okay—to be blunt—for a person to sell their body, but when that action begins to impede on others, fundamental moral values are impacted." Alan Young, an Osgoode Hall law professor representing the SPOC members in the case, denounced the attempt to inject moral values as a factor for the court to consider when making its determination. "What these three groups want is a freestanding airing of their grievance that drugs, homosexual bathhouses and prostitution are spoiling the fabric of Canadian society. What you really have are three groups that have very strong opinions about the immorality of prostitution."[81]

Initially a judge of the Ontario Superior Court, Justice Ted Matlow, agreed with Young's point of view and denied the request for intervenor status. He expressed concern that the groups might use the trial as a forum to advance their religious views, which would be inconsistent with a strictly legal proceeding. He added that the challenge "does not provide a political platform where interested persons are permitted to speak in order to advance their personal views, beliefs, policies and interests at large."[82] The groups appealed, however, and the Ontario Court of Appeal overturned Matlow's decision. Three appeal court judges declared that there was a moral dimension to the issue of prostitution. The groups seeking intervenor status had a legitimate contribution to make to the case. Commenting on that decision, Derek Bell, another lawyer for the groups, agreed: "The criminal law has been, and always will be, grounded in morality."[83]

The constitutional challenge to the prostitution laws was argued in October 2009 at the Ontario Superior Court, with a decision expected to be released sometime in 2010. Regardless of the decision, it is likely that an appeal will be launched by one side or the other, with the case ultimately ending up at the Supreme Court of Canada.

The social conservative groups have sought stronger laws against prostitution and tried to become actively involved in Charter challenge cases because of a well-grounded fear that the courts, as they have done with abortion and pornography, will ultimately take action in regard to the prostitution laws—action that the politicians have so assiduously avoided. Those fears were heightened by a December 2005 judgment of the Supreme Court of Canada regarding a challenge to the bawdy house laws. To their alarm, seven out of nine justices ruled in two cases known as *R. v Labaye* and *R. v. Kouri* that consenting adults engaging in group sex in sex clubs or swingers clubs did not commit acts of indecency. The clubs therefore were not common bawdy houses under the Criminal Code. The cases arose from bawdy house charges laid against the owners of two Montreal swingers clubs in which clients engaged in heterosexual group sex and partner-swapping.

The judgments significantly changed the legal definition of indecency. They ruled that the meaning of indecency should not depend on what is acceptable to the community at large, but rather should be based on the harm that a particular activity might cause. There was no evidence in the cases before the Court that harm was caused to any individual or to society. The majority judgment noted that no one was pressured into having sex, paid for sex, or was treated as a mere sexual object for the gratification of others. Significantly, the justices stated, although the clubs were businesses this did not mean that the acts that took place within them were "commercial," which meant in turn that the acts did not constitute prostitution.[84] Accordingly, while they did not strike down the provisions of the Criminal Code dealing with prostitution, the judgments significantly narrowed the circumstances in which sexual activity that social conservatives would brand as immoral or sexual sin would result in criminal convictions.

Claiming to speak for Canadians as a whole, the EFC's Buckingham was quick to denounce the Supreme Court judgment as being "beyond what most Canadians would find tolerable. This kind of thing offends Canadian standards of decency." Richard Bastien of the Catholic Civil Rights League (National Capital Region) criticized the judgment for effectively declaring "that one of the basic principles underpinning the Canadian legal system is that the law should never be used to enforce morality. In other words, the law should be morally neutral. This is not only wrong, it is absurd. It is impossible to conceive of any law that does not have a moral basis."[85]

The Supreme Court's decision on swingers clubs was released in the middle of the January 2006 federal election campaign, and Harper wasted no time in currying favour with social conservative voters. He pledged to have a Conservative government look at the decision to see what could be done "to plug that loophole" opened by the change in the definition of indecency. "I think a lot of Canadians are troubled by that decision," he solemnly intoned.[86] Tellingly, Harper was the only leader of a federal political party to make any statement about the judgment during the election campaign.

Following the election of the minority Conservative government, social conservative groups began a campaign to ensure that Harper lived up to his commitment. The Evangelical Fellowship called for amendment of the Criminal Code to reinstate the community standards of tolerance test for indecency that had been changed by the Supreme Court's decision. Swingers clubs, the EFC contended, "are beyond Canadian community standards of tolerance. And these decisions will have ripple effects on other sex-related businesses." Among the effects, the EFC predicted, would be public advertising by swingers clubs to "encourage more couples to consider consensual adultery" and a negative impact on some marriages and relationships. Other ripple effects would be public sex acts performed in strip clubs. As well, "Bath houses and massage parlours will be able to operate as legitimate businesses, publicly offering sexual services, unless someone can prove 'harm.'" It was imperative that there be a response to the decision by Parliament, the EFC argued. "There is a strong moral argument and strong community support for Members of Parliament to address this issue."[87]

The Harper government, though, did not go on to state any intention to amend the Criminal Code to reinstate the indecency definition as it existed before the Supreme Court justices amended it. Its inaction has been significant, given that a number of other Criminal Code amendments have been introduced and adopted since the judgment was issued, and the government could easily have included the indecency definition among those other amendments. Perhaps Harper realized that the promise delivered to shore up the votes of the social conservative electorate during the election campaign was easier to make than to actually implement as legislation. Perhaps the cause remained an item for implementation by the government at some future date, possibly after it secured a majority and would be able to ensure the enactment of its legislation. Given the presence of a strong social conservative faction within the Conservative parliamentary caucus, perhaps the best that can be hoped is that the government will decide to continue to at least acquiesce to the Court's decision. In the long term, it can only be hoped that the Harper government and any future administrations will accept that the Supreme Court has finally removed the indecency sections of the Criminal Code from the nineteenth-century context of regulating religious morality and given them a twenty-first-century interpretation reflecting the secular morality of not causing harm.

Sadly, there is no realistic reason to believe that members of Parliament will take the next logical step and actually decriminalize prostitution and repeal the repressive bawdy house sections of the Criminal Code. As has so often been the case in the past, the best hope for progress on those issues rests with the justices of the Supreme Court and their interpretations of the rights guaranteed by the Charter.

Meanwhile evangelicals and others in the social conservative movement remain deadly serious about the imperative of state regulation of morality, and of sexual morality in particular. They are convinced that nothing short of a cultural war, encouraged and supported by the instruments of the state, is required to ensure that their moral standards will prevail over sexual permissiveness and the immorality of secularism.

FOUR

Anti-Gay Activism in the Age of Rights

Even though the media, the courts and the
educational system are straining to normalize
homosexuality, the fact is that it is <u>not</u> normal.
The simple fact is that nature did not create
the human body to express itself in a same-sex
manner: society does not have to abandon
common sense and accept this abnormality
as acceptable.

– REAL Women of Canada, 2009

Of all the sexual sins, homosexuality has attracted the most attention from modern social conservatism. Armed with the Bible, their religious fervour, and substantial financial and human resources, social conservatives have strenuously rejected both the positive social acceptance of homosexuality as a healthy, normal alternative sexuality and the notion that the state should acknowledge and protect the rights and relationships of gays and lesbians.

The conservatives base their condemnation of homosexual acts on a close reading of certain Bible passages. Leviticus 18:22 and 20:13 (of the King James Version) refer to the acts as "an abomination." Leviticus 20:13 declares, "And if a man also lie with mankind, as he lieth with a woman, both of them have committed an abomination: they shall surely be put to death; their blood *shall be* upon them." Especially for evangelical Protestants, the biblical account of the destruction of Sodom and Gomorrah became God's retribution for homosexual activity by the men of the two towns. Homosexuality historically was, and even in some references today is referred to as, "the sin of Sodom." In the New Testament—although Jesus Christ, as represented in the scriptures, had nothing whatsoever to say on the specific subject of sexual relations between members of the same sex—the proscriptions on same-sex sexuality, as articulated by the apostle Paul in Romans and I Corinthians, refer to "vile affections" that are "against nature" and "unseemly."

For evangelical Protestants, if the Bible scriptures say homosexuality is a sin and an abomination, it must be so, and no further interpretation or explanation is required. Focus on the Family (Canada) asserts, "Relying on what the Bible clearly teaches about homosexuality to form our views is critical." It cites various scriptures to declare: "Any discussion about homosexuality in the Bible must be placed within the context of the Biblical view of sexuality and marriage in general.... The Bible clearly affirms heterosexual monogamy, and prohibits all sexual activities outside the marriage relationship." Various Bible passages, the organization states, "make clear the point that homosexuality is in violation of God's plan for humanity."[1]

The Roman Catholic Church bases its condemnations of homosexuality on the biblical scriptures augmented by interpretations of the Church's leadership. It takes into account, among other factors, the concept of "natural law," which it contends is part of the eternal or divine law of the universe. In accordance with natural law, the purpose of sex is procreation. It is to be confined to two persons of the opposite gender who are married. Good and moral sex occurs only within marriage. All other sex is immoral and sinful. Homosexuality, which cannot result in procreation, is unnatural and immoral. That view was expressed unequivocally in a 1986 "Pastoral Letter to Homosexuals" published by the Vatican's Congregation for the Doctrine of the Faith. The document declared that the homosexual inclination "is a more or less strong tendency ordered toward an intrinsic moral evil." For the Catholic Church, sexual relations between members of the same sex are unacceptable under any circumstances. The *Catechism of the Catholic Church*, updated in 1992, commands that "homosexual persons are called to chastity," and that "by the virtues of self-mastery that teach them inner freedom, at times by the support of disinterested friendship, by prayer and sacramental grace, they can and should gradually and resolutely approach Christian perfection."[2] In other words, it is acceptable to have a "homosexual inclination," but it is a sin to act upon that inclination in any way other than by lifelong abstinence from sexual relationships with members of the same sex.

Yet while the religious view of homosexuality as gravely immoral lies at the root of social conservatism's anti-gay advocacy, its attack on homosexuality has involved much more than simply following the strict path of religious dogma.

The movement's leaders understand that merely casting homosexuals as morally depraved sinners appeals only to a very limited audience of the devout. Thus they have broadened their pitch to include other, non-religious arguments—drawing upon the "scientific" support provided by a small minority of psychiatrists and other mental health professionals who hold tenaciously to the view that homosexuality is deviant, abnormal, and disordered. The *Catechism*, for example, combines the language of psychiatry with traditional religious beliefs to refer to homosexual acts as both "grave depravity" and "intrinsically disordered."

Given this direction, social conservative anti-gay advocacy has sought to generate revulsion and alarm by painting the homosexual "lifestyle" as medically and psychologically harmful to those entrapped by it. They have described purportedly disgusting and disease-producing sexual practices to paint homosexuals as ominous threats to the health and well-being of the whole of society. They have portrayed homosexuals as threats to marriage, family, and the social order—by extension, and even more dangerously, fanning hatred towards and fear of homosexuals and homosexuality. As a 2003 Focus on the Family position paper setting out "a Christian response" to marriage and homosexuality asserts (in presenting "The facts about homosexuality"): "Homosexual practices are intrinsically more risky than heterosexual practices." The paper states, "Homosexual practices are strongly associated with a wide variety of health risks (including AIDS) which are related to the tendency to have anonymous sexual encounters." The organization attributed the increased risk for homosexuals to three contributors: increased promiscuity, anal intercourse, and, perhaps most astoundingly, "the *unique desire to acquire HIV within certain aspects of the homosexual community.*"[3]

Social conservative zealots have malevolently appealed to and played upon fears of homosexuals as child molesters and corrupters of and threats to youth—with REAL Women being one of the most persistent groups in this regard. In a position paper published in 1994 REAL Women posited, "If homosexuals are successful in obtaining legal recognition of their relationships, the very fabric of Canadian society will be irreparably damaged." The group repeatedly offered this rationale:

> When REAL Women speaks out against homosexuality, it is not from hatred, but from love and concern: concern for the well-being of our country; concern for our vulnerable youth; concern for the freedoms of Canadians to express their religious and social beliefs.... No matter how unpalatable they may be, the facts about the homosexual lifestyle must be presented to the public. We owe our young people the truth about a lifestyle that is unhealthy and dangerous.[4]

In pursuit of their objective, REAL Women and other groups have cited the contested and propagandistic materials produced by U.S. religious right groups such as the Family Research Institute (FRI), founded in 1985 by psychologist Paul Cameron, and the Family Research Council (FRC), established in 1983 by James Dobson of Focus on the Family—organizations that added the apparent imprimatur of scientific research and authority to support the traditional religious condemnations of homosexuality. Cameron became a prominent national spokesperson for social conservatism in the United States during the 1980s. His purported research studies and anti-gay polemics were heralded by social conservative groups, even though leading professional bodies in the United States had resoundingly condemned his work.[5] In its 1994 position paper REAL Women cited an FRI article co-authored by Cameron that presented data on death from AIDS compiled by studying the obituaries in sixteen gay newspapers in the United States. REAL Women declared: "The average age of men dying from AIDS is 39; the average age of homosexuals dying from other causes is a revealing 41 years of age."[6]

In a series of pamphlets Cameron characterized homosexuals as evil child molesters and dangerous threats to both the social order and the personal health of the rest of the population—pointing in particular to diseases spread through promiscuity and unsanitary sexual activities. Among the most pernicious of his assertions was a statement indicating that "evidence suggests that the 1%-to-3% of adults who practice homosexuality account for between a fifth and a third of all child molestation."[7] REAL Women cited this "evidence" many times in its publications and advocacy materials, including in its 1994 position paper, concluding, "The propensity for paedophila is proportionately far higher among homosexuals." In a number of studies and reports the FRC has made exactly the same claim.[8]

In briefs to governments and in advocacy materials various social conservative groups have endlessly repeated this assertion—that homosexual pedophiles sexually molest children at a far greater rate compared to the percentage of homosexuals in the general population—as a purportedly compelling reason why rights should not be granted to gays and lesbians. The deliberate and repeated assertions of "gays as child molesters" amount to fear-mongering. It is an argument that is completely unsupported by the preponderance of credible scientific research done on the subject of the sexual exploitation of children, and is rejected by all of the leading medical health professions. The research and studies have established that most pedophiles and child molesters identify as heterosexual in their adult sexual relationships and are attracted to children of both sexes, not specifically to male children or female children.

Other manifestations of social conservative hate-mongering have been the oft-expressed contentions of the movement's advocates that homosexuals are broken or defective sexually and emotionally, that they suffer from a deviant and abnormal sexual proclivity. Social conservatives have sought to portray homosexuality as neither an innate nor an immutable characteristic. They emphatically reject one of the fundamental tenets of gay liberation—that same-sex attraction can and should shape one's identity and sense of self in a positive and affirming way. They argue that homosexuality is merely a sexual practice, a base genital reaction to immoral and unnatural stimulations—something that should bring a sense of guilt or shame to those who experience it.

REAL Women of Canada, Focus on the Family, and the Evangelical Fellowship of Canada all enthusiastically promote the notion that gays can be cured of this illness. As a "psychological disorder," REAL Women argues, homosexuality can be "reversed"—"If a person is willing to change." First of all these people need to be determined to change, and then they need to avail themselves of Christian counselling services, which "have worked successfully in changing sexual orientation. The idea that homosexuals cannot change is a myth like the popular view at the turn of the century that alcoholics could never change." On its website Focus on the Family has appealed to homosexuals who seek to be cured: "You're not simply 'wired that way.' Indeed, you don't have to be gay—there is hope for those who want to change." The group proudly proclaims, "Focus on the Family is promoting the truth that homosexuality is preventable and treatable."[9]

An EFC leaflet widely circulated in the 1990s asserted, "The social sciences simply do not provide the evidence to prove that homosexuality is genetically or biologically based. And even if a genetic or biological component is ever demonstrated this would not prove that homosexuality is normal. Many abnormal conditions have a genetic or biological origin." EFC also took up the "myth" that homosexuality could not be changed: "The fact is that there is a long list of psychotherapists and religious counsellors who have helped persons of homosexual orientation move into a heterosexual orientation and a much happier life." Calling on all Christians to reach out and to convert homosexuals, EFC proclaimed, "Any person with a compulsive neurotic condition deserves help, if help is available." That help should come from "all morally serious Christians [who] must see that this is made known and available. When help is available, it is cruel, not loving, to tell homosexuals that they were born that way and no change is possible.... The Church, as a loving and redeeming community, should be in the forefront of proclaiming this good news."[10]

The "long list of psychiatrists and religious counsellors" may well have been a reference to a U.S.-based advocacy group, the National Association for Research and Therapy of Homosexuality (NARTH), a group of mental health professionals whose purpose is "to provide psychological understanding of the cause, treatment and behavior patterns associated with homosexuality." Founded in 1992, NARTH has championed the view that gays can be cured through conversion therapy, which is also sometimes referred to as reorientation or reparative therapy. In advancing its mission, NARTH operates "an international referral service of therapists offering sexual reorientation treatment in the United States, Canada, Europe and Australia." It reaches out to "lay organizations, including religious groups, which turn to us for scientific evidence which may support their traditional doctrines." It maintains close ties with the Interfaith Committee on Theological Concerns and Focus on the Family in the United States.[11] NARTH's claim that gays can be cured is entirely consistent with the religious belief that homosexual behaviour is a grave sin that can be overcome through abstinence or atoned for by repentance—coupled with a commitment, aided by prayer and religious faith, to cease engaging in the behaviour.

NARTH's emergence to prominence in the North American social conservative movement represented a rebellion by embittered psychiatrists, psychologists, and other mental health professionals, many with strong religious beliefs, who had become increasingly marginalized within their professions for clinging to the view that homosexuality can be cured through psychological therapy—a view that had long been the prevailing view of psychiatry and other health professions. The historic decision of the American Psychiatric Association (APA) in 1973 to remove homosexuality from the list of mental disorders officially altered that perception. Later, in 1997, the APA formally announced its opposition to therapy that attempts to turn gays straight, as well as to portrayals of lesbian, gay, and bisexual people as mentally ill and in need of treatment due to their sexual orientation. Reiterating that position in a 2001 news release, APA president Rodrigo Muñoz declared, "There is no scientific evidence that reparative or conversion therapy is effective in changing a person's sexual orientation. There is, however, evidence that this type of therapy can be destructive." The APA also pointed out, "Reparative therapy runs the risk of harming patients by causing depression, anxiety, and self-destructive behavior."[12]

The American Psychological Association, American Association of Social Workers, and American Academy of Pediatrics have also taken positions opposing reparative therapy. The American Psychological Association states:

> Although much research has examined the possible genetic, hormonal, developmental, social, and cultural influences on sexual orientation, no findings have emerged that permit scientists to conclude that sexual orientation is determined by any particular factor or factors.... To date, there has been no scientifically adequate research to show that therapy

aimed at changing sexual orientation (sometimes called reparative or conversion therapy) is safe or effective.[13]

Still, as the existence of NARTH attests, a sizable number of practitioners within the mental health professions did not accept the general shift to a new way of thinking. The unrepentant and increasingly renegade practitioners embraced the social conservative assault on the positive acceptance of homosexuality, providing the movement with purportedly scientific evidence to support the notion that gays could be cured; and the social conservatives in turn embraced the "cure the gays" practitioners and their theories to bolster their essentially religious-based rejection of homosexuality as a natural and normal form of sexual orientation. For the social conservative groups, reparative therapy represented an opportunity to secularize and medicalize their anti-homosexual positioning. This approach, they hoped, would make opposition to gay rights more palatable to the lawmakers and to a large segment of the general population not explicitly motivated by religion or questions of morality.

The answer to addressing discrimination against gays and lesbians, then, was not to grant them legal rights that condoned or approved of their homosexuality and lifestyle. Rather, the humane and compassionate approach would be to offer admitted homosexuals the prospect of treatment and therapy that would help them to find their true heterosexual selves. They could then become accepted as "normal and moral" and could integrate into society without fear of discrimination or reprisal. All they had to do was make the decision to change and commit to a course of reparative therapy. The Evangelical Fellowship of Canada exultantly proclaimed that view in a 1993 leaflet dealing with "common myths about homosexuality." It outlined the organization's opposition to amending the Canadian Human Rights Act (CHRA) to prohibit sexual-orientation discrimination:

> Another myth which must be sustained to uphold the homosexual ideology is that homosexual orientation cannot be changed.... If it can be demonstrated not only that homosexual practice can be changed to heterosexual practice, but that the underlying homosexual orientation can be changed to heterosexual orientation, then the whole homosexual ideology collapses. That is why homosexual lobbyists have very mixed feelings about research into the causes of homosexuality. What if a cure is found![14]

To that end a whole industry has sprung up to cure homosexuals by use of reparative therapies. Focus on the Family, NARTH, and other groups produce and sell books, publications, and slick videotapes and audiotapes on the subject. They market these to gays and lesbians hoping to escape the "enslavement of homosexual desire" and to the parents and families of gays and lesbians who hope their "afflicted loved ones" can be cured. Focus on the Family has become particularly prolific, holding "Love Won Out" conferences and rallies that specifically target gays and lesbians who, they claim, want to hear the truth about "moving out of homosexuality."[15] "Love Won Out" events also seek the participation of those who must "deal with the heartbreak of learning about a gay loved one, with no one to turn to for answers." By attending "Love Won Out," Focus on the Family contends, these people will be learning how to "respond to misinformation in our culture, defend biblical beliefs and prevent your child from embracing this destructive way of life. Most importantly, you'll be reminded of the power of God's love and His desire to transform the life of a struggling homosexual to find freedom in Jesus Christ."[16]

So-called transformational ministries and ex-gay groups are also part of the mix. To achieve their goals of changing sexual orientation and turning homosexuals into healthy and godly heterosexuals, they use a variety of tactics such as prayer, religious conversion, and individual and group counselling. The first "ex-gay" group, using the biblically symbolic name of Exodus International, was founded in 1976 in the United States, with affiliated ministries forming in Canada soon afterwards. Exodus proclaims itself an "interdenominational Christian organization promoting the message, 'Freedom from homosexuality through the power of Jesus Christ.'" Exodus boasts that it "upholds heterosexuality as God's creative intent for humanity, and subsequently views homosexuality as outside of God's will"—as being "destructive" and "sinful." But a "reorientation of same sex attraction is possible." The end goal is "a lifelong and healthy" heterosexual marriage or "a Godly single life."[17] A Canadian affiliate, New Direction for Life Ministries, has partnered with the EFC in conducting training workshops for "pastors and church leaders to equip their congregations for discipleship in the area of sexual attraction."[18]

Another "ex-gay" group, Homosexuals Anonymous (HA), has affiliations with evangelical Protestants. Founded in 1980, it claims to be able to "free" individuals from homosexuality by helping them with "recovery from the spiritual, psychological and relational distortions of homosexuality." Human Life International (HLI), a Catholic lay group founded in 1972, has gained notoriety for its militant anti-abortion campaigns and anti-gay advocacy and virulent opposition to sex education in the schools. Courage, another Catholic group, with chapters in Vancouver, Winnipeg, and Toronto, professes to show how "an interior life of chastity" can lead practitioners "beyond the confines of the homosexual identity to a more complete one in Christ."[19]

Lesbian and gay activists, among others, have resoundingly condemned these various initiatives to cure gays as nothing more than promoting hatred. Social conservatives and their "ex-gay" group allies respond that they hate the sin but love the sinner. Yet advocating that homosexuality is sinful, abnormal, deviant, and evil is by no means an act of love. Telling gays and lesbians that they should remain chaste or, worse, should repair their damaged and depraved sexuality through prayer and therapy in order to be reoriented as heterosexual is anything but professing love. Establishing an entire industry devoted to curing gays and turning them straight is nothing more than the merchandising of hatred, no matter how the various groups attempt to dress it up in the language of compassion and caring.

The lesbian and gay rights agenda

In their own response to the social and cultural oppression that had historically cast them as sinful, sick, pathetic, or criminal, advocacy groups within the gay liberation movement organized to secure the amendment of provincial and federal human rights laws to include the term "sexual orientation" as a prohibited ground of discrimination. They faced a daunting challenge. Virulent anti-homosexual attitudes were pervasive and freely expressed—even by the very politicians that the lesbian and gay activists had to convince of the need to change the laws. One of those was the Progressive Conservative attorney general of Ontario, Allan Lawrence. When asked at a public meeting in 1971 whether he supported amending the Ontario Human Rights Code to prohibit discrimination against homosexuals, Lawrence replied: "A homosexual is a pervert and this perversion should not be legally recognized in any way, shape or form."[20] In Manitoba a similar question posed by Gays for Equality, Winnipeg, at an all-candidates meeting during the 1973 provincial election prompted Joe Borowski to blurt out that "homos and perverts" had taken over the provincial NDP. "I don't regard homos as human beings," he said.[21] Lawrence's and Borowski's comments provide a representative indication of how freely at this time politicians—of various stripes, and not just conservatives—felt they could with impunity make derogatory and condemnatory statements about homosexuality.[22]

Indeed, no government took action on the issue until 1977, when the first Parti Québécois government under Premier René Lévesque, after an initial period of resistance to legislating human rights protections for gays and lesbians, acted hastily in the aftermath of a police raid on a gay bar in Montreal. A stunning act of police repression, the raid on Truxx—with 146 patrons arrested on bawdy house and other charges—generated a massive public demonstration of protest in the streets of downtown Montreal. During the demonstration the police compounded the anger and outrage with acts of violence inflicted on demonstrators. Television newscasts captured the event, and within a matter of days the PQ, fearing that its progressive reputation would be damaged, introduced and secured the adoption of a bill that added sexual orientation to the provincial Charter of Human Rights and Freedoms. The bill, given final legislative approval on December 15, 1977, was proclaimed to be in force four days later.[23]

For the next eleven years Quebec remained the only province to enact such legislation as the new social conservative groups continued to raise the alarm among politicians and the broader public about the long-term adverse impacts that they claimed would arise from prohibiting sexual-orientation discrimination in human rights acts: the employment of openly gay/lesbian teachers and other professionals working with children, the legal recognition of same-sex relationships, possibly even gay marriage, and, for them, the horrific prospect of adoption of children by homosexuals.

Federally, the Liberal government of Pierre Trudeau ignored the calls of gay and lesbian rights groups to include sexual orientation when it introduced, and Parliament enacted, the Canadian Human Rights Act in 1976. That act consciously omitted the issue of sexual orientation, despite concerted lobbying by the National Gay Rights Coalition (NGRC). At the time, opposition to the amendment came principally from the armed forces, the RCMP, and the Department of External Affairs, which all maintained discriminatory policies of not hiring or continuing to employ gays and lesbians. The main reason cited for the ban was that gays and lesbians posed risks to national security because of the secretive and furtive nature of their lifestyle. That lifestyle, it was argued, made them susceptible to blackmail and placed them at risk of being recruited for espionage purposes by hostile foreign governments. Until its demise in 1981, NGRC made amendment of the CHRA one of its main advocacy objectives, organizing demonstrations, submitting briefs and petitions, lobbying members of Parliament, publicizing instances of discrimination in the federal public sector, especially the expulsion of gays and lesbians from the armed forces, and enlisting the support of other equality-seeking groups.[24]

The evangelical backlash

The new counter-movement to gay liberation, led by Ken Campbell, Hudson Hilsden, and David Mainse, remained in relative obscurity until 1977, when its champions suddenly burst into prominence in mobilizing fiercely homophobic sentiment in response to the public release of a groundbreaking report of a committee established by the Ontario government to review and propose changes to the Human Rights Code.

The Ontario Human Rights Code Review Committee, in a report called *Life Together*, recommended, among other measures intended to expand and strengthen the Code, that sexual orientation be added to the prohibited grounds of discrimination. It was a legislative measure that gay rights groups in Ontario had been demanding since 1972. The Coalition for Gay Rights in Ontario (CGRO) had concertedly lobbied both the Progressive Conservative government of Bill Davis and the Ontario Human Rights Commission for an amendment since the group's founding in 1975. As part of those efforts, CGRO made submissions to the Review Committee that cited documented cases of discrimination against gays and lesbians in employment, housing, and access to services. The Committee heard them, stating in the report that, "Homosexuals have never received the same protection from discrimination that is extended to their fellow citizens.... As a result, they are subjected to blackmail, to arbitrary dismissal from their jobs, and to summary eviction."[25] This was not only an acknowledgement by a government-appointed committee that discrimination against gays and lesbians was a reality that must be addressed by way of legislation, but also a ringing validation of the principal political demand made by the lesbian and gay rights groups.

In reaction to the *Life Together* report, CGRO devised a strategy to use the sexual-orientation recommendation as the means to pressure the government to finally amend the Human Rights Code.[26] Principally, it concentrated on the opposition parties in the legislature, in recognition that the Davis government, despite the recommendation, remained adamantly opposed. But even among the opposition it found the proposition of a sexual-orientation amendment to be a hard sell. At a November 1977 meeting with members of the Liberal Party caucus, CGRO was confronted with deep divisions among the members of the provincial parliament, with many, especially from small urban and rural areas, being staunchly opposed. Indeed, CGRO was asked during the meeting whether it would support an amendment to the Code that would ban discrimination against homosexuals in general but would permit discrimination in cases of employing teachers or child-care workers. CGRO's rejection of that as a viable option removed any realistic prospect of significant support from the Liberals. Indeed, in his report of the meeting, *Toronto Sun* columnist Claire Hoy confirmed that widespread opposition existed within the party. He noted, in a column provocatively headlined "The Limp Wrist Lobby," that Liberal MPPs he had spoken with privately "have no sympathy with the notion of institutionalizing homosexualism either in the human rights code or elsewhere."[27]

Outside the legislature, the release of the *Life Together* report with its recommendation for a sexual-orientation amendment sent shock waves through the large and politically influential social conservative constituency. Campbell, Hilsden, and other social conservative activists organized a campaign to persuade the Progressive Conservative government to reject the recommendation. In one especially nasty incident, Hilsden publicly circulated a letter calling on the "morally respectable people of Ontario" to organize against the "satanic" gay rights movement. Citing the horror of gay teachers and gay speakers being allowed in schools, Hilsden urged his followers to write letters to members of the provincial legislature demanding that lesbians and gays not be protected under the human rights legislation.[28]

In late 1977 and throughout 1978, Campbell and other social conservative leaders intensified their crusade. In one very high-profile move, they brought U.S. activist Anita Bryant to Canada to help generate public opposition to the amendment. Bryant, a fervent evangelical Protestant, well-known recording artist (with three gold records), and primary spokesperson in television advertisements for Florida orange juice, claimed to have been called by God to lead a crusade against gay rights. Her high profile as spokesperson for one of the first U.S. anti-gay rights initiatives, the Save Our Children campaign, had helped bring the social conservative movement to prominence in the United States. In Canada Campbell, through Renaissance International, organized prayer rallies and church services, with Bryant as the star attraction, in Toronto, Peterborough, London, Winnipeg, Moose Jaw, and Edmonton. The rallies became headline news—especially when they were countered by angry demonstrations by gays and lesbians protesting "born-again bigotry."[29]

With Bryant's appearances in the various cities generating enormous media coverage, and with gays and lesbians organizing in protest, the news media were obliged to tell another side of the story. The visits gave lesbian and gay activists a kind of access to the media that they simply had not previously been able to gain through presenting briefs to legislatures and meeting with politicians. Ironically, Campbell and Bryant did as much to advance the cause of securing public support for gay rights legislation as they did to generate opposition to such measures. Many Canadians who had never heard about the drive to amend human rights laws to prohibit discrimination against gays and lesbians were now being informed of the issue on radio and television, and in newspapers, by proud out of the closet gays and lesbians.

Campbell's Renaissance group, for its part, also aggressively targeted politicians who spoke in support of legislative initiatives to prohibit sexual orientation discrimination. It accused such politicians of being complicit in the undermining of moral values and contributing to social decay. In short order, Campbell, collaborating with an assortment of other social conservative advocates, along with powerful political forces, managed to turn Toronto's 1980 municipal elections into a referendum on gay rights—attacking what they saw as the gay-positive bent of a

Toronto city council dominated by leftist and progressive councillors. Those councillors, in response to lobbying by the Gay Alliance Toward Equality–Toronto, had adopted, in 1976, Canada's first municipal anti-discrimination policy prohibiting sexual-orientation discrimination in respect of employment and the provision of municipal services. As a representative of Toronto's growing and increasingly visible gay and lesbian community, George Hislop was running for city councillor in a downtown ward. Toronto mayor John Sewell, a member of the reform faction on city council, was once again running for the mayorality; he publicly and actively supported Hislop's candidacy.

During the election, a motley collection of social conservative groups organized a massive campaign to defeat Sewell, Hislop, and other candidates supportive of gay rights. Campbell's Renaissance International distributed a publication to 100,000 households condemning the gay rights agenda and its nefarious supporters. It was joined by some smaller local organizations—Metro's Moral Majority, Positive Parents, and the League Against Homosexuals—as well as certain business interests and members of the Toronto Police Association. In the race for major, candidate Art Eggleton lambasted Sewell for "facilitating San Francisco–style gay power politics in Toronto" and condemned what he asserted was "flaunting sexual preference." Eggleton rode a wave of anti-gay sentiment to victory, defeating Sewell in the race for mayor. Hislop was also defeated, failing in his bid to become the first openly gay city councillor.[30]

Emboldened by their success in the Toronto municipal elections, the social conservative groups turned their efforts to defeating CGRO's drive to amend the Ontario Human Rights Code. They united in common cause during the 1981 provincial election under the name of the Pro-Family Coalition, working to defeat candidates from the Liberal Party and NDP who were on public record as supporting an amendment. Perceiving that support for lesbian and gay rights had caused the defeat of Sewell and Hislop, many Liberal and NDP members of the legislature who had previously supported an amendment became fearful of invoking voter backlash. Margaret Campbell, a Liberal MPP who had publicly called for an amendment, commented that skittish provincial politicians were being held back by "the terrible controversy in the municipal elections and the stirring up of people." NDP leader Michael Cassidy, who had also been supporting an amendment of the Human Rights Code, backtracked from that position, declaring that gay rights were no longer a priority.[31]

The Progressive Conservatives capitalized on the surging pro-family sentiment, returning to a majority government after nearly five years of minority rule. Shortly after the election, the Davis government finally introduced amendments to the Human Rights Code based on the recommendations in *Life Together*, but it refused to add sexual orientation to the Code. Labour Minister Robert Elgie declared in response to a question on the subject, "The government does not feel [sexual preference] should be enshrined as an acceptable or normal lifestyle."[32] Elgie's statement was a tacit acknowledgement that it was social conservatives and not gay activists who had influence with the government. The omission of sexual orientation from the amended Human Rights Code was the Davis government's payback for the support that social conservatives had given it during the election.

In 1981, then, the social conservative views of homosexuality and opposition to legislating rights for gays and lesbians were clearly still within mainstream opinion, commanding the support of politicians. Political leaders were not yet willing to accept that discrimination against homosexuals was unjustifiable and unacceptable. They simply did not accept that gays and lesbians constituted a legitimate minority as deserving of the rights and protections afforded by law as any other recognized minority groups. Amending human rights legislation to include prohibitions on sexual-orientation discrimination was seen as a huge public step towards the positive acceptance of homosexuality: that is, as a moral issue. The state could still not condone or encourage the open expression of homosexuality— the "flaunting" of it in public or the open presence of an abnormal and immoral/ unacceptable lifestyle.

But within a year the social and judicial landscape would be changed forever. The patriation of the Canadian Constitution and adoption of the Canadian Charter of Rights and Freedoms would usher in the "age of rights." One of the most dramatic indications of that profound change would be the incremental recognition in law of human rights protections and guarantees of equal treatment for gays and lesbians in the ensuing years.

The social conservative response to calls for the enactment of human rights for gays and lesbians contrasted sharply with the reactions of some other Christians. In 1977 the United Church of Canada publicly called for the amendment of human rights laws to prohibit discrimination against gays and lesbians. Indeed, Bruce McLeod, a former United Church Moderator, had been a member of the Ontario Human Rights Code Review Committee and became a public advocate of a sexual-orientation amendment. He had notably joined with other clergy in expressing opposition to the Campbell and Bryant crusade against the *Life Together* recommendation. A more contemplative approach to the question was also taking place within the Anglican Church of Canada. A 1976 editorial in the *Canadian Churchman*, the national Anglican publication, suggested:

> There is a role for the church to play. It could join ranks with those in the gay community working towards changes in provincial and federal law.

It could work towards changing the public attitude that makes the gay man or woman an outcast in society. It could remove the terror of those within its own ranks who live a double life in daily fear that their homosexuality will be discovered. It could do all these things—and it should. It's a simple case of human rights.[33]

In 1979 the Anglican Church officially called for human rights laws to be amended to prohibit discrimination against homosexuals.

Special rights and family values

Despite the transformative nature of Canadian society in the new age of rights, symbolized most demonstrably by the Charter—and indeed in reaction to it—social conservative advocates remained steadfastly committed to basing their objection to rights for gays and lesbians on their religious and moral objections to homosexuality and to the portrayal of the "homosexual lifestyle" as dangerous and destructive. At the same time they attempted to respond to the new judicial and social frames of rights and equality by characterizing the rights that gays and lesbians sought as illegitimate "special rights." Those special rights, they contended, merely disguised the true objective of the "gay agenda": the positive acceptance of homosexuality as a natural and normal alternative to heterosexuality. They endeavoured to overlay their fundamental religious and moral objections with a more secular patina of preserving the traditional heterosexual family.

By the mid-1980s social conservative advocates were arguing that homosexuals were not a legitimate minority, as the gay rights advocates claimed, but were instead a deviant segment of society, undeserving of legislated rights that would protect their immoral and destructive behaviour. Fundamentally, according to that argumentation, the state's positive recognition of gays and lesbians as a legitimate minority would be tantamount to approving of homosexual behaviour. Moreover, they argued disingenuously, gays and lesbians already had in law all the same rights and protections as other citizens—which meant that there was no need to introduce sexual-orientation amendments to human rights laws.

"Social acceptance that will follow 'gay rights' laws will give homosexual behaviour a favourable climate to spread even more easily," advised REAL Women of Canada in a 1986 leaflet. "As homosexuality becomes publicly accepted as a valid life-style, traditional moral standards are further undermined." Addressing the question of special rights, REAL Women maintained: "Including 'sexual orientation' as a prohibited ground of discrimination would mean that, in addition to the rights shared by everyone, homosexuals would have *special rights* recognizing in law their lifestyle and behaviour. That is, amending the Human Rights legislation would mean society 'condoning' homosexual activity." Because it deemed homosexuality to be a behaviour that could be curtailed or even changed—cured—REAL Women also reasoned that the rights sought by gays and lesbians were illegitimate.

> "Sexual orientation" or homosexual legislation does not fall within the standards of human rights laws which protect morally neutral and unchangeable status, NOT behaviour. That is, standard human rights laws or codes protect unchangeable characteristics that are based on biology, sex, race, national origin or belief system (religion). None of these narrowly defined exceptions protect sexual preference.

Another leaflet pointed out: "Homosexuals have the same civil rights every other Canadian has. They are protected by the Charter of Rights and by federal and provincial human rights legislation." The group did not provide any evidence to support this claim.[34]

In a 1986 submission opposing the amendment of the Canadian Human Rights Act, the Evangelical Fellowship of Canada weighed in with: "Homosexuals have the same legal and constitutional rights as do all Canadians. They are protected by the Charter of Rights and existing human rights codes and enjoy the same equal protection and benefit of all statutory and common law remedies.... What they want is special recognition of their lifestyle and sexual preference." Later, in a 1993 fundraising solicitation, the EFC charged that homosexuals were seeking the "*special* status of a protected group and, indeed, the public acceptance of their lifestyle." Declared the group: "The implication for the family in all of this is frightening."[35]

There was more than a little hypocrisy and some considerable irony in the social conservative groups' accusation that the drive for gay rights was simply a ploy to force on society the recognition of special status for homosexual activity and the granting of special rights to the homosexual lifestyle. Indeed, it can be equally argued that it is Christianity—and the lifestyle it promotes and indeed demands—that has historically been given special status and special rights by the state in Canada. Christianity is a particular belief system of faith and values that is merely one among many in the world. Tellingly, the social conservative groups were not arguing that the state should not grant special status or special rights to any particular group or groups because of their system of faith and values or the religion-influenced lifestyles of their members. To do so would have been to argue that Christians should relinquish the special status and special rights that they and their belief system had enjoyed since the first days of colonial rule in Canada. What the social conservative groups really objected to and fought so strenuously against was the recognition by the state of any values and lifestyles other than their own. Homosexuality and the "homosexual lifestyle" were simply the most immediate and, for them, the most egregious threat to the preservation and protection of their own special status and special rights.

The claim that gays and lesbians already had the same legal and constitutional rights as other Canadians, that they were already protected under the Charter and human rights laws, was simply untrue. The courts had not yet determined that sexual orientation was a ground analogous to those specifically enumerated in the Charter. The statutory and common law remedies then available to gays and lesbians included being able, upon being fired from a job, to sue for wrongful dismissal and for payment of damages, or being able to sue for breach of contract; and those remedies had distinctly proven inadequate in effectively providing redress for discrimination. After all, that is why, in the period from the late 1940s to the 1970s, provincial governments began introducing, first, legislation prescribing fair employment and accommodation practices and, later, human rights acts.

Another social conservative claim—that same-sex and same-gender behaviour was neither an obvious nor a distinguishing characteristic—was undermined by the great amount of time and effort put into railing and organizing against both homosexuality and the homosexual lifestyle. Additionally, the gays and lesbians who were being fired from their jobs or evicted from their residences when their employers or landlords discovered they were homosexual would have strongly disagreed that their homosexuality was not seen as a distinguishing characteristic that led to discriminatory treatment by others. Further, by declaring that same-sex attraction is not innate or immutable, meaning that it is acquired and changeable, the social conservative groups put homosexuality in the same category as religion, which is also acquired and can be changed—or for that matter may not be possessed at all. Yet they did not argue that human rights laws should decline to prohibit religious discrimination. Fundamentally, the argument against gay rights was premised on the belief that censure and discrimination were justifiable if they were manifested for reasons of morality. Of course, what is moral and what is not is a matter of personal belief, whether rational or not. In the age of rights, many other people held the view that permitting, condoning, or acquiescing to discrimination against any group, including gays and lesbians, for religious or moral reasons was neither rational nor moral.

By the late 1980s, social conservative opposition to legislated human rights for gays and lesbians was also increasingly articulated using the dialectic of family,

family relationships, and family values. The issue in that context was cast in stark terms: providing human rights protections in law to gays and lesbians would undermine the traditional family, the foundation of society. Consequentially, the changes would endanger society and the social order. Yet the underpinnings of what became in the public consciousness a movement in support of "family values" were the same old religious teachings about sexual morality and sexual relationships that had formed part of the Canadian character and identity from the outset, and that had been intricately woven into the laws and institutions of the state. Social conservative advocates held tenaciously to the belief that the family, as exemplified by marriage, was the fundamental, God-given unit of society. For them, the state and state institutions must continue to promote the family through laws and public policy. In addition, the inseparability of sexuality and marriage and sexuality's exclusivity to holy matrimony were essential to ensuring social order and regulation.

"Family values" thus became the modern political expression of the traditional Christian belief that sex is a sacred act between a man and a woman that must be reserved to marriage and that has procreation as its principal purpose. For modern social conservatives, the stability of marriage and family—indeed, of a moral society—becomes imperilled by actions such as liberal (no-fault) divorce laws, recognition of unmarried, common-law relationships, relaxation of criminal sanctions on prostitution and pornography, and most especially by legislated rights for gays and lesbians and the legal recognition of same-sex relationships. For them, the gay rights movement and its drive to have governments amend human rights laws to prohibit sexual-orientation discrimination more than anything else became the embodiment of the threat to the traditional family anchored on traditional Judeo-Christian values.

In the phraseology of REAL Women:

> The homosexual movement aims to redefine the family away from the traditional model of husband, wife and children. It seeks a more "functional definition" which does not require heterosexuality as its foundation. In other words, homosexuals want an "open-ended" definition of the family. This would include persons *unrelated* by blood, marriage or adoption who live or cohabit together.[36]

The EFC issued a comparable declaration in a 1995 leaflet calling on evangelicals to enlist in the battle to defeat the amendment of the Canadian Human Rights Act. It urged the devout to "protect family values" and oppose equality rights legislation for gays: "Marriage and family have been given special status because of their unique role in providing for a stable relationship between a man and a woman and a setting for the begetting and nurturing of children. As Christians we are called to take a stand against the forces that challenge these biblical foundations."[37]

That traditional or natural family is the same one that was based on patriarchy and male supremacy—conditions also apparently ordained by God in the Bible. Historically, women who were not wives and mothers were viewed as having failed to meet their sacred duty and accordingly had little value and a lowly stature. Girls were socialized to be wives and mothers, to be cooks and cleaners and caregivers, to glory in being housewives and homemakers. They had to be chaste and feminine, and thus desirable commodities for marriage. Within Christian denominations, traditional religious marriage vows contained the requirement that the bride pledge to "obey" her groom.

Until 1982 it was not possible under the provisions of Canada's Criminal Code for husbands to be charged with raping their wives. Until the last couple of decades the domestic abuse of wives and sexual abuse of female children within traditional families had a low profile and carried few consequences. Women were economically dependent on men, first their fathers and then their husbands. Wives had no legal right to matrimonial property that was not in their own names or that they had not purchased. They could not take out bank loans or possess credit cards without the consent of their husbands. Until the 1970s, women had no right to an equal division of matrimonial assets in the event of a divorce, despite having contributed towards the acquisition of such assets, or in recognition of their role in supporting the husband and nurturing the family. Few measures were in place to ensure that men who abandoned or separated from their wives and families paid financial support to them.

The social conservative constructions of family and family values also adamantly insisted that the masculine and feminine genders and the roles ascribed to each are God-given and preordained; they are intended for procreation within monogamous, life-long marriage. "Heterosexual gender is a divine creation," asserts Focus on the Family.[38] According to the social conservative mindset, men and women have significant and inherent differences that are the result of biology, God's grand design, and other factors. Woman was created as the "helper" of man, according to the book of Genesis in the Bible. She was created from one of Adam's ribs and thus "taken out of man" and brought to the man to be his wife. Within the traditional family, men were dominant, as husbands, fathers, and providers, the heads of the households, and the ultimate authority figures. The biblical family, as expressed by God in Genesis, made women into little more than incubators who were perpetually subservient to men: "Unto the woman he said, I will greatly multiply thy sorrow and thy conception; in sorrow thou shalt bring forth children; and thy desire *shall be* to thy husband, and he shall rule over thee."[39]

Social conservatives contend that rigid, and correct, gender roles are essential to marriage and the family and to social well-being. In its "Guidelines for Education within the Family," the Roman Catholic Church's Pontifical Council of the Family exhorts parents to be examples to their children by displaying proper gender behaviour:

> A mother who values her maternal vocation and her place in the home greatly helps develop the qualities of femininity and motherhood in her daughters, and sets a clear, strong and noble example of womanhood for her sons. A father, whose behaviour is inspired by masculine dignity without "machismo," will be an attractive model for his sons, and inspire respect, admiration and security in his daughters.[40]

Homosexuality and especially same-sex relationships, social conservatives contend, violate and corrupt God's divine intent and dangerously disturb and pervert the "complementarity" of women and men that are fundamental to marriage and the family and, in the words of Focus on the Family, "the foundation for every civilized society."[41]

In regard to the family, family values, and family relationships, social conservative advocates also saw amending human rights codes to outlaw sexual-orientation discrimination as a dangerous wedge issue. Their briefs, letters, and petitions frequently spoke in foreboding terms about gay adoption of children and the legal recognition of same-sex marriages as shocking consequences. "But protecting citizens' rights to a homosexual lifestyle would lay the groundwork for same-sex marriages; it will eventually be argued that to deny such 'marriages' would be discriminatory," the EFC noted in a 1986 brief. "Right now, as the human rights legislation does not forbid discrimination on the basis of sexual orientation, no court will find the statutes [governing marriage] discriminatory. But under the proposed changes, the Marriage Law itself will be challenged as discriminatory and become legislatively vulnerable."[42] The Coalition for Family Values drew the same connection between the human rights issue and the status of the traditional family: "More fundamentally, however, is that the status of the family in society is threatened [by the proposed amendment to the Human Rights Code]."[43]

The expressed fears about the consequences for the preferential and privileged legal status of heterosexual marriage and the traditional family proved to be well founded. Amending the human rights laws to prohibit discrimination against gays and lesbians in employment, housing, and access to services would set the stage for expanding the ambit of legal rights into areas of law dealing with marriage and the family. It would establish the principle that gays and lesbians were a recognized minority who faced discrimination that was no longer tolerable. If discriminating against them in some aspects of their daily lives such as employment and housing was to be prohibited, it logically followed that discrimination should be prohibited in all other aspects of their lives. In fact, as early as the 1970s, CGRO and the other groups pursuing human rights amendments had set a broader agenda. CGRO's original list of legislative priorities included guaranteeing gay couples the same medical coverage under provincial health insurance plans as heterosexual couples; legislating that a parent's sexual orientation not be held against him or her in cases of child custody; or ensuring that a prospective parent's sexual orientation not be held against him or her in cases of child adoption.[44]

The social conservative advocates had incisively deduced that much more was at stake, that the very nature of marriage and family, as defined both in law and within the broader social context, would probably be altered forever as the battle for the legal recognition of the rights of gays and lesbians moved inevitably to the next round. For them, only one kind of family mattered—the family as based on the Judeo-Christian notions of a man and a woman, married and monogamous, with children. They would fight tenaciously and uncompromisingly on all fronts to protect and strengthen that family, the values that framed it, and the exclusivity and privilege that the law afforded to heterosexual marriage and family relationships.

"Save our children"

Anita's Bryant's crusade against homosexuality and gay rights under the Save Our Children banner served as a model for social conservative groups throughout North America. Social conservative advocates complained bitterly against and warned ominously about the dangerous consequences for children and youth should the legislators acquiesce to the demands of the gay rights groups and introduce laws prohibiting sexual-orientation discrimination. In addition to promoting the purported linking of homosexuals with disproportionately high incidences of pedophilia and child molestation, they focused more generally on ensuring that impressionable and vulnerable children were not presented with gay people or homosexuality in ways that were positive or affirming. They attempted to raise the alarm that children and youth might be deceived, lured, or recruited into homosexuality and the homosexual lifestyle. If, they reasoned, homosexuality was approved or condoned through the granting of human rights protections in law, children and young people would be led to believe that homosexuality was a normal, alternative sexual orientation equal in all respects to heterosexuality. Another oft-repeated concern was that lesbians and gay men would be permitted to have custody of or to adopt children. They contended that these groups and their lifestyles would be undesirable and dangerous for the raising of children.

The Evangelical Fellowship's 1986 brief expressed alarm that amending human rights legislation would mean that Big Brothers groups would no longer be able to maintain their policy of not permitting homosexuals to be big brothers for young boys. In addition, the EFC warned, such action would substantially increase the likelihood of a same-sex couple being permitted to adopt a child. The organization postulated that "such legislation will give rise to a trend in which the assumption will be made that it is discriminatory either to suppose or to act on the supposition that a homosexual atmosphere is undesirable for the raising of children." The EFC stated:

> Public and private schools will be pressured to teach that the homosexual lifestyle is a viable and normal alternative to traditional marriage and family life. It is not unrealistic to expect, if sexual orientation legislation is passed, that a school refusing to condone other sexual orientations would be considered discriminatory by the courts. Almost certainly, schools would be pressured to teach in such a way as to imply that homosexual activity is equal to and just as desirable as marriage and family life.[45]

REAL Women of Canada raised the spectre of children being "recruited" by homosexuals, proclaiming, "Many homosexuals, because they cannot procreate, must recruit—often the young. . . . With new legislation such seduction becomes permissible and acceptable." It cited examples of people who, in their estimation, would be hurt by amending human rights laws to include sexual orientation: "Athletic associations, colleges, university campuses, churches, schools, day-care centres, boy's clubs, parents of school-age children, Children's Aid Societies, counselling agencies and all professions in physical contact with the public."[46]

The Coalition for Family Values speculated that an amendment of the Ontario Human Rights Code could lead to the horror of a parent being forced to hire a homosexual as a child-care worker. Like the EFC, it warned about the dire consequences in store for social agencies "that provide services and companionship to children and single parents" and for schools, day-care centres, and group homes forced to hire homosexual employees. Then too, CFV noted, "'Homosexual rights' lobbyists could use the amendment to acquire the right to legally 'marry' and adopt children."[47]

The turning of the tide: from Ottawa to the provinces

After 1985 the guarantee of equality rights enshrined in the Constitution challenged the state's historic right to permit discrimination and unequal treatment of individuals, either through explicit statutory provision or the simple absence of statutory prohibition on discrimination. In this new age in Canadian public policy, the moral imperative of complying with the Charter would ultimately overrule the reticence or resistance of politicians on issues such as lesbian and gay rights.

Still, the political environment in which the equality rights guaranteed by the Charter came into fruition was not initially propitious for the gay and lesbian rights groups. Federally the ruling Progressive Conservatives had long been the least receptive of all of the mainstream political parties on gay rights issues. Now, under Mulroney's leadership, the social conservative faction was both influential and obstreperous. They were not impressed when a group of parliamentarians, the Equality Rights Subcommittee, called upon the government to amend the CHRA to prohibit sexual-orientation discrimination and to remove the prohibition on gays and lesbians in the armed forces.

In 1985 Justice Minister John Crosbie initially responded to the recommendations with an apparently positive statement that the federal government would "take whatever measures are necessary to ensure that sexual orientation is a prohibited ground of discrimination in relation to all areas of federal jurisdiction." As Crosbie later noted in his memoirs, the issue met with fierce resistance from evangelical Christians within the federal caucus and among the party's grassroots supporters.[48] An extremely influential committee on family values within the caucus sought, among other things, the entrenchment of a declaration on the "importance of the family" in the preamble to the Constitution and the introduction of a legislative definition of a "traditional family."[49] REAL Women of Canada, EFC, Focus on the Family, and other social conservative groups continued their persistent lobbying. Despite Crosbie's pledge, the Mulroney government never did enact the CHRA amendment, although within a few years' time Ottawa would be forced by a court decision to remove the ban on gays and lesbians serving openly in the armed forces.

In Ontario in 1986 the minority Liberal government under David Peterson—backed by the NDP—faced the usual controversy when it attempted to add sexual orientation to the Human Rights Code by way of an amendment to Bill 7, government legislation that adjusted various provincial laws to comply with section 15 of the Charter. Headed by Hilsden, the CFV mounted a full-scale assault on the measure. Professing to be "committed to basic moral and family values," CFV objected to "the use of legislation to interfere with the moral choices and values of Canadians."[50]

The CFV's well-organized, well-funded lobby reached its full stride in the fall of 1986, just as Bill 7 was to be introduced for final approval in the legislature. Hilsden was unequivocal in stating that the group opposed "any legal measure to recognize and protect homosexuals in this province."[51] Thousands of church congregation members wrote and telephoned their MPPs and sent in petitions opposing Bill 7, in the process flooding the parliamentary offices with angry denunciations of the amendment. Many Liberal MPPs, fearing the consequences of a backlash from Christian constituents, reconsidered their earlier support for Bill 7. At a press conference in early November Hilsden revealed that he had written to all MPPs explaining that the legislation would have a negative impact on schools, churches, religious institutions, marriage, and social values. Acknowledging that some homosexuals face discrimination, Hilsden charged that it would be "immensely unfair to a much larger segment of Canadians to be forced into courts to defend their moral values and standards." He also argued that the amendment, if adopted, would force evangelical Christians to hire homosexuals and thus condone a practice that would be contrary to their moral fabric. In addition, as the Supreme Court of Canada had not ruled on whether sexual-orientation discrimination should be outlawed, Hilsden contended that it would be premature for Ontario to amend its Human Rights Code to achieve that objective.[52]

Progressive Conservative MPPs dutifully read the letters and petitions from churches and took care to cite the positions of CFV, Ontario Conference of Catholic Bishops, and other groups. The Bishops had declared, "Any law that leaves the door open to such a life-style [homosexuality] will cause great harm to society." Conservative MPP Robert Runciman, representing the largely rural constituency of Leeds, did not mince words in taking up the cause. He denounced the amendment as "trendy" and not needed. "Homosexuality is essentially anti-family. It encourages promiscuous sexuality, self-centred morality and socially irresponsible behavior that extracts huge costs from society," he added, reading from the script of the social conservative groups.[53]

Shortly after Hilsden's press conference, sensitive to the outpouring of opposition, the Liberal Party's house leader, Robert Nixon, publicly backtracked from an earlier statement that Liberal MPPs would be required to support all parts of Bill 7. He mused that the government was considering a free vote on the sexual-orientation amendment.[54]

In alliance with another gay rights group in Toronto, the Right to Privacy Committee (RTPC), CGRO attempted to counter the CFV campaign with a letter-writing campaign of its own. To support Bill 7 the groups held a press conference at Queen's Park and organized a public rally that was attended by one thousand people.[55] The challenge was enormous. They could not match the organizing of the CFV among church groups across the province. Despite substantial majority support by Ontarians for the amendment (a recent Gallup Poll had indicated that 69 per cent supported the amendment), that backing was not being expressed to MPPs. Another type of crucial support, though, came from progressive Christians. Reverend Brent Hawkes, the pastor of the Metropolitan Community Church of Toronto, which ministered to gay and lesbian people, succeeded in obtaining the support of forty clergy from various denominations in a letter sent to Peterson calling for the adoption of the sexual-orientation amendment. On the same day as the CGRO-RTPC rally, the General Council of the United Church of Canada passed a motion strongly endorsing Bill 7. These endorsements were not only an indication of growing support within the broader community for legislative action to prohibit sexual-orientation discrimination, but also timely and dramatic statements from a substantial body of Christians that they did not share the religion-based bigotry of the family values opposition to Bill 7.[56]

In the end a majority of members of the legislature passed the amendment to Bill 7—which marked the first significant political defeat for the family values forces and a rare victory for gay rights advocates. Yet for the forces of social conservatism, their impressive organizing had dramatically demonstrated their ability to command public and media attention. They had clearly identified their political supporters and solidified their position as a powerful electoral constituency. They had received sympathetic responses to their foreboding about the detrimental consequences that would result from protecting gays and lesbians from discrimination. Premier Peterson himself diligently acknowledged the social conservative groups' success on this front. In letters sent even to supporters of the sexual-orientation amendment, he took pains to state, "The amendment does not constitute government support of a particular lifestyle or mode of sexual conduct."[57]

Peterson also took steps to reassure social conservatives that the sexual-orientation amendment would not lead to a change in the definition of "marital status" or "spouse." In a letter to the EFC, he stressed that Bill 7 "would not enable a homosexual couple to receive the service of the solemnization of marriage." Going further, he sought to console EFC by stating:

> An adoption must be in the best interests of the child. Although many factors are taken into consideration in assessing whether a particular adoption would be in the best interests of the child, it is unlikely that a homosexual parent or parents would be deemed to be in the best interests of the child in most cases.[58]

Peterson's assurances did not mollify the family values activists. In their view, Bill 7 was a wedge driven into the masonry that cemented the foundation of moral society—the traditional family. They feared cracks and crevices would soon open up and weaken it irreparably. Hilsden vowed, "If necessary, we'll go to the courts.... We don't intend to change our moral values because of legislative pressure." He speculated whether a religious publishing house would be able to insist that "the staff should share the same theological beliefs [as the owner], including the belief that homosexuality is a sin?" Another scenario that concerned him was whether "a church-run senior citizens' home which was partly funded by the province" would be able to refuse "a couple of lesbian ladies who wanted to live there."[59]

Contrary to Hilsden's opinion, the new law did not require anyone to change their moral values, their religious beliefs, or their view of the family and family values. What the amended Human Rights Code prohibited was acting upon those values and beliefs in a manner that discriminated against gays and lesbians in such fundamental aspects of everyday life as employment, housing, and access to services. But for social conservatives, the amendment of the Ontario Human Rights Code was an alarm bell, a signal that the nature of Canada was fundamentally changing, and not in a good way. Another indication of that change was action by retailers in the province to defy the law that deemed Sunday as God's day of rest and prohibited them from being open for business on that day. It was the beginning of a movement that would lead within a short time to the adoption of so-called Sunday shopping laws that brought an end to the old Lord's Day law that had been one of the great successes of social conservatism in the late nineteenth and early twentieth centuries.

Dorothy Lipovenko, writing in the *Globe and Mail* just days after the adoption of Bill 7 and citing "several of Ontario's foremost social observers and historians," noted that the recent developments would have been "unthinkable 10 or 15 years ago." Remarkably, these changes were occurring "at a particularly unusual time, just when many North Americans are attempting to remake their culture and politics in the simpler image of the 1950s." Such North Americans, of course, were the legions of social conservatives among which CFV, REAL Women, and EFC were now leading players. "Gay rights and Sunday openings," Lipovenko observed, "join abortion in the trilogy of social battles being fought in Ontario on the grounds of freedom of choice—a freedom that opponents say conflicts with traditional community values." Personal freedom was taking precedence over community standards. "This notion clashes with Ontario's traditional ethic of subordinating individual rights and privileges to community or traditional family values."[60]

Despite their fervent hope for the contrary, the forces of social conservatism would witness, over the next several years, the tide of Charter rights flowing inexorably across the whole of the land, and changing it forever. Next in line for change in this regard were the Yukon and Manitoba, both of them with NDP governments. The Yukon's commitment to act, announced in 1985, had actually preceded any of the Bill 7 developments in Ontario. But the NDP had virtually no support for the amendment and faced the opposition of a well-organized lobby led by Anglican, Baptist, and Pentecostal clerics. Nonetheless, following a public consultation process that exposed widespread public opposition, the NDP forged ahead, in 1987 passing a new human rights act that included a prohibition on sexual-orientation discrimination.[61] In the same year, in Manitoba, the NDP government of Premier Howard Pawley introduced a new human rights act that reflected the equality rights provisions in the Charter and specifically included sexual orientation. An ad hoc group of gays and lesbians called the Lobby for Inclusion of Sexual Orientation in the Human Rights Act (LISO) forged a coalition with some sixty non-gay groups—one of which, crucially, was the United Church—to press for adoption of the new act.

Other churches and social conservative groups mounted a counter-campaign, joined by Progressive Conservative members of the legislature, including Opposition leader Gary Filmon and some members of the NDP caucus. The opponents' messages were, in the words of LISO activist Margie Coghill, full of "hellfire, damnation and sinfulness." In an attempt to placate the religiously motivated opponents of the legislation, the Pawley government added a declaration to the bill stating that it "neither condones nor condemns the lifestyle of those it intends to protect." It also defined sexual orientation as "heterosexual, homosexual or bisexual," and noted that the designation "refers only to consenting adults acting within the law." With that concession, the Manitoba legislature finally adopted the bill.[62]

Elsewhere politicians were not as inclined to arouse their social conservative constituencies by taking up the cause of gay rights. Several years passed before other provinces and territories amended their human rights laws. Several provinces, like Ontario, had strong social conservative lobbies supported by politicians who either personally shared the objections to legislating prohibitions on sexual-orientation discrimination or believed that they could not alienate an important voting bloc. In Nova Scotia the Progressive Conservative premier John Buchanan opposed such measures on religious grounds. It was not until 1991, under a different Tory premier, Donald Campbell, and in response to persistent lobbying by the province's gay and lesbian activist groups and pressure from the human rights commission, that the province amended its human rights act.

New Brunswick, under the Liberal government of Frank McKenna, amended its human rights act in 1992, following a prolonged and well-organized campaign by gays and lesbians led by the New Brunswick Campaign for Human Rights Reform. In Newfoundland, both Progressive Conservative and Liberal governments remained strongly opposed to a sexual-orientation amendment until 1997, when the Liberal government of Brian Tobin finally acted. Prince Edward Island's Progressive Conservative government of Premier Pat Binns followed suit in 1998. On the West Coast, in British Columbia, the Social Credit governments of first William Bennett and then William Vander Zalm, with their deep roots in social conservatism and evangelicalism, were adamantly against amending the province's human rights law. It was only in 1992, after the election of the NDP government of Michael Harcourt, that the province's human rights law was amended to include sexual orientation. The Northwest Territories included a prohibition on sexual-orientation discrimination in its new human rights law enacted in 2002, as did Nunavut in 2003.

In Saskatchewan, despite the province's image as a haven for social democracy, evidenced by its long periods of governance by the CCF and NDP, social conservative opposition to amending human rights legislation was particularly strong. Evangelical Protestants were numerous, and the Roman Catholic and Greek Orthodox churches were highly influential in many communities. Legislators, many of them once again seeing homosexuality as a "moral issue," resisted all efforts made by the province's gay and lesbian groups to amend the provincial human rights law. To be ensured of election they depended on the votes of God-fearing Christians in countless church congregations scattered across their sparsely populated electoral districts. Although the Saskatchewan New Democratic Party had made a sexual-orientation amendment official party policy in the late 1970s, the NDP government of Allan Blakeney had failed to act on the issue. Under a Progressive Conservative Party government that took power in 1982, cabinet ministers made periodic public statements condemning homosexuality, making clear that they did not intend to amend the human rights act. Social Services Minister Grant Schmidt stated publicly in 1987 that homosexuality was a "deviant lifestyle" and, comparing homosexuals to thieves, stated that employers should have the right to not hire them. At another point, Schmidt opined that treating gay couples as families was "contrary to the rules of Allah, God, and the Great Spirit" and that he "always put the rules of God before the rules of men."[63]

In response, two organizations—the newly formed Coalition for Human Equality (CHE) and Equality for Gays and Lesbians Everywhere (Egale) Regina—organized doggedly and conducted public education on the issue. NDP leader and future provincial premier Roy Romanow finally declared publicly in 1990 that an NDP government would enact legislation to add sexual orientation to the provincial Human Rights Code.[64]

In the provincial election of 1991 Grant Devine presented the Progressive Conservatives as the only party willing to stand up for family values. One Tory candidate in Regina, John Bergen, a minister of the Christian and Missionary Alliance, asserted that homosexuality would cause the end of society. He also declared that the homosexual lifestyle was "very dangerous from a disease standpoint," claiming that gays transmitted syphilis, gonorrhoea, tuberculosis, hepatitis, and AIDS. He called for mandatory AIDS testing and suggested that restaurants should be allowed to post signs stating that their premises were AIDS-free.[65] The election also saw the emergence of the Coalition in Support of the Family (CSF), led by Dale Hassett, an associate pastor of a church in the small town of Leader who was well connected with the Tory government.[66] CSF ran ads in newspapers and circulated 170,000 copies of a booklet that raised the spectre of the "sweeping special rights for homosexuals and lesbians" that would be granted if the NDP were to be elected.

Although the subsequent election of an NDP government led by Romanow generated frenetic lobbying by the CSF and other groups, including REAL Women Saskatchewan and a group called Community Impact Saskatchewan, the Romanow government held firm, and in 1993 introduced a bill amending the Human Rights Code to include sexual orientation. The social conservative forces counterattacked. A vigil on the steps of the Saskatchewan legislature drew a hundred Christians who prayed for the bill's defeat and "the preservation of family values." Opponents of the amendment inundated members of the legislature with their expressions of concern, and a number of NDP backbenchers became increasingly nervous about the bill. One of them, Lorne Scott, the MLA for Indian Head–Wolsely, reportedly told the press, "I've had hundreds of phone calls from people from all political stripes expressing concern about the issue, and I'm their representative." Justice Minister Bob Mitchell, in response to the mounting opposition to the bill, stated that he was contemplating amending it to ensure that it did not foster gay instruction in the schools or affirmative action programs for gays and lesbians.[67] In newspaper advertisements opponents of the bill posed the question, "Does this mean teaching our children that the homosexual lifestyle is natural and normal (maybe even *preferable* to the heterosexual lifestyle) as they're now doing in Toronto?" Others asked, "How will this affect daycares, schools, Big Brothers, Boy Scouts and Brownies? Can they continue to screen the people who work with our kids?" Such questions tended to be followed up with the old hateful allegation that gays are predators and corruptors of youth: "These amendments need to go all the way to protect our children from gays who are out to increase their numbers any way they can."[68] The CSF and Community Impact Saskatchewan mounted a petition campaign that sought to garner the 100,000 signatures needed under provincial legislation to force the government to hold a plebiscite on the issue of amending the Human Rights Code. Although they failed to get the requisite number of signatures, they did manage to collect over 50,000 names—an astonishing number that evidenced widespread opposition to gay rights initiatives among the population of the province.[69]

When finally passed in 1993, the legislation included a provision stating that it did not in any way protect behaviour that was illegal under the Criminal Code—a clear and appalling reference to the unfounded fears about incest and pedophilia, and just as clearly an attempt to respond to the hysterical and hateful arguments made by the bill's opponents.[70]

Amending the CHRA in Ottawa

Shortly before the Saskatchewan bill was passed, a major court decision ruled that sexual-orientation discrimination was contrary to the equality rights guaranteed by the Charter. The 1992 case *Haig v. Canada* involved a challenge to the Canadian Human Rights Act by two openly gay members of the armed forces, Graham Haig and Joshua Birch. Haig had been told that he would not be promoted to a higher rank because of the ban on homosexuals serving in the forces. The Ontario Court of Appeal ruled that the omission of sexual orientation from the CHRA contravened section 15 of the Charter. It also ruled that the CHRA was to be "interpreted, applied and administered as though it contained 'sexual orientation' as a prohibited ground of discrimination."[71] The immediate effect was to force the Mulroney government to enact a policy change that permitted gays and lesbians to serve in the armed forces. The government decided not to appeal the decision, which thus remained in place as an important new judicial precedent.

In the long term the *Haig* case was significant because of what became known as "reading in" sexual orientation as a prohibited ground of discrimination in statutes in which the omission of that term caused unjustifiable discrimination. Although the *Haig* case did not involve religious rights, the principles established by the judgment came to symbolize the "activism" of judges in the use of the Charter's provisions to strike down laws. *Haig* was cited in subsequent judicial pronouncements on gay rights issues that were in total few in number but large in impact. The perceived activism of the judiciary as a result became almost exclusively associated in the public mind—and most definitely in the minds of social conservative leaders—with the extraparliamentary imposition of gay rights by the courts "reading in" anti-discrimination provisions that had not been enacted by Parliament or a legislature.

The *Haig* decision also put pressure on the Mulroney government to amend the CHRA to explicitly prohibit sexual orientation. But the power of the Tory family committee was such that when federal justice minister Kim Campbell announced that she would table a bill amending the CHRA, she felt obliged to offer a concession. The legislation would clearly stipulate that the definitions of spouse and marriage would not be changed to recognize same-sex relationships. "I think it's important to make the distinction between legal marriage and other kinds of relationships," Campbell declared. "I think the definition is very consistent with Canadian public opinion and values."[72]

Outside Parliament, social conservative activists intensified their opposition to amending the CHRA. After Campbell became prime minister the Evangelical Fellowship of Canada targeted the new justice minister, Pierre Blais, with a petition opposing the amendment. It also launched a campaign that attacked "the homosexual community" for wanting "the public acceptance of their lifestyle."[73] The Tories ultimately dropped amendment of the CHRA from their legislative agenda.

When the Liberals took over after the 1993 election they too—despite expressed support for the CHRA amendment on the part of both Prime Minister Jean Chrétien and Justice Minister Allan Rock—began feeling the pressure and, as a result, dragging their feet. By the end of 1994 the media were reporting that Chrétien no longer supported amending the CHRA because the Liberal caucus was deeply divided on the issue.[74] Among the most militant MPs were Roseanne Skoke and Tom Wappel, devout Roman Catholics. Skoke publicly expressed the view that homosexuality "is undermining the inherent rights and values of our Canadian families and it must not and should not be condoned." Wappel, a right-to-life advocate, described the potential evils of the CHRA amendment as being the legalization of same-sex marriages and adoption of children by homosexuals—even though the amendment would not have any impact on the marriage laws; and the adoption laws were the responsibility of the provincial legislatures and not the Parliament of Canada.[75]

Members of the parliamentary opposition, especially those in the Reform Party, were staunchly opposed. Indeed, opposition to gay rights was fundamental Reform Party policy, and the party's MPs were renowned for making homophobic and bigoted comments and defending "family values." The party supported replacing the Charter with the limited Bill of Rights as adopted by Parliament in 1960. This agenda item represented a longing to return to simpler times. A news report on a Reform Party policy conference made the case: "When Canada recognized the supremacy of God, the law was tougher on criminals, English was the only language you needed to do anything in, and family meant Adam and Eve, not Adam and Steve."[76]

Only a scathing denunciation of the government's inaction by the chief commissioner of the Canadian Human Rights Commission, Maxwell Yalden, in March 1996, prodded the Chrétien government into action. The Liberals finally introduced an amendment to the CHRA in the form of Bill C-33.[77] Even then, sensitivity to social conservative sentiment and the Liberal caucus opposition resulted in a preamble to the bill stating that the government "recognizes and affirms the importance of family as the foundation of Canadian society and that nothing in this act alters its fundamental role in society."[78] That was not enough for the social conservatives. A mysterious group called the Coalition of Concerned Canadians quickly placed a full-page advertisement in the *Globe and Mail* accusing Chrétien and Rock of being anti-family. It stated, "Bill C-33 is the product of myth and is a serious threat to marriage and family." The coalition members were not named in the ad, and the Coalition itself was exceptionally ephemeral, vanishing from public view immediately afterwards.[79]

Other familiar social conservative groups also organized against Bill C-33. The EFC, Canadian Conference of Catholic Bishops, REAL Women, and Focus on the Family all made presentations to the parliamentary committee that considered the bill, with all of them making the by now familiar arguments: that including sexual orientation in the CHRA would effectively open the door to granting benefits to same-sex couples as spouses through the eventual redefinition of "marital status" and "family status"; that sexual orientation is "a complex moral issue" and not a human rights issue; and that homosexuality is not a distinguishing, immutable characteristic but rather a behaviour, a conduct, or a sexual practice that can be changed. Diane Watts, speaking on behalf of REAL Women, restated the organization's belief in the illegitimacy of the gay rights activists' demands for special rights: "Homosexual activists pushing for special recognition and protection are a powerful special interest group that are using their considerable wealth and political clout to piggyback on the legitimate claims of others." Repeating the fallacy that gays and lesbians had all of the fundamental rights of other Canadians, she opined: "Persons who identify themselves as homosexuals are not being singled out for unfair treatment. In fact, they have singled themselves out for privileged treatment by aggressively pursuing special protective status to which they demonstrably have no valid claim."[80]

Jim Solera, representing Focus on the Family, informed the committee that "discrimination, in some situations, occurs for good reasons" and "the pursuit of so-called gay rights is leading to a systematic devaluation of heterosexual marriage and family in society." Lamenting the loss of the historic Christian Canada based on Judeo-Christian morality, Solera declared:

> What is there, though, at this time in our country's history, at a time of weakness in our sense of national identify and unity and heritage, that would warrant the tearing down of thousands of years of wisdom and moral and religious conviction? What is there in 1996 that makes this the year to tear down the social and moral restrictions regarding human sexual expression that have existed throughout human history and are

rooted in various millennia of philosophical and moral teaching? What is it? Why is it time?

Taking up the threats to children and "gays can be cured" themes that remained so central to Focus on the Family's anti-gay advocacy, he implored the committee:

> I plead with you, for the sake of the Canadians and their upcoming generations, for mothers and fathers and their young children, do not enshrine a lifestyle, not even defined, of some 3% or 5%, whatever percentage it may be, in the highest human rights code of our land. Do not open the door to teaching this lifestyle in our schools. It's already being taught. Don't throw the doors wide open. Do not make it harder for homosexuals to get the help many are looking for to leave this lifestyle. Do not make it harder for those who are seeking to leave the homosexual lifestyle to find the help they would like to have.[81]

Gay and lesbian groups lobbied just as hard in support of the amendment. Egale Canada and the Metropolitan Community Church of Canada, Canadian Human Rights Campaign, and both Dignity, the group for gay and lesbian Catholics, and Integrity, for gay and lesbian Anglicans, appeared before the parliamentary committee. So too did the Canadian Jewish Congress and B'nai Brith Canada. In keeping with its two-decade-long leadership in supporting legislated human rights protections for gays and lesbians, the United Church of Canada also spoke strongly in support of Bill C-33. In vivid contrast with the religion-based justification of the social conservative groups for opposing the bill, Dr. David Hallman, representing the moderator of the United Church of Canada, told the committee, "Much of the opposition to this bill comes with religious dimensions attached to it and religious arguments associated with it. We want to indicate clearly that those perspectives are not the only religious perspectives that people of faith can have. Our United Church support for the bill is firmly grounded in our theology, spirituality, and faith."[82]

Bill C-33 was finally adopted on May 9, 1996—although twenty-three Liberal MPs voted against it. Yet the Bill C-33 saga confirmed that social conservative intransigence continued to present a political obstacle to the enactment of equality rights for gays and lesbians. A large number of politicians clearly shared and acted on the views of the social conservative groups. Too many others simply feared invoking the wrath of a powerful constituency at the polls. The homage to the family in the preamble to Bill C-33 served notice that gays and lesbians were indeed not considered to be the equal of heterosexuals in all respects. Parliament had simply redrawn the line beyond which discrimination was still legally permissible. It was a signal that the legal recognition of same-sex relationships—of gay and lesbian families—was still out of bounds, that Parliament, at least for the time being, was siding with the social conservatives in legislating the perseveration of the traditional family and heterosexual marriage.

Alberta and the "imposition of morality"

In Alberta by the 1990s, two decades of successive Progressive Conservative governments vowing not to amend the province's human rights legislation had left gays and lesbians frustrated and discouraged. All of that would change in 1991, when Delwin Vriend, an openly gay man, was fired from his job with King's College (now King's University College) in Edmonton. An evangelical Protestant educational institution offering degrees "from a Christian perspective" and with a philosophy "rooted in the historic Christian faith," King's College professed to have a view of the world and daily life "informed by the Bible, the authoritative Word of God as confessed by the early church and in the creeds of the Protestant Reformation." Vriend was fired when his employment with the college became public knowledge as a result of his involvement as a gay activist—and because "homosexual practice goes against the Bible, and the college's statement of faith."[83]

The Alberta Human Rights Commission refused to deal with a complaint filed by Vriend against King's College because the province's human rights law, the Individual Rights Protection Act (IRPA), did not include sexual orientation as a prohibited ground of discrimination. Vriend launched a legal challenge charging that Alberta's failure to include sexual orientation in the law contravened the rights guaranteed by section 15 of the Charter. He was supported by Edmonton's Gay and Lesbian Awareness (GALA), Dignity, and the Gay and Lesbian Community Centre of Edmonton. They also used Vriend's firing and his Charter challenge litigation to renew their lobbying to have sexual orientation added to the IRPA.[84]

Vriend's case wound its way through various levels of the judicial system, finally reaching the Supreme Court of Canada in November 1997. At the Supreme Court hearing his position citing Charter rights was opposed by an assortment of social conservative groups: Focus on the Family (Canada), Evangelical Fellowship of Canada, Alberta Federation of Women United for Families, and the Christian Legal Fellowship. A factum filed with the Court by the EFC argued that the rights sought by Vriend "may adversely impact on the rights and freedoms of other groups or individuals within society, including the right of religious groups to establish moral standards consistent with the deeply held religious beliefs of those groups."[85] If Vriend was successful in his challenge, they noted, their religious freedom would inevitably be undermined. They argued that religious institutions like King's College should be able to discriminate when the discrimination is based on religious beliefs.

The EFC factum also contended that the courts should not overrule the legislatures in determining which rights should have precedence: "It is the task of the legislature to weigh competing values and interests when enacting social policy legislation. It is not for the courts to second guess the value choices of the legislature where those choices are the result of principled weighing of those competing interests."[86] In other words, legislatures had the ultimate authority to pick and choose which groups should be advantaged or disadvantaged, privileged or discriminated against, and the courts should butt out, leaving the discrimination intact.

Despite the arguments put forward by the social conservative intervenors, the Vriend case did not deal directly with a determination of whether King's College had unlawfully discriminated against Vriend or, for that matter, with the broader question of religious freedom. The case before the Supreme Court was ultimately one of judicial interpretation of the extent to which the Charter governed laws adopted by a provincial legislature. On that issue, the social conservative groups contended, along with the Alberta government, that the IRPA dealt with private activity, namely employment policy and practices, and therefore was not subject to the Charter. Earlier court decisions had in fact determined that the Charter did not apply to private activity. The fear was that adding sexual orientation to the IRPA would open the door for complaints against religious institutions and churches to be dealt with through what the social conservative groups considered to be an unfair and unaccountable human rights process. Once the law was amended, it would only be a matter of time, they argued, before religious entities adhering to religious teachings would be forced to hire homosexuals.

The Supreme Court issued its judgment on April 2, 1998, finding unanimously that the IRPA's omission of sexual orientation infringed or denied rights guaranteed by section 15 of the Charter. Of the eight justices, seven agreed that the most appropriate remedy was to "read in" sexual orientation to the IRPA. The decision of the majority pointedly noted that "private activity" was not the subject of the appeal. "It does not concern the acts of King's College or any other private entity or person," the justices observed. However, laws that regulate private activity are "obviously" subject to the Charter and, they ruled, the IRPA's omission of sexual orientation was a valid ground for a constitutional challenge.[87]

Condemning this decision—even though the Court did not rule on whether King's College had discriminated against Vriend—the social conservative groups waged a sustained and impressive campaign aimed at forcing the Conservative government of Premier Ralph Klein to take actions to override it. The newly formed Canada Family Action Coalition distributed 35,000 leaflets claiming that the Court decision would force the government to "promote homosexuality." CFAC also ran full-page advertisements in two daily newspapers urging the government to invoke the "notwithstanding" provision of the Charter to override the Court's decision. Under that provision, a legislature could pass a law to last for five years that would permit the offending law to continue, but would have to re-enact the override every five years thereafter for it to continue indefinitely. "It's not too late! If Vriend Wins . . . Who Loses?" asked the headline on the CFAC newspaper ad. The moral and social decline being witnessed in other provinces because of gay rights would soon befall God-fearing Alberta, CFAC charged, if the Vriend decision was allowed to stand. Based on what had recently occurred in British Columbia and Ontario, they warned, "The natural family, the fabric of our society will be seriously undermined." Among the dire consequences, CFAC warned, was the prospect that schools would be forced to teach, and students would be forced to attend, classes taught by "gay role models" in which "they are forced to approve of and discuss explicitly, homosexual activity."[88]

Hermina Dykxhoorn, executive director of the Alberta Federation of Women United for Families, voiced similar sentiments: "It's a battle for legal acceptance and approval—complete equality with heterosexual marriage and family." Gay activists were attempting to use the Charter "to gain their ends without going through the legislative assembly." Her group, along with CFAC and the Catholic Civil Rights League, held a demonstration in Calgary to protest the Supreme Court decision and to urge the invocation of the notwithstanding clause. During the demonstration Dykxhoorn linked the recognition of legal rights for gays and lesbians with broader social developments that were irreparably damaging Canadian society. She complained: "The family has been battered in the last 30 years with the lack of commitment, easy divorce, that sort of thing. . . . This is something that goes to the very heart of who we are and we do not want this." She warned that if the Alberta government accepted the Vriend decision, "There's going to be some very angry Albertans out there."[89]

Elsewhere, Ken Campbell, through his pro-life group Choose Life Canada and his other advocacy vehicle, Canada's Civilized Majority, ran a full-page advertisement in the *Globe and Mail* that bore the blazing headline: "'CANADA'S SUPREME COURT HAS NO BUSINESS IMPOSING 'BATHHOUSE MORALITY' ON THE CHURCHES AND IN THE NATION'S LIVING ROOM!'" The ad contained an unrestrained denunciation of the Supreme Court's decision: "*In decreeing the abandonment in public policy* of DISCRIMINATION between the creative and the destructive in sexual conduct, the Supreme Court judgment in Vriend replaces 'the supremacy of God' [in the preamble to the Charter] with the permissiveness, lawlessness and tyranny of ATHEISTIC secular fundamentalism as the principles setting public policy in Canada." The ad also condemned "buggery or sodomy—homosexual genital conduct" as one of the "destructive disorientations," along with drunkenness, as "conduct which no civilized society embraces as normal in its legislative agenda." Like its cohorts in Alberta, Canada's Civilized Majority called upon "Premier Ralph Klein and the Alberta Legislature to take a stand for the principles of a civilized society and for a restoration of the dynamics of democracy to Canadian public life."[90]

The Alberta Civil Society Association, headed by University of Calgary professor Ted Morton, placed advertisements on several radio and television stations—spreading the word that the decision would infringe religious freedom and undermine the family. A popular radio call-in show was swamped by calls from listeners who cited biblical justifications for refusing to protect gays and lesbians from discrimination. Premier Klein and MLAs, mainly from rural areas, were bombarded with hundreds of phone calls from furious citizens. Cabinet ministers reported that the outpouring was unprecedented. Many callers read "church bulletins or scripted comments verbatim over the phone."[91]

The Klein government did not buckle under the pressure. Klein even went so far as to publicly blast the anti-gay forces. "I abhor discrimination," he declared. "We have people writing letters that quite frankly make your stomach churn."[92] His government, like those elsewhere, was generally reluctant to use the notwithstanding measure, which would have amounted to repudiating the Supreme Court in the exercise of its responsibility as the guardian and interpreter of constitutional rights. That role, after all, had been conferred on the Supreme Court by the Constitution with the approval of the provincial legislatures and the Parliament of Canada. Contrary to what the forces of social conservatism were so angrily claiming, the justices of the Supreme Court had not usurped the legislatures either in taking on that role or in the exercise of their authority to interpret the provisions of the Charter.

Klein tacitly acknowledged that fact and opted to let the Supreme Court decision stand. In doing so, he permitted the IRPA to be amended by the hated, non-elected, activist judges rather than by means of a vote in the legislature. As it turned out, Alberta's human rights legislation was not altered to explicitly include sexual orientation in the prohibited grounds of discrimination until the Human Rights, Citizenship and Multiculturalism Act was amended in 2009.

Klein's decision profoundly disappointed members of the social conservative movement, who remained resentful about the Vriend decision for many years after. They often cited the instance in their submissions to government as a leading example of how religious freedom was being destroyed by judges in what they saw as dubious gay rights cases. In truth, the Vriend decision, along with the enact-ment of human rights code amendments provincially and federally, meant that in future, social conservatives would be on the defensive. Their assertion of the right to be free to discriminate for reasons of religious belief and morality—even when presented in the guise of defending marriage, the traditional family, and family values—was no longer legal or socially acceptable. In the age of rights, even in the social conservative heartland of Alberta, the new morality was increasingly trumping the old.

Opposing the hate crimes law and hate literature legislation

While the social conservative groups were organizing in opposition to leg-islation prohibiting sexual-orientation discrimination, another of their tenets—that they loved the sinner (the homosexual) but hated the sin (homosexuality)—came more and more under challenge. In opposing the extension of human rights protections to gays and lesbians, and especially in the tactics and arguments deployed in mounting their campaigns, social conservatives were clearly engaging in undiluted hate-mongering. That prevailing tendency became especially appar-ent in the 1990s as they turned their advocacy towards blocking the adoption of legislative measures to deal with the hatred and violence being experienced by gays and lesbians.

In conjunction with human rights code amendments, the addition of sexual orientation to the hate law provisions of the Criminal Code had gained political prominence as lesbian and gay rights activists succeeded in pressuring police forces in urban centres to begin taking seriously acts of homophobic violence, known as gay bashing. Such acts should be seen for what they are, they argued: as violent assaults motivated by a hatred of homosexuals. At the same time, advocacy groups for racial, ethnic, and religious groups were similarly urging more effective action in the investigation and prosecution of hate-motivated crimes. Police forces in some of the largest cities started to collect data on crimes in which the sexual orientation of the victim had been a motivating factor.

Impetus for a legislative response was quickened when the federal Depart-ment of Justice took up the view that laws dealing with hate crimes generally should specifically address hate crimes directed towards gays and lesbians. The solution would be the provision of tougher penalties in the Criminal Code. The federal Liberal Party, supporting that approach, pledged in its 1993 election plat-form to take such action if it formed the government; and in fall 1994, after the election, the new Chrétien government kept its promise. Its Bill C-41 established a new hate crimes section of the Criminal Code. The law required courts, when sentencing a person found guilty of a crime, to take into consideration whether there was evidence that the offence had been motivated by bias, prejudice, or hate based on specified grounds, one of which was sexual orientation. The new law permitted a court to increase the penalty imposed on the convicted person if such evidence existed.

Social conservative groups reacted with alarm. They argued that Bill C-41 would infringe on their right of religious freedom. Acts of homophobic violence should be dealt with through criminal laws, they said, only if that could be done without granting state approval of immoral homosexual activity. The social conservative groups rejected claims made by gay and lesbian activists that homophobic violence could be attributed to promotion of the view that homosexuals are variously sinful, immoral, deviant, abnormal, disgusting, menacing, or threats to the family and society.

In November 1994 REAL Women appeared before the House of Commons Committee on Justice and Legal Affairs to oppose the inclusion of sexual orientation in the new law. Part of the strategy was to diminish the significance of violent crimes motivated by homophobia and hatred towards gays and lesbians. The group also argued that the term "sexual orientation" was vague and undefined and might therefore include pedophilia or necrophilia. It submitted that lobbying by gay activists for the inclusion of sexual orientation in the hate crimes law was nothing more than an attempt to obtain special rights and recognition for their deviant and immoral lifestyle.

In Parliament the Reform Party and a large social conservative faction of Liberal MPs waged a furious battle to have sexual orientation removed from Bill C-41. Liberal dissidents, led by Wappel, Skoke, and Dan McTeague, decried the bill, parroting the social conservative accusations that it was merely an attempt to give gays and lesbians "special rights." At one point McTeague disclosed that forty-six Liberal MPs had expressed "serious concerns" about the bill. In the end the government prevailed and Bill C-41 was adopted, with sexual orientation included, in June 1995.[93]

In the years following the passage of Bill C-41, REAL Women remained adamant that there was no proven need for it, declaring that the hate crimes statistics that had prompted it were phoney. Citing the statistics prepared by police forces on incidents of hate crimes directed at gays and lesbians, its members continued to debunk the extent of the problem and its importance as an issue. The November–December 2000 issue of the organization's newsletter, *REALity*, noted, for example, that "to claim that large numbers of homosexuals/lesbians are targets of hate-motivated crimes is simply not true."[94]

Once established, though, the Criminal Code section about which REAL Women and the other social conservatives groups vented so persistently was in practical terms largely ineffective and rarely used. It served more as window-dressing for the government, which could cite the section as evidence that it took seriously the growing social problem of hate-motivated crimes. But judges are not compelled to use the law to impose a stronger penalty on an offender even in cases in which there is evidence firmly suggesting that hatred expressed towards the victim was a motivating factor. Douglas Victor Janoff, in *Pink Blood: Homophobic Violence in Canada*, notes that in the years 1995 to 2003 the hate crime law was not used by judges to increase the sentences of individuals convicted of "gay-bashing" crimes against over one hundred gays and lesbians in the country.[95]

Another issue that distressed social conservative groups was the call made by gay rights groups and openly gay member of Parliament Svend Robinson for the amendment of section 318 of the Criminal Code (advocating genocide) and section 319 (public incitement of hatred) to include sexual orientation within the listing of grounds that distinguish identifiable groups. In fall 1998 the federal and provincial attorneys general had agreed that the grounds should be expanded to include sex, sexual orientation, age, and mental disability. When legislation on that matter was not forthcoming, Robinson introduced his private member's Bill C-415 in 2002. It simply proposed that sexual orientation be added to section 318. The social conservative groups once again swung into action to oppose the bill. The Catholic Civil Rights League, in an exhortation to its supporters to lobby hard to defeat Bill C-415, argued, "The term 'sexual orientation' is inherently problematic because it does not distinguish between the 'person and the 'sexual activity.' Unlike the morally neutral characteristics of race and ethnicity, sexual behaviour is fraught with moral and religious significance because it refers to what a person does, not what they are."[96]

Although Parliament did not adopt Robinson's private member's bill, the Liberal government subsequently introduced Bill C-250, which reflected the recommendations of the attorneys general and thus prompted a huge outpouring of social conservative resistance. In its formal presentation to Parliament on the bill, the EFC again objected to the term "sexual orientation" along the same lines as the Catholic Civil Rights League's earlier complaint. "When practice and characteristics are fused and are argued to be inseparable, moral objections to practices are interpreted as moral objections to persons."[97] It would be better, the EFC argued, to omit sexual orientation from the particular sections of the Criminal Code to ensure that a person could not be accused of promoting hatred for publicly acting upon or expressing their religious and moral views on homosexual activity. In other words, according to the EFC it should be permissible to spread hatred or even advocate genocide against homosexuals so long as this is done as an expression of religious or moral views. So much for the professed love of the sinner and hatred only for the sin.

The EFC also queried whether, under the new law, it might be

> argued that the Christian message that gays and lesbians have a choice as to whether to act on their sexual inclinations is a message that advocates "genocide"? That is not a violent message, nor is it intended to induce violence. However, some promote therapy that enables people to change their sexual orientation. Is this considered "advocating genocide" within the meaning of s. 318?

This expressed fear was both exaggerated and provocative, seemingly more intended to stir evangelicals into righteous outrage against the sexual-orientation provision. For "genocide" in section 318 (then and now) means only specific "acts committed with intent to destroy in whole or in part any identifiable group." The only acts specified as meeting the intent to destroy are "killing members of the group" or "deliberately inflicting on the group conditions of life calculated to bring about its physical destruction." Unless a Christian group was actually engaged in rounding up gays and lesbians, placing them in internment camps, hospitals, or prisons, and subjecting them to conditions of life calculated to bring about their extermination, they would not be engaged in genocide. Promoting therapy purportedly enabling people to change their sexual orientation would not be an act of genocide. In addition, EFC and the other social conservative groups conveniently ignored another provision of section 318 stating that no proceeding for an offence under the section shall be instituted without the consent of the attorney general.

The EFC went even further, raising the prospect that Christians would be silenced for expressing within their religious traditions their moral disapproval of homosexuality or engaging in "socially and culturally important conversations" on such issues as premarital sex, sex outside and inside marriage, or permissible sexual partners. "Canada's diverse religious groups need to be free to continue to publicly discuss sexual ethics without fear of criminal sanction or censure," the EFC asserted, as if the ability for them to speak out on any of those issues was actually endangered.[98]

The EFC and Catholic Civil Rights League, along with REAL Women, Focus on the Family, and Canada Family Action Coalition, organized letter-writing, petition-signings, and publicity campaigns to generate opposition to Bill C-250. They were particularly vexed about the effect that amending the definition of "identifiable group" to include sexual orientation would have on the interpretation that would be given to the public incitement of hatred. They argued that quoting the Bible and the *Catechism* of the Roman Catholic Church in public venues such as churches would be branded hate literature because of their condemnations of homosexuality. The fear, as expressed in an article published in *Christian Week*, was that "many in Canada's religious community worry the legislation will curb their right to speak openly about homosexuality—and could even result in their sacred texts being banned as 'hate propaganda.'"[99] Again, as in the case of the fears expressed about being accused of genocide, the social conservative critics of Bill C-250 ignored or failed to mention the provision within section 319 (public incitement of hatred) stating that the attorney general had to consent to a proceeding under the offence. No attorney general would ever agree to the laying of charges in the circumstances being cited so loudly and persistently by the EFC and the other social conservative groups: that is, in the public discussion of sexual ethics, including the biblical condemnations of homosexuality or the immorality of same-sex relationships.

More germane to the issue was that evangelical preachers and social conservative ideologues, armed with the Bible, have been among the most egregious hate-mongers, often using radio and television religious broadcasts to that effect. One of the most prominent was Jerry Falwell, who regularly used his religious programs—often broadcast in Canada—to make virulent anti-gay remarks. Homosexuals are "anti-family moral perverts," he once said, "who want the right to violate any child of any age."[100] Focus on the Family, in both its U.S. and Canadian branches, has also had a long history of publicly fomenting hatred. In 1997 a panel of the Canadian Broadcast Standards Council investigated a complaint made against a Focus on the Family radio program that featured "abusively discriminatory comment on the basis of sexual orientation." During the program, Dr. Anthony Falzerano, executive director of Transformation Ministries and a declared "ex-homosexual," stated, "Gays are using the AIDS epidemic to push the gay agenda onto our country right now and in essence it is really the spirit of the anti-Christ." The Broadcast Standards panel found that the program attributed to the gay movement "a malevolent, insidious and conspiratorial purpose." In another decision, released in 2002, a Council panel reprimanded the religious television channel VisionTV for airing an edition of *Power Today*, produced in the United States, that featured evangelist R.W. Schambach. In the show Schambach referred to "homosexual devils" and to homosexuals as being "demon possessed." "Homosexuality is not another lifestyle," he declared. "It's a demon spirit."[101]

Nor were the religious groups satisfied with the adequacy of the protection afforded by the exception from conviction already specified in section 319. That exception applied when, in good faith, a person expressed or attempted to establish, by argument, an opinion on a religious subject. They charged that human rights commissions, the courts, and militant gays and lesbians would use the sexual-orientation provision to persecute Christians and members of other faiths for expressing any negative views about homosexuality. "If passed into law," declared REAL Women, "Bill C-250 will be a useful tool for organized homosexual rights activists to intimidate their adversaries." In *The Interim*, prominent social conservative advocate Peter Stock stated, "Any Christian church, school, hospital or social service agency with an orthodox understanding of the Scriptures can anticipate trouble with radical homosexuals over everything from hiring practices to the content of the liturgy." Millions for Marriage, a group operating out of the Canada Christian College, ran full-page newspaper ads combining opposition to same-sex marriage and Bill C-250. It charged, "This week the Government may pass Bill C-250 that could make the Bible illegal."[102]

As Bill C-250 proceeded through the various stages of parliamentary approval, social conservative advocates intensified their efforts, growing ever more desperate and strident in their opposition. On April 17, 2004, several religious groups mounted a last-ditch public action campaign, holding a rally on Parliament Hill with the provocative title of "National Liberty Day Rally." Vowing to "resist the totalitarian impulse currently asserting itself in the legislative and judicial branches of our government," they repudiated Bill C-250, while professing to categorically reject all forms of hatred against any person. The protesters called on "our government officials to uphold freedom of speech and religious liberty for all Canadians, and to reject legislation which attempts to intimidate and suppress dissenting opinion."[103]

Parliament enacted Bill C-250 in April 2004, but not before amending it in an effort to address one of the concerns raised by the social conservative groups. A new provision was added to the Criminal Code to expand the exemption for good faith expression of an opinion on a religious subject. It exempted a person from conviction "if in good faith, the person expressed or attempted to establish by an argument an opinion on a religious subject or an opinion based on a belief in a religious text." The inclusion of the phrase "a belief in a religious text" was clearly an attempt to address the concerns of the EFC and other groups about providing for an explicit exemption for sacred texts. By such means, passages in the Bible—like the one in Leviticus that calls for homosexuals to be put to death—would not be seen as promoting hatred.

Despite that concession, the objectors to Bill C-250 remained unsatisfied. The EFC spoke of the possible "chilling effect" of the legislation: "We no longer trust that the guarantee of religious freedom in the Charter is necessarily going to apply to protect religious freedom of speech." Derek Rogusky of Focus on the Family decried the prospect that "a lot of law-abiding citizens" would have to be "very, very careful about what they say." As an example he added, quite preposterously, "Now you have the risk of criminal sanctions for just simply talking about something like same-sex marriage or the immorality of homosexuality." The Catholic Civil Rights League likewise condemned the legislation: "Canada has now embarked upon a course of criminalization of dissent." It warned, "We suspect Canadians will soon discover the extent of the new peril imposed on their freedom of speech only after they receive that knock on the door to answer to the authorities."[104]

FIVE

The Defence of Family and Marriage

> We, the people of Canada who support marriage solely as the union of a man and a woman, apologize to the people of the world for harm done through Canada's legislation of homosexual marriage. We are grieved and troubled as we consider the impact this is having in weakening the fundamental institution of marriage in countries and cultures around the world.... Our warning to you, the people of the world, is to learn from our mistakes and avoid repeating them in your own countries.
>
> – REAL Women of Canada, apology presented to the World Congress of Families, Warsaw, Poland, May 2007

By the late 1980s the various skirmishes over amending human rights laws had evolved into a more specific political and cultural concern: the controversial issue of whether same-sex relationships should be granted legal recognition. The social conservative groups had rightly anticipated that a victory by gay activists on the human rights front would inevitably lead to an assault on marriage and the traditional family—this time backed by the human rights commissions and the courts.

Indeed, in August 1989 the Coalition for Lesbian and Gay Rights in Ontario (CLGRO) held the first conference in Canada to deal with the issue of spousal rights for gay and lesbian couples. The meeting provided an impetus for mapping out a strategy and agenda to pursue that objective.[1] The CLGRO conference was followed by a lobbying campaign aimed at amending a large number of Ontario laws that defined "spouse" and similar terms. For CLGRO as a political strategy and, increasingly, for individual lesbians and gays, challenging the exclusive and discriminatory recognition of heterosexual relationships in laws and public policy and the privileging of heterosexual marriage, legally and socially, became a new rights imperative. In medical situations, one member of a same-sex couple would not be recognized as the spouse for visitation rights when the other was hospitalized or was a patient in a care facility. A same-sex partner was not recognized for the purpose of making decisions on behalf of the other partner unable to make decisions about his or her own care or treatment, or in the event of the partner's death. As CLGRO noted in a leaflet produced to generate support for its campaign, Ontario's Bill 7, which amended the Ontario Human Rights Code, was "only the first step in gaining full equality."

> Lesbians and gay men still encounter discrimination in areas which affect our personal lives and our personal relationships. Many government acts define spouse as a member of the opposite sex, thereby denying gays and lesbians access to spousal benefits. We regularly confront discrimination in matters related to housing and domestic arrangements, wills and other contracts. Our relationships are often ignored or used against us in disputes over custody rights.[2]

The CLGRO campaign to change the laws would continue for a decade. In 1990, with a provincial election looming, CLGRO sent letters to members of the legislature seeking their support for legal recognition of same-sex common-law relationships. Liberal Attorney General Ian Scott responded that the government was reviewing "over seventy" laws that would have to be amended to recognize same-sex relationships. NDP leader Bob Rae replied that the tax and legal implications of what CLGRO was proposing had to be worked out, but his party was committed to supporting equal treatment of same-sex couples.[3] Within a few months—following the election of the NDP as Ontario's government in September 1990—Rae's comment would take on added significance.

The courts and the religious view of homosexuality

Scott's acknowledgement of the Ontario government's review of various laws was a recognition that the heterosexual definition of spouse and spousal relationships was under increasing challenge in human rights cases and before the courts. A number of gays and lesbians in same-sex relationships had filed complaints with the human rights commissions or undertaken court challenges alleging that various laws were discriminatory because they restricted the provision of pension, health, and social benefits to spouses in heterosexual relationships. The lesbian and gay litigants advocated for acceptance of a new construct, the non-traditional or "functional family," to challenge the legal exclusivity and special status of traditional (heterosexual) family and marriage based on ancient religious moral values. Families, they contended, should instead be defined by the interdependence and interactions of the individuals who comprised them. They should be distinguished by such indicia as emotional and economic interdependence and a shared responsibility to support and care for each other, often also including the nurturing of and caring for children. A functional family was a group of two or more people living together as a single household or unit that displayed all of the characteristics and behaviours of families and family relationships. That these families were not structured in accordance with the traditional religious ideal of two married heterosexuals, a husband/father and a wife/mother, and their biological children, was argued as being irrelevant in determining whether they should be legally recognized and afforded all of the same rights and obligations of heterosexual family units.

Even more so than the efforts to include sexual orientation in human rights laws, the attainment of legal recognition for same-sex relationships was seen by the courts, at least initially, and by legislators as fundamentally a moral issue. The earliest cases to be argued before the courts revealed what law professor Kathleen Lahey has described as the "heterosexual presumption."[4] That presumption was based on Judeo-Christian religious beliefs, with its absolutist construct of marriage and family as the epitome of moral (and social) uprightness, proper conduct, and acceptable behaviour. Heterosexual marriage was the idealized relationship. Everyone was supposed to dutifully strive for that ideal, and the state was to ardently and unwaveringly support it in myriad ways through laws, public policies, services, and programs. Not surprisingly, the heterosexual presumption permeated all aspects of the law, as well as social and cultural institutions and interaction. According to the heterosexual presumption, it was, quite simply, impossible and, indeed, preposterous that same-sex couples could be "spouses" in any real or meaningful sense—and certainly not ever in any legal sense. Their couplings properly could not be considered families under the law.

There was also not any judicial framework within which the courts could or would expand the constructs of spousal relationships and family to encompass same-sex relationships. The new morality of rights and equality was still in the early stages of evolution and development. Indeed, the principal focus within both the judicial and political realms had only very recently and somewhat hesitantly shifted to include the necessity of enshrining in law the right of gays and lesbians to be free from discrimination, and then only in limited and prescribed areas. To preserve and protect marriage and the traditional family, politicians in particular had been at pains to draw a line beyond which they would not transgress in enacting any expansion of legal rights for gays and lesbians. The justice system's idea of homosexuality and same-sex relationships was also firmly rooted in the prevailing religious beliefs and morality. The religious standard of morality, not the secular standard of rights and equality of treatment, was used as the test to determine the cases that were coming before the courts from individuals in same-sex relationships; and traditional religious values provided the most convenient and familiar standard for the courts to apply in such cases.[5]

In cases initiated by gays and lesbians in the late 1980s and early 1990s the courts reaffirmed the privileged status of opposite-sex relationships in law. One of the first and most important of such cases was launched by Brian Mossop, a translator for the federal government and a gay activist involved with a number of groups, including the Gay Alliance Toward Equality, Toronto and the Coalition for Gay Rights in Ontario. Mossop was denied bereavement leave when he wanted to attend the funeral of the father of his same-sex partner, Ken Popert. The collective agreement between his union and the federal Treasury Board recognized only opposite-sex relationships. Mossop filed a grievance, and in 1985, after being denied at all levels within the federal bureaucracy, he filed a complaint with the Canadian Human Rights Commission under the provisions of the Canadian Human Rights Act.

Although the CHRA did not at the time contain sexual orientation as a prohibited ground of discrimination, the term "family status" was not defined and Mossop argued discrimination on that basis. His complaint did not cite Charter grounds, although section 15 had come into effect earlier in the same year. Sexual orientation was not specifically enumerated in section 15, and given the newness of the section there was an absence of jurisprudence on whether sexual-orientation discrimination was prohibited. Instead, Mossop's case was argued on the statutory definition of "family." The issue was whether that term could be defined broadly to include non-conjugal and non-spousal relationships. A human rights tribunal ultimately found that the denial of the bereavement leave was discrimination. When the federal government appealed that finding, the stage was set for a historic legal skirmish between the aspirations of gays and lesbians and the defenders of the traditional notion of family and marriage. Not surprisingly, the government sided with the forces of tradition.

REAL Women of Canada, Focus on the Family (Canada), Evangelical Fellowship of Canada, Pentecostal Assemblies of Canada, and the Salvation Army intervened in the case. Defining "family" to include gay couples "would be wrong, on a biblical basis," asserted Reverend Hilsden. REAL Women's Landolt added, "The traditional family contributes a service to society by raising the next generation and has certain legal obligations to each other, which homosexual couples do not." She argued that the traditional family deserved special advantages and treatment. That view was supported in a June 1990 judgment of the Federal Court of Canada, which stated that gay couples did not constitute a family in law. The issue raised in the case, the Court contended, was rightly to be determined by Parliament and was not for the courts to decide.[6]

Mossop appealed the decision, in the end taking his case all the way to the Supreme Court. A majority of justices of the Supreme Court, in a 1993 judgment, *Canada (Attorney General) v. Mossop*, agreed that family status in the CHRA could not be interpreted to include same-sex relationships. They maintained that Parliament, at the time the CHRA was adopted, had not intended that the term would have any meaning other than its normal (heterosexual) meaning. That view was supported, they argued, by the fact that the legislators had specifically not included sexual orientation as a ground of prohibited discrimination in the CHRA. The majority also ruled that in the absence of a Charter challenge of the CHRA's constitutionality, "when parliamentary intent is clear, courts and administrative tribunals are not empowered to do anything else but to apply the law." However, the justices also invited Mossop to reformulate his complaint on the ground of sexual orientation and pursue it as a constitutional challenge of the CHRA under section 15.[7]

Earlier legal cases had covered some of the same ground, with disappointing results from the point of view of gay and lesbian activists. In 1986 the B.C. Supreme Court heard a case involving Penny Anderson, a woman who sought maintenance and child support from her former partner. The couple, while together, had two children born by artificial insemination. The Court dismissed arguments that the family law provisions recognizing only opposite-sex couples contravened the Charter. The court ruled that Anderson was not entitled to support under the law because the law had not been intended to apply to providing support to a child born to another woman through artificial insemination. In a 1985 Ontario case involving the application of the publicly funded Ontario Health Insurance Plan (OHIP), the provincial government contended that two persons of the same sex who were cohabiting could not in law be spouses; and the Ontario Supreme Court agreed that the term "spouse" in law "always refers to a person of the opposite sex." The court, exercising the heterosexual presumption, read that definition into the Health Insurance Act.[8]

Perhaps the most significant of the cases in which the heterosexual presumption and the traditional religious understanding of marriage and family trumped the claim of same-sex couples to be treated without discrimination came when Jim Egan attempted without success to have his partner, Jack Nesbit, provided with a spousal allowance under the Old Age Security Act (OASA). Like other federal laws, the OASA defined spouse as meaning a person of the opposite sex. A 1991 Federal Court of Canada ruling maintained that same-sex couples did not qualify for OASA benefits because Parliament had intended that act to apply only to "traditional" married couples, a basic unit upon which "society depends for its continued existence." Furthermore, same-sex couples could not expect to receive the same spousal recognition as heterosexual couples, not because of the sexual orientation of the individuals, but because they were not married in the eyes of the law.[9] Of course, the laws of the country also prohibited same-sex couples from legally marrying, a factor that seemed not to matter to the Court.

Egan and Nesbit appealed without success to the Federal Court of Appeal and then to the Supreme Court of Canada, where, as in the *Mossop* case, an assortment of social conservative groups intervened to oppose the couple under the name of the Interfaith Coalition on Marriage and the Family. Supporting Egan and Nesbit were Egale Canada and the Metropolitan Community Church of Toronto. On May 25, 1995, the Supreme Court issued a mixed decision. All nine justices held that sexual orientation must be read into the Charter as a ground of discrimination analogous to existing grounds such as race, sex, or religion—thus marking the first time that Canada's highest court had ruled on that question, making it an important milestone. But more importantly for the social conservative groups, a majority of five justices dismissed the appeal. They ruled that the OASA was constitutional under section 1 of the Charter—that the discrimination evidenced by the refusal to recognize same-sex couples was justifiable because it placed a reasonable limitation on the rights otherwise guaranteed in the Constitution. The social conservatives were particularly gratified that four of the five majority justices offered a ringing endorsement of marriage as exclusive to heterosexual unions and deserving of special recognition in law. One of them noted that marriage had "from time immemorial" been

> firmly anchored in the biological and social realities that heterosexual couples have the unique ability to procreate, that most children are the product of these relationships, and that they are generally cared for and

nurtured by those who live in that relationship. In this sense, marriage
is by nature heterosexual. It would be possible to legally define marriage
to include homosexual couples, but this would not change the biological
and social realities that underlie the traditional marriage. [10]

The justices were equally firm on the subject of recognizing unmarried same-sex
relationships. "Homosexual couples differ from other excluded couples in that
their relationships include a sexual aspect, but this sexual aspect has nothing to
do with the social objectives for which Parliament affords a measure of support to
married couples and those who live in a common law relationship."

Here was the expression in the most resounding terms possible, by the highest court of the land, of the adoption—indeed the championing—of the religious
view of marriage and family as the judicial standard by which the rights claims
of same-sex couples were to be adjudged—and ultimately denied. The judgment
could very well have been written by one of the social conservative groups that so
vehemently asserted that Judeo-Christian morality should remain the bedrock of
Canada's laws regulating sexuality and conjugal relationships. These justices, at
least, had not yet embraced in respect of same-sex relationships the new secular
morality of equality rights and its antithesis that discrimination is immoral and
unacceptable in a free and democratic society. For them, the privileging of heterosexual marriage evidenced by the affordance to it of special rights and recogni-
tions in law remained a fundamental precept of the state, central to the national
identity of Canadians, and vital to social stability and well-being.

Social conservative criticism of the *Egan* decision, not surprisingly, was
muted. Comments centred on the contradictions that they saw within the ruling
and on the dilemma that the courts faced in attempting to mitigate the impact of
the Charter. Essentially, the primary negative aspect of the decision for them was
the determination by all nine judges that sexual orientation must be read into the
Charter as a ground of discrimination analogous to existing grounds. Overall, however, social conservative groups expressed satisfaction with the *Egan* decision's
finding on the essential question: that, at least for the time being, Parliament was
under no obligation to treat same-sex relationships in the same way as marriage
in law. In an article published on the website of the Canada Family Action Coalition, social conservative journalist Rory Leishman deplored the "tangle of contradictions" presented by the *Egan* decision, but nonetheless welcomed the majority opinion that Parliament's support of heterosexual marriage and common-law
relationships was essential because of their critical task of nurturing children.
Similarly, the Canadian Conference of Catholic Bishops commended the *Egan*
decision's finding: "It is appropriate to make distinctions between heterosexual

and homosexual couples because of the unique and important contribution that heterosexual couples make to the future of society."[11]

Organizing for legal recognition of same-sex relationships

The triumph of heterosexual presumption and the stifling pervasiveness of the Judeo-Christian religious views of homosexuality, marriage, and family were also dramatically evident in the legislative realm throughout the 1990s. The first cataclysmic confrontation between the rights asserted by same-sex couples and the defence of traditional heterosexual marriage and family erupted in Ontario, following the surprise election in 1990 of the NDP government under Rae. Almost immediately CLGRO pressed for amendment of the estimated seventy laws dealing with spousal relationships and family rights. The government responded by announcing an intention to review all provincial laws with a view to amending the definition of "spouse"—in all likelihood the same review already initiated by the former Liberal government. Nonetheless, it was a positive gesture by the Rae government, which also stated that medical and other benefits would be granted to same-sex partners of provincial government employees.[12]

At first the social conservative groups did not rise up en masse in opposition. The exception was the Family Coalition Party (FCP), a small fringe party made up of evangelical Protestants. One of the more prominent members of the FCP was Ken Campbell, who had been a candidate for the party in the 1990 election. The FCP slammed the announcement as an attack on the family, "the demolition of the fundamental building block of society." FCP spokesperson Giuseppe Gori asserted, "People shouldn't be ashamed to say the traditional family deserves privileges."[13] The denunciation was a warning sign of more to come. The NDP would soon face a storm of mounting and increasingly militant opposition from the forces of social conservatism; and despite its purported progressivism, the ruling party remained politically sensitive to the views of social conservatives on the issue. It took little concrete action in the first years of its mandate.

Many NDP caucus members, especially those from rural areas, small urban centres, and suburban communities, were strongly opposed to their government's potential policy change. Even members of the government who were generally seen as being more supportive of rights for lesbians and gays were decidedly reticent about acting on the issue. Rae later commented in his book *From Protest to Power* that he hoped enough cases would be determined by the courts to provide impetus to force the government to take legislative action.[14] In stark political terms, acting proactively would incite the large social conservative population of

the province, whereas reneging on a promise made to the gay and lesbian community would have little electoral impact. The NDP cold-bloodedly calculated that it
could sustain whatever pressure was forthcoming from an increasingly angry gay
and lesbian community. That anger was expressed in petition and postcard campaigns, in demonstrations, and on two occasions, most dramatically, by sit-ins that
CLGRO held at the offices of both Rae and Attorney General Howard Hampton.[15]

Some two years after the NDP was elected, an Ontario Human Rights Board
of Inquiry ruling in a case launched by provincial civil servant Michael Leshner
increased the pressure to act. Leshner charged that the failure to recognize his
same-sex partner for survivor benefits under the government's pension plan was
sexual-orientation discrimination under the Human Rights Code.[16] In a historic
and precedent-setting decision released in September 1992, the Board of Inquiry
agreed. It ordered the government to provide pension benefits to surviving partners of same-sex couples. The decision put the Rae government in an awkward
position: whatever action it took would have political ramifications. An appeal of
the decision would have further infuriated an already antagonized gay and lesbian
community—and would also have exposed as hypocritical the party's profuse and
public proclamations made over many years that it (and only it) was the party that
championed human rights, including in particular rights for gays and lesbians.
Alternatively, the government could belatedly follow through on its commitment
to legislate recognition of same-sex rights, which would unleash a cyclone of social
conservative invective and mobilization.

CLGRO cited the tribunal's decision as evidence that all of the similar Ontario
laws were discriminatory and needed to be amended. Its leaders met with Hampton, urging him not to appeal and pressing him for immediate enactment of legislation. Social conservative groups, for their part, waged a massive campaign, targeting Hampton and the Human Rights Commission with hundreds of phone calls,
faxes, and letters from church groups denouncing the Leshner decision. Hampton
responded in September 1992, stating that the government would not appeal the
decision. But he went no further, stating only that the government was continuing
to review the question of amending provincial laws.[17]

Over the next couple of years two private member's bills—one intended to
bring Ontario laws into line with the Leshner decision and the other dealing with
hatred directed towards identifiable groups—failed to proceed to final votes in the
legislature. The Evangelical Fellowship of Canada organized petitions and letter-
writing campaigns against the bills. Members of church congregations confronted
MPPs in their local communities. It was not until March 1994, in the waning days
of a now hugely unpopular Rae government, that the NDP finally decided to act,
announcing the introduction of legislation to recognize same-sex common-law

relationships. But the government was at first perplexingly and distressingly vague as to whether the legislation would be limited to the extension of medical and pension benefits to same-sex spouses or would go further and amend other laws, including those dealing with spousal support, child custody, and adoption. Furthermore, it did nothing to create either public or political support for what was clearly controversial legislation. Its Bill 167—which proposed to amend all of some seventy acts to change the definition of spouse and other similar terms—succeeded only in creating a clash of major proportions between gay and lesbian activists and the social conservative groups.[18]

Leading a broadly based campaign with the support of arts and cultural groups and organized labour, CLGRO formed a new group, the Campaign for Equal Families (CEF), organizing under the slogan "We are Family." But it proved no match for an aggressive social conservative mobilization against the bill. The EFC and Roman Catholic clergy issued alerts to galvanize church members across the province, urging them to phone and send letters to MPPs to protest Bill 167. A flyer issued by Stew Newton of Positive Parents screamed: "If you vote for this pro homosexual legislation, your schools! your churches! your daycare centres! will soon become recruiting centres for homosexuals." MPPs from all parties were bombarded with phone calls, letters, and petitions. One Liberal MPP reported that expressed opinion in his constituency was running fifty to one against the bill. Other MPPs reported sentiment as running one hundred to one against. Some four thousand negative letters were received by one rural MPP. Politicians going back to their home constituencies, as one observer noted, were getting "the crap kicked out of them."[19] Support for the bill in the legislature was fragile, at best. The NDP caucus was bitterly divided, with a large number of backbench MPPs openly defying the government.

In the end the NDP responded like a deer caught in the highlights of a fast-approaching transport truck. Responding to the pervasive objections to Bill 167, the NDP committed a fatal tactical error and decided to hold a free vote. The rationale for doing so, Rae later wrote, was "because there would be those with religious objections to the government's official sanctioning of gay and lesbian relationships."[20] Unlike other government bills, for which members of the government caucus were expected and instructed to vote in favour or face disciplinary action, NDP MPPs would be free to vote according to their "conscience." It thus became, bizarrely, a government bill that the government was not prepared to wholeheartedly support. Bill 167 only narrowly passed on first reading, at which point, in a desperate attempt to salvage some semblance of what the legislation was intended to achieve, the government announced that it would replace the definitions of "spouse" and "marital status" that included same-sex relationships with a new term, "domestic partner." The new domestic partnerships would have the same legal status as common-law heterosexual relationships. The right of same-sex couples to adopt children would be removed.

The new strategy was a colossal flop. The NDP caucus opponents remained firm. The Liberals were not persuaded to vote in favour of Bill 167. Among the general public, the move was simply seen as a staggering retreat. It failed to placate social conservative opponents while only further angering the gay and lesbian community. The hapless, bungling government was left without supporters on any side.[21] Bill 167 suffered a crushing defeat on second reading and never became law.

Social conservatives were elated by the outcome. Campbell, speaking on behalf of Renaissance Canada, presumptuously claimed that the defeat reflected the views of the majority of people in Ontario. "If the government took its cue from the grassroots, this legislation would never have been brought forward," he crowed. Gays and lesbians were furious and felt betrayed. The NDP, their erstwhile political friend that had made so many promises and raised so many expectations, had cruelly and cravenly acquiesced when confronted by homophobia and religiously motivated intolerance. After silently witnessing the vote from the legislature's public gallery, a large group of gays and lesbians stormed into the main foyer and refused, when asked, to leave the building. Their shouts of "Shame! Shame! Shame!" reverberated through the halls before they were forcibly driven out of the building by Ontario Provincial Police officers. Some of the officers wore rubber gloves, presumably in an effort to protect themselves from being infected with AIDS.[22] That evening ten thousand people demonstrated in the streets of Toronto to protest the bill's defeat.

The defeat of Bill 167 was indisputably an important political victory for the social conservative movement in its ardent defence of the traditional family and marriage. It would have ripple effects in both the federal jurisdiction and other provinces. The heterosexual presumption and the state's assertion of the old morality based on religious beliefs and values had seemingly demolished the assertion of gays and lesbians that legal recognition of their relationships was a vital issue of ensuring fairness and equality and removing unjustifiable discrimination. Still, Bill 167, though unquestionably a debacle, was nonetheless merely an interregnum; and the social conservative victory was to be ultimately ephemeral.

Breakthrough and retreat

In the immediate aftermath of Bill 167, politicians who had appeared to be supportive of establishing legal equality for same-sex relationships backed off, fearful of facing the same fate as the Ontario NDP. Even the NDP government in

British Columbia, which had seemed poised to follow the lead of its Ontario colleagues, became more cautious on the issue. Premier Glen Clark's government had been assiduously lobbied to legally recognize same-sex relationships by the December 9th Coalition, a Vancouver-based advocacy group for gays and lesbians formed in 1992. Now the Clark government decided to amend one statute at a time rather than attempting the omnibus route that had failed in Ontario. In 1995 it amended by administrative order the regulations to the Adoption Act to permit single persons, including homosexuals, and same-sex couples to adopt. Liberal leader Gordon Campbell voiced his opposition, and petitions against the change bearing a few thousand names were presented in the legislature. Otherwise there was no huge public outcry.[23]

In 1997 the Clark government introduced two other bills changing the definition of spouse in the Family Relations Act and Family Maintenance Enforcement Act. Same-sex couples thus became subject to the provisions dealing with child support, custody, and maintenance. But this time social conservative groups and religious leaders quickly organized to oppose the bills. REAL Women of British Columbia mounted a concerted letter-writing and lobbying campaign. The Roman Catholic Archbishop of Vancouver, Adam Exner, urged Catholics to send letters and faxes and make phone calls in protest. Calling homosexual relationships "gravely immoral," he denounced the bills as attacking the sacredness of marriage and weakening the fabric of society. The archbishop was joined by other religious leaders, including the heads of the Conference of Mennonites, Akali Singh Sikh Society, Orthodox Rabbinical Council, and Council of Muslims of Canada. Their opposition to the legislation, they contended, was an affirmation of a universal truth of their faiths about marriage and marital relationships. They pressed the political parties to hold a free vote on the issue, in the hope of repeating the events that had led to the defeat of the Ontario bill. Despite these interventions, the B.C. bills were eventually enacted.[24]

In Quebec the Parti Québécois government of Premier Lucien Bouchard amended provincial laws and regulations in June 1996 to provide for same-sex benefits for employees in the private sector. Unlike the experience in Ontario and British Columbia, the amendments encountered little opposition.[25] As in other provinces, the Quebec government's action had followed several years of lobbying by gay and lesbian groups in the province, notably by the Coalition des organismes Montréal métropolitain. The PQ government's action also responded to a call made by the Quebec Human Rights Commission in 1994 for the amendment of Quebec laws to recognize same-sex relationships. Still, the amendments did not extend recognition to same-sex relationships in all areas of Quebec law. To pressure the government to take that next step, ten lesbian and gay groups and other supportive organizations formed the Coalition pour la reconnaissance des conjointes et conjoints de même sexe to lobby the government on the issue. In 1999 Quebec became the first province to establish full legal recognition for all common-law relationships, whether opposite-sex or same-sex.

In contrast, the political climate in Ottawa regarding the amendment of federal laws became demonstrably chilly following the rancorous debate and defeat of Bill 167. Federal politicians, including those who had previously expressed support, were now in full throttle retreat on the issue. The most important of backtrackers was federal justice minister Allan Rock. Following the 1993 federal election, Rock had made positive statements about introducing a sexual-orientation amendment to the Canadian Human Rights Act and, as the logical next step, enacting extension of spousal benefit provisions to same-sex couples. But in spring 1994, Rock, obviously leery of invoking an outcry similar to that spurred by the events in Ontario, stated flatly, "I don't favour the approach that involves redefining family and spouse." He condemned the approach taken by Ontario's NDP government as "unduly provocative." By spring 1995 Rock was retreating even further, stressing that he had no plans to move on legal recognition of same-sex relationships in the near future.[26]

The federal Liberal government's reluctance was coupled with a general lack of support in Parliament for recognizing same-sex relationships. In September 1995, openly gay Bloc Québécois MP Réal Ménard introduced a private member's motion calling for the legal recognition of same-sex couples. The members of Parliament, including all Liberals who voted, decisively defeated the measure.[27] The federal government was also not under any pressure from the courts to act on the question. As evidenced by the *Egan* decision, the courts were either content to leave the issue to Parliament to resolve or had issued judgments defending the special status and recognition given in law to heterosexual relationships.

Nevertheless, the introduction and demise of Bill 167 and other similar measures had occurred on the cusp of a truly transformative change in the judicial and, increasingly, the social landscape. More and more Canadians were coming to accept the rightness of recognizing same-sex relationships. Employers of all kinds were taking action by including same-sex partners and in many cases their children within their health and dental benefit plans. They were extending survival pension rights to same-sex partners, even though the laws had not changed.[28] As the age of rights continued to evolve in the post-Charter era, the new morality based on equality and respect for diversity was slowly and irreversibly gaining the ascendancy. While some progress had been seen on the part of legislators in British Columbia and Quebec, it would, within a few short years, be the courts that would force the legislators elsewhere to gradually, if reluctantly, amend a vast array of laws to recognize same-sex relationships.

Inclusion and accommodation

By the end of the 1990s, the courts had begun to move away from the religious view of homosexuality, marriage, and family as the standard by which to consider the rights and obligations of same-sex relationships. As the result of an increasing body of cases that were using the equality rights guaranteed by section 15 of the Charter to strike down discrimination and establish equal treatment on the basis of sexual orientation, the courts were evolving what Bruce MacDougall describes as the "inclusive-accommodation approach." Under that approach, Mac-Dougall notes, the courts sought compromise and accommodation rather than a conflict resulting in winners and losers. They strove to accommodate same-sex relationships within the definitions of spouse and family status while at the same time attempting to respect and accommodate religious views and religious freedom of expression.[29]

This new accommodation approach became evident when the Supreme Court dramatically reversed its stance in a landmark judgment dealing with the legal recognition of same-sex common-law relationships. The case, known as *M. v. H.*, involved two Ontario lesbians. One of them, M, following the breakup of the relationship, sought spousal support payments under the provisions of Ontario's Family Law Act (FLA). A judge of the Ontario Court (General Division) had initially ruled in the case that the FLA discriminated because of sexual orientation under section 15, and "read in" to the FLA definition of spouse the words "any two persons" while striking out the phrase "a man and a woman."[30] The other partner, H, and the provincial government appealed. When the Ontario Court of Appeal upheld the lower court decision, the Ontario government appealed to the Supreme Court of Canada, which heard the case in March 1998.

REAL Women and the Interfaith Coalition—made up of Focus on the Family, EFC, Ontario Council of Sikhs, and Islamic Society of North America—supported the Ontario government as intervenors in the case. The Interfaith Coalition argued the necessity of protecting heterosexual marriage, even though the case did not contest the provisions of the Marriage Act. The FLA, it maintained, did not contravene section 15 of the Charter because of the "fundamental and foundational role in our society and other societies" played by heterosexual spousal units. Rejecting the notion that "spousal rights" ought to be granted to anyone who seeks them on the basis of "coupleness," the Interfaith Coalition arued: "It is legitimate for law and social policy to make certain distinctions based on historical, biological and sociological grounds which reflect underlying religious and philosophical tradition." It warned the Supreme Court against redefining "spouse" to encompass same-sex relationships: "Such a radical change to legal, social and public policy, which reflects millennia of religious and philosophical understanding, is beyond the intended scope of Charter review, and would improperly require the exercise of a judicial 'legislative' function."[31]

On the other side as intervenors were Egale Canada, Foundation for Equal Families, Women's Legal Education and Action Fund, United Church of Canada, and Ontario Human Rights Commission. In a backgrounder on the case Egale Canada noted that it was intervening because "the Supreme Court has never before ruled that a law is unconstitutional because it fails to treat same-sex couples equally." Its expectation was that the Supreme Court would "be clarifying its position on the proper constitutional application of ss.15 [equality rights] and 1 [the 'justifiable' discrimination clause] of the Charter of Rights." It was proven correct in that expectation. The Supreme Court released its historic *M. v. H.* decision in May 1999, with eight of nine justices ruling that the definition of spouse in the FLA contravened section 15. The Court imposed a six-month time frame in which the Ontario government could amend the FLA to comply with the Charter. If it did not do so, the offending section of the act would be deemed to no longer have any force or effect.[32]

Significantly, the decision represented the rejection of the heterosexual presumption in regard to spousal and conjugal relationships and the assertion of the new moral imperative enshrined in section 15 of the Charter of ensuring equality and freedom from discrimination. In their written decision six justices concluded that the FLA discriminated on the basis of sexual orientation because it specifically accorded rights to members of unmarried cohabiting opposite-sex couples and omitted to accord such rights to members of cohabiting same-sex couples. The judges struck a blow against "differential treatment" that "imposes a burden upon or withholds a benefit" on a claimant "in a manner that reflects the stereotypical application of presumed group or personal characteristics, or which otherwise has the effect of perpetuating or promoting the view that the individual is less capable or worthy of recognition or value as a human being or as a member of Canadian society, equally deserving of concern, respect, and consideration."[33]

Noting that the FLA extended the obligation to provide spousal support to include opposite-sex relationships that "have a specific degree of permanence and are conjugal," and that same-sex relationships are capable of meeting the same "temporal requirements," the judges held that the differential treatment imposed by the FLA was discriminatory. The description of the requirements as "temporal," a synonym for "secular," was deliberate and particularly significant. The FLA, they declared, set a secular and not a religious standard by which the state was recognizing spousal relationships and bestowing them with legal rights and obligations. According to that secular standard, the exclusion of same-sex relationships from the FLA "implies that they are judged to be incapable of forming intimate relationships of economic interdependence as compared to opposite-sex couples, without regard to their actual circumstances. Such exclusion perpetuates the disadvantages suffered by individuals in same-sex relationships and contributes to the erasure of their existence."[34] The only just and constitutionally permissible solution therefore was to accommodate a member of a same-sex conjugal relationship by including him or her within the definition of "spouse."

Darrel Reid of Focus on the Family charged that the decision had "overturned centuries of social tradition." Changing the definition of spouse to recognize same-sex relationships would no longer address "the unique needs of marriage and heterosexual spousal relationships," lamented Bruce Clemenger of the EFC. Peter Stock of the Canada Family Action Coalition called upon Ontario and other provinces to use the notwithstanding clause of the Charter to override the decision.[35] The Roman Catholic Archbishop of Toronto, Aloysius Ambrozic, complained:

> The long-term consequences of the decision of the Supreme Court of Canada in *M. v. H.* are difficult to predict, but cannot be good because the decision is based on flawed philosophical, theological and biological premises. The Court adopts an approach that may serve to undermine our traditional understandings of marriage and family, and the nature of spousal and conjugal relationships.[36]

The judicial landscape for recognizing rights and relationships had been undeniably altered. The Supreme Court had rejected the traditional, familiar, and pervasive constructs of spousal and family relationships based on Judeo-Christian religious views and its moral code. With the *M. v. H.* judgment, the Supreme Court had declared that Charter rights and equality of treatment were paramount, in effect declaring, in respect of spousal and family relationships, that the Charter was the new, secular moral code and the state was obligated to comply with that code. Furthermore, if the legislators would not act to ensure the equality of gay and lesbian common-law relationships by amending statutes that violated the rights guaranteed by the Charter, the laws would be struck down. The *M. v. H.* decision was thus a major defeat for social conservatism, overturning the political victory scored with the defeat of Bill 167.

The reluctant legislators finally act

The social conservative movement and its vigorous defence of traditional marriage and morality would never recover from the body blow inflicted
by *M. v. H.* In no way was that more evident than in the response of Ontario's
Progressive Conservative government headed by Mike Harris. Elected in 1995, the
economically conservative Harris government had assiduously and successfully
wooed the province's large social conservative constituency in its bid for power;
and the social conservative groups hoped that their role in helping to elect the
Harris government would result in Ontario remaining a bulwark of family values.
Following the *M. v. H.* decision, they lobbied the government intensely, urging it
to do everything in its power to resist the dictate of the activist Supreme Court
judges, or at least to mitigate the horrific impact of the judgment. Instead, Harris
announced that the government would comply with the *M. v. H.* decision. In doing
so, the government adopted the same accommodation and compromise approach
that the courts were now championing.

The Harris government had a delicate political issue to manage. It needed
the continued electoral support of social conservatives but also had to be seen to
be showing respect for the Constitution of the country and its guarantee of equality rights. Thus the legislative response, when it came, was framed politically to
send a message that the government had been forced to act by the Supreme Court.
In October 1999, the conservatives introduced Bill 5, which created a new category of "same sex partner." Under that category, same-sex couples were granted
all of the legal rights and responsibilities that common-law heterosexual couples
had under sixty-seven provincial statutes. But, in a gesture to social conservative
sentiment, the definition of "spouse" would remain applicable only to heterosexual couples. This protection of the definition of "spouse" in Ontario law, Attorney
General James Flaherty pointed out to the legislature, would serve to preserve
"the traditional values of the family."[37]

Social conservatives were not placated by the Ontario government's clever
dialectical dancing. An article by Rory Leishman in the CFAC newsletter accused
the Harris government of caving in to "judicial blackmail." Derek Rogusky of Focus
on the Family warned that Bill 5 "has major ramifications for the traditional family
and people of faith who view homosexual activity to be morally wrong." Rogusky
lamented, "Bill 5 goes a long way in establishing the rights of homosexuals and
providing their relationships legal recognition." REAL Women's Landolt thundered
that the Ontario government's action "will result in damage to the fabric of our
society by undermining the traditional family." She characterized the Harris government's action as a "betrayal of Canadian values and principles."[38]

In Ottawa, parliamentarians feared that even though the *M. v. H.* decision did not deal explicitly with the constitutionality of the traditional definition of marriage, it was a troubling indication of the direction in which the Supreme Court was moving. MPs moved quickly to send a strong message that marriage would be reserved exclusively for heterosexuals. The Reform Party introduced a resolution stating:

> That in the opinion of this House, it is necessary, in light of public debate around recent court decisions, to state that marriage is and should remain the union of one man and one woman to the exclusion of all others, and that Parliament will take all necessary steps within the jurisdiction of the Parliament of Canada to preserve this definition of marriage in Canada.

The "take all necessary steps" provision was widely interpreted as meaning that Parliament would invoke the notwithstanding clause of the Charter if necessary to block any judicial decision recognizing same-sex marriage. The resolution was overwhelmingly supported by the governing Liberals, and passed on June 8, 1999, by a vote of 216 to 55. It was a solid, although ultimately short-lived, victory for social conservatism.

The federal legislators clearly faced a conundrum. They could not ignore the pronouncements of the courts and especially of the Supreme Court. They would have to act to remove unlawful discrimination against same-sex common-law relationships without, they hoped, threatening the perpetuation in law of the privileged status granted to heterosexual marriage. Adding to the necessity to act were an estimated thirty lawsuits against the federal government that were working their way through the courts, challenging the definition of spouse in various laws.[39] Accepting the inevitable, the Chrétien government finally introduced Bill C-23, The Modernization of Benefits and Obligations Act, in February 2000. It amended the definition of "common-law partner" to recognize same-sex partners in conjugal relationships in the same way in law as common-law opposite-sex relationships. It was a "different but equal" approach that left "marital status" and "spouse" defined in exclusively heterosexual terms. Following the example of the Harris government in Ontario, Ottawa was attempting to appease social conservatives both inside and outside of Parliament.[40]

Although Egale Canada called upon MPs to adopt Bill C-23 without amendment, opponents of same-sex relationships immediately went on the attack in hope of having it defeated. The EFC condemned the "impropriety of extending rights, obligations and benefits on the basis of 'conjugality.'" They argued that the term "cannot be extended to same-sex partners" because same-sex couplings were not procreative. The Canadian Conference of Catholic Bishops held firmly to their Church's belief that "sexual relations outside marriage, whether heterosexual or homosexual, [are] morally unacceptable." What the state had historically supported, the Catholic bishops argued, was the bearing and nurturing of children by heterosexual couples.[41]

The social conservative interventions to defeat Bill C-23 included the active involvement of Muslim objectors. The Toronto District Muslim Education Assembly (TDMEA), in a submission to the standing committee that reviewed Bill C-23, declared: "We from the Muslim community strongly object to Bill C-23 because it constitutes a direct attack, ridicule and assault on the sacred institution of marriage, the family and the valued traditions of a healthy society." To confer "rights, privileges and benefits" to relationships between unmarried people, TDMEA asserted, "would be malignant, unfair and unjust and does not serve any real benefit to society. On the contrary, only great harm and evil would ensue from such abuse and usurpation." Specifically regarding same-sex relationships, the TDMEA brief did not pull any punches: "Homosexual/lesbian relationship does not only negate the higher societal duty of procreation, but it is the promotion of moral corruption and degradation of human beings. Promoting such a life style is wrong and unacceptable and constitutes grave dangers to society."[42]

As Bill C-23 proceeded through Parliament, several Liberal MPs threatened to vote against it. The government dealt with this political problem by making a further concession. It inserted a ringing declaration into the preamble to Bill C-23 that marriage remained in law the exclusive right of heterosexual couples: "For greater certainty, the amendments made by this Act do not affect the meaning of the word 'marriage,' that is, the lawful union of one man and one woman to the exclusion of all others." With that amendment, and the separation of common-law relationships from marriage, Bill C-23 was adopted on April 11, 2000. Nonetheless, seventeen Liberal MPs remained defiant and voted against it.

By the year 2000, then, the social conservative movement and its political champions had failed to stop same-sex common-law relationships from being legally recognized. Gradually the laws in every province and territory were amended. While marriage and marital status remained in law the exclusive right of heterosexual couples, social conservatives feared, rightly as it would turn out, that such would not be the case for very much longer.

The desperate defence of marriage

Armed with a growing number of favourable court decisions ruling that the Charter required legal recognition of same-sex common-law relationships, gay and lesbian couples launched Charter challenges of the marriage laws. Egale Canada made changing the legal definition of marriage to include same-sex couples its top priority, organizing political and public education campaigns to secure support for legislative action. It also effectively intervened in various Charter challenge cases that were wending their way through the courts. For Egale, legal recognition of same-sex marriage was "a simple question of equal dignity and respect." Furthermore, it noted, "Many same-sex couples raise children, and those children are entitled to the benefit of a family unit that is recognized and respected by the state." Legalizing same-sex marriage, Egale emphasized, would not impinge upon freedom of religion: "Any religion would have the choice not to marry same-sex couples, but civil marriage would be equally available to all couples who choose it."[43]

Egale Canada and the other like-minded groups adopted the accommodation and compromise approach of the judicial pronouncements. More fundamentally, what they were seeking was not to destroy or debase marriage and family, as their social conservative protagonists so frequently claimed. They were seeking to be accommodated and included within essentially traditional constructs of marriage and family based on conjugal relationships of longevity, if not permanence, that looked very much like many heterosexual marriages and families except when it came to the gender of the spouses. Many of the gays and lesbians actively involved in the campaign, as either advocates or litigants, were Christians who wanted to retain their faith and involvement in their churches. Members of the United Church or other Protestant denominations sought to have their marriages performed within those churches recognized in law. Indeed, in 2003 the United Church of Canada adopted a resolution calling upon the federal government to recognize same-sex marriages in law.

Reverend Brent Hawkes of the Metropolitan Community Church of Toronto was not only one of the leading advocates in the campaign, but was also notable for generating considerable publicity by performing marriage ceremonies at his church—marriages that the Ontario government refused to recognize as being legal on the grounds that same-sex marriages did not meet the common-law definition of marriage. The Metropolitan Community Church thus began to challenge the law governing solemnization of marriages, arguing that the law violated the equality rights guaranteed by the Charter.[44]

The opponents of same-sex marriage formed a broad coalition to intervene in the various marriage challenge cases, joining with governments in opposing the litigants. The by now familiar antagonists—including the EFC, Catholic Civil Rights League, B.C. Coalition for Marriage and Family, Association for Marriage and the Family, Ontario Conference of Catholic Bishops, Focus on the Family, and REAL Women—were joined in the cause by the Islamic Society of North America,

B.C. Council of Sikhs, B.C. Muslim Association, and Ontario Council of Sikhs. Organized social conservatism was successfully branching out beyond evangelical Protestants and conservative Catholics, at least insofar as the defence of marriage was concerned.

Initially the interventions proved to be successful. The first pronouncement of a court, in a 2001 case known as *Barbeau v. British Columbia (Attorney General)*, was extremely negative towards the legalization of gay marriage—ruling that only legislatures, and not judges, could make the decision to include same-sex couples in the common-law definition of marriage. Not only that, the judge in this case opined that even Parliament could not amend the definition of marriage because that would involve amending the Constitution. In effect, he concluded, the meaning of marriage had been definitively determined in 1867 and could not be legally defined to include same-sex couples without recourse to the process for amending the Constitution. The judge accepted the argument put forward by the social conservative intervenors that granting same-sex couples the right to legally marry would diminish heterosexual marriage and indeed the institution of marriage itself. The social conservative groups embraced the judgment and cited it often in their entreaties to politicians. An article in *The Interim* boasted that the decision was a "stinging defeat for supporters of homosexual marriage."[45] Not surprisingly, the same-sex couples in British Columbia appealed the decision.

Courts in other parts of the country took a different approach on the marriage question. In an Ontario case, *Halpern v. Canada (Attorney General)*, a Divisional Court decision in July 2002 found that the common-law definition of marriage infringed the equality rights of same-sex couples under section 15 of the Charter. Similarly, in a Quebec case, *Hendricks v. Canada*, the Quebec Superior Court ruled in September 2002 that the statutory definition of marriage contained in the Quebec Civil Code and the federal harmonization legislation were discriminatory and contravened section 15. Both courts held that the discrimination could not be justified under section 1 of the Charter and gave the legislatures twenty-four months in which to amend the respective statutes.

In response the Catholic Civil Rights League's Philip Horgan charged that the Ontario court was "dictating to Parliament, and all Canadians, a radically different approach to the shared understanding of an institution which is at the core of society." He attacked the court for its failure "to provide explicit protection to religious communities and other conscientious objectors to a definition of marriage which is sinful or which they would find objectionable." The result was, moreover, "intrusion of a new definition of marriage by court fiat."[46]

Egale, meanwhile, used the judgments to denounce the federal government for "wasting taxpayers' money fighting to discriminate against its own citizens."

Egale called on the federal government to respect the decisions and immediately bring in legislation to recognize same-sex marriages.[47] The Chrétien government instead announced that it would appeal the Ontario decision. Indeed, in documents filed with the appeal courts in support of its arguments, the federal government sided squarely with the social conservative groups. Its core argument was that heterosexual procreation is the "fundamental objective" of marriage. To which Egale executive director John Fisher responded, "The government's attempt to portray marriage as nothing more than *a breeding program for heterosexuals* is completely offensive" and "an *insult to Canadians*."[48]

In arguing its case, the federal government was continuing to uphold the old moral standard of the Christian church and the heterosexual presumption about marriage that the courts, for the most part, had recently rejected. The Liberal government, which loudly touted itself as the champion of Charter rights, was hypocritically attempting to thwart the expansion of those rights, apparently content to argue that religious rather than secular moral values should dictate what rights were accorded to individuals whose sexuality and lifestyles were contrary to the teachings of the churches. Most ironically, Chrétien as prime minister was now heading a government vigorously defending discriminatory marriage laws in opposition to the new morality of rights and equality of treatment that the courts were saying the Charter required to be reflected in law—a Charter that, as justice minister in the 1980s, Chrétien had played a key role in drafting and enacting.

The courts did not support the position of the government and its social conservative allies. B.C. and Ontario Appeal Court decisions issued in May and June 2003 ruled that the opposite-sex definition of marriage established by common law contravened section 15 of the Charter and could not be justified under section 1. The B.C. Appeal Court gave the government a date in 2004 by which to rewrite the definition to comply with the Charter. The Ontario Court of Appeal took a different approach. Its decision took effect immediately, which meant that same-sex marriages would be legal in Ontario unless the federal government appealed to the Supreme Court. In Quebec the Catholic Civil Rights League had appealed the marriage decision because the Quebec government refused to do so. The Quebec Court of Appeal dismissed the CCRL's appeal in a decision issued in March 2004.

Sensing that they were on the losing side of the issue, social conservative groups had attempted, in their various submissions to the courts, to broaden the matter by complaining bitterly that their religious rights would be infringed should same-sex marriage become legal. They argued that denying same-sex couples the opportunity to marry in their churches would put them into conflict with the state and with the values of Canadian society as reflected in the laws. That in turn would marginalize the churches and their devout followers. They also asserted that religious practitioners should be able to continue to condemn homosexuality with impunity. In other words, they adopted a rights argument for themselves and at the same time defended their own intolerant calls for denial of the rights of gays and lesbians. In doing so, they created a dynamic in which the right of gays and lesbians to be free from discrimination was put in conflict with their own right to religious freedom and expression. The courts would be required, they hoped, to choose which right should be paramount.

Indeed, the grave threat to religious freedom cited by the social conservative advocacy leaders was an important feature of their exhortations to their followers to support the defence of marriage campaign both financially and politically. Darrel Reid and Focus on the Family founder James C. Dobson called upon supporters to help in their efforts by asserting that there was a campaign afoot "to deprive religious Canadians—particularly those of us who hold the Word of God as our guide—of their constitutional freedom to speak and act in faithful obedience to their Creator."[49] The EFC adopted the same tactic. Among the dire consequences that confronted the religious, the EFC declared, was that clergy, acting "as agents of the provincial government," would lose "their ability, as a matter of conscience and religious freedom, to refuse to marry same-sex couples." The clergy would be "challenged under human rights codes" and "it is unlikely that churches, clergy and religious institutions that do not recognize same-sex marriage will escape legal action."[50]

The contention—that religious freedom would be threatened or infringed by granting legal recognition to same-sex couples—was something that the various court decisions on marriage had directly addressed; and it was in this regard that they most demonstrably exercised the accommodation and compromise approach. The Quebec Superior Court judgment noted:

> No-one would deny that religions have played an important role in marriage—indeed, their beliefs and their rites have framed the institution. The secularization of marriage, however, requires government to recognize that the institution is a civil one, and cannot be defined exclusively by religion.... The State must ensure respect for every citizen, but no group has the right to impose its values on others or to define a civil institution.[51]

The Quebec Court of Appeal also pointedly noted, "On the one hand, the sole question at issue is that of civil marriage, and on the other, an explicit provision of law allows any member of the clergy to refuse to solemnize a marriage when a religious impediment exists."[52]

Similarly, the B.C. Court of Appeal pronounced with clarity and certainty:

> Contrary to the assertion of the Interfaith Coalition—I cannot conclude
> that freedom of religion would be threatened or jeopardized by legally
> sanctioning same-sex marriage. No religious body would be compelled
> to solemnize same-sex marriage against its wishes and all religious
> people—of any faith—would continue to enjoy the freedom to hold and
> espouse their beliefs.[53]

The Ontario judgment in *Halpern v. Canada* made exactly the same point:

> Nor is this a case of balancing the rights of same-sex couples against
> the rights of religious groups who oppose same-sex marriage. Freedom
> of religion under s. 2(a) of the Charter ensures that religious groups
> have the option of refusing to solemnize same-sex marriages. The
> equality guarantee, however, ensures that the beliefs and practices of
> various religious groups are not imposed on persons who do not share
> those views.[54]

Ignoring the reassurances, social conservative activists condemned the marriage decisions. REAL Women attacked the Ontario Court of Appeal justices as "political appointees" who "used their unelected positions to impose their own vision on the country—a vision based not on law, but on their own politically correct ideology." These judges "had the arrogance to change the definition of marriage." Appealing to the politicians to abandon the courts altogether on the question, REAL Women declared, "To restore democracy to Canada, Parliament must undertake a pre-emptive strike by assuming its proper role in determining public policy, by defining the legal definition of marriage, rather than relinquishing this role to unscreened, unscrutinized judges."[55] For REAL Women, the solution rested with Parliament leapfrogging over the despicable judges, taking matters into its own hand, and legislating unequivocally the opposite-sex definition of marriage. In effect, the organization was arguing that Christian religious dictates about marriage should be imposed on all Canadians.

Charles McVety, president of the Canada Family Action Coalition, also condemned the marriage decisions and called on the federal government to appeal *Halpern* to the Supreme Court. Rogusky of Focus on the Family charged that the Ontario Court of Appeal "has devalued the institution of marriage." He lashed out at the activism of judges: "Our unelected judiciary has taken upon itself the powers of the legislative branch of government and has created an edict for Parliament to enforce." Rogusky urged the federal government to appeal the decision. Otherwise "the democratic process has been rewritten by a judiciary eager to re-engineer society."[56]

Urging an appeal to the Supreme Court seemed to be a curious tactic. After all, the social conservative groups had stridently denounced the judicial activism of such groundbreaking decisions as *Vriend* and *M. v. H.* as a hijacking of the democratic process by unaccountable judges. Now they were calling upon that same maligned judiciary to give a further and final determination of the issue of same-sex marriage. Politically, however, the call for an appeal made a great deal of sense. An appeal to the Supreme Court would have the benefit of postponing any move by the federal government to introduce a statutory change to the definition of marriage. It would give the social conservative forces more time to mount a campaign of political opposition. Despite *M. v. H.*, which had not addressed the question of marriage, there was always the prospect that the Supreme Court might adopt the approach of the B.C. trial judge who found that the definition of marriage could not be changed by the courts.

The members of the social conservative movement launched a desperate, last-ditch campaign to defend traditional marriage, pouring their religious fervor into the cause and devoting their considerable human and financial resources in hope of securing a victory. They ardently hoped to sway public opinion and a majority of elected politicians that religious rights must necessarily trump the purported human rights of gays and lesbians—if marriage, as understood in the old world of Christendom and historically supported by the state, was to be saved.

The government responds

In the midst of the heightening battle to transform marriage, the political wing of social conservatism experienced its own transformative change. After the Reform Party evolved into the Canadian Alliance in 2000, the new party's policy statement proudly proclaimed: "We believe that the family unit is essential to the well being of individuals and society because that is where children learn values and develop a sense of responsibility. Therefore, government legislation and programs should support and respect the Canadian family." Bills and regulations would be evaluated to ensure that their effect on the family was positive. The family, the Canadian Alliance emphasized so that there could be no uncertainty, meant "individuals related by blood, adoption or marriage," with marriage being understood to mean "the union of a man and woman" as recognized by the state.[57]

The leader of the Canadian Alliance, Stockwell Day, was an evangelical Protestant active in his local Pentecostal church in Alberta. During the leadership convention, groups militantly opposed to lesbian and gay rights had publicly endorsed Day for leader through the Alberta-based Families for Day. As a member of the Progressive Conservative government in Alberta, Day had strongly supported the traditional heterosexual family and opposed equality rights for gays. Families for Day enlisted the support of evangelical clergy across the country, urging them to solicit members of their churches to take out Canadian Alliance party memberships in order to be able to vote in the leadership ballot.[58]

Day's tenure as Canadian Alliance leader was short-lived. He led the new party in what was generally considered to be an inept and disastrous campaign during the federal election of November 2000. Having seen him as squandering the opportunity to defeat the Liberals, party members organized to oust Day as leader. A new leadership vote in early 2002 led to the victory of Stephen Harper, a former Reform Party MP. Like Day, Harper was also an evangelical Protestant, a congregant of Christian and Missionary Alliance churches. During the leadership contest, he had accepted the endorsement of the Concerned Christian Coalition, a group that had supported Day during the 2000 leadership campaign. The coalition, consisting of individuals and small Christian businesses, organized a drive to encourage Pentecostal and other evangelical church members to support Harper.[59] Under the leadership of Harper, the defence of traditional, heterosexual marriage remained central to Canadian Alliance policy.

So armed, the Canadian Alliance was soon presented with an opportunity to exploit the same-sex marriage issue for electoral gain by catering to the all-important social conservative constituency. That opportunity came when Chrétien announced that the federal government would not further appeal the Ontario Court of Appeal decision: "Rather, we will be proposing legislation that includes and legally recognizes the union of same-sex couples." Yet, fully aware of the extent of social conservative opposition to the measure inside and outside of Parliament, Chrétien also stated that the legislation would reflect the accommodation and compromise approach by at the same time protecting "the right of churches to sanctify marriage as they define it."[60]

To strike such a balance, the text of the proposed Civil Marriage Act unveiled by the government stated: "Nothing in this Act affects the freedom of officials of religious groups to refuse to perform marriages that are not in accordance with their religious beliefs." The draft legislation was then referred to the Supreme Court of Canada for review to determine three questions: whether defining marriage in law was within the exclusive legislative authority of Parliament; whether extending the capacity to marry to persons of the same sex would be consistent with the Charter; and whether the freedom of religion guaranteed by the Charter protected religious officials from being compelled to perform a same-sex marriage if that was contrary to their religious beliefs.[61]

Although all of the social conservative groups organized massively to defeat the legal redefinition of marriage, their approaches showed significant differences. REAL Women and the EFC announced that they would intervene in the Supreme Court reference case. The EFC intervention would argue against same-sex marriage, citing "the broader freedom of individuals and organizations, religious or otherwise, to promote and support the common understanding of marriage as only a union of one man and one woman." In contrast, the Canada Family Action Coalition, ever mistrustful of the courts and activist judges, opted not to intervene in the reference case. Instead, CFAC began feverishly lobbying MPs. It preferred to focus on "the people who really matter—our elected representatives." CFAC's efforts apparently had an immediate impact. Over the weeks that followed Chrétien's announcement, Liberal MPs reported that their offices were flooded with calls and letters from "furious" constituents. "In the six years I've been in Parliament, no issue, not even remotely, has generated the calls and e-mails that this one has," said John McKay, a Liberal MP who opposed the bill.[62]

The Canadian Conference of Catholic Bishops also mobilized on the question, complaining in a letter to Chrétien that the proposed legislation "would mean devaluation of traditional marriage as the basis of the family and as an essential institution for the stability and equilibrium of society." The Calgary Roman Catholic bishop Fred Henry went even further, publicly declaring that the prime minister would burn in hell if he legalized same-sex marriage. Archbishop Marcel Gervais of Ottawa reprimanded the prime minister, warning him that he had lost his way as a Catholic.[63]

The government's announcement also generated a storm within the Liberal parliamentary caucus. A total of forty-eight Liberal MPs publicly declared their opposition to the proposed bill.[64] The Canadian Alliance introduced another motion calling on Parliament to affirm that marriage should remain a union of one man and one woman to the exclusion of all others, and said that Parliament should take all necessary steps to preserve traditional marriage. In contrast with the outcome on the identical motion adopted in 1999, MPs narrowly defeated this motion, with 137 MPs voting against and 132 voting in support, including 53 Liberals. It appears that MPs, especially in the Liberal Party, who had once opposed same-sex marriage had been persuaded by the rulings of the courts that the Charter required equal treatment of same-sex couples. Yet while the defeat of the marriage motion had great symbolic and political significance, in practical terms it changed nothing. A law would still be required to explicitly provide legal recognition for same-sex marriages.

The opposing sides gear up

A full-scale, national advocacy campaign to defend the privileged legal status of heterosexual marriage and oppose same-sex marriage was launched with great fanfare during the summer and fall of 2003. The Canadian Conference of Catholic Bishops called upon Catholic politicians and lay persons alike to do everything possible to resist the legalization of same-sex marriage. Priests across the country urged parishioners to lobby against same-sex marriage by writing, faxing, or phoning their MPs. In Toronto Archbishop Ambrozic sent a letter to 223 congregations advising that it was "imperative" that priests use the pulpit to speak out against same-sex marriage legislation.[65]

A national campaign, Millions for Marriage, was organized "to defend the traditional definition of marriage." Supported by REAL Women, CFAC, and other groups, and organized by McVety, Millions for Marriage held Sanctity of Marriage Week rallies throughout Canada in September 2003. The events included assembling in front of offices of MPs "for prayer and proclamation." The members also announced their intention to target for defeat in the next election thirty federal MPs who had failed to oppose same-sex marriage and won their seats by small margins. Legions of the devout were enlisted as "all assemblies of worship" were urged to distribute a Family Action Bulletin that provided suggestions for lobbying MPs and provincial representatives. A Rally Declaration proclaimed:

> The redefinition of the sacred term marriage would mean a devaluation of traditional marriage as the basis of the family and as an essential institution for the stability and equilibrium of society.... Because it pre-exists the State and because it is fundamental for society, the institution of marriage cannot be modified, whether by the Charter of Rights, the State or a court of law.[66]

In July 2003 Harper attacked the government's move to introduce legislation to recognize same-sex marriage. Arguing that Parliament should vote on the bill before it was presented to the Supreme Court, Harper expressed grave concern over what he charged was the erosion of religious freedom embodied in the legislation. In harmony with his social conservative constituents, he also opined that the issue of same-sex marriage was one of "social values, and not, as some have been saying, a matter of human rights or equality."[67] He maintained the anti-gay marriage stance in fall 2003 following the successful merger of the Canadian Alliance Party with the Progressive Conservative Party to form the new Conservative Party of Canada. Led by Harper, the new party inherited a strong social conservative core among party activists and a huge social conservative electoral constituency that it could draw on for support. Opposition to legally recognizing same-sex marriage was an important plank in the party's political platform.

Developments within the Liberal Party also encouraged the leaders of the movement for the defence of marriage. Chrétien was replaced as Liberal leader and prime minister in late 2003 by Paul Martin, who was reportedly uncomfortable with the issue of legalizing same-sex marriage.[68] Indeed, for the first few months of the Martin government, it looked as if the social conservative lobbying and the opposition within the Liberal caucus were prompting serious reconsideration of legislative options. Early in 2004 the Supreme Court was asked to address a fourth question: whether the opposite-sex requirement for marriage was consistent with the Charter. Adding this option broadened the scope of solutions that might be available to the government. If the Court were to rule that retaining the traditional definition of marriage did not violate the equality rights of the Charter, the door would be opened for establishing a marriage-like same-sex union status while reserving marriage exclusively for heterosexuals. It would create a viable "separate but equal" option as a compromise. It would also establish in law that same-sex relationships were significantly different from heterosexual marriages, while according equal treatment to same-sex relationships in terms of rights and responsibilities. Same-sex couples would be recognized, but the definition of marriage would be unchanged and retain its privileged status in law.

For the Martin government, the modified reference to the Supreme Court conveniently put off the need to take any political action until after a federal election could be held. But at the same time, it guaranteed that same-sex marriage would be a hot and divisive issue in that election. While the government awaited the Supreme Court's pronouncement, a nasty defence of marriage campaign raged throughout 2004. Social conservative advocates became shriller, issuing dark threats about the imminent decline of godly Canadian society. Demonstrations, prayer vigils, petitions, and public advertising campaigns attempted to sway public opinion against same-sex marriage and to persuade enough members of Parliament to vote against the government's bill.

Egale Canada also intensified its efforts to secure political support for same-sex marriage. In July 2003 a group of religious leaders from several faiths spoke out publicly in support of same-sex marriage. In doing so, they sent a strong message that not all Christians supported the doctrinaire and intolerant position of the social conservative groups. Individual clergy within the Anglican, United Church, Unitarian, Religious Society of Friends (Quakers), and Lutheran churches joined with the Canadian Coalition of Liberal Rabbis for Same-Sex Marriage to support the proposed civil marriage law granting legal recognition to same-sex marriage. As importantly, they contradicted the views of the social conservative groups by agreeing that "the federal Bill affirms religious freedom by recognizing the right of all religions to marry or not marry same-sex couples in accordance with the principles of their faith."[69]

The Roman Catholic Church was also experiencing dissent on the issue. A small number of Catholic priests who spoke out in support of same-sex marriage invoked the wrath of the Church's hierarchy, and faced swift retribution. Reverend Tim Ryan was suspended by the Archbishop of Toronto from being permitted to celebrate mass in public or to preach in a church after he signed an affidavit as part of a Metropolitan Community Church Toronto submission that supported same-sex marriage. Ryan had volunteered for over thirty years with gay and lesbian Catholics, holding mass and offering counselling. He lamented in a news report after his disciplining, "I've struggled hard for 42 years to stay in the Church. It's really not a tradition friendly to dissent." Reverend Paul Lundrigan, a Catholic priest in a parish outside of St. John's, Newfoundland, was "silenced and censored" and ordered not to speak out on the issue. Lundrigan had criticized the Church's campaign against same-sex marriage as hypocritical when it had remained silent on cases of priests sexually abusing children. "It's either the party line, or say nothing at all," Lundrigan commented. In Thunder Bay, Ontario, Reverend Scott Gale told his parishioners that they should not just "parrot" the Pope's position on same-sex marriage. He was admonished by the Church for urging parishioners "to think for themselves about the debate."[70]

In response to the Sanctity of Marriage coalition, Egale Canada also established its own broadly based coalition in support of same-sex marriage. Canadians for Equal Marriage was launched in September 2003, in recognition that Egale "cannot fight this battle alone." In addition to Egale, Canadians for Equal Marriage included Parents and Friends of Lesbians and Gays, Canada, Canadian Federation of Students, Canadian Labour Congress, Canadian Psychological Association, and Canadian Association of University Teachers. It immediately presented a petition to MPs calling for the adoption of the same-sex marriage bill. The petition was signed by 20,000 people in communities large and small across Canada. The coalition also undertook a vigorous campaign to lobby and educate MPs on the issue. In its first two weeks of organizing, Canadians for Equal Marriage generated through its website a phenomenal 1.3 million e-mail messages to MPs supporting the passage of same-sex marriage legislation.[71]

Despite these impressive efforts, the enormity of the opposition within Parliament, especially among MPs from outside Quebec, spoke volumes about the influence of social conservative advocates, as well as the volatility of Canadian public opinion on the question of same-sex marriage. Except in Quebec, where there was majority support for legalizing same-sex marriage, Canadians were almost equally divided in their positions. Public opinion polls during this period had consistently shown fluctuations in support and opposition within a narrow range of about 5 to 10 per cent. At best, a bare majority was supportive; at worst, the number of Canadians either for or against gay marriage was divided, with support and opposition generally being in the low 40 per cent range.[72] This split in public opinion allowed social conservatives to rightfully claim that their opposition was consistent with the views of a significant cross-section, if not a majority, of the Canadian population. Indeed, the number of Canadians opposed to same-sex marriage far surpassed the number of members of evangelical Protestant congregations, and included large numbers of Catholics and, ever more demonstrably, the ranks of conservatives of Muslim, Jewish, Hindu, and Sikh faiths. A substantial opposition also existed among older Canadians and those living in small and rural communities. These various factors gave the organized social conservatives the benefit of more mainstream support.

The political clash over the legal definition of marriage reached a crescendo during the federal election of 2004. The social conservative groups went all out to ensure that candidates who opposed same-sex marriage were elected and those who supported it were not. Among the more high-profile efforts was a Focus on the Family advocacy campaign that featured a series of radio and newspaper advertisements urging Canadians to vote for candidates who supported traditional marriage. A number of MPs in tight races who had supported same-sex marriage were targeted for defeat. The Conservative Party, along with a substantial number of Liberal candidates, aggressively staked out anti-same-sex marriage positions.

The Conservatives in particular attempted to use the same-sex marriage issue to their advantage in the hope of toppling Martin's Liberal government, and the Conservative election platform was committed to giving Parliament, not the courts, the final decision on the question. Harper stated that he would withdraw the Liberal government's marriage reference to the Supreme Court. Instead of legislating same-sex marriage, a Conservative government would introduce a law upholding the traditional definition of marriage, in conjunction with establishing a separate civil union status for same-sex relationships.[73]

These developments emboldened and encouraged the defence of marriage advocates. Victory, they thought, would take the form of a Conservative government headed by the pro-marriage, evangelical Harper, who would be supported on the crucial issue by a sizable number of Liberal opposition MPs.

In the June 2004 election the Liberals barely staved off defeat. Their extremely precarious minority meant that they needed significant opposition support to ensure the passage of their legislation in general, and in particular to pass any same-sex marriage bill that they might want to eventually introduce. With the staunch opposition of Conservative MPs and the continuing presence of about forty anti-gay-marriage MPs within the reduced Liberal caucus, support for the government's bill would have to be obtained from the NDP and Bloc Québécois. While both of these parties had emerged with significant increases in the numbers of their MPs, the passage of the same-sex marriage bill was by no means certain.

Social conservative groups and their parliamentary supporters, accordingly, continued to organize against the proposed civil marriage bill, while waiting for the outcome of the Supreme Court reference. Meanwhile, the courts in several other provinces followed the direction set by Ontario, British Columbia, and Quebec and issued judgments recognizing same-sex marriages. By summer 2005, only Alberta, Prince Edward Island, and the Northwest Territories retained a legal definition of marriage that exclusively recognized opposite-sex couples.

The Supreme Court opines

The Supreme Court finally heard the marriage reference case in October 2004. The stakes were high for both same-sex marriage advocates and for their social conservative opponents.

A parade of social conservative groups intervened in defence of the traditional definition of marriage.[74] A prominent argument was that God's ideal of opposite-sex marriage predated civil law and was not by its very nature discriminatory or in contravention of the Charter. Legalizing same-sex marriage would destabilize society. According to the submission of the Interfaith Coalition, it would have "uncertain and unanticipated effects upon these religious communities and society as a whole." A common refrain was that religious freedom would be gravely and irreparably harmed. People of faith, particularly officials of religious groups who refused to perform marriages that were not in accordance with their religious faith, would be dragged before human rights commissions or the courts and punished.

Other adverse consequences, the Interfaith Coalition argued, would be denial of public benefits, including a loss of charitable status, memberships, accreditations, licences, and other regulatory approvals from public institutions. Religious institutions might be required to make their physical facilities (houses of worship, schools, recreational halls, camps) available for same-sex weddings or for wedding receptions. Clergy might be required to make premarriage counselling available to same-sex couples. Human rights commissions might require religious institutions to recognize the same-sex marriages of their members or employees. Most horrifically of all, they contended, parents might be "compelled to acquiesce in their children being inculcated in a doctrine of marriage contrary or hostile to their religious beliefs." The Canadian Conference of Catholic Bishops declared in its submission: "The Federal government's proposed legislation would result in two grave harms: it would eliminate the state's interest in protecting and promoting, for its benefit, the institution of marriage and it would impose an orthodoxy that contravenes freedom of conscience and religion."[75]

A long list of intervenors argued in support of the same-sex marriage law.[76] Both the Canadian Civil Liberties Association and the B.C. Civil Liberties Association specifically dismissed concerns about infringement of religious freedom. The CCLA stated, "Defining the secular institution of civil marriage in terms that do not happen to coincide with a particular conception of a divine will does not threaten the legitimate interests of religious groups or individuals." In addition, BCCLA argued, "Government sanctioned same-sex marriages will not compel religious officials to perform marriages of same-sex couples that are contrary to their religious beliefs because church officials are not required to solemnize marriages which their religion does not condone."[77]

The Supreme Court's historic decision, released on December 9, 2004, was a blow to the hopes of the social conservative groups that marriage would remain a privileged heterosexual institution in law. A unanimous decision by nine justices found that the proposed same-sex marriage law was consistent with the Charter and that the federal Parliament had exclusive authority to legislate a change in the definition of marriage. The justices also resoundingly rejected the argument that the opposite-sex definition of marriage enunciated in the common law "spoke to a society of shared social values where marriage and religion were thought to be inseparable. This is no longer the case. Canada is a pluralistic society. Marriage, from the perspective of the state, is a civil institution." The Court had not only demarcated the separation of religious faith from law and public policy, but also once more articulated that the new morality of rights and equality of treatment had replaced the old religious morality as the dominant condition that the state must take into consideration. Noting that Canada's Constitution is "a living tree," which, by way of progressive interpretation, accommodates and addresses the realities of modern life, the justices held that the word "marriage" in the Constitution did not exclude same-sex marriage.[78]

Still, the justices offered some solace to the social conservative groups on the question of religious freedom. They stated, "Absent unique circumstances with respect to which the Court will not speculate, the guarantee of religious freedom in s. 2(a) of the Charter, is broad enough to protect religious officials from being compelled by the state to perform civil or religious same-sex marriages that are contrary to their religious beliefs." The justices also rejected the contention that "the mere legislative recognition of the right of same-sex couples to marry would have the effect of discriminating against (1) religious groups who do not recognize the right of same-sex couples to marry (religiously) and/or (2) opposite-sex married couples." No submissions had been made to show how the proposed act might be seen to draw such a distinction, they noted, "nor can the Court surmise how it might be seen to do so." However, they added, "The mere recognition of equality rights of one group cannot, in itself, constitute a violation of rights of another."

The justices also dismissed the argument that the proposed act would impose a dominant social ethos and thereby limit the freedom to hold religious beliefs to the contrary. They noted, "The protection of freedom of religion afforded by s. 2(a) of the Charter is broad and jealously guarded in our Charter jurisprudence." They also observed that it was the provinces and not the federal parliament that had the authority to legislate the rights of religious officials who provide for the solemnization of marriages. But they expressed the view that any law enacted that compelled religious officials to perform same-sex marriage "would almost certainly run afoul of the Charter guarantee of freedom of religion." It would also be contrary to the Charter to require "compulsory use of sacred places for the celebration of such marriages."[79]

Despite the careful reasoning and assurances of the Supreme Court, social conservative groups responded with fury to the decision. The most extreme reaction came from a new group, Enshrine Marriage Canada, which had dedicated itself to securing a constitutional amendment to establish a heterosexual definition of marriage. "Canadians should refuse to acknowledge the moral validity of any law that attempts to redefine marriage. Instead, they should enshrine the historic definition of marriage as the union of one man and one woman in Canada's Constitution."[80] The organization's objective was wildly impractical. Obtaining a constitutional amendment on any matter, let alone the definition of marriage, is nearly impossible—it requires the support of at least seven provinces with at least 50 per cent of the population. Enshrine Marriage Canada's proposition found no support outside a small coterie of the most extreme and incensed social conservatives.

The utterances of the more well-known social conservative groups were only slightly less extreme. The Catholic Civil Rights League denounced the decision "as an unprecedented pre-empting of parliamentary debate by the judiciary." Phil Horgan, now the league's president, asserted, "Involving the court at this stage was an attempt to circumvent the democratic process in order to impose a fundamental social change that many Canadians do not want. This is a bad and dangerous precedent."[81] Brian Rushfeldt, executive director of the Canada Family Action Coalition, called for a national referendum on the matter: "The process for a fair decision on the definition of marriage has been so corrupted, polluted and politicized by less than 30 judges and maneuvers by the Liberal government, that the only way to resolve this divisive matter is a full vote by Canadians." Claiming to speak for all heterosexually married Canadians, Rushfeldt added, "It is offensive to all married people to be told their unique and sacred relationship is now the same as homosexual relations." Added CFAC president McVety, "You do not need to desecrate the sacred institution of marriage to protect the rights of others."[82]

Other groups were more muted in their responses. Some of them attempted to find justification for their pro-marriage positions in the Supreme Court's decision. The EFC welcomed "the strong affirmation of religious freedom in the Court's reply." It opined, "While the Supreme Court has said that Parliament may redefine marriage, it has not said that it must redefine marriage to include same-sex couples." Terence Rolston, president of Focus on the Family, also noted positively that the ruling held that Parliament was not compelled to take such action.[83] But the Supreme Court decision left room for only a faint hope.

Egale Canada and Canadians for Equal Marriage both called on the government to act immediately to introduce legislation. Alex Munter, co-chair of Canadians for Equal Marriage, speaking in the language of the new secular morality, characterized the decision as "a green light to the government's proposed equal marriage legislation, reflecting Canadian values and Canadians' commitment to fairness." Gilles Marchildon, Egale's executive director, commented: "Equal marriage is something whose time has come.... Same-sex couples have been marrying for over a year and a half, and support for equal marriage is higher than it's ever been."[84] Their optimism would prove to be well-founded, although not immediately. The forces of social conservatism and their political cohorts in the Conservative Party were not yet quite finished.

Legislating same-sex marriage

The Canada Family Action Coalition, Focus on the Family, and REAL Women of Canada called for a referendum on same-sex marriage to be held at the time of the next federal election. Declaring that he was "thoroughly disappointed" with the Supreme Court decision, Alberta premier Ralph Klein lent his support to the referendum idea. He was joined by a number of federal Conservative Party MPs. Prime Minister Paul Martin ruled out a referendum as an option, declaring, "I think that this is an issue that parliamentarians ought to decide." Even Stephen

Harper supported that view, despite a strong sentiment for a referendum within his caucus. Gilles Duceppe of the Bloc Québécois and Jack Layton of the New Democratic Party went further in their rejection, arguing that it is wrong to subject minority rights to a majority vote in a referendum.[85]

With the referendum idea clearly rejected as an option, the social conservative groups mounted an intense lobbying campaign intended to pressure the Martin government to abandon any attempt to introduce same-sex marriage legislation. Focus on the Family used broadcasts on 130 radio stations to stir up opposition to same-sex marriage legislation. During December 2004 and January 2005 the Prime Minister's Office received 22,000 letters, 26,000 e-mails, and 1,000 telephone calls, about 90 per cent of them opposed to same-sex marriage. A large number of these quoted from the Bible. Other MPs also reported high volumes of mail and phone calls on the subject.[86] Early in 2005 the Canadian Conference of Catholic Bishops appealed to its followers in the churches of the country to lobby the government. Bishop Fred Henry of Calgary subsequently issued a pastoral letter that was widely condemned as an expression of outright hatred directed at homosexuals:

> Since homosexuality, adultery, prostitution and pornography undermine the foundations of the family, the basis of society, then the State must use its coercive power to proscribe or curtail them in the interests of the common good. It is sometimes argued that what we do in the privacy of our home is nobody's business. While the privacy of the home is undoubtedly sacred, it is not absolute. Furthermore, an evil act remains an evil act whether it is performed in public or private.[87]

Bishop Henry asked the devout to send letters, e-mails, and faxes to government leaders and other members of Parliament, "registering your objection to the proposal to reinvent the institution of marriage."

A few days later Cardinal Ambrozic publicly released a letter he had sent to Martin calling on him to maintain the heterosexual definition of marriage. Among other disastrous outcomes, legalizing same-sex marriage, Ambrozic contended, would force public schools to present heterosexuality and homosexuality as morally equal. A few days after that, Cardinal Marc Ouellet, Archbishop of Quebec and Primate of Canada, issued an open letter in which he stated alarmingly that youth would be irreparably harmed by the "confusion" that would be sown and would "trouble their minds" as a result of same-sex marriage. Declaring that a turning point in the evolution of Canadian society had been reached, he asserted, "The bill announced by the Government threatens to unleash nothing less than a cultural upheaval whose negative consequences are still impossible to predict." Taking his scare-mongering to a higher level, Ouellet suggested, "The choice to be made could bring in its wake bitter and unpredictable demographic, social, cultural, and religious consequences."[88]

In the midst of this opposition, and confronted with a bitterly divided Liberal caucus, the Martin government, on February 1, 2005, introduced Bill C-38, the Civil Marriage Act. It declared, "Marriage, for civil purposes only, is the lawful union of two persons to the exclusion of all others." In acknowledgement of the concerns expressed by religious groups, the bill also contained a provision stating, "It is recognized that officials of religious groups are free to refuse to perform marriages that are not in accordance with their religious beliefs." That qualification failed to appease critics. Bruce Clemenger, EFC president, dismissed the clause as "bland assertions." The Campaign Life Coalition condemned the bill as seeking to destroy marriage. Focus on the Family responded with a slick and impressive national newspaper advertising campaign. Eye-catching and attempting to project a moderate image of reasonableness and tolerance, the ads featured wholesome-looking young Canadians expressing the firm belief that "marriage is between a man and a woman" and urging like-minded citizens to write to their MPs.[89]

A new group headed by McVety called Defend Marriage Coalition launched a "marriage bus" resplendent with a red and white logo resembling Canada's maple leaf flag. The bus was deployed to rallies and demonstrations, especially targeting MPs, mostly from the Liberal Party, who might be undecided or at least open to changing their positions. For distribution to church congregations, the group also produced one million brochures advocating "traditional marriage." Half of the brochures were printed in Chinese, Spanish, Korean, and Tamil to reach out to members of minority communities. The Knights of Columbus joined in the cause, producing two million postcards that were circulated to Catholic parishes for mailing to MPs.[90]

The federal Conservative Party continued to campaign aggressively against same-sex marriage. Harper promised that should the Liberal's proposed bill not be adopted, the Conservatives, if elected to government, would enact legislation to ban same-sex marriage and maintain the opposite-sex definition. He also refused to rule out invoking the notwithstanding clause to maintain the ban, if the Supreme Court at some future date were to rule that an opposite-sex definition contravenes equality rights guaranteed by the Charter. Conservative Party newspaper advertisements featured Harper promising to preserve marriage as a right for heterosexual couples only and accusing Martin of "imposing" same-sex marriage on Canadians.[91]

In spring 2005, when Bill C-38 went before a parliamentary committee, the Conservatives, disregarding the pronouncement of the Supreme Court in the marriage reference case, accused the government of deceiving Canadians into believing that the bill would protect religious freedom. They denounced the clause added to the preamble as unconstitutional. A procession of social conservative advocates who appeared before the committee made similar arguments. McVety expressed the fear that people of faith would be "ghettoized" by the new law.[92] Douglas Farrow, representing Enshrine Marriage Canada, bitterly disparaged the religious freedom clause as hypocritical:

> C-38 places the vast majority of religious communities in this country—
> and this means the majority of Canadians—squarely on the side of the
> bigot. It makes them out to be purveyors of discrimination and, by some
> accounts, of hatred. What is more, it leaves them no option, if they wish
> to avoid this slur, but to keep their religious opinions to themselves and
> to conform their visible practices to those of the state. ... C-38 is the
> beginning of the end of religious freedom in Canada.[93]

Other social conservative presenters spoke with alarm about the profoundly negative change that would come to the country through the bill. Roy Beyer of the Defend Marriage Coalition said Bill C-38 would bring disruption to the harmony of Canada: "The spirit behind C-38 is profoundly anti-religious and motivated by a radical secularist agenda." It would lead to an "ongoing cultural war." Picking up on the refrain of persecution that formed the essence of many social conservative submissions, Beyer added, "Illegitimate lower court rulings (made by radical secularist, activist judges) forcing same-sex marriage upon Canadians have triggered an attitude of intolerance from individuals and governments towards those who disagree, on conscientious or religious grounds, with so-called 'same-sex marriage.'"[94]

The submissions made to the parliamentary committee had an impact. The committee adopted amendments that were responding to the arguments about the infringement of religious freedom. They added a new reassuring statement to the preamble: "It is not against the public interest to hold and publicly express diverse views on marriage." The act itself was amended to include a new clause that expressly addressed freedom of conscience and religion and expression of beliefs. It stated that no person or organization would be deprived of any benefit, or be subjected to any obligation or sanction under federal law solely for exercising their freedom of conscience and religion rights as guaranteed under the Charter or for expressing their religious beliefs regarding marriage. Given the strong and clearly articulated protections for freedom of religion and freedom of expression found in the various pronouncements of the courts, this inclusion seemed intended more to placate the social conservative opponents of the law than to

provide greater protection for the expression of religious beliefs. Social conservatives continued to be seen as an important electoral constituency that was best not
left totally alienated.

Still, that concession was clearly not enough. To keep the pressure on, Defend
Marriage Coalition held rallies and prayer vigils across the country. One of the
largest, held at Queen's Park in Toronto in May, was attended by a crowd estimated at about 3,000 to 5,000 people. Participants expressed the fear that priests
and other clergy would be "charged" for refusing to marry same-sex couples in
churches.[95] Just days before the final vote on Bill C-38 in the House of Commons,
in an "Immediate Call for Prayer," Rushfeldt urged "all of us as God's Church"
to "Pray that the political leaders do not open themselves and this nation to the
enemy in this matter." One of the specific areas cited for prayer focus was that "MPs
will not be influenced and directed by an anti-Christ spirit, but will be influenced
by the Spirit of God and righteousness."[96]

Those prayers proved to be futile. On June 28, 2005, following a long and
acrimonious debate, Bill C-38 was passed in the House of Commons on final reading by a vote of 158 to 133. The Senate gave approval to Bill C-38 in less than a
month, and Royal Assent was given on July 20, 2005.

The aftermath

REAL Women denounced Bill C-38 as "contemptible." For social conservatives, the forces of evil had been (temporarily) victorious over the righteous and
the godly, but the defence of heterosexual marriage would be continued with resolution and vigour. "Parliament is embarking on a social experiment that removes
the language of husband and wife from the law and eclipses its ability to champion
the rights of children to know and be raised by a mother and a father," declared
Clemenger. People of faith, he lamented, "have been made to feel our beliefs about
marriage are unCanadian and contrary to the Charter." The Canadian Conference
of Catholic Bishops decried Bill C-38's dangerous potential: "What is also at risk
is the future of marriage as a fundamental social institution, together with the
importance that society accords the irreplaceable role of a husband and wife in
conceiving and raising children." The Defend Marriage Coalition called on supporters to not forget June 28, 2005, "the day that Paul Martin broke faith with the
citizens of Canada with his agenda to destroy the sacred and precious institution
of marriage."[97]

Social conservatives were urged to disregard this "undemocratic" new law.
In a public statement the Canadian Conference of Catholic Bishops urged defi-
ance on the part of the faithful, pronouncing that "the new federal statute falsifies

moral values and principles. Catholics are to continue to oppose it." Douglas Farrow of Enshrine Marriage encouraged Canadians to reject the law: "Canadians are under no obligation to adopt the positivist view that a law is valid simply because it is passed by a duly constituted authority." As for the way forward for those refusing to recognize same-sex marriage, "For all, it will mean vigilance against the growing statism that, under the cover of a perverted 'rights' discourse, now threatens us with a new and dangerous Leviathan." The Canada Family Action Coalition condemned "the dictatorial imposition of homosexual marriage [that] began with a few judges overriding Parliament." Rushfeldt made an astonishing claim: "This is the most illegitimate legislation a Canadian government has ever passed. When legislation is illegitimate, then it is likely that most Canadians will continue to oppose it and even ignore it. . . . The people of Canada will not forget this mockery of justice and democracy."[98]

Several of the social conservative responses included a vow to punish politicians who voted in support of Bill C-38. They "will be held accountable," declared Horgan of the Catholic Civil Rights League. REAL Women predicted that imposing same-sex marriage, "which is unacceptable to the majority of Canadians," would lead to the defeat of the Liberals in the next election and to the downfall of "this despotic Prime Minister and his cronies."[99]

The leaders of social conservatism clearly wanted to demonstrate to their members and supporters that they had not given up the fight to save marriage. After all, the grassroots of their movement had fought for nearly three decades to defend and preserve family values and traditional marriage. They had written the letters, signed the petitions, sent in their financial contributions, attended the countless prayer rallies and demonstrations, and prayed for their God to recognize and reward their efforts. The adoption of Bill C-38 was a crushing defeat for a movement that had progressed and indeed prospered by bashing homosexuals and what they considered the grotesque notion of gay rights. Now, without the defence of marriage as a call to arms, the advocacy agenda of the social conservative groups suddenly looked a little scant—raising the question of whether the movement had sufficient ground on which to sustain itself in the long term.

Despite the denunciations and bold predictions of the social conservative leadership, the Canadian population was apparently content to put to rest the same-sex marriage issue once and for all. A poll conducted following the adoption of Bill C-38 revealed that 55 per cent of Canadians surveyed stated that the next government should let the legislation stand. Only 39 per cent expressed the view that efforts should be made to repeal it, and 6 per cent gave no opinion. In any event, by the end of 2004 same-sex marriages had already become legal in all but five provinces and territories. As a result of Bill C-38 coming into effect, the remaining provinces and territories now conceded the issue. Those jurisdictions accepted the federal legislation as the means by which same-sex marriages would be recognized within their boundaries.[100]

Even social conservative stalwart Ralph Klein announced that the Alberta government had no choice but to issue marriage licences to same-sex couples: "Our chances of winning are virtually none. The fact is the government can give hope as long it's legitimate hope, but we can't give false hope." Yet, unrepentant in his devotion to the cause, and on the day that the first same-sex marriage licence was issued in the province, Klein meanspiritedly declared, "It's a sad day for the majority of Albertans who believe in the traditional definition of marriage. We have to obey the law of the land, and it's unfortunate that such a law would be passed."[101]

Nonetheless, the various social conservative groups had a glimmer of hope. They remained optimistic that if the Conservative Party managed to form the next government, Harper and his MPs would fulfil their promise to repeal Bill C-38. In that case, the political battle over same-sex marriage would be engaged anew, and possibly have a different outcome. The Conservatives, for their part, vowed that, if elected, they would hold a vote in Parliament that would determine if MPs wanted to overturn the same-sex marriage law.

Indeed, shortly after winning the 2006 federal election and forming a minority government, Prime Minister Harper kept the promise made to hold a free vote on same-sex marriage, which he announced for later that year. A positive outcome on the question would result in the introduction of legislation to repeal the Civil Marriage Act created by Bill C-38 and establish instead a legal category of civil unions for same-sex relationships. The commitment was loudly cheered by social conservative groups, who mounted a new round of public advocacy and political lobbying that lasted for several months. Finally, in December 2006, the Conservative government introduced a resolution that "the House call on the government to introduce legislation to restore the traditional definition of marriage without affecting civil unions and while respecting existing same-sex marriages."

Although Harper kept his promise, he did so, apparently, with the knowledge that the resolution would be defeated. Public opinion by that time had become solidly supportive of not revisiting the legal definition of marriage. A new poll, published just days before, indicated that now fully 58 per cent of Canadians would vote to retain the same-sex marriage law while only 36 per cent favoured its repeal. More practically, the minority Conservative government depended on securing the support of a significant number of opposition members in Parliament to pass any legislation. Unless a sizable number of Liberals joined with the government in supporting the resolution, it was doomed to defeat. Not surprisingly, when the vote on the same-sex marriage resolution was held in the House of Commons, 175 MPs, including a small number of Conservatives, voted against it and only 123 MPs voted in favour. Harper calmly accepted the outcome. The question of same-sex marriage had been firmly and finally determined. There would be no going back. Parliament would not be asked again to deal with the issue.

Outside Parliament, same-sex marriage had become for most Canadians a non-issue. The apocalyptic predictions of the histrionic social conservative ideologues about the consequences that would result from same-sex marriage failed to come true. The vast majority of Canadians appear to have accepted with relative ease and tranquillity the idea that same-sex couples who wish to do so may now marry. And these couples are doing so in ways that are remarkably similar to their heterosexual friends and relatives—without any discernible effect on heterosexual families and marriages, on the status or recognition afforded to marriage, or on Canada as a whole.

Conflicting Rights and Clashing Values

Education continues to be a bastion of secular
foolishness. Promiscuity and even perverted
sexual practices are promoted to your children
as normal and healthy. Humanism is the
religion of public schools, teaching children
that mankind can create his own destiny
and morality.

– Brian Rushfeldt, 2001

Throughout its various campaigns and crusades, modern social conservatism has impressively kept its essence undiluted and virtually unchanged—and that essence, whether expressed through Protestant or Catholic activism, remains firmly rooted in Christian evangelicalism. As evangelicals, social conservative activists continue to take seriously the obligation to live their faith in all facets of their lives. Through the paradigm of evangelicalism, they stubbornly do not accept that religious belief can be separated from public policy, the political process, or the objectives of the state. They adamantly refuse to acquiesce to rampant secularism, the new morality of rights and equality of treatment, or the imperatives of what they would call "political correctness."

In response to the shifting winds, social conservatives have ascribed to themselves the role of the victimized and the persecuted—a beleaguered and increasingly repressed minority, believers who are no longer able to express their honestly held religious views and act in accordance with their moral values.

During its intervention before the Supreme Court of Canada in the consideration of same-sex marriage, the Interfaith Coalition on Marriage and the Family articulated this fundamental principle:

> Religion is, in part, an attempt to ascertain whether there is a universal order of reason and human freedom, and to align oneself with that order. Where a person is prevented from carrying out actions that he or she believes to be necessary to bring that order to his or her life, that person's integrity and moral character are harmed. For the state to force a person to carry out actions which are contrary to that order, is to force the person to forego the benefits from acting according to conscience, and to instead alienate that person from their actions.[1]

In particular, a protracted warfare in the public school systems of the country has fully, and dramatically, evidenced this grim resolve to take back control of the moral agenda and restore Judeo-Christian values as the defining values of Canada. In the education system social conservatives have battled tenaciously against a new moral mandate to teach and to ensure equality and tolerance for diversity, including, increasingly, sexual orientation diversity.

Fighting to control the moral agenda in the schools

The social conservative activism on this front has been nurtured by a profound resentment towards the transformation of the public schools from primary loci of indoctrination of children with religious values to indoctrination of secular values.[2] The movement activists have condemned the mutation of the public education system into what they have characterized as a morally barren wasteland without values based on any religion. They complain bitterly that these new imperatives are changing both the nature and the mandates of the public schools and are unacceptably infringing their religious freedom. According to Focus on the Family, in a 2003 statement, parents became angered because "the fundamentals are being sacrificed as schools focus on material they consider secondary and at odds with strongly held personal and family values." Years earlier the Evangelical Fellowship of Canada similarly declared, "A secular worldview, which restricts religion to private life, has become the prevailing framework of many public school systems."[3]

Over the last nearly forty years, through various campaigns and political advocacy, social conservative groups have fought tenaciously to reassert the mandate first given to public education in the 1850s to instil religion-based morality and values in children. They have advocated that schools must uphold the right of parents to dictate what their children are or are not taught regarding such matters as morality, values, sexuality, and family. They have contended that not only must religious and spiritual values be taught in the schools to ensure the proper indoctrination of children, but the children should also be taught the religious and spiritual values of their parents. Teachers and schools should do nothing to teach children or to inform them about anything that conflicts with those values. As the EFC pointed out, "Religion and spirituality are foundational to a student's quest for identity"—a claim the organization makes as if the statement were irrefutable fact or true for all children. "Further, students are to be encouraged to explore their own particular religious or spiritual traditions and the impact those have on shaping their own beliefs, values and visions of life."[4]

To the consternation of the EFC and the other social conservative groups, the relegation of religion to private life and the emphasis now placed on secular morality in the schools reflect the evolution of Canada into a vibrantly diverse society bearing little resemblance to what they characterize as the devoutly Christian country of old. In the area of school prayers, for example, it was once commonplace for children in public schools to be required to recite the Christian Lord's Prayer—even if the pupils were not Christians or had no religion. In 1988 the Ontario Court of Appeal ruled that practice to be unconstitutional, striking down a section of Ontario's Education Act that made the prayer mandatory for all students. The judgment resulted from a challenge by parents of Jewish children who argued that the Act contravened the right to freedom of religion and to equal treatment and benefit under the law guaranteed by the Charter. Similarly, and also in 1988, another Ontario regulation mandating Bible-based teachings in public school classrooms was ruled unconstitutional on Charter grounds. Reacting to the Court's decision, the Ontario government introduced a directive that banned all religious instruction from the public schools, even if the instruction was optional. In 1990 an Ontario Court of Appeal decision banned classes exclusively teaching Christian religious values in the public schools. The court ruled this practice to be a form of religious coercion.[5]

In Quebec the secularization of schools followed rapidly after the enactment in 1997 of legislation that reorganized the province's schools along linguistic rather than denominational lines. The denominational rights and privileges of both Roman Catholics and Protestants were removed by an amendment of the Constitution Act, 1867. At the same time, however, the Quebec Charter of Human

Rights and Freedoms granted the right of freedom of choice in regard to religious instruction and moral education in the public schools. In a pluralistic society in which equality of treatment was also guaranteed, this step meant that the schools of Quebec had to accommodate the religious and moral values of parents who subscribed to religions other than Christianity. To do otherwise would be discriminatory. Quebec established a policy that gave parents the choice of enrolling their children in Catholic, Protestant, or non-religious moral education.

To address the volatile issue of religion and moral instruction in the schools, the Parti Québécois government initiated a public consultation and a Task Force on the Place of Religion in Schools in Quebec. In its report, released in 2000, the task force recommended the establishment of "open, secular schools that would draw on the common values of citizens and include the study of both religious and secular world views." It also put forth the principle that "state policy on the question of religion in the schools must be subject to the requirement of egalitarian neutrality." It acknowledged, "Religion may have a place in schools, as a contribution to the development of the child as a whole person, provided its teaching is organized in a way that is consistent with the principle of fundamental equality of all citizens."[6]

In 2005 the Quebec legislature amended the Charter of Human Rights and Freedoms to delete from the "parental rights" section a reference to "in the public educational establishments," thus removing the right of parents to determine the type of religious instruction that would be given to their children in public schools. In 2008 the Liberal government implemented a non-denominational Ethics and Religious Culture Program to be taught at all levels within Quebec's elementary and secondary schools. The ethics portion of the program focused on the diversity and pluralism of society and on values such as freedom, equity, equality and justice, respect, and integrity. The "religious culture" portion of the program, while allowing students to become familiar with the religious heritage of Quebec, also taught them to become "open to religious diversity" and to "recognize that some people derive their view of life, death, suffering, etc. from sources other than religion."[7] The new program became mandatory for all students regardless of parents' preferences.

The Roman Catholic Church condemned the Ethics and Religious Culture Program. The Assembly of Quebec Catholic Bishops lamented that the school was "no longer a place for confessional religious instruction. Instead this responsibility has primarily been assigned to parishes and families."[8] Evangelical Protestant parents in Quebec joined Roman Catholics in the concern that parents had lost freedom of choice. They accused the Ethics and Religious Culture Program of being essentially anti-religious and undermining Quebec's Judeo-Christian heritage. A new conservative group, the Canadian Constitution Foundation, lent its support to these parents. In the words of John Carpay, its executive director, the program "denigrates and trivializes religions by portraying all of them as mere folklore." In 2009 the parents launched a court challenge to the Ethics and Religious Culture Program, citing infringement of their rights of freedom of religion and conscience in contravention of the Canadian Charter, Quebec Charter, and United Nations Universal Declaration of Human Rights.[9]

Certainly, though, other factors had propelled the secularization of public schools, including a recognition of the need to provide sex-education programs to youth. Another factor was the need to ensure that the schools teach, respect, and promote diversity, tolerance of differences, equality of treatment, and human rights. Gay and lesbian activists sought the eradication of homophobia in the schools and changes to curricula towards bias-free presentations of homosexuality and same-sex relationships (free from the biases of sin, sickness, and criminality that had historically characterized discussion). They also advocated for the establishment of proactive policies and programs to ensure safe and welcoming environments for openly gay and lesbian students and teachers in the school system.[10]

Social conservatives responded by defending their purported rights as parents to keep schools from indoctrinating their children with a "pro-homosexual" agenda. School boards in a number of cities became the sites of conflict and confrontation. Social conservative groups such as Renaissance Canada and Citizens United for Responsible Education (CURE) were joined by others, including REAL Women and EFC, in opposing the establishment of sexual-orientation anti-discrimination and anti-harassment policies, and the creation of programs and policies to address homophobia and acts of violence against gays and lesbians in the schools. They fought against changes to curricula that presented homosexuality and gay and lesbian people in morally non-judgmental ways. The result, once more, was a momentous conflict between the two oppositional social movements over what children should be taught.

REAL Women contended in 2005 that changes to school curricula sought by "homosexual activists" on the pretence of promoting "diversity" and "tolerance" and to "protect homosexual students from harassment and prejudice" were actually efforts to "indoctrinate our children." The inclusion of sexual orientation along with the "traditional categories" on which discrimination is prohibited had nothing to do with the "safety" of students, the critics said. Instead, it was a political tactic on the part of its advocates.

> When harassment based on sexual orientation is explicitly banned, schools' staff and students are inevitably trained to believe that the reason that such harassment is wrong is not because all harassment is wrong or because all people should be treated with respect, but because

there is nothing wrong with being gay or lesbian. Such an assertion is
not only offensive to the moral standards of most Canadians ... and to
the historical teachings of most major religions, it flies in the face of
hard scientific data showing high rates of promiscuity, physical disease,
mental illness, substance abuse, child sexual abuse, and domestic violence that often accompany homosexual behaviour.[11]

In addition, REAL Women charged, the homosexual activists were being aided and
abetted in their sinister plot to indoctrinate children by the courts, especially the
Supreme Court of Canada, human rights commissions, and "some school boards
[that] have betrayed this trust [that is, the authority delegated by parents to
school board trustees to teach their children] and instead are using their position
to *indoctrinate* children on the issue of homosexuality as a matter of fact." The way
to fight against "the homosexual agenda in schools," REAL Women argued, was
for parents who are concerned about "school boards across the country [that] are
also jumping on the pro-homosexual bandwagon" to assert their parents' rights by
writing to the schools to express concerns about "the promotion of homosexuality," and "object to your child being involved in any presentation which portrays
homosexuality as a normal, equal lifestyle choice." According to REAL Women,
parents needed to demand that their children be exempted from any such presentations, and parents should be prepared to face serious resistance from teachers
and the school administration when standing up for their rights.[12]

The EFC and Canada Family Action Coalition took up the same cause. CFAC
spokesperson Brian Rushfeldt asked, "Will schools be forced to teach children that
homosexual behaviour and same-sex marriages are normal and healthy?"[13] Ted
Morton, now a Progressive Conservative member of the Alberta legislature, had
warned in 2005, "The next battleground is the schools. We'll see teachers fired,
[church] schools losing public funding and hate-crimes litigation for refusing to
go along with 'tolerance education.'"[14]

Parents' rights, social conservative militants contend, are to be supreme over
any rights that may be claimed by other persons and most especially by gays and
lesbians. Parents' rights must thus be resolutely promoted and defended by the
state and its agent, the public school system. According to the EFC, "Parents have
the privilege and unique responsibility of leading their children to know God and
His ways as well as the world around them." CFAC declares, "We believe in policies
which protect the inherent right and responsibility of parents in the raising and
education of children."[15]

The Roman Catholic Church has also strongly asserted the right of parental
authority over children, especially in regard to education: "Since they have con-

ferred life on their children, parents have the original, primary and inalienable right to educate them; hence they must be acknowledged as the first and foremost educators of their children." The rights of parents, according to the Church's Charter of the Rights of the Family, include "the right to educate their children in conformity with their moral and religious convictions." The rights also include "the right to ensure that their children are not compelled to attend classes which are not in agreement with their own moral and religious convictions." Striking directly at what it considers the odious secularism of modern public education, the charter of family rights also asserts, "The rights of parents are violated when a compulsory system of education is imposed by the State from which all religious formation is excluded."[16]

For their part, according to this way of thinking, children receive no choice in how they are educated, or what values they are taught; they are primarily the property of the parents. For the kids, parents' rights demand compliance with the directive, given by the apostle Paul in the New Testament: "Children, obey your parents in all things; for this is well pleasing unto the Lord."[17] The interests of the parents are the best interests of the children. The parents know best and can impose their values and beliefs on the children, who must obey. The state has no role or right in determining what is in the best interests of the child, because only the parents have that right and the authority to exercise it.

In defence of parents' rights, social conservative groups have opposed sex education in public schools, as well as any teachings about contraception, abortion, homosexuality, or same-sex marriage that conflict with or contradict their religious views on those subjects. Pursuing an agenda to desecularize the schools, they have presumptuously styled their campaigns as reflective of mainstream opinion and themselves as broadly typical of concerned parents, rather than as the zealous advocacy of a small minority of religious absolutists. At the local community level, they have formed purportedly grassroots organizations bearing "parents" in their names. These groups work closely with the larger and more well-known social conservative organizations. They target school boards and ministries of education, engaging in homophobia and fear-mongering justified on the grounds of promoting moral values and defending religious freedom.

A prominent agenda item has been the question of how homosexuality and same-sex relationships should be presented—if presented at all—within the curricula for sex education or family issues courses. Policies and programs to make schools safer for gays and lesbians by combating homophobia in particular have come under fierce attack. Parents' rights groups have posited that the religious and moral right to disapprove of homosexuality and the homosexual lifestyle is being infringed. They have charged that their children are being harmed by being taught to positively accept homosexuality as an alternative sexual orientation.

In Calgary evangelical Protestants founded Parents' Rights in Education (PRE) in 1996 as a means to oppose a decision by the city's Board of Education to establish an Action Plan for the Safety of Gay/Lesbian/Bisexual Youth and Staff Safety. The organization was headed by Tom Crites, assistant pastor of Centre Street Church (affiliated with the Evangelical Missionary Church of Canada). Critics purported to counsel "recovering homosexuals." He accused the school board of teaching children that "homosexuality is a healthy, acceptable lifestyle. We don't want our kids brought into a gay lifestyle." Crites also expressed alarm that under the policy school counsellors would refer a student to an outside agency without notifying the parents; and he condemned the prospect that a student might be referred to a group that presented homosexuality positively rather than being referred to an organization that said it could cure gays, such as the National Association for Research and Therapy of Homosexuality. PRE also took strong stances against sex education and abortion information and counselling in public schools.[18]

In 1997 Crites and PRE mounted another campaign to have the school board remove two books dealing with gay themes from public school libraries. One was an anthology of lesbian and gay fiction for teens; the other was a novel about a teenager who comes to terms with being gay. Accused by PRE of allowing a "gay agenda," the Board buckled under the pressure and removed the books from the libraries. Following a public furor over the banning, a panel was appointed to review the decision. It eventually ruled that one of the books was to be reinstated to library collections, but not the other.[19]

In British Columbia, the Citizens' Research Institute (CRI), based in Surrey, began in 1996 to conduct initiatives in various communities to gain support for a Declaration of Family Rights aimed at "parents who wish to exercise their authority over the education of their children." The declaration gave notice to schools that the child identified in it must not be exposed to and/or involved with any activity or program that "discusses or portrays the lifestyles of gays, lesbians, bisexual and/or transgendered individuals as one which is normal, accepted or must be tolerated." It threatened legal action against any teachers, administrators, or employers who violated it. "The school's focus on social engineering has got out of control," CRI's founder and executive director, Kari Simpson, stated in 2003. "Not just with homosexuality but also feminism, unionism and sexism," she continued, lambasting what she described as "the sexualization of our education system."[20]

Simpson had gained particular notoriety in 1997 after she publicly opposed a resolution adopted by the B.C. Teachers' Federation that sought elimination of homophobia and heterosexism from the province's schools. But she also became renowned for her unsuccessful campaign to have two NDP members of the B.C.

legislature, Helmut Giesbrecht and Paul Ramsey, removed by their electors in recall initiatives made possible under provincial legislation. Ramsey, education minister in the NDP government, had sought to reform the public school curriculum, presenting approaches such as the promotion of anti-homophobia programs and presentation of non-traditional family structures that included families with parents in same-sex relationships.[21]

Another long-lasting parents' rights group, British Columbia Parents and Teachers for Life—founded as an informal network in 1985 and more formally constituted in 1990—aims among other things "to promote a positive attitude towards human life." That positive attitude does not extend to gays and lesbians. Its website boasts, "We have opposed the introduction of school programs that would promote a favourable attitude towards homosexual behaviour." The organization also works "to support the legitimate rights of parents as the prime educators of their children to determine the nature of their children's education" and, furthermore, "to seek to have teachers' organizations refrain from the promotion of abortion and euthanasia, and to promote freedom of conscience and justice for teachers in the public work-place."[22] B.C. Parents and Teachers for Life encouraged parents to sign and present to school administrators a "Parents' Directive," to be brought to the attention of teachers and other school staff. The directive ordered that nothing taught to the children should undermine respect for the "ideal concept of the family as founded on the life-long commitment of one man and one woman to another in marriage and their commitment to the welfare of their children." It also asserted a strong anti-abortion stance: "We hold to the belief that human life is sacred from conception to natural death, and nothing taught to our child or children in the school should undermine respect for this principle."[23]

Citizens' Research Institute, B.C. Parents and Teachers for Life, and a panoply of other groups succeeded in 1997 in orchestrating the adoption of a resolution by the B.C. Confederation of Parents Advisory Councils calling for a ban from all school curricula of any material dealing with homosexuality. Various social conservative groups also organized to oppose a motion presented in the year 2000 to the convention of the B.C. Teachers' Federation. The motion called for support of "gay/straight alliances" to bring gay and straight students in Grades 7 to 12 together to achieve mutual understanding and tolerance. Hundreds of protesters, including parents, evangelical Christians, and educators argued that the establishment of such alliances "would promote alcoholism, attract pedophiles, and lure straight kids into homosexuality." A resource guide developed in the same year by the B.C. Teachers' Federation, called "Challenging Homophobia in the Schools," became the focus of a sustained social conservative attack when it was introduced for use in public schools.[24]

A skirmish over this issue occurred in 2006. Murray Corren, a gay teacher in Coquitlam, and his partner, Peter Corren, had filed a successful human rights complaint againts the B.C. Ministry of Education after Murray was turned down in his efforts to have the curriculum of public schools add teaching about sexual orientation and positive, affirming content about gays and lesbians. A member of Gay and Lesbian Educators of British Columbia, Murray Corren was aiming to force the schools to teach "Queer history and historical figures, the presence of positive queer role models—past and present—and the contributions made by queers to various epochs, societies and civilizations and legal issues relating to (lesbian, gay, bisexual, transgendered) people, same-sex marriage and adoption." The eventual settlement committed the Ministry to establish a social justice resource package for use in Grade 12 classes in public schools, the purpose of which would be "to explore, from legal, political, ethical and economic perspectives, the concept of a just and equitable society in which there is full participation of all peoples. One topic of study ... will address issues of sexual orientation/gender identity."[25]

As part of the settlement, the Correns were to be provided with a draft of the sexual orientation/gender identity portion of the resource package for review, and the Ministry agreed to make revisions that it deemed appropriate to reflect any comments they made.[26] The end result was a curriculum guide, *Making Space, Giving Voice*, that was condemned by social conservative groups in the province. B.C. Parents and Teachers for Life was one of a number of groups that responded with thunderous fury and dire predictions about children being harmed and morals being undermined. The organization denounced the settlement as "a serious threat to the children and youth of our society.... Parents can no longer take for granted—if they ever could—that the schools their children attend are safe." Clearly, for these critics, acknowledging in a positive way the mere presence of gays and lesbians in the schools, or the positive contributions of gays and lesbians to society and culture, created an unsafe and dangerous environment for children. Another B.C. group, the Canadian Alliance for Social Justice and Family Values Association, organized a petition condemning the settlement, with 15,000 people signing it. B.C. Parents and Teachers for Life, the Alliance, and other groups organized an event to protest the settlement and the curriculum guide. More familiar stalwarts of Canadian social conservatism—the Catholic Civil Rights League, REAL Women, and Canada Family Action Coalition—lent their support to the demonstration and rally in Vancouver, which was attended by 800 people.[27]

Social conservative skirmishes with school boards over the introduction of equity and other policies dealing with sexual orientation show no signs of abating. Throughout 2007 and 2008, the Hamilton-Wentworth Family Action Council, affiliated with the Canada Family Action Coalition, waged a vigorous campaign against the establishment of a sexual orientation equity policy by the Hamilton-Wentworth District School Board. The group, "Dedicated to preserving family values," complained that there was inadequate public and parent awareness of the development and approval of the policy. An important element of their opposition was that the policy would "affirm homosexual/bi-sexual bias" that "amounts to homosexual/bi-sexual indoctrination." They particularly objected to what they said were "measures [put] in place to silence students and families who view homosexual/bisexual conduct as high-risk conduct physically, emotionally and spiritually."[28] The Family Action Council urged parents to submit a Declaration of Spiritual Values to their child's teacher, instructing the teacher not to discuss "sexual orientation indoctrination" with the child.

Alberta became the first province to take an official stand on the issue of parental rights. In 2009 the provincial government legislated the right of parents to pull their children out of a classroom or place of instruction in which "courses of study, educational programs or instructional materials, or instruction or exercises ... include subject-matter that deals explicitly with religion, sexuality or sexual orientation." It enshrined this right in the province's Human Rights, Citizenship and Multiculturalism Act following years of pressure from Tory caucus members, including Morton, and social conservative groups. Progressive Conservative culture minister Lindsay Blackett acknowledged that the gesture was intended to placate religious groups and conservative voters who might be angered over the province's long overdue amendment to the Act to prohibit discrimination on the basis of sexual orientation (following from the 1998 Supreme Court decision in *Vriend*). CFAC's Rushfeldt saluted the amendment and attempted to cast it as being important for more than just evangelical Protestants: "I don't think you have to be a religious person to decide that you don't want certain things taught to your child."[29]

Some ten years earlier, in Surrey, B.C., the same issue led to a groundbreaking legal challenge that ultimately wound up at the Supreme Court of Canada. In a 1996 election a social conservative group, the Surrey Electors' Team (SET), had dominated the school board, electing five of the seven trustees. One of the new trustees was a member of the radical anti-abortion group Operation Rescue. Another, who later became chair, was Heather Stilwell, a former president of both the Christian Heritage Party (CHP) and Alliance for Life, and a member of REAL Women of Canada. The election of the SET trustees transformed the Surrey board into a laboratory for social conservative activism with a focus on sexuality in general and homosexuality in particular. A Board decision to bar any sex education that did not focus on abstinence created obstacles for AIDS educators seeking access to Surrey schools to conduct education on safer sex practices. Administrators in one

Surrey school removed a child from the classroom of an openly gay teacher, James Chamberlain, after the parents objected to their child having a gay teacher.

But it was a 1997 decision of the Board to ban three books featuring children with same-sex parents from use in kindergarten and Grade 1 classes that escalated the Board's moral agenda into an issue of national significance. The Board deemed the books, *Asha's Mums*, *Belinda's Bouquet*, and *One Dad, Two Dads, Brown Dad, Blue Dad*, to be inappropriate because they dealt with "a sensitive and contentious matter inappropriate to children aged five and six." Not only that, the books would be "potentially offensive to the various cultural and religious groups in the region."[30] In response Chamberlain and the Gay and Lesbian Educators of British Columbia (GALE), an advocacy group based in Nelson, B.C., launched a court challenge. They argued that the ban violated the Human Rights Code and the School Act provisions stating that public schools should be non-sectarian.

The Surrey Board suffered an initial setback in 1998, when Justice Mary Saunders of the B.C. Supreme Court held that school policies must be governed strictly by secular principles. She found that the trustees opposed to the use of the books had acted on their personal beliefs in contravention of the B. C. School Act. Board members fared better when they took the case to the B.C. Court of Appeal, which upheld their contention that strictly secular principles should not govern public education policies. The appeal court judges stated that religious and other beliefs could properly inform decisions about moral issues of education. In addition, they asserted, a prudent teacher would use professional judgment and consult with various parents, other teachers, and the principal before taking up sensitive materials in the classroom.[31]

Members of GALE and other individuals appealed the decisions to the Supreme Court of Canada, with the support of Egale Canada, B.C. Civil Liberties Association, Canadian Civil Liberties Association, Families in Partnership, and Elementary Teachers' Federation of Ontario. Egale Canada argued, "Banning of the books violates the right of children with same-sex parents or family-members to see their reality reflected in the curriculum, and contributes to the invisibility and marginalisation of those who are lesbian, gay, bisexual and transgendered." The B.C. Civil Liberties Association opposed the ban on books as being contrary to the B.C. School Act, which provided that all schools must be "conducted on strictly secular and non-sectarian principles" and that "the highest moral values must be inculcated but no religious dogma or creed is to be taught."[32]

Supporting the Surrey Board as intervenors were EFC, Roman Catholic Archdiocese of Vancouver, Catholic Civil Rights League, and Canadian Alliance for Social Justice and Family Values. In their submission to the Court these organizations attempted to blur the lines between secular and religious morality and values.

They argued that the appellants were attempting to use the equality rights guaranteed under section 15 of the Charter to advance their own political and moral agenda—the implication being that neither the intervenors nor the Surrey Board had any such nefarious intentions. Their factum to the court maintained that the term "secular" in the School Act "is intended to mean non-denominational and that is not intended to exclude moral values flowing from religious conviction." Further, they maintained, "Nor does the secularization of the public school system remove the question of morality from decisions concerning the conduct of the public school system or 'make religious unbelief a condition of participation in the setting of the moral agenda.'" The Surrey Board, they argued, was entitled and, in fact, mandated by the School Act "to have regard to the common moral goals expressed by the community, irrespective of whether those goals are influenced by religion." The Board's resolution, they argued, did not put at risk the appellants' right to remain free from discrimination based on sexual orientation. Rather, the relief sought by the appellants was aimed at garnering social acceptance for homosexual conduct generally and as expressed in the context of families headed by same-sex couples. They asserted that if, "in setting the moral agenda for schools," public officials were not able to take into account the community's moral views—even if those views were "informed by religion"—that would be an infringement of the "religious liberty interests and equality rights" guaranteed under the Charter.[33]

For the social conservatives, only the moral dictates of Christianity (and other similar religions such as Judaism and Islam) provided what they cited as the "common moral goals expressed by the community." Moral teaching informed by religion, which they asserted was neither religious indoctrination nor representative of a moral agenda, was acceptable and should be permitted. In contrast, teaching that gays and lesbians should be treated with equality and without moral condemnation was a "political and moral agenda" that should not be allowed in the schools. The argument was a restatement, in a rights context, of the imperative of granting religion, and Christianity above all other religions, a privileged status within a state committed to reflecting the supremacy of God.

In a rebuke of those arguments, in its judgment *Chamberlain v. Surrey School Board District No. 36*, the Supreme Court overturned the appeal court's decision. The December 2002 judgment by a majority of seven to two instructed the Surrey Board to reconsider its decision to ban the books. The majority decision, written by Chief Justice Beverley McLachlin, emphatically declared, "Tolerance is always age-appropriate." The judgment also noted that the curriculum for the K–1 level had a goal that children be able to discuss their family models and that all children be made aware of the diversity of family models in society. It noted pointedly that behind all the Board's considerations "hovered the moral and religious concerns of some parents and the Board with the morality of homosexual relationships." Ruling that the Board's decision was unreasonable, the majority justices noted that it "failed to proceed as required by the secular mandate of the School Act by letting the religious views of a certain part of the community trump the need to show equal respect for the values of other members of the community."[34]

James Chamberlain and the intervenors who supported him were thrilled with the resounding decision, declaring that it would benefit every child in Canada. The social conservative groups thought otherwise. Their opinions were by no means altered by the Supreme Court reasoning. Focus on the Family spokesperson Anne Marie White charged that the decision would leave schoolchildren vulnerable to unwelcome discussions of complex social issues that they could not hope to comprehend. The Catholic Civil Rights League complained that the judgment "effectively trumps expectations of tolerance and equal respect which religious parents expect from the publicly funded school system." It went on to declare that the Court's "reasoning fails to recognize that the allowance of such materials likewise offends others in a pluralistic society, who have reason to expect that their views will not be trumped by the promotion of gay parenting relationships by gay activist educators as normative." REAL Women joined the chorus. Denouncing the decision as "explosive," the organization stated, "The result allows homosexual propaganda to be included in the curriculum." For Rushfeldt,"This is possibly the most offensive and discriminatory ruling that has ever come from Canada's Supreme Court.... It is bad enough to impose upon five and six-year-old children the idea that homosexuality is appropriate sexual behavior. But to impose the denial of all opinions that are based on religion is even more bizarre."[35]

For those on the other side of the question, the Court's decision delivered an important message to school boards: "that they need to teach acceptance of same-sex families and have their educators teach kids about homophobia." For the B.C. Civil Liberties Association, the decision made it clear that, in weighing the issues of religious convictions and beliefs of parents against "the requirements of tolerance and strictly secular curriculum—which are key elements of the Act—tolerance must come first." For John Fisher of Egale Canada, the victory affirmed "the right of children to a bias-free curriculum."[36]

In response to the Supreme Court decision, the Surrey Board did review its decision to ban the books. But it ended up finding new grounds on which to continue the ban. Heeding the order of the Supreme Court to avoid religious arguments, the Board seized upon some rather flimsy reasons to keep the books out of Surrey classrooms. They argued that the books in question were inappropriate because of bad grammar, confusing scenarios, and unfair depictions of authority figures. The trustees went so far as to cite words spelled in the U.S. rather than the Canadian manner.[37] The Board members thus thumbed their collective noses at the Supreme Court decision. The views and beliefs of evangelical Christians would, in practice, if not in law, trump the rights of gays and lesbians. The activist judges could go to hell.

Private religious schools

Many social conservatives, disillusioned or merely dissatisfied with the removal of religious morality as the touchstone for public schools, have sought to shelter the minds and protect the morality of their children by sending them to private schools that are enthusiastically committed to a purely Christian education. For these parents, the secular public schools have an immoral curriculum. The parents object to the "anti-biblical" teaching, particularly sex education and lessons about evolution and the origin of the species. They want, as an administrator of a Quebec private school put it, "a curriculum based on a Christian world view rather than humanistic world view." Rather than sex education, students are taught abstinence; and rather than evolution they learn about creationism, styled as "intelligent design." Within that theory students learn about "what's wrong with the theory" of evolution."[38]

The parents interested in this alternative kind of education have formed and financed a burgeoning movement to build and sustain private religious schools. The focus is singularly on the rights of parents to determine what and how their children should be taught. The approach represents an emphatic rejection of the principle, reflected in the laws and policies of the state as well as in the pronouncements of the courts, that the interests of the children should be paramount and that children are not mere property or chattel without rights of their own. The children educated in private religious schools often face a serious disadvantage. The schools are not licensed or accredited by provincial ministries of education, which means that their diplomas are not recognized by public colleges or universities or even for occupational or vocational purposes. In that regard, the religious beliefs of parents are being recklessly put ahead of the best interests and long-term welfare of the children.

Not content with simply exercising their right to send their children to private religious schools, social conservative organizations have advocated to secure or enhance tax funding for them as a matter of human rights and equality of treatment. It is discriminatory, they charge, for the state not to support such private schools in the same way that it supports the public schools, through the tax system. They strenuously object to the notion that receiving tax funds from the state should necessarily require adherence to terms and conditions set by the state, such as promotion of equity and non-discrimination, when doing so conflicts with their religious beliefs. They equally object to curriculum requirements that the theory of evolution be taught.

One of the problems in this regard for social conservative groups is that Canada's provinces and territories have no uniformity of treatment on the question. Some provide varying degrees of tax-funded support, while others provide funding only to Catholic schools. Others do not provide any public funding of any kind to private schools.[39] Ontario provides public funding only to Catholic schools because of a constitutional guarantee given to schools under the 1867 Constitution. That policy has been decried as discriminatory, and a group called the Ontario Multi-Faith Group for Equity in Education has called for public funding for alternative religious schools. Mohammad Ashraf of the Islamic Society of North America asked, "If Catholics can get it [funding], why can't we?"[40]

For several years, despite persistent lobbying by the Multi-Faith Group, the Ontario government declined to legislate public funding for non-Catholic private schools. In an attempt to force the issue, Susie Adler, a parent of children in a private Jewish school, decided to challenge the constitutionality of the policy, and her case eventually found its way to the Supreme Court of Canada. Adler's challenge was supported by the Canadian Jewish Congress, parents in schools belonging to the Ontario Alliance of Christian Schools, and the Ontario Multi-Faith Coalition for Equity in Education. They argued that funding other religious schools in the same manner as Catholic schools was just and equitable in modern Ontario society. Unhappily for them, the Supreme Court of Canada, in a 1996 judgment known as *Adler v. Ontario,* strongly disagreed. It ruled that refusing to fund independent religious schools is not an infringement of religious freedom. Ontario, the Court stated, had no constitutional obligation to fund such schools, but could provide such funding if it wished to do so.[41]

After the Supreme Court's rebuff, another member of the Jewish faith, Arieh Hollis Waldman, filed a complaint (also in 1996) with the United Nations Human Rights Committee. It alleged that Canada was contravening the International Covenant on Civil and Political Rights because Ontario provided tax funds to support Catholic schools but did not similarly fund other denominational schools. In a decision released in November 1999, the UN Committee ruled that the Ontario government's funding policy was discriminatory because it was not based on "objective and reasonable criteria." The Committee held that Ontario violated Article 26 of the Covenant, which states that all persons must be treated equally under the law on the ground of religion, among others. Significantly, however, the UN Committee's decision did not state that Canada and Ontario must provide public funding for private religious schools. It was clear in declaring, "The *Covenant* does not oblige States parties to fund schools which are established on a religious basis. However, if a State party chooses to provide public funding to religious schools, it should make this funding available without discrimination." The decision, although not binding, bolstered the case made by the non-Catholic religious groups. Reference to it appeared often in submissions made by groups such as the EFC and Canadian Jewish Congress when they pressed their case for tax-supported religious schools.[42]

The Ontario government took no action on the UN Committee's decision until the Progressive Conservative government of Mike Harris announced a shift in the policy on private religious schools in 2001. Responding to pressure from social conservative members of the Tory caucus, the government announced that it would introduce a tax credit for parents of children in private schools, including religious schools. It justified the decision using the same fairness argument that had been repeatedly made by social conservative groups, contending that it was a matter of restoring equity. If the government supported Roman Catholic schools, it should also support parents who send their children to other religious-based schools.[43]

The tax credit proved to be a highly controversial initiative that alarmed human rights advocates. No conditions, such as ensuring compliance with the Human Rights Code, were imposed on private schools in exchange for benefiting from the tax credits policy. Keith Norton, Chief Commissioner of the Human Rights Commission, expressed concern that the tax credits would "result in racial, ethnic and religious apartheid in our educational environment as well as intolerance and ignorance among our children unless some appropriate standards and oversight are provided." Earl Manners, the president of the Ontario Secondary School Teachers' Federation, strongly condemned the new policy, stating apprehensively that "in the name of choice, this government may be supporting ... racism, homophobia and sexism" within private schools because of the religious beliefs that would be taught within them.[44]

Despite the criticism, and with the support of religious groups, the government enacted a refundable tax credit for parents who enrol their children in private schools. Happily, the measure was short-lived. The Conservatives were defeated in the 2003 election by the Liberals under Dalton McGuinty, and one of the new government's first actions was to repeal the tax credit. With that action, it seemed that the private schools issue was effectively killed. But the faith communities were determined not to abandon the issue and continued to lobby the government and opposition parties, citing the finding of the UN Committee. The Multi-Faith Coalition for Equal Funding for Faith-Based Schools in Toronto denounced the Ontario government's refusal to extend funding to private religious schools as "odious discrimination."[45]

The efforts of the faith communities once more found favour with the Progressive Conservative Party, now led by John Tory. The 2007 Conservative election platform contained a pledge to "Take action to bring faith-based schools into the public system"—a promise that went far beyond the old tax credit scheme. If elected, the Tories were committing to provide full tax-funding to all faith-based schools so that there would be "an opportunity for non-Catholic, faith-based schools to choose to join our publicly funded education system the same way Catholic schools have already done." For added measure, the platform emphasized, "The best results will be achieved through direct funding rather than tax credits." While the election platform also contained some vague commitments to ensure "strict criteria and accountability requirements" for faith-based schools, there would not be any requirement to adhere to the provisions of the Human Rights Code or to avoid the "racial, ethnic and religious apartheid" that Norton had warned about.[46]

The faith-based schools pledge became the dominant issue in the 2007 provincial election, and it was an issue that the McGuinty Liberals adroitly exploited to secure another majority government. They supported maintaining the status quo of funding for Catholic schools but not for schools of any other faiths. At the same time, McGuinty firmly ruled out a constitutional amendment to remove the funding for Catholic schools as the means to achieve absolute fairness through a completely secular public school system. The NDP also supported maintaining the status quo. Only the Green Party, which did not have any members elected to the legislature, was bold enough to commit to remove public funding for the Catholic school system.[47]

The Tory plan met with considerable and massive opposition among the Ontario electorate. Gay and lesbian advocacy groups spoke out forcefully against the policy. The Canadian Civil Liberties Association, supported by the Ontario Secondary Schools Teachers' Federation District 12, Elementary Teachers of Toronto, Canadian Union of Public Employees Local 4400, and Peel Elementary Teachers' Local, took out full-page newspaper advertisements condemning the funding proposal. Public opinion also swiftly swung decisively against faith-based funding. During the election campaign, opposition to the proposal among the general population soared to more than 71 per cent and remained at that level until election day.[48] Conservative election candidates repeatedly faced hostile reactions to the policy during their door-knocking campaigns. Finally recognizing the folly of his policy, Tory, a week before the election, backtracked and jettisoned it altogether.

As an issue, the funding of private religious schools through taxation is starkly and irreconcilably at odds with the otherwise highly secularized and pluralistic nature of Canada today. But so long as the provincial governments do not have a consistent approach and the Catholic school system in Ontario is funded by tax-payers, the question is not likely to go away. Social conservative groups (and their allies such as the Canadian Jewish Congress) will continue to press the issue, using the argument of parents' rights and allegations of discrimination and unfairness.

A case involving an openly gay student in an Ontario Catholic secondary school vividly illustrates the dynamics of the issue. In 2001 Marc Hall, a seventeen-year-old Grade 12 student in a Catholic school in Oshawa, Ontario, wanted to take his same-sex date to the end-of-year prom and asked his principal, Mike Powers, about it. He was denied permission. Powers, following Roman Catholic doctrine, stated that interaction between partners at a prom is sexual activity. Granting per-mission to Hall to bring his date would be endorsing and condoning conduct that is contrary to Catholic Church teachings, he argued. Powers's decision was upheld by the Durham Catholic School Board. Mary Ann Martin, chair of the Board, issued a statement declaring, "The teaching of the Catholic Church on homosexuality is very clear and well understood by Catholics and many others ... the catechism notes that homosexual behaviour is unacceptable and cannot be approved."[49]

Hall fought back, enlisting the support of George Smitherman, an openly gay member of the Ontario legislature, and a diverse array of nineteen community and advocacy groups that formed the Coalition in Support of Marc Hall. Significantly, among the supporters were two Catholic lay advocacy groups, Catholics for Free Choice and Challenge the Church. The Ontario English Catholic Teachers' Associa-tion, representing separate school teachers, also supported Hall, clearly putting the teachers in the Catholic school system at odds with both the School Board and the Roman Catholic Church. Hall and his supporters went to court to seek an injunction restraining the school and the Board from preventing his attendance at the prom with his boyfriend. In their legal factum, the Coalition argued that the Durham Catholic School Board had discriminated against Hall in violation of his rights under the Charter. They argued that the case not only was a manifestation of systemic discrimination against gays and lesbians but also had broader social implications and impact. They said the case "presents the challenge of upholding Canada's public policy that forbids discrimination on the basis of sexual orienta-tion while respecting its commitment to religious freedom."[50]

The Durham Catholic Board was supported in the case only by the Ontario Catholic School Trustees' Association. Their argument followed a familiar line: that Powers's decision was not personally targeted against Hall or homosexuals. Attempting to illustrate an analogous situation, they held that a student would also be prohibited from bringing a married date to the prom because that would be considered immoral in the eyes of the Church and could not culminate in the sac-rament of marriage between the two people. In addition, the trustees contended, it was in the public interest to uphold the decision of the principal in the exercise of his statutory duties.[51]

In essence the case hinged on which rights would have precedence: the right of religious schools to discriminate—and to justify that discrimination citing their religious beliefs—versus the rights of students to be free from such discrimination. Justice Robert MacKinnon of the Superior Court of Justice, in a landmark ruling, agreed with Hall's claim of discrimination, and issued the injunction. The judgment stated, among other things: "If individuals in Canada were permitted to simply assert that their religious beliefs require them to discriminate against homosexuals without objective scrutiny, there would be no protection at all from discrimination for gays and lesbians in Canada because everyone who wished to discriminate against them could make that assertion."[52] The discrimination against Hall, he concluded, was unjustified under section 15 of the Charter. As one of Hall's lawyers, David Corbett, pithily commented, the judgment was evidence that "even Catholic students have human rights."[53] The Durham Catholic School Board and the principal of the school complied with the injunction. Hall attended the prom, in the glare of national publicity, without incident—though the Board served notice that it would appeal to a higher court. The Catholic School Board—and behind it, the Catholic Church—could not "condone or promote ... the exercise of a homosexual lifestyle" and would remain steadfast on that issue.[54] As Catholic Civil Rights League president Thomas Langan stated, "The court is sending the message that it knows better than Catholics, and their bishops, what they can and can't believe. The judge is sending the message to Catholic students and their parents that the values of the Charter trump the teachings of your faith within your Catholic schools."[55] In deciding on what is in the interests of its faithful, the Roman Catholic Church would not take a back seat to the secular state.

Religious teachers in secular schools

In the education sector this issue—the right of religious freedom and its conflict with the rights of gay and lesbian students—extends beyond Catholic schools into the public school system.

In one case in the 1990s involving Trinity Western University (TWU), an evangelical Protestant educational institution located in Langley, B.C., the question revolved around whether the university should receive official accreditation for its teaching program. Affiliated with the Evangelical Free Church of Canada, TWU strictly enforced adherence to the religious and moral teachings of its parent denomination. For one thing, all students, faculty, and staff were required to sign a pledge to refrain from engaging in sinful practices that are "Biblically condemned." The prohibition included engaging in homosexual acts, premarital sex, adultery, viewing pornography, and such other "practices" as drunkenness or using profane language. Because of this strict policy, the B.C. College of Teachers decided that the TWU policy displayed an inherent bias against homosexuals and therefore TWU graduates would not be certified as public school teachers. In its decision, the BCCT stated that it "believes the proposed program follows discriminatory practices which are contrary to the public interest and public policy."[56]

TWU took legal action, arguing that the College of Teachers did not have the legal authority to make a judgment on the acceptability of religious beliefs or to enforce human rights legislation. TWU also alleged infringement of its right of religious freedom guaranteed by the Charter. TWU's executive vice-president, Guy Safford, characterized the College's decision as the actions of "thought police," and said that the right to certify teachers had been denied because the College "doesn't like the way we think." He argued that the decision rested on "the unsupportable assumption that if people's religious beliefs include viewing sex as a matter between a husband and a wife, they may, therefore, be bigoted and incapable of 'correct' thinking on the issue of homosexuality." He denounced the College's actions as abhorrent and "a very dangerous precedent for religious freedom—and for civil liberties—in Canada."[57]

In 1998 the B.C. Supreme Court held that the College of Teachers did not have the jurisdiction to determine whether the university followed discriminatory practices and ruled that it had acted in a "patently unreasonable" manner. The court ordered the College to approve the TWU teaching training program. Following an appeal by the College, the B.C. Court of Appeal concluded that the College had acted within its statutory authority, but also ruled that the TWU should be approved because there was no reasonable foundation for the finding of discrimination. In November 2000 the BCCT appealed that decision to the Supreme Court of Canada.

In its appeal to the Supreme Court the College was supported by the Ontario Secondary School Teachers' Federation and Egale Canada. TWU was supported by a coalition of social conservative groups and, more significantly, the B.C. Civil Liberties Association. Both the social conservative and Civil Liberties spokespersons argued that the religious beliefs of TWU graduates should not prevent them from being certified as public school teachers. They maintained that adherence to TWU's strict policy did not mean that the graduates would treat gays and lesbians within the school system in a discriminatory manner, that the question of whether a teacher contravenes the law should be based on actual conduct and not beliefs on matters of conscience. The Civil Liberties Association added that the right to be free from discrimination on the basis of sexual orientation had to be weighed against and balanced with TWU's freedom of religion and association. The College, the association argued, "erroneously concluded that equality of rights on the basis of sexual orientation trump freedom of religion and association. They do not."[58]

The Supreme Court of Canada agreed. In a judgement released on May 17, 2001, it dismissed the appeal. A majority of eight justices, with the ninth dissenting, found that the College of Teachers had acted unfairly. The Court held that College, acting solely on a perception that the religious precepts of the TWU would result in discriminatory actions by its graduates, had not considered the actual impact of those beliefs on the public school environment. At the same time, the Court held, there had been no violation of TWU's Charter rights. On the question of balancing conflicting rights guaranteed by the Charter, the majority of justices opined:

> Neither freedom of religion nor the guarantee against discrimination based on sexual orientation is absolute. The proper place to draw the line is between belief and conduct. The freedom to hold beliefs is broader than the freedom to act on them. Absent concrete evidence that training teachers at TWU fosters discrimination in the public schools in B.C., the freedom of individuals to adhere to certain religious beliefs while at TWU should be respected. Acting on those beliefs, however, is a different matter. If a teacher in the public school system engages in discriminatory conduct, that teacher can be subject to disciplinary proceedings before the BCCT. In this way, the scope of the freedom of religion and equality rights that have come into conflict can be circumscribed and thereby reconciled.[59]

It was a carefully reasoned and adroitly balanced decision. TWU and its graduates had the right to hold strongly anti-homosexual religious beliefs, but could not act on those beliefs as teachers in the school system without facing the prospect of disciplinary action.

A subsequent case in the public school realm addressed the difficult question of when a teacher holding anti-homosexual beliefs goes too far by acting on those beliefs in a discriminatory manner. Chris Kempling, a public school teacher and guidance counsellor in Quesnel, B.C., was a member of a Christian and Missionary Alliance of Canada denomination (the local Maple Park Alliance Church) and had a long social conservative pedigree. In addition to being active in B.C. Parents and Teachers for Life, he was a member of and federal election candidate for the Christian Heritage Party—a party guided by "Biblical principles," including a belief in the Bible as "the inspired, inerrant written word of God and the final authority above all man's laws and governments." As a Registered Clinical Counsellor and a member of the National Association of Research and Therapy of Homosexuality, he believed gays could be cured, arguing that "results for orientation reparative therapy are quite impressive."[60]

Kempling had gone public with his views. In a series of letters to the Quesnel *Cariboo-Observer* and in published articles he expressed the view that homosexual acts are immoral. He also wrote letters to members of the city council objecting to Quesnel's declaration of a gay pride day, arguing that the proclamation disrespected the views of local Christians. In one of his published articles he defiantly declared: "I refuse to be a false teacher, saying that promiscuity is acceptable, perversion is normal, and immorality is simply 'cultural diversity' of which we should be proud.... Teachers must inculcate the highest moral standards."[61]

As a result of these public utterances, the B.C. College of Teachers undertook disciplinary action against Kempling, suspending him for one month for engaging in conduct unbecoming for a teacher. A disciplinary panel ruled that statements made in published articles demonstrated that Kempling was not prepared to uphold the education system's core values, one of which is non-discrimination and which includes recognizing the right of homosexuals to equality, dignity, and respect. Further, the panel held, the "reasonable and probable consequences of his published writings" would have an adverse impact on the environment of the schools in which he taught. His statements represented a clear declaration that he did not separate his personal moral and religious beliefs from how he conducted himself in his capacity as a teacher in the public school system.

Social conservative advocates belligerently defended Kempling's right to teach bigotry and intolerance in the public schools and condemned the disciplinary action as an outrageous infringement of the right of religious freedom. When he sought a judicial review to have the discipline decision overturned, hoping for a ruling that the discipline violated the Charter protections of freedom of expression and religion, the Catholic Civil Rights League, the Canadian Alliance for Social Justice and Family Values, and other social conservative groups lined up solidly in support. Rallies and demonstrations were organized and social conservative polemicists penned articles for journals and websites condemning the College's finding. REAL Women lambasted the College for being "bent on turning the BC educational system into a haven for homosexuality by forcing its legitimization on the school system by every means possible.... Mr. Kempling quite rightly questions whether the Gay and Lesbian Educators of BC (GALE) and their allies in the BC College of Teachers had a right to indoctrinate with homosexual propaganda Christian children and those of other faith communities, such as Sikhs, Jews, and Muslims."[62]

In an unequivocal decision released in January 2004, Justice R.R. Holmes of the B.C. Supreme Court upheld the College's disciplinary decision. He concluded that Kempling's "published writings provided ample evidence that could reasonably support the finding that he made and published discriminatory and derogatory statements against homosexuals." Readers of one of Kempling's published papers "might reasonably apprehend the appellant as insinuating that homosexuals are pedophiles or become homosexual as a result of pedophilia." Further, Holmes found that the college could properly discipline Kempling for conduct occurring off-duty when that conduct "negatively impacts the school system" or has an effect "on the appellant's ability to carry out his professional and legal obligations as a teacher fully and fairly." He found that Kempling's Charter rights had not been infringed. Kempling could express his religious views about homosexuality, but could not do so publicly in a way that drew upon his role and stature as a teacher in order to give those views credibility.[63]

"It is a black day for religious freedom in Canada," Kempling declared in a letter to his supporters the day after the court's decision was released. Distorting the judgment's meaning, he charged that the decision "means that teachers who happen to be Christians or who belong to other religions proscribing homosexuality may not comment publicly on this issue." An indignant response from the Catholic Civil Rights League reflected a similar distortion: "But if the shadow of authoritarian rule is not troubling enough, Mr. Justice Holmes clearly implies that authentic Christian teaching about homosexual conduct is a harmful lie, and that anyone who spreads such lies—Christian or not—deserves to be punished. The implications of this decision are ominous." The Christian Heritage Party condemned the "persecution" of Kempling as "a warning to all of us that free speech and religious liberties in Canada are under attack by pro-homosexual fascists and their deluded sympathizers."[64]

Kempling appealed the decision, with interventions on his behalf being made by the Canadian Religious Freedom Alliance (CRFA), made up of the Catholic Civil Rights League, Evangelical Fellowship of Canada, Christian Teachers Association, and Christian Legal Fellowship. The CRFA complained that the lower court had created two kinds of citizens: "those who enjoy fundamental freedoms and those who do not because they have chosen to pursue a professional occupation." It was a new assertion of the right and obligation claimed by evangelicals to live their faith in all facets of their life, and to have that accepted as a fundamental right under the Charter. In addition, the CRFA argued, the court's decision "eviscerates" the sections of the Charter dealing with freedom of expression and religion by removing their protection from "where it is most needed: unpopular or controversial beliefs and speech."[65]

In a decision released on June 13, 2005, three justices of the B.C. Court of Appeal unanimously agreed that the lower court judge had not erred in his decision. While Kempling's rights of freedom of expression under the Charter were infringed by the suspension of his teaching certificate, the infringement was not beyond what could be justified in a free and democratic society under section 1 of the Charter. In particular, the justices noted, "There is no evidence that establishes that his ability to practice his religion would in any way be compromised by his being restricted from making discriminatory public statements about homosexuals." The justices also ruled that a finding that conduct is unbecoming could be justified on the basis that a teacher's conduct caused harm to the education system:

> Non-discrimination is a core value of the public education system; the integrity of that system is dependent upon teachers upholding that value by ensuring the school environment is accepting of all students. When a teacher makes public statements espousing discriminatory views, and when such views are linked to his or her professional position as a teacher, harm to the integrity of the school system is a necessary result.[66]

Phil Horgan of the Catholic Civil Rights League predicted that "the net result" of the judgment "will be a chilling effect on free speech." Kempling, supported by the CRFA, applied to the Supreme Court of Canada to hear an appeal of the decision. When the Court refused to do so, Kempling bitterly declared: "This is a victory for the enemies of free speech and a sad day for all Canadians who value the free exchange of ideas in the public square." With "no regrets," he maintained that he "was simply expressing a social conservative point of view shared by millions of Canadians."[67]

Champions of religious freedom

By the time of the Kempling decision, social conservatives generally were casting themselves publicly as the self-styled champions of religious freedom fighting against the tyranny of atheistic secularism and moral relativism in the age of rights. That stance was nothing new: protestations about a loss of religious freedom had been a large part of the social conservative rhetoric since the 1970s. Now, however, as a substantial number of human rights tribunal decisions and pronouncements of the courts, including most importantly the Supreme Court of Canada, attested, their worst fears were being confirmed. The state, and its intrusive and anti-democratic laws, unaccountable and out-of-control human rights commissions, and unelected activist judges were imposing a secular morality while spurning people of religious faith and declaring that their religious and moral values were no longer "Canadian values."

An Ontario Human Rights Board of Inquiry decision issued in 2000 particularly riled social conservatives. The decision found that Scott Brockie and his family-owned printing business Imaging Excellence had contravened the rights of Ray Brillinger and the Canadian Lesbian and Gay Archives by refusing to print letterhead, envelopes, and business cards for the group. Brockie cited, as justification for his actions, his sincerely held religious beliefs that homosexuality is sinful and detestable. He argued that he must not assist in the dissemination of information intended to promote acceptance of the homosexual lifestyle. Providing printing services to homosexual organizations, he maintained, would be in direct opposition to his beliefs, as he strove to live according to biblical principles. The Board of Inquiry did not agree. Brockie and Imaging Excellence were ordered to provide to lesbians and gays, and to organizations in existence for the benefit of those groups, the printing services that they provide to others. Brockie was also ordered to pay damages of $5,000 to Brillinger and the Archives.[68]

In an appeal to the Ontario Superior Court of Justice, Brockie argued, among other things, that "a person's dignity should not be demeaned by being conscripted to support a cause with which he disagrees because of an honestly held and sincere religious belief. There should be a defence to discrimination based on the *bona fides* of the reason for the discrimination to permit a right of dissent."[69] The Canadian Religious Freedom Alliance intervened in support of Brockie's appeal. In its factum to the court the CRFA noted that Ontario's Human Rights Code "does not make it discriminatory to refuse to provide services to a cause to which one conscientiously objects." Addressing the question of the limits on freedom of conscience and religion, the factum argued that the Board of Inquiry "erred in law in its delineation of the guarantee of freedom of conscience and religion by failing to recognize that the freedom ensures the public practice of one's beliefs and that laws are required to extend reasonable accommodation to such public practices 'up to the point of undue hardship.'" To accept the remedy of the Board of Inquiry would mean that "freedom of conscience and religion is subordinated to equality rights based on sexual orientation. . . . It marks a 'zero tolerance' approach to the public exercise of conscientious or religious belief." The CRFA argued that the court should interpret the Code as extending protection to persons but not to causes (gay rights), and that "the law must accord some place to conscientious objectors."[70]

Brockie and CRFA scored a partial victory when the court determined that the Board of Inquiry's order had gone beyond what was reasonably necessary to ensure the right of Brillinger and the Archives to freedom from discrimination. The three presiding judges amended the order to "balance the conflicting rights" inherent in the case. They added a condition specifying that Brockie or Imaging Excellence would not be required "to print material of a nature which could reasonably be considered to be in direct conflict with the core elements of his religious beliefs or creed." But they did not agree with the contention that an outright exemption from the Human Rights Code should apply when persons act in accordance with their religious beliefs. Instead, the court noted that limitations on the right to freedom of religion in the "commercial marketplace are justified where the exercise of that freedom causes harm to others; in the present case, by infringing the Code right to be free from discrimination based on sexual orientation in obtaining commercial services." The court conceded the need for a balancing of the right of religious freedom with the right to be free from discrimination on the basis of sexual orientation. However, the justices concluded, "There can be no appropriate balance if the protection of one right means the total disregard of another."[71]

Brockie ultimately decided not to appeal the Superior Court's decision. Citing an e-mail he sent to his supporters, Focus on the Family quoted him as saying the decision was "a very important, qualified victory." His lawyer also stated that the decision was "extraordinarily significant in that it affirms the public right of religious expression and belief against those who claim that religious conduct is limited to home and church." Janet Epp Buckingham, speaking for the EFC, agreed with that assessment. "This is the first time this kind of right of freedom of conscience or religion has been recognized for business owners under human rights codes. This is a significant step forward for religious freedom in Canada."[72]

Still, the balancing of rights approach articulated by the court did not mollify all social conservative advocates. The Catholic Civil Rights League's Langan complained in a press release, "It is a disconcerting message to suggest that one's religious views must be silenced, or limited to avoiding express support for an organization's message, especially in circumstances where the proposed customer is an organization established to advocate for a way of life which cannot be condoned by one's faith."[73] REAL Women seized upon the Brockie decision to renew its bashing of human rights commissions:

> The Court has enabled the Human Rights Commissions to be the arbitrator of core religious values. What do such Commissions know? They are notorious for their bias and prejudice. We can draw no comfort from the fact these Commissions will be deciding matters of conscience and assessing one's core religious beliefs, in order to assess this defence to charges of discrimination by homosexual activists. It should be up [to] the individual believer to determine what actions do or do not violate one's conscience—not up to the majority vote of the Human Rights Commissions or to judges on the bench.[74]

As careful as the Brockie judgment was in attempting to strike a balance between the right to freedom of religion and the right to be free from discrimination, other cases soon gave credence to the social conservative concerns about human rights tribunals. In some provinces, notably Alberta and Saskatchewan, the human rights acts contain provisions that prohibit the publication, distribution, or display of materials that are likely to expose a person or class of persons to hatred, contempt, or ridicule. These provisions extend the ambit of human rights complaints and adjudication processes well beyond actual instances of prohibited discrimination—in housing, employment, or access to services—or the incitement of persons to discriminate against other persons because of specified characteristics such as race, religion, or sexual orientation. The provisions in effect restrict or restrain the free expression of opinion. Regrettably, gays and lesbians and their supporters have in recent years sought to use these vague and subjective provisions to censor and stifle various social conservative zealots who have spread hatred against homosexuality and homosexuals under the guise of expressing their legitimate religious and moral beliefs.

One such case involved Hugh Owens, an evangelical Christian who paid to have the Saskatoon *StarPhoenix* publish an advertisement to promote bumper stickers that he was producing. The left side of the advertisement displayed references to Bible passages condemning homosexuality. One of the cited scriptures, Leviticus 20:13, states that homosexuals should be put to death. An equal sign (=) appeared in the centre. On the right side was an image of two stick men holding hands. Superimposed over the figures was a red circle with a diagonal bar, connoting forbidden or prohibited. It was a crude but simple message reflecting the absolutist evangelical view of homosexuality. It infuriated gay activists Gens Hellquist, Jason Roy, and Jeff Dodds, who filed a complaint with the Saskatchewan Human Rights Commission against Owens and the newspaper.

In his defence, Owens argued that the advertisement expressed his honestly held religious belief as it related to his interpretation of the Bible and its portrayal of homosexuality. After an investigation, the complaint was referred to a Board of Inquiry for a hearing. The Board of Inquiry ruled that Owens's advertisement violated the Human Rights Code by exposing homosexuals to hatred and ridicule. It also held that the right to freedom of religion and freedom of expression did not protect the advertisement from being in violation of the Code. Owens and the *StarPhoenix* were each ordered to pay $1,500 to each of three complainants.

Social conservative groups rightly denounced the Board's decision, but they did so with an excessive and distorted rhetoric that only fuelled more volatility in the debate over freedom of religious expression. "Saskatchewan Human Rights Tribunal Bans the Bible" screamed the headline on an article in REAL Women's newsletter.

Grossly distorting the Board's decision, the article charged, "A one-woman Human Rights Board of Inquiry ordered all parts of the Bible referring to homosexuality be publicly banned in Saskatchewan." It characterized the decision as "the pinnacle of the many absurdities that Canadians have had to endure from reckless and uncontrollable Human Rights Tribunals." An article published in the *Western Catholic Reporter* under the headline "Bible Declared Hate Literature" complained with alarm, "Hugh Owens may well be the first Canadian ever fined for quoting the Bible." The writer warned darkly: "Activist courts and human rights commissions are no longer the thin edge of the wedge in the persecution of Christians for their faith, and of everyone else who holds opinions unacceptable to the political correctness mafia. They are the battering ram crashing through the door."[75]

Owens, supported by the CRFA, appealed the decision (the *StarPhoenix* did not appeal), at first unsuccessfully to the Saskatchewan Court of Queen's Bench, but then with success to the Saskatchewan Court of Appeal. In April 2006 three justices unanimously held that the publication of the advertisement, when properly considered in its full context, did not offend the Human Rights Code. They noted that the advertisement had appeared in the middle of an ongoing national debate about "how Canadian legal and constitutional regimes should or should not accommodate sexual identities." It was also "published in conjunction with gay pride week— an event promoted by the gay community as a celebration of diversity and used in part as a platform for the advancement of gay rights." Seen in that broader context, the "advertisement tends to take on the character of a position advanced in a continuing public policy debate." The Inquiry Board and the lower court had erred by taking the Bible passages cited in the advertisement "at face value, making no allowance for the fact they are ancient and fundamental religious text." They could not be assessed "in the same way as one might consider a contemporary poster, notice or publication saying, 'Homosexuals should be killed.'"[76]

Between the time of the Board of Inquiry decision and the appeal court judgment in the Owens case, the Saskatchewan Human Rights Commission dealt with another highly controversial complaint against William G. (Bill) Whatcott, who had gained a certain notoriety as a member of the Christian Truth Activists. The media had characterized Whatcott as "Saskatchewan's most visible and vocal anti-gay, anti-abortion activist." Described in a newspaper article as a former drug addict and male prostitute and now an evangelical Catholic, Whatcott had committed himself to waging a "war" to have homosexual acts recriminalized and funding for abortions stopped. He believed that homosexuals could be cured through reparative therapy—and cited himself as an example of the success of such measures.[77]

The human rights complaints came from four Saskatchewan residents who were angered and offended by various flyers that Whatcott distributed publicly.

In the material, among other things Whatcott condemned homosexuals as "sodomites" and linked homosexuality to the corruption and endangerment of children. The complaints charged that the materials promoted hatred of gays and lesbians by characterizing them as sick and predatory and as living a filthy and perverted lifestyle, and by claiming that "sodomites are 430 times more likely to acquire AIDS and 3 times more likely to sexually abuse children." According to an Agreed Statement of Facts submitted by the parties before the tribunal, Whatcott's flyers made such obnoxious statements as "Our children will pay the price in disease, death, abuse ... if we do not say no to the sodomite desire to socialize your children into accepting something that is clearly wrong." And this gem: "Our acceptance of homosexuality and our toleration of its promotion in our school system will lead to the early death and morbidity of many children."[78]

The Board of Inquiry found that the materials circulated by Whatcott could be objectively viewed as exposing homosexuals to hatred and ridicule. Further, it held that the provisions of the Human Rights Code prohibiting the display of hate material were a reasonable restriction on Whatcott's right to freedom of religion and freedom of expression. Whatcott was ordered to pay a total of $17,500 to the four complainants. Both he and the Christian Truth Activists were prohibited from distributing the offending flyers "or any similar material which promotes hatred against individuals because of their sexual orientation."[79]

Oddly, unlike the case of Owens and Brockie, Whatcott's case was not formally supported by the prominent social conservative groups. The expressions of support that he did receive came mostly from social conservative media and several Internet blogs. One of those was by Rory Leishman, writing for Catholic-Insight.com, an online newsletter. Leishman commented:

> All Christians should take note. In numerous cases like Whatcott's, human rights tribunals and the courts have made clear that in their opinion, the equality rights of homosexuals in human rights codes and s.15 of the Charter trump the ostensible guarantees of freedom of religion in the laws and the Constitution of Canada. Thanks to these judicial rulings, Canadians no longer have a legal right to make a public statement that is liable to expose homosexuals to hatred or contempt, even if the statement is true and reflects the Christian convictions of the speaker.... Whatcott is on a course for jail as a Christian prisoner of conscience.[80]

Leishman provocatively exaggerated the consequences for Whatcott arising from the decision. No person could ever be sent to jail for violating the provisions of a human rights code. Nonetheless, Leishman expressed the widespread sentiment among social conservatives that judges and unaccountable and uncontrollable human rights commissions were stripping away the right of Christians to freely and publicly express their religious beliefs. As for Whatcott himself, he remained unbowed, dismissing the Board of Inquiry decision and the requirement to pay the complainants as "quite frankly garbage" and "not something I am going to abide by."[81] He also appealed the decision to the Saskatchewan Court of Queen's Bench, which in December 2007 dismissed the appeal and upheld the Board of Inquiry decision. Whatcott then proceeded with an appeal to the Saskatchewan Court of Appeal, which heard the case in September 2008.

By that time Whatcott's battle had attracted substantial support around the issue of free speech and free expression, although not for what he actually had to say. As intervenors in the appeal, the Canadian Constitution Foundation defended Whatcott's right to peacefully express his views while at the same time stating that it "does not argue in favour of the content of the speech."[82] The Canadian Civil Liberties Association categorized Whatcott's messages as "confrontational, extreme and polemical" and, repudiating their content, argued for the need to robustly protect freedom of expression. It contended that comment on the morality of others' behaviour is fundamental to democracy. The CCLA called on the court to strike down the section of the Human Rights Code that Whatcott was accused of violating as being an unjustifiable limit on freedom of expression. Alternatively, it urged the court to "read down" the section and thereby limit it to an expression that "signals an intention to engage in otherwise unlawful discriminatory behaviour, or seeks to persuade another person to do so, such as a sign on a store saying 'No Gays Allowed.'" If the court decided to do neither, it should overturn the Board of Inquiry's order against Whatcott.[83]

In a February 2010 decision the Court of Appeal overturned the Tribunal's decision. It found that the language used in Whatcott's flyers did not meet the judicial test of promoting hatred and therefore could not be prohibited or limited by the Human Rights Code. Citing the earlier decision in the Owens case, the Court held that the Tribunal and the lower court had failed to read the statements in the context of the documents as a whole or the larger context of protecting freedom of expression in regard to matters of public policy.

The Owens and Whatcott cases did not stand alone. Complaints were also made against the Roman Catholic Bishop of Calgary, Frederick Henry, who in a January 2005 pastoral letter condemning the legal recognition of same-sex marriage made several provocative—some would say extreme and hateful—statements, such as "an evil act remains an evil act whether it is performed in public or private."[84] The complaints were later withdrawn. Another complaint was made against Stephen Boissoin, an Alberta pastor and the former executive director of Concerned Christians Canada, Inc., who publicly condemned the "wickedness" of the "homosexual machine." The gay rights activists "and those who defend them," Boissoin declared, "are just as immoral as the pedophiles, drug dealers and pimps that plague our communities." He claimed that children in the school system were being "strategically targeted, psychologically abused and brainwashed by homosexual and pro-homosexual educators," and he appealed to young people who may be struggling with their sexuality to realize that "enslavement to homosexuality can be remedied."[85]

The Alberta Human Rights Commission ruled in November 2007 that Boissoin had contravened the human rights law by publishing "statements which were likely to expose homosexuals, as a vulnerable group, to hatred and contempt due to their sexual preference, effectively making it more acceptable to others to manifest hatred against homosexuals. The letter's content exposed homosexuals to contempt and reinforced existing stereotypes." Boissoin appealed the decision, presenting the case as a defence of freedom of expression and himself as a victim of abusive and out of control human rights commissions. In a judgment released in December 2009, the Alberta Court of Queen's Bench found that Boissoin had not violated the provisions of the Human Rights, Citizenship and Multiculturalism Act dealing with the publication of statements that expose a person or class of persons to hatred or contempt. The court also held that the penalties imposed on Boissoin by the panel were either unlawful or unconstitutional.[86]

In all of these cases, the appeal to a human rights tribunal is just as troubling as the extremely problematic statements themselves. In a free and democratic society, people of faith who feel compelled to publish or circulate hateful tracts quoting the Bible or other sacred texts must have the right to do so; and that right should be vigorously defended—no matter how offensive or reprehensible some of that expression may be to gays and lesbians or other identifiable groups. On that question, social conservatives and those they so militantly oppose should be able to find common ground, and common cause. In the words of the Canadian Civil Liberties Association, "Human rights commissions should not be in the business of restricting free expression of opinion."[87] What is more, the continued existence and use of these anti-free speech provisions simply provide unnecessary fodder for social conservative groups, which have for many years condemned the mere existence of human rights laws and commissions. To the bitter end, it seems, they will continue to call for their abolition.

Faith, Politics, and the Transformation of Canada

In recent years, some politicians and commentators have asserted that in order to maintain separation of church and state, legislators should not be influenced by religious belief.... The notion of separation refers to the state not interfering in religious practice and treating all faith communities impartially. It does not mean that faith has no place in public life or the public square.

– Stephen Harper, 2006

After four decades of concerted political and social action, the modern social conservative movement has experienced more defeats than victories. It has fought a losing battle to stem the tide of secularism, to halt the severing of the historic link between church and state. It has been resoundingly set back in its desperate efforts to reclaim Canada as a staunchly Christian democracy in which the laws, culture, and institutions preserve and promote Judeo-Christian values and identity. Social conservatism has failed in its substantial and persistent efforts to recriminalize abortion. It was defeated in its campaigns to prevent legislated human rights for gays and lesbians, the legal recognition of same-sex relationships, and the state's recognition of same-sex marriage. While the social conservative movement was a leading participant in the successful campaigns to achieve tough child pornography legislation, new criminal offences purportedly to address child sexual exploitation, and an increased age of consent, it was the new morality of rights and equality of treatment, especially as applied to women and children, that formed the basis of new laws to regulate sexual behaviour; it was not the old Christian religious morality. Nevertheless, by continuing to agitate, not just through those intensive campaigns focusing on key issues and through court challenges but also in the political arena proper, social conservatives remain hopeful that eventually the tide may be turned: that Canada will be taken back from the atheists and secularists and restored as a religiously moral state in which God and God's laws have supremacy.

As social conservatives sensed that they were losing control over the moral agenda of the country they sought to increase their influence on the political agenda. Happily for them, in electoral politics they have found no shortage of political support—primarily but not exclusively among the various conservative parties, from the old Progressive Conservative Party through the Reform Party and its successor, the Canadian Alliance, to the united-right Conservative Party of Canada. Indeed, social conservatives were the founders, leaders, and dominant forces within the Reform Party and Canadian Alliance and carried that involvement into the Conservative Party under Stephen Harper.

Just as importantly, social conservatives have constituted an indispensible electoral constituency that can be marshalled at election time to support their favoured candidates. While, as the various opinion polls show, social conservatives represent a minority of Canadians overall, their numbers, strategically dispersed across the country, remain significant. A survey carried out during the 2000 federal election by academics from three Canadian universities indicated that fully 27 per cent of voters identified as social conservative. According to a 2003 poll conducted for the Evangelical Fellowship of Canada, 19 per cent of Protestants and 7 per cent of Catholics identified themselves as "evangelical."[1] As the election of both the Mulroney and Harper governments attest, the path to power requires forming and sustaining a coalition of both social and economic conservatives. That goal in turn requires that close attention be paid to the moral issues that social conservatives view as primary.

In "Rediscovering the Right Agenda," Harper articulated the importance of social conservatives as an electoral constituency. In the article Harper called for a union of economic and social conservatives in a new political movement: "In this environment, serious conservative parties simply cannot shy away from values questions. On a wide range of public-policy questions, including foreign affairs and defence, criminal justice and corrections, family and child care, and healthcare and social services, social values are increasingly the really big issues."

Uniting the right, he emphasized, required rediscovering the conservative agenda, which means that "we must give greater place to social values and social conservatism, broadly defined and properly understood."[2]

Harper's appeal to include social conservatives and their moral issues within a political coalition of the right was also a pragmatic recognition that, as an electoral constituency, social conservatives have been passionately motivated to use partisan politics and the political process to advance their agenda. In contrast, the majority of Canadians are not similarly motivated. A Carleton University study conducted in 2003 found that most Canadians do not feel a similar need to get involved in the political process and generally decline to become politically involved. Indeed, in the years leading up to 2003, the number of Canadians who had attended political rallies, signed petitions, or joined political parties had actually declined.[3] In contrast, members of the social conservative movement in Canada are active in all of these political pursuits, as well as in making financial donations to their political allies.

Social conservatives also have allies among legislators who accept the notion that religious faith should guide public policy decisions. A number of current members of Parliament have publicly expressed the importance of drawing upon their religious faith to influence their political decision-making. Conservative Party MP and cabinet minister Jason Kenney, a former director of the Catholic Civil Rights League, has spoken out against the removal of faith from the public square and its replacement with "the absolute value of secularism." Liberal MP Dan McTeague told a forum on faith and politics organized by the Canada Family Action Coalition and Catholic Civil Rights League that "faith is a moral guide which steers him through important issues." New Democratic Party MP Chris Duncanson-Hales acknowledged a movement by some NDP caucus members to bring religious faith more within the mainstream of the party. "It's the idea that you are there for something bigger than yourself," he commented.[4] During the 2006 federal election Harper told the EFC:

> In recent years, some politicians and commentators have asserted that in order to maintain separation of church and state, legislators should not be influenced by religious belief. Leaving aside the fact that the separation of church and state is an American constitutional doctrine, not part of Canada's legal or political tradition, the notion of separation refers to the state not interfering in religious practice and treating all faith communities impartially. *It does not mean that faith has no place in public life or the public square....* On an issue like the definition of marriage, for example, citizens and legislators can certainly make

reference to the fact that almost all faith communities—not only Catholic, Protestant and Jewish, but Sikh, Muslim, and Hindu and native religions as well—consider marriage to be the union of a man and a woman,
and to call for this moral consensus to be reflected in civil law.[5]

The leaders of social conservatism have also encouraged Christians involved
in the political process to bring their religious beliefs to that role. In a 2002 edict
the Roman Catholic Church commanded Catholics involved in the political process not to espouse "ethical pluralism." It declared, "A well-formed Christian conscience does not permit one to vote for a political program or an individual law
which contradicts the fundamental contents of faith and morals."[6] In a 2004 position paper, the Catholic Civil Rights League articulated the obligation of the faithful to follow the laws of God if those rules collide with the laws of the state:

> Even when public authority becomes oppressive, Catholics are bound
> to obey the laws of the state *insofar as they do not conflict with divine
> law.* But no parliament, no legislature and no court has the authority to
> set aside the commandments of God, nor to command obedience to
> laws and regulations that are contrary to the natural moral law. When
> this abuse of authority occurs in a democracy, Catholics must take all
> legal and political steps necessary to defend ourselves and our fellow
> citizens, and may, in addition, resort to conscientious objection, civil dis-
> obedience, non-co-operation and other forms of non-violent resistance
> in accordance with the natural moral law and the Gospel.[7]

Evangelical Protestants have been equally insistent about the imperative of bringing religious faith to political involvement. In a 2006 position paper the EFC's
Bruce Clemenger exhorted evangelicals to become politically active. "The Church
has a political task," he said. "We should be politically engaged, as individuals
and as churches. The participation of churches in politics is part of its mission,
but its participation is that of a church in fulfilment of a broader mandate under
the sovereignty of God and Lordship of Christ." In a similar vein, the CFAC's Brian
Rushfeldt lambasted governments for promoting the "negative moral and financial consequences of social liberalism." He lamented, "The family—God's fundamental institution for society—is labelled destructive by feminists, discriminatory
by homosexuals, outdated and unnecessary by liberals." To address this alarming
situation, and to defend "the biblical view of humanity," Rushfeldt encouraged
people of faith to become "an elected official or other public servant in your community and influence decision-making."[8]

Towards an electoral breakthrough

To this end social conservatives have assiduously pursued their objective of regaining control of the moral agenda through activism within conservative political parties—an effort that has been going on since at least the Mulroney years, if not longer. But it was a basic dissatisfaction with the Mulroney government that, in 1987, led social conservatives, especially in Western Canada, to establish the Reform Party, which would more faithfully reflect their ideology, especially in regard to moral issues. Its first leader, Preston Manning, was a fervent evangelical Protestant. Manning and his father Ernest, an evangelist and former Social Credit premier of Alberta, had authored books advocating the establishment of a new right-wing party that would adopt a philosophy of both social and economic conservatism emphasizing individualism and greater free enterprise. They sought the privatization of most services provided by government, including health care, regional development, and education. Those beliefs formed the basis of the Reform Party platform. Reform called for strong opposition to abortion; support for traditional family values and measures to strengthen and support the family unit, which included strong opposition to legislating rights for gays and lesbians; opposition to affirmative action; the cessation of government support for women's and advocacy groups; tightening of immigration laws; opposition to state-funded day care; a reduction in taxes; and the slashing of social assistance programs.[9]

The Reform Party scored a stunning political success in the 1993 federal election campaign. The result was due in no small measure to the shattering of the coalition that had elected Mulroney a decade earlier. The Quebec nationalists had split from the Progressive Conservatives to form the Bloc Québécois. Angry and disillusioned social conservatives embraced the new Reform Party. The Tories were decimated, electing only two members of Parliament. In contrast, the Reform Party emerged from the election as the third-largest political party in Parliament (after the governing Liberal Party and Bloc Québécois). Like their leader, Manning, the Reform MPs were, as Brooke Jeffrey noted, "quite unrepresentative of Canadian society as a whole." They were made up of "predominantly older, middle-class, white males." In addition, wrote Jeffrey, "Their religious commitments far exceeded those of legislators from other parties, with at least 40 per cent indicating they were connected with fundamentalist or evangelical religious groups and many of them claiming experience in formal or lay positions."[10] The Reform Party immediately became the preferred political entity of social conservative activists, gaining the support of REAL Women of Canada and other groups. Later, Manning's executive assistant, Darrel Reid, went on to become president of Focus on the Family (Canada).

Still, a couple of elections later the Reform Party had failed to make the electoral breakthrough it needed to become a truly national party. It was not able to attract in any significant numbers the support of economic conservatives in Eastern Canada, especially Ontario, and its support in Quebec was practically nonexistent. Political scientists and the news media held that a major cause for the failure was its social conservative agenda. The party had become identified in the public mind with bigotry and intolerance. Many political conservatives saw this image as an obstacle to the movement to unite the right. In response, Manning and others conceived of a new political party. The Canadian Reform Conservative Alliance, popularly known as the Canadian Alliance, was founded at a convention in March 2000.

The Canadian Alliance proved to be short-lived, lasting only three years and failing, like the Reform Party before it, to establish itself as a national party capable of forming a government. Like its predecessor, the Canadian Alliance was fundamentally a social conservative phenomenon in its political orientation and its membership—exemplified by its first leader Stockwell Day, who had long been a ferocious social conservative champion. After the calamity of the federal election of 2000, Day was replaced as leader by fellow evangelical Protestant Harper. Both Day and Harper were massively supported by social conservative groups during their leadership campaigns. Equally important, the Canadian Alliance retained within its ranks a strong social conservative core of former Reform Party MPs.[11]

In late 2003 the Progressive Conservative Party and Canadian Alliance merged to form the Conservative Party of Canada. Social conservative groups organized aggressively to sign up members and to influence both the policies of the new party and the choice of its leader. The Canada Family Action Coalition mounted a campaign urging its members to join the new party to ensure that it opposed same-sex marriage and other "progressive" issues.[12] A few weeks later the Social Conservative Caucus for Members of the Conservative Party of Canada was formed. Its mission was to "bring together various groups such as pro-life and pro-family advocacy organizations." The group would "cross religious lines," including "Muslims, Christians, Jews and even non-religious social conservatives"—anyone who shared objectives on issues such as gay marriage, the defeat of legislation such as Bill C-250, euthanasia, and abortion. "United we can ensure that the values we all share are recognized and adequately represented." One of the organization's stated objectives was to recruit as many social conservatives as possible to become members of the Conservative Party during the leadership campaign and policy discussions.[13] These efforts were rewarded not just through the election of Harper to party leadership, but by the party's official policy statements. The party decided, among other concessions to social conservative sentiment, to make a commitment to give Parliament, not the courts, the final decision on issues such as marriage.

Conservative Party candidates in the 2004 election also reflected the strong social conservative bent of the new party. Ottawa-area candidate Cheryl Gallant stated that abortions were "absolutely no different" from a recent beheading of a hostage in Iraq by Islamic militants. She told CBC News that the Conservative caucus "as a whole" wanted to repeal Bill C-250. Other Conservative candidates supported the return of the death penalty. They promised that bilingual services would be reduced by a Conservative government, and suggested that women considering abortions should first seek out independent counselling.[14] Although the election returned the Liberals to power with a fragile minority government, the new Conservative Party formed the official opposition and stood as the only other party in Parliament with a realistic chance of forming a government.

At the party's grassroots level, an intense battle erupted between social moderates and social conservatives over policy. The first policy conference, held in early 2005, featured organizing by social conservatives to secure the party's support for policies opposing abortion and for an opposite-sex definition of marriage. The Campaign Life Coalition and REAL Women, among other groups, urged their members to become involved in the party and to secure election as delegates to the policy conference. REAL Women exhorted its supporters to resist the efforts of the "Red Tories" to move the new party towards the centre of the political spectrum. That tendency must be stopped, the group said, by "ensuring that the Conservative National Convention in Montreal in March is filled with true conservatives who are prepared to stand up for genuine conservative values."[15] In the end the social conservatives lost on the abortion question. The party members pledged that a Conservative government would not introduce a new law to ban abortions. But the social conservative faction scored a victory on same-sex marriage. The party committed itself to holding a free vote in Parliament on the question of defining marriage in law as the union of one man and one woman.

The battle within the party continued at the local constituency level as prominent social conservatives were nominated to be Conservative Party candidates in the next election. In British Columbia, Darrel Reid and Cindy Silver, a former executive director of Christian Legal Fellowship, were elected as candidates. Rondo Thomas, an official with the Canadian Christian College, and David Sweet, former president of Promise Keepers, secured Conservative nominations in Ontario. So too did Harold Albrecht, a Kitchener, Ontario, evangelical pastor. In a letter sent to his local newspaper, Albrecht had charged that recognition of same-sex marriage would destroy society within a generation. In Nova Scotia the party nominated three candidates, including a church minister, who had received strong public support from Tristan Emmanuel, the head of a new social conservative group called Equipping Christians for the Public Square.[16]

During the 2006 federal election the Conservative Party made a number of commitments intended to retain the support of its social conservative constituency. It was on the very first day of the election campaign that Harper made his promise about the holding of a free vote on whether or not the same-sex marriage law adopted by the Liberals should be overturned and replaced with a law stating that marriage would be limited to opposite sex couples. He restated his intention that, upon receiving a positive outcome from such a vote, the government would establish a new category of civil union for same-sex couples.[17] The Conservatives also campaigned on other policies designed to appeal to social conservative electors: increasing the age of consent for sexual activity to sixteen years (from fourteen years) and to ending "all defence loopholes for child pornography." Focus on the Family, Canada Family Action Coalition, and Evangelical Fellowship of Canada had aggressively promoted both measures. Similarly, the Conservative child-care policy catered strongly to social conservatives. The party promised to rescind an agreement between Martin's Liberal government and the provinces to create and publicly fund a national child-care program. Instead, a Conservative government would introduce a tax credit for parents of young children—something that would purportedly provide families with choice in child care. After one political rally Harper took time to meet with Charles McVety of Defend Marriage Canada in yet another attempt to court the social conservative vote.[18]

Despite these manoeuvres, the Conservatives succeeded in presenting Harper as a moderate conservative, as someone who was not an extremist on social issues and looked "prime ministerial." The party strategists effectively muzzled the social conservative ideologues, and rumblings about activist judges, threats to recriminalize abortion, and even the policy to repeal the same-sex marriage law were noticeably absent in the rest of the campaign. The strategy succeeded: the Conservatives won enough votes to secure a minority government. Indeed, one study of the 2006 election results found that while Harper continued to be viewed as "too extreme" by a significant 48 per cent of Canadians, that negative perception had declined by 5 per cent since a previous survey in 2004. The study noted, "The modest shift may well have contributed to the Conservative victory."[19] Outright expressions of concern about what a Conservative government would do on social issues were replaced, for many Canadians, with a more benign suspicion that perhaps Harper and his crew of evangelical Christians had a hidden agenda that would be revealed only after they took command of government.

That suspicion remained a feature of public discourse following the election and was certainly not alleviated by the exultant nature of social conservative commentary on the outcome of the vote. For social conservatives, the arrival of the Harper government presented the prospect of securing victory over the secularists, social engineers, and activist judiciary who had brought the country so perilously close to ruin. Noting that about thirty Liberal MPs who had voted in favour of same-sex marriage had gone down to defeat in the 2006 election, McVety declared the outcome a "tremendous victory for families nationwide ... and a great victory for marriage." The Catholic Civil Rights League's Horgan noted pointedly in a press release, "The League, our individual members, and our colleagues in inter-faith coalitions, devoted a great deal of time and effort to electing candidates who support the traditional definition of marriage, and whose views on moral issues are in line with those of the majority of Canadians." The EFC also expressed optimism about the new Conservative regime. "We now have a government that will be more sympathetic to a number of the issues of concern to evangelicals," Clemenger stated. For Rushfeldt the election of the Conservative government opened up the prospect of reclaiming the moral agenda: "Let us build on the hope that Election 2006 gave us for change in the moral and spiritual levels of Canada."[20]

The social conservatives in power

After assuming office as prime minister, Harper kept his election promises. The motion on same-sex marriage was introduced in the House of Commons but defeated as a result of the combined opposition of the other parties. Harper's government also moved quickly to introduce legislation to increase the age of consent for sexual activity to sixteen years from fourteen years, a move that Janet Epp Buckingham of the EFC saluted: "We took it as a message that we were being heard." The Conservatives also quickly honoured their commitment on child care by introducing, in their first budget, a so-called Choice in Childcare Allowance that provided all families with a taxable $1,200 allowance per year for each child under six. The Liberal Party's plan for a national child-care program was abandoned. Tellingly, the government enlisted social conservative advocates in a public campaign to secure support for the new policy.[21]

Social conservative groups had long been vociferously opposed to tax-funded child care. REAL Women in particular had advocated for a tax-credit scheme for child care similar to the one introduced by the Harper government. "REAL Women of Canada does not support the concept of universally available, government subsidized day care," the group's statement on child care proclaimed.

We do *not* believe that it is a 'fundamental right' for all women, regardless of circumstances, to have universal day care, but rather day care
should be available according to need.... We believe, therefore, that
child care funds should be paid *directly* to the parents to allow them
to choose the kind of care of their children, whether home, private or
institutional care. *Equal* child care tax credits should be paid to parents
regardless of which type of care they choose—whether home care or
substitute care.[22]

It is no wonder that REAL Women and other social conservative groups proved to
be so supportive of the Harper government's child-care policy: the Conservatives
simply adopted as their own the policy that REAL Women had been promoting for
many years.

The Harper government also dismantled some of the federally funded,
socially liberal, and secularist infrastructure that it and its social conservative constituents had long attacked. They ended the world-renowned Law Commission of
Canada, which had over many years generated a significant volume of studies and
reports calling for a modernization of Canada's laws, including those that criminalize various forms of consensual sex. In 2001 the Law Commission had produced
a ground-breaking report, *Beyond Conjugality*, which recommended that the federal government review the laws dealing with recognizing and supporting close
personal adult relationships to ensure that they reflected the diversity of conditions in modern-day Canada. Social conservatives had branded the Commission
as "anti-family."

Also axed was the Court Challenges Program, which provided funding for
legal challenges alleging that a law or government policy contravened the equality rights guaranteed in the Charter. The program had invoked the wrath of social
conservative groups because it had, in particular, provided funding to a number of
successful Charter challenge cases launched by gays and lesbians to strike down
discriminatory laws, including the laws that gave legal recognition only to opposite-sex spousal relationships. The decision to kill the program was clearly driven
by the ideology of the Harper government and not by economics. The budget for
the program was, in government terms, insignificant at $5.6 million annually,
especially in a time when the government had a $13-billion budget surplus. Yet the
impact of the program in helping to reshape modern Canada in the age of Charter
rights had been profound.

For social conservatives, it had been profoundly negative. They gleefully celebrated its death. No longer would they have to confront in court various groups
representing gays and lesbians, or other "special interests," asserting nefarious

anti-family and anti-religion Charter rights while being funded by the taxpayers through odious grants. The program, complained REAL Women in a press release that applauded its demise,

> constantly funded only left of centre organizations and by way of this abuse of the taxpayers' money has carried out social restructuring by way of the courts. The promotion of social changes by way of judicial fiat funded by the Court Challenges Program has resulted in the bypassing of the democratic process of public debate in Parliament.... The elimination of the Court Challenges Program will go a long way to promoting democracy in Canada.[23]

More social conservative joy greeted a sizable cut in funding for another one of the movement's targets: Status of Women Canada (SWC), the federal commission with a mandate to promote equality for women. At the same time the Harper government changed the mandate and funding guidelines for the grants awarded by the SWC, thus ending the funding of women's organizations that advocate for or conduct research on rights for women. These actions by the government catered to the demands of REAL Women and other social conservative groups opposed to feminism. In April 2006 REAL Women had mounted a concerted lobbying campaign directed at Harper and selected MPs that called for an examination of the need for the SWC's continued existence. REAL Women denounced SWC as a "serious abuse of taxpayers' money" because of its promotion of "feminist policies on the false premise that women in Canada are victims of patriarchal society." What REAL Women sought was "to disband the Status of Women and its outrageous policies and funding." Although the Harper government's response fell short of disbanding Status of Women, its action left the organization significantly diminished as an agent of social change. A few weeks after slashing its funding, the government announced the closure of three-quarters of the organization's regional offices. Bev Oda, the heritage minister, declared, "What these offices don't necessarily provide is the help directly to women. There was a lot of lobbying groups, there was a lot of advocacy."[24]

One of the other significant consequences of the government's funding decision was the closing of the office of the National Association of Women and the Law (NAWL). NAWL had been active on such issues as combating violence against women, improving the lot of women on low income, pay equity, and publicly funded, universal child care. NAWL would no longer receive the $300,000 a year in government funding on which it depended. "These are ideologically driven cuts that demonstrate a defective concept of women's equality and democracy," commented Pamela Cross, a NAWL board member. Cross also accused the Harper government of "trying to silence women's groups who speak out against its right-wing agenda."[25]

Ideology, whether of a social conservative bent or one that simply despised government funding for social service and equity programs—especially those focused on equality for women or that were directed towards queer communities—manifested itself in other Harper government decisions. The Canadian Rainbow Health Coalition (CRHC), established to advocate for better access to health care for gay, lesbian, bisexual, and transgendered (LGBT) communities, issued urgent fundraising appeals in 2007 as a result of being confronted with the removal of federal government funding. Under the previous Liberal government, CRHC had received funding for a multi-year project to conduct education into health issues for LGBT communities and to provide resource materials for health-care professionals and organizations. But CRHC was unable to obtain funding under the Harper government to continue the project. "While we have applied for a number of federal grants we're finding that the current political climate in Ottawa does not bode well for any organization wanting to address health issues that are endemic to our communities. Homophobia is rife within the federal government and the federal bureaucracy," wrote Gens Hellquist, CRHC's executive director, in a November 2007 fundraising letter. "Those few programs that have benefited our communities in the past have been cut or will be cut in the next budget."[26]

Ideological considerations also appear to have led in 2007 to reduced funding for HIV/AIDS community education programs in Ontario. The Harper government defended its action as part of its overall objective to reduce spending by realigning federal government investments. The added factor cited by the government was its commitment to fund research into an AIDS vaccine by the Bill & Melinda Gates Foundation. However, the principles of the Foundation required that donations to it by governments not result in a reduction of existing funding for AIDS programs—and the Harper government was breaking those principles. The cuts, amounting to 30 per cent of total federal government funding of HIV/AIDS programs in Ontario, would, according to AIDS organizations, have their most severe impact on the gay male population, which had become the focus of renewed education efforts aimed at reversing an increase in the rate of HIV/AIDS. Other changes to federal funding provisions introduced by the Harper government had resulted in the loss of funding for operating AIDS organizations, with the focus being placed instead on funding certain kinds of projects. Funding had been removed, for instance, from the Legal, Ethical and Human Rights Fund of the Canadian HIV/AIDS Legal Network.[27]

For the Harper government it was neither necessary nor politically advisable to articulate in anything other than fiscal terms its funding policies in relation to women's organizations that had a feminist bent, to gay and lesbian organizations, or to HIV/AIDS organizations. There was no political advantage in admitting that it was targeting certain groups and communities because of a strong social conservative tendency or even as a way of placating its most fervent social conservative supporters. The members of that important constituency would know what was motivating the cuts to programs, and would applaud those measures; and there was little likelihood that any of the groups or communities hurt by the funding cuts would in any significant way be or become supporters or allies of the Harper Conservatives. Few votes would be lost through such actions. The cutting of government funding of programs and projects is simply one of the many ways in which an ideological agenda can be effectively advanced without the need to introduce legislation or seek the approval of the electorate. It can also be defended as fiscally prudent. Moreover, it is also an effective means of helping social conservatives in their constant struggle against secularism and immorality.

In December 2006 the Harper government once more placed the interests of social conservatives in the foreground when it appointed members of the board of Assisted Human Reproduction Canada, a federal agency established to influence Parliament and medical practice on issues of fertility treatments and research on human embryonic stem cells. The appointees included pro-life anti-abortion advocates and opponents of embryonic stem cell research, including Suzanne Rozell Scorsone, a prominent public advocate for over two decades of the views of the Roman Catholic Church. At the same time, no scientists involved with embryonic stem cell research or fertility medicine were appointed to the board.[28]

The appointments to Assisted Human Reproduction Canada were especially concerning given the strident advocacy of social conservative groups on the issues of reproductive technologies, or assisted human reproduction, and research into the use of embryonic stem cells. As with other issues, their religious beliefs have strongly influenced their positions and advocacy on these issues. For instance, both the EFC and REAL Women have actively urged strict, some would say draconian, laws to prohibit or strictly regulate such practices. REAL Women has supported a total ban on embryonic stem cell research. So too has Campaign Life Coalition, which in 2006 called upon Harper and the Government of Canada to "stop the use of and experimentation on human embryos by the scientific community." The statement was issued in response to an announcement by the Canadian Institutes of Health Research that it would approve the use for scientific research of human embryos left over from in vitro fertilization.[29]

The EFC has actively lobbied for stringent laws dealing with reproductive technologies. In successive briefs and submissions to the federal government, the organization has argued that Parliament should protect the dignity of every human life, which "includes prohibiting research on human zygotes and embryos, in addition to adopting legislative terminology which reflects respect for human dignity." The group has also been adamant in opposing sperm donations: "One reproductive practice we find objectionable is that of sperm 'donation,' particularly anonymous sperm donation, which breaks biological ties and denies children the answers to basic questions of identity." As for embryonic stem cell research, the EFC maintains, "We affirm again our deep moral opposition to any research that causes the destruction of the embryo." It has called for an outright ban on such research.[30]

Similarly, Harper's government moved, in a small but symbolic way, to address the evil of judicial activism. In September 2006 Harper appointed a prominent social conservative lawyer, David Brown, as a judge on the Ontario Superior Court. Brown had represented social conservative groups in a number of anti-abortion and anti-gay rights interventions in significant court cases in recent years. Among those groups was the Association for Marriage and the Family in Ontario, which opposed a challenge by same-sex couples to the legal definition of marriage. In welcoming Brown's appointment Mary Ellen Douglas, a spokesperson for Campaign Life Coalition, declared, "It's high time we had some balance on the bench."[31]

In 2007 Harper's government drew cheers from social conservatives and generated a furor among the arts community and civil libertarians when it attempted to enact Bill C-10, an omnibus bill amending the Income Tax Act. The change in question would have allowed the heritage minister to withdraw tax credits from film productions determined to be "contrary to public policy." The bill was passed by the House of Commons with no attention being given to the film tax credit provision. It would have given the minister authority to establish guidelines for film and television producers addressing violence, hatred, and sexual content in film and TV productions, or anything else the minister believed should not be financed by Canadian taxpayers. Committees within the Heritage and Justice departments would be charged with vetting productions and implementing the guidelines. Any film or television program found to have contravened the guidelines would have its tax credits withdrawn and could be required to repay funding given through federal film and television funding agencies.

Bill C-10 was supported by social conservative groups that expressed concern about alleged pornographic material in films or television programs being funded by the tax system. REAL Women saluted the bill as an attempt "to prevent the abuse of taxpayers' money by requesting that those receiving government grants or tax credits be made accountable for the money received. It is little to ask." What was good, according to the group, was that film producers who wanted to depict violence or sex would "no longer be able to do this with the use of money from overtaxed Canadians" because of "how detrimental such material may be, especially to women, children and adolescents." The CFAC's McVety also championed the adoption of Bill C-10, pointing out that taxpayers should not "subsidize pornography." As he put it, "No one can give a good reason to allow tax dollars to fund pornography, or to fund films focusing on sex with corpses, or others with memorable names such as Young People F—king and The Masturbators."[32]

Even more disturbing than the content of the film-financing provision of Bill C-10 was how the outcry over it erupted only after news reports disclosed the provision when the bill was being considered by the Senate—that is, after it had already been adopted by the House of Commons. Arts and creative groups, including the producers' associations, the performers' union ACTRA, the Writers Guild of Canada, and the Canadian Civil Liberties Association, condemned the measure as censorship. They also charged that the refusal of government agencies to provide grants to film productions would work against the necessary obtaining of private funding because the ability of the donors to receive tax credits would be removed. The Canadian film industry would be seriously damaged, they contended, because it depended on both government funding and private donations for which tax credits could be received. Luminaries such as film producer David Cronenberg and actress and director Sarah Polley were among those who led the public opposition to Bill C-10.

Initially the Harper government defended the bill by denying that its purpose was to censor films. "Bill C-10 has nothing to do with censorship and everything to do with the integrity of the tax system," Heritage Minister Josée Verner protested. "The goal is to ensure public trust in how tax dollars are spent." But by fall 2008, in the midst of a federal election in which the Conservatives were desperately seeking to win a majority government, Harper finally bowed to the growing opposition to Bill C-10 and announced that the contentious provision would be removed.[33]

The importance of being incremental

The various actions of the Harper government led to considerable speculation on what it all meant for the future of social conservatism. In that regard, some insight might be gleaned by looking once more at Harper's musings in "Rediscovering the Right Agenda."

"We must realize that real gains are inevitably incremental," Harper wrote. "This, in my experience, is harder for social conservatives than for economic conservatives. The explicitly moral orientation of social conservatives makes it difficult for many to accept the incremental approach. Yet, in democratic politics, any other approach will certainly fail.... Conservatives should be satisfied if the agenda is moving in the right direction, even if slowly."[34]

If incrementalism is indeed Harper's strategy, but the real agenda remains, as he stated, one of "social values," clearly there are grounds for concern among those who have a different vision for the future of the country.

Clearly, as well, the path taken by the movement must continue to appeal to a broad spectrum of conservatives, whose unity and support are essential to the long-term success of Harper's Conservative Party. Tom Flanagan, one of Harper's ideological mentors and his chief campaign organizer, has described the Conservative Party as containing libertarians, social conservatives, populists, and Red Tories from the old Progressive Conservative Party as well as both Quebec and Canadian nationalists. As he noted in his book *Harper's Team: Behind the Scenes in the Conservative Rise to Power*: "They all need each other each. They can never win unless they try to understand each other and reach compromises that they can all live with."

Proposing an agenda for Conservative electoral success in tellingly biblical terms—a "Ten Commandments of Conservative Campaigning"— Flanagan observed: "Canada is not yet a conservative or Conservative country. We can't win if we veer too far to the right of the median voter." The task of conservatives and Conservatives over time, he contended, is to preserve the "traditional Conservative base of Anglophone Protestants" and draw in "Francophones, Roman Catholics (44 per cent in the 2001 Census of Canada), and other racial and religious groups." Echoing Harper's call for incrementalism, Flanagan declared, "We have to be willing to progress in small, practical steps." Noting approvingly that "incrementalism has marked Harper's leadership throughout," Flanagan lauded it as "intrinsically the right approach for a conservative party."[35]

Incrementalism as a guiding principle not just for a conservative movement but also for a Conservative Party bent on retaining political power and over time using that power to reshape the country—all of this recognizes that, in Flanagan's words, "conservatism is not yet the dominant public policy" in Canada. The implication is clear: Harper and his cohort believe that through many small and possibly imperceptible steps—what Flanagan has termed "small conservative reforms [that] are less likely to scare voters than grand conservative schemes"—Canada can be transformed from a socially liberal into a socially conservative country.[36] That is the real objective—and in pursuit of that goal, issues such as same-sex marriage and abortion that may no longer have any immediate political traction will be replaced with a range of other issues or initiatives, presented as seemingly moderate and unthreatening.

Social conservatives have not universally embraced incrementalism. Some see it as simply a cynical and opportunistic political tactic to avoid taking stands on the issues that are most of concern to them. Despite the Harper government's various initiatives, these social conservatives have remained sceptical about the veracity of the administration's commitment to their values and issues. They have cited in particular the capitulation on the same-sex marriage legislation, the failure to take a strong stance in opposion to abortion, and a refusal to support pro-life legislation. That scepticism was expressed publicly in the months prior to the 2008 federal election. A March 2008 editorial in *Catholic Insight* contained a blunt warning for Harper:

> The government had better recognize the strong support it has received from social conservatives. But, instead, it looks more and more like Harper has no intention—now or in future—of doing anything about the killing of the unborn through abortion; halting the attacks on the family and school children though the equality of same-sex "marriage"; changing Canada's pro-abortion delegation at the United Nations; cutting the funding of secularist feminists and, now, also reforming the HRC's [human rights commissions].

In any upcoming election, the editorial declared, "These topics should be front and centre in the questioning of candidates. If answers are not forthcoming, moves should be made for replacement of Stephen Harper as party leader."[37]

A few weeks later Charles McVety pointed out that "the honeymoon" with Harper had "ended quite quickly" after the defeat of the same-sex marriage resolution and the prime minister's declaration that the issue was closed. Link Byfield, a long-time social conservative polemicist and founder of the Alberta-based Citizens Centre for Freedom and Democracy, lambasted Harper for scuttling Ken Epp's fetal homicide bill and for making a "promise to suppress pro-life activity in the new Parliament." Those actions, Byfield declared, "were a harder slap in the face than anything social conservatives suffered from Jean Chretien." As a result, "An exodus of social conservatives has begun, and if Harper does nothing to end it soon, a large chunk of his base will inevitably disappear." Some deserters would go to the Liberals, others to the Christian Heritage Party, "but most will probably just stop voting."[38]

Another self-described social conservative, Ted Hewlett, also expressed disgust with Harper's incrementalism and its impact on the imperative of regaining control of the moral agenda. Accusing conservative politicians such as Harper of "working against social conservatives" by refusing to take action on abortion, Hewlett stated: "Until we have a strong movement to spread the idea of supporting traditional morality and political leaders who will vocally support positions rooted in that morality, it is hard to see how Canada can become a truly socially conservative nation once more."[39]

Confronted with growing disenchantment within his social conservative constituency, Harper persisted in promoting incrementalism as the way of achieving Canada's transformation into a conservative country. During the 2008 federal election campaign he told *Maclean's* magazine that the long-term objective was to hold his conservative coalition together and "to make Conservatives the natural governing party of the country." They needed, he said, "to pull conservatives, to pull the party, to the centre of the political spectrum. But what you also have to do, if you're really serious about making transformation, is you have to pull the centre of the political spectrum toward conservatism." Harper's agenda for change included a number of important elements: tax reduction, focusing on "delivering benefits to people and families," and "restoring pride in the country." That last goal included "pride in things like our institutions, our military, our history." He declared, "We are also building the country towards a definition of itself that is more in line with conservatism."[40]

Most social conservatives apparently took solace from Harper's comments. The Prime Minster seemed to be speaking in code that they readily understood. He offered assurance that in the long term his government's objective of moving the political spectrum rightward included facilitation of an incremental shift in the national ethos to social conservatism, which would occur through the restoration of pride in the national institutions and the history of the old Christian Canada. In the end, enough social conservatives stuck with Harper and his Conservative Party to help ensure re-election, albeit without the majority that party members so desperately wanted.

The objective of casting Canadian values and identity in more traditional and conservative hues featured prominently in one of the government's more significant initiatives following re-election. Citizenship and Immigration Minister Jason Kenney put it forth that the government was reviewing the content of the civic literacy questions used on the test written by persons applying to become Canadian citizens— "with a mind to improving the test to ensure that it demonstrates a real knowledge of Canadian institutions, values, and symbols, and history."[41]

In fall 2009 Kenney introduced a new study guide for the citizenship test that placed a renewed emphasis on the importance of Christianity and religious faith in the development of "a common Canadian identity." *Discover Canada: The Rights and Responsibilities of Citizenship* noted that "the great majority of Canadians identify as Christians," while acknowledging in passing that members of other religions "as well as atheists" were increasing in numbers. Using language that undoubtedly appealed to ardent social conservatives, the guide emphasized, "In

Canada the state has traditionally partnered with faith communities to promote social welfare, harmony and mutual respect; to provide schools and health care; to resettle refugees; and to uphold religious freedom and freedom of conscience." Similarly, the section describing the rights and responsibilities of citizenship presented the Canadian Charter of Rights and Freedoms in a manner that social conservatives would applaud. It noted that the Charter "begins with the words, 'Whereas Canada is founded upon principles that recognize the supremacy of God and the rule of law.' This phrase underlines the importance of religious traditions to Canadian society and the dignity and worth of the human person." In contrast, *Discover Canada* made no mention of the equality rights guaranteed by section 15. It tellingly omitted them from its short listing of the "most important" rights and freedoms set out in the Charter.[42]

The continuing presence of social conservative activists among Harper's circle of closest advisers also provided evidence that fostering social conservatism would remain an important element of the Conservative government's agenda. Early in 2009 Harper appointed Darrel Reid as his deputy chief of staff. Reid had previously served as director of policy, and replacing him in that position was Paul Wilson, a former executive director of Trinity Western University who had worked for Preston Manning and Stockwell Day. In fall 2009 Nigel Hannaford became a speech writer for Harper. As a former columnist with the *Calgary Herald*, Hannaford had championed social conservatism, disparaging equality rights for gays and lesbians and attacking human rights commissions.

These appointments caused alarm in gay and lesbian communities that were already apprehensive about the Harper government's agenda. Helen Kennedy, executive director of Egale Canada, cited the Reid and Wilson appointments as an acknowledgement of what "we've suspected for a long time—that Harper has deep roots with the religious right." She added, "We don't expect to see a lot of favourable recommendations coming out of the PM's office with respect to lesbian, gay, bisexual and trans human rights." Commenting on Hannaford's appointment, Michael Phair, a gay activist and former city councillor in Edmonton, worried that much of what Hannaford expressed in his newspaper column "reflects Prime Minister Harper's and his party's position on what they would like for Canadian society to be, and I think it harks back to a 1950s approach." Gay NDP member of Parliament Bill Siksay said he was not surprised by the appointments. "Lots of folks within the Conservative Party and Conservative parliamentary caucus," he said, "are not friends of the queer community."[43]

Lesbian and gay activist suspicions about social conservative influence on the Harper government were heightened in June 2009 following controversy generated over a $400,000 federal tourism stimulus grant awarded to help fund the annual pride celebrations in Toronto. The grant, approved and personally presented to Pride Toronto by Diane Ablonczy, the minister of State for Tourism, was condemned by outraged social conservatives. REAL Women urged its supporters to write to Harper and MPs in protest. The Institute for Canadian Values, a social conservative "think tank" launched in 2005 at the instigation of McVety, presented a petition to protest government funding for "sex parades" that added fuel to "a dangerous sex trade." "Unrepentant" conservative spokesperson Joseph Ben-Ami cited the grant as "the latest indication of how detached the Harper Conservatives have become from their key supporters and how incoherent their evolving electoral strategy is as a result." The Harper government, he lamented, "has ignored, obstructed or jettisoned virtually every prudent policy initiative that social conservatives have championed." According to Ben-Ami, the time had come "for rank and file members of the party to let their leaders and elected representatives know that they're mad as hell and they're not going to take it any more." The outcry led to a sharp rebuke of Ablonczy by the Harper government. Conservative MP Brad Trost stated on a pro-life website that the grant was not supported "by a large majority of the MPs," and that Ablonczy was being punished for awarding it. Responsibility for tourism stimulus grants was abruptly taken away from her and given to Industry Minister Tony Clement, who was swift in declaring that the funding program would be reviewed to ensure that "we have value for taxpayer money." Sure enough, shortly afterwards, the Harper government denied a tourism grant for Diverse Cité, Montreal's pride event.[44]

Organizing to reclaim the moral agenda

Whatever the immediate strategic objectives of a Conservative government, social conservatives are hopeful that they are on the cusp of achieving a historic retransformation of Canada. For despite the many defeats and setbacks suffered over the last couple of decades, social conservatism in Canada is neither dying nor beaten. It has survived with astonishing resilience and tenacity. Indeed, it seems that the enactment of legislation recognizing same-sex marriage and the many perceived assaults on religious freedom by the courts and human rights commissions have galvanized social conservatives anew. They have spiked their determination to restore Judeo-Christian religious beliefs and moral values as the bedrock of Canada's laws and public policy.

In pursuit of that objective they have cast their eyes to their counterparts in the United States to find the means through which they can reclaim the moral agenda. They see the American social conservative movement as being fabulously successful in controlling the political and social agenda in that country. They hope that by adopting the strategies used south of the border they can enjoy the same degree of success here—although, like Harper, they also believe that the key to their success must also involve incrementalism. REAL Women, in its 2004 polemic "The Silencing of the Conservative Voice in Canada," acknowledged as much, stating: "It may take several generations to institutionalize a rightward trend in Canada. But we have to begin somewhere and it should begin now. Years ago, American conservatives began this journey. Do conservative Canadians have the will to do the same?"[45]

Social conservative and *National Post* scribe Adam Daifallah similarly wrote in a July 2004 opinion piece that what the country needs is "an overt campaign to shift the Canadian political goalposts to the right." The model for doing so, he suggested, could be found in the United States, where conservatives had built a powerful institutional structure:

> If conservatism is ever to take hold here, the U.S. model must be replicated. Wealthy, conservative-minded benefactors must come forward with the dedication and resources necessary to fund alternative media. New foundations and think-tanks must be endowed. Political campaign schools must be started to find and train Canada's [Ronald] Reagan. Without a stable of intelligent, articulate and ideological writers, thinkers and political activists, conservative ideas are bound to continue to fall on deaf ears.[46]

The need to build a U.S.-style movement of social conservatism in Canada was also touted in a December 2005 essay published by Paul Tuns of the Christian think tank Work Research Foundation. Tuns suggested that politically viable social conservatism has been absent in Canada primarily because of three interrelated reasons: the lack of a conservative infrastructure such as foundations, think tanks, and publications; the failure to organize and become part of a larger conservative coalition; and Charter-era politics. Although the task confronting people of faith to bring moral issues into the political arena was daunting, Tuns optimistically noted:

> The marriage question may have begun a political awakening among people of faith. The attention being paid to the need for a conservative infrastructure is a development that could bear fruit. Whatever the hurdles social conservatives face, it is important that they do not give up and that they begin the hard work of organizing, becoming intellectually equipped and politically active.[47]

Social conservative advocates remain optimistic that they will be able to succeed in the long run through continued agitation, public education, and involvement in the political process. Commenting in a December 2007 *Canadian Christianity* online article, Brian Stiller declared, "The pendulum of secularism has swung as far as it can, and now it's in retreat." Bruce Clemenger expressed a similar sentiment: "We are living in a post-Christian society which is secularized yet very religious and highly individualistic.... In the aftermath of a period of rapid secularization, Canada is searching for a clearer sense of its identity amidst the diversity of culture, race, religion, lifestyle, social and political visions."[48]

Around the same time, Joseph Ben-Ami, then the executive director of the Institute of Canadian Values, proclaimed the determination of social conservatives to fight back against contemporary secularism, which he condemned as a "supremacist, fundamentalist religion." He stated:

These fundamentalists have taken control of the apparatus of government in Canada, and are using its power to impose their creed on unsuspecting Canadians, all under the guise of separation of church and state. Standing in the way of this post-modern crusade is a growing number of committed Christians who recognize the threat, not just to their own communities, but to all Canadians. Increasingly persecuted, these Christians have begun to fight back. And they're not alone—many committed Jews, sensing the threat to their own freedoms posed by the suppression of Canada's Judeo-Christian heritage, are joining the fight.[49]

Richard Bastien of the Catholic Civil Rights League asserted:

The renewal of Canadian conservatism is a long-term project requiring conversion of both hearts and minds. Some claim that holding such a project is delusional because it involves "turning back the clock." In fairness, social conservatives do seek to "turn back the clock" because they believe that we are better served by the logic of past generations, i.e., tradition, than by that of utopian dreamers, i.e., ideologies. Why should that be delusional?

Bastien contended that "Canada, like most other Western countries, has been on the wrong road for quite some time and that our current social model is simply not viable in the long run." Taking a U-turn would be a progressive act resulting in a rediscovery of "the permanent human virtues" without which "no democracy can survive."[50]

Conservative mainstay Preston Manning also weighed in, expressing optimism that social conservatives had it within their power to gain control of the political agenda in the long run. They could do so by presenting a more moderate image and adopting more pragmatic tactics that would allow them to successfully navigate "the faith/political interface." The first step, according to Manning, must be "'legitimating the discussion' of faith-based convictions and issues in the Canadian political arena, including Parliament and the legislatures." Even though public opinion surveys "consistently reveal that the overwhelming majority of us [Canadians] profess to hold and be guided by various religious convictions," Manning noted, "Most Canadian politicians are very uncomfortable in dealing with expressions of faith in the political arena." There was, he argued, an "unwritten taboo" caused by invoking the separation of church and state that constrains members of Parliament from talking about their personal religious convictions or those of their constituents.

For Manning, an important element of "legitimating the discussion" was for "members and spokespersons for faith perspectives to express their convictions wisely, responsibly, and non-threateningly." Doing so would assuage the fears of secular politicians that religious discussion in the public arena would—as it did in the past—lead to "a flood of ill-considered, ill-tempered, and contradictory statements, animosities, and positions, accompanied by shrill demands that such positions be imposed on others whether they subscribe to them or not." The tactics that must be adopted to be wise and unthreatening, Manning suggested, include abandoning "moralizing self-righteously or legalistically against the evil to be remedied" and instead "identifying with and publicizing the human *suffering* which will be caused if it is not." They would also include using the existing law, including the Charter, attempting to divide and conquer opponents, and finding and training the "right" spokespersons who would be seen as credible. Choosing the "right" public arena in which to advance the cause would also be necessary, followed by effectively using that forum to present the case.[51]

Canada is now indeed witnessing the persistent building of an organizational infrastructure that will support and sustain a social conservative resurgence. New political action groups and think tanks have formed. They join with and in some instances are spawned by the more established groups. Their mandates revolve around the challenge of restoring the union of church and state. One such group is the web-based Social Conservatives United. Founded in August 2006 by John Pacheco, a Catholic anti-gay marriage militant, it is dedicated to "faith family freedom." Its objective is to become a "network of social conservative groups to advance the principles of social conservatism in Canada through political and social activism." Another online venture, *C2C: Canada's Journal of Ideas*, launched in 2007, publishes quarterly issues containing analysis and opinion on both economic and social conservatism. Preponderantly made up of lawyers, academics, and journalists, *C2C*'s editorial and advisory boards are a who's who of Canadian conservatism. They include Preston Manning, Tom Flanagan, Adam Daifallah, and David Frum (prominent North American social conservative and former speech writer for George W. Bush). Some have also served as policy advisers or political aides to conservative politicians.[52]

The more prominent Manning Centre for Building Democracy, founded in 2005 by Preston Manning, is another instance of the social conservative effort to promote both an active engagement in the political process and the construction of an infrastructure to enable movement members to do so. The Centre's mission is "the creation of a democratic society in Canada whose governments are guided by conservative ideas and principles—individual worth, free markets, freedom of choice, acceptance of responsibility, limited government, and respect for Canada's cultural, religious, and democratic values." Among the Manning Centre's projects is "A Faith and Politics program to assist faith-oriented Canadians to better understand, manage and involve themselves responsibly at the interface of faith and politics." The program claims to have partnerships with organizations and individuals within the various faith and cultural communities, faith-based volunteers, media and communication professionals, and others. Its seminars for Christian, Jewish, and Muslim communities have included, as speakers, social conservative politicians at both the federal and provincial levels. "The intended output of our seminars," the Manning Centre's website boasts, "is a personal analysis and plan for credible political involvement at all stages—citizenship, voting, formal education, lifelong study, volunteering, employment, holding political office, mentoring, and political infrastructure building."[53]

The Manning Centre offers a number of certificate programs. One focuses on policy implementation aimed at individuals aspiring to hold senior staff positions in ministerial and parliamentary offices, and another aims at student activists on university campuses—providing training and basic skills for everything from "constituency organization and campaign organization and campaigning to public policy analysis and communications." Through these various means, the Centre built and maintains strong ties to the Conservative Party and serves as a training ground for both social conservative and party activists. An inaugural fundraising dinner in April 2007 honoured the first graduates of the Certificate Program in Political Management. Stephen Harper and his wife were in attendance.[54]

Meanwhile, too, the Roman Catholic Church remains adamantly committed to the "evangelization of culture," as dictated by Pope Benedict XVI, and to combating the "the split between the Gospel and culture, with the exclusion of God from the public sphere." In addresses made during a 2006 visit of Canada's Catholic bishops to the Vatican, the Pope lamented: "Certain values detached from their moral roots and full significance found in Christ have evolved in the most disturbing of ways. In the name of 'tolerance' your country has had to endure the folly of the redefinition of spouse, and in the name of 'freedom of choice' it is confronted with the daily destruction of unborn children." Benedict XVI warned about the "false dichotomies" that "are particularly damaging when Christian civic leaders sacrifice the unity of faith and sanction the disintegration of reason and the principles of natural ethics, by yielding to ephemeral social trends and the spurious demands of opinion polls."[55]

Apparently august think tanks and institutes play their part, making a concerted effort to present social conservative values and beliefs to the Canadian public with a patina of academic respectability. McVety's Institute for Canadian Values, for instance, is "dedicated to advancing knowledge of public policy issues from Judeo-Christian intellectual and moral perspectives, as well as promoting awareness of how such perspectives contribute to a modern, free and democratic society."[56]

In February 2006, amidst great fanfare, Focus on the Family also launched its own think tank, the Institute of Marriage and Family Canada, tasked with "presenting solid family-based policy research and ideas to Canada's decision makers." Several members of Parliament attended the opening of its Ottawa office, including Stockwell Day and Jason Kenney. The Institute's executive director, the evangelical Christian Dave Quist, was formerly a Conservative Party candidate and worked as a political aide to Harper.[57] Yet another social conservative think tank, the Institute for the Study of Marriage, Law and Culture, founded in 2003, includes contributions from high-profile academics who have crusaded against the legalization of same-sex marriage.[58]

The Canadian Constitution Foundation, formed in 2005, describes itself as "a voice for freedom in Canada's courtrooms." Adhering, like the Manning Centre, to both a socially conservative and economically conservative agenda, it asserts support for individual freedoms (including freedom of conscience and freedom of religion), economic liberty ("the right to earn a living, and to own and enjoy property") and equality before the law ("equal rights and equal opportunities for all Canadians, special privileges for none"). It holds annual conferences on legal issues that provide forums for various social conservative legalists and activists. The Foundation has also intervened in Charter cases in support of social conservatives such as Stephen Boissoin and Bill Whatcott and in the defence of religious freedom and freedom of expression.[59]

Other social conservative projects have been set in place specifically to train the movement's future advocates. In 2003 a consortium of REAL Women, Catholic

Civil Rights League, Christian Legal Fellowship, Focus on the Family, EFC, and Home Schooling Legal Defence Association of Canada formed the Faith and Freedom Alliance as a charitable not-for-profit organization. Its purpose is to "promote and defend the Christian faith in our justice system, especially in areas of freedom of religion, conscience and opinion, the sanctity of life and promotion of the natural family." Among its activities is hosting the Christian Legal Intervention Academy, which "trains lawyers and legal students in regard to arguing the pro-life, pro-family perspective before Human Rights Tribunals, as well as in the courts."[60]

A similar group, Trinity Western University's Laurentian Leadership Centre, based in Ottawa, is "geared towards third and fourth year students who plan a career in business, communications, history, international studies or political studies." The Centre's program includes internships working on Parliament Hill, at the *Ottawa Citizen* newspaper, or in government and non-government organizations. Guest speakers have included Preston Manning and other social conservative politicians such as Stockwell Day, Deborah Grey, Chuck Strahl, and Sharon Hayes.[61]

The construction of this more durable infrastructure will support continuing efforts on a broad range of issues that the leaders believe will, in the long term, result in the retransformation of Canada. The "sanctity of life" remains foremost among those issues—an umbrella term that covers the recriminalization of abortion, strong prohibitions on reproductive technologies, and opposition to any efforts to decriminalize euthanasia and assisted suicide. In January 2008 Stiller expressed his belief that "abortion will surface again" as a political issue, along with "the larger issues of the sanctity of life of the human person in the various forms of cloning and embryo manipulation that will inevitably come down the pipeline." In November 2009 Bastien emphasized the "imperative" of mounting "resistance to the growing pressures in support of legalizing euthanasia. Such legalization would be tantamount to giving government bureaucrats the power to determine who should live and who should not." He added, "Given the increasing pressures exerted on medical practitioners to perform acts that they morally object to, freedom of consciences must also be reinforced."[62]

In 2009 the EFC and other groups mounted a vigorous lobby to block Bill C-384, a private member's bill that would have decriminalized euthanasia in certain tightly restricted circumstances. Introduced for first reading by Bloc Québécois MP Francine Lalonde, the bill proposed an amendment of the Criminal Code "to allow a medical practitioner, subject to certain conditions, to aid a person who is experiencing severe physical or mental pain without any prospect of relief or is suffering from a terminal illness to die with dignity once the person has expressed his or her free and informed consent to die." An EFC letter-writing campaign urged people of faith to write their MPs calling on them to "uphold the current prohibitions against euthanasia and assisted suicide."[63]

At the same time, social conservative groups swung their support behind a private member's motion introduced by pro-life Conservative MP Harold Albrecht, who called for an amendment to the Criminal Code to establish a criminal offence for using the Internet to counsel a person to commit suicide. The motion was passed unanimously by MPs on November 19, 2009. Although not a bill that would have actually amended the Criminal Code, it was the advice of the House of Commons to the government. Albrecht and his supporters hoped that it would provide the impetus for the government to introduce a bill to establish such an offence. [64]

The pro-life groups remain formidably active. At the annual March for Life held on Parliament Hill on May 14, 2009, twelve thousand people called for the introduction of right-to-life legislation. That same year the Campaign Life Coalition launched a petition calling on members of Parliament to "pass legislation for the protection of human life from the time of conception (fertilization) until natural death." The Coalition claimed that by December of that year that it had collected some thirty thousand signatures on "the first round" of its petition drive. It promised to forward the signed petitions to pro-life politicians in the House of Commons.[65]

Pro-life groups also redoubled their public education activities in the hope that, over time, they will be able to convert a majority of people to their view on abortion. Alliance for Life Ontario mounted an impressive media campaign in fall 2009 that featured television commercials "designed to reach out to women experiencing a crisis pregnancy and to challenge and reshape people's thinking and emotions on the societal acceptance of abortion." The Alliance claimed that, in the forty years since decriminalization, "Three million unborn Canadians" had been killed through abortions—"a national disgrace."[66]

The alleged decline of marriage and family remains a critical issue. As Bastien declared, "In addition to being today's major cause of social instability, family breakdown compromises civic freedom." To reduce family breakdown, he stated, young couples needed to be made more aware of the dangers of common-law unions, which are "much less likely to survive the test of time." The best way of strengthening the family is by "doing away with unilateral divorce, also known as easy divorce." REAL Women of Canada, among other groups, renewed the call for repeal of "no fault divorce" and its replacement with a system based on "mutual consent." Under a fault system, both spouses would be required to "negotiate mutually agreeable arrangements regarding child custody and the division of assets and finances." Failing such a change, a "fault" should be reinstated "in order to prevent the easy walk-away from marriage currently permitted."[67]

The Institute of Marriage and Family in Canada has urged government action to "make marriages stronger." In addition to laws that would make divorce harder to obtain, it advocates for "the incorporation of the positive attributes of marriage into school curriculum, the eradication of so-called marriage penalties in taxes, and legal protection for marriage, as distinguished from living common-law." The elimination of perceived tax penalties for married couples—a long-time social conservative issue—gained renewed impetus under the Harper government. The introduction of "family taxation," which would allow "the splitting of work income," Bastien and other social conservatives argue, would "be of great help to families with a stay-at-home parent."[68]

For social conservatives, the strengthening of marriage and family also involves stronger laws against prostitution and one of its current manifestations, human trafficking. REAL Women, the EFC, and other groups campaigned intensively during 2009 for stronger Criminal Code provisions dealing with human trafficking, linking that issue to the need to retain or strengthen laws against prostitution. Decriminalizing prostitution, they maintained, would only create a social climate in which the trafficking of young girls and women would proliferate.[69]

The social conservative agenda also includes the abolition of the despised human rights commissions. In 2008 both REAL Women and the Canada Family Action Coalition ratcheted up their campaigns against the commissions. In calling for their abolition, REAL Women complained, "For far too long [they have] intimidated Canadians by attempting to herd them into mindless obedience to their arbitrary dictates.... The self-righteous appointed members of the Commissions should not be allowed to continue to torment Canadians." CFAC has been even more extreme. In May 2008 it accused human rights activists and commissions of being influenced by "communist socialists" and having "immorality as an ethos." The human rights commissions, the group contended, have "a bias bordering on hatred of moral principals"—and especially if these morals emanate from a Christian organization. "We citizens who have rights, hold to religious beliefs and have a sense of morality must force governments to rescind the Human Rights Acts that interfere with normal functions of a civilized society and democracy."[70]

The war to recapture the public square for people of faith and to reclaim the moral agenda is not, then, a momentary or short-lived phenomenon. The social conservative leadership in Canada, whether prescient or simply deluded, has concluded that the changing consensus of Canadians about sexuality and moral issues, the pronouncements of the courts, and the actions of legislatures are merely transitory and changeable. They do not see the growing separation of church and state that has produced the incremental secularization of Canada's laws and public policy over the last several decades as being irreversible. They want more, not less, religious faith influence on the nation's public policy. They are determined to wage their war for the long term, convinced that they can still prevail over the forces of immorality, secularism, and "political correctness."

Social conservatism as a movement does face immense challenges. A crucial question is whether movement activists will attempt to position themselves more within the mainstream of a broad conservative renewal movement—and whether they will succeed if they do. Will they truly embrace the "moderation" and "incrementalism" championed by Harper and Flanagan in the interests of achieving significant and long-term progress? Can the coalition of political conservatives maintain a place for social conservatives? As Tashha Kheiriddin and Adam Daifallah observed, "Let's be clear: an overtly socially conservative platform calling for implementing so-con ideas through legislative means—i.e., through laws restricting abortion, outlawing gay marriage, etc.—will not resonate with a majority of Canadian voters. Unlike the United States, we are not a socially conservative, God-fearing nation."[71]

Indeed, the pluralistic, multicultural, multi-religious country of the twenty-first century is not the old Canada of predominantly European colonialists, firmly indoctrinated with Judeo-Christian beliefs and morality. Attempting to desecularize the state would be somewhat like trying to unscramble eggs. Myriad laws and public policies, as well as social and cultural institutions, would have to be repealed and replaced or at least substantially altered.

The biggest obstacle of all for the forces of social conservatism remains the Charter of Rights and Freedoms and the rights that it guarantees to every citizen, notwithstanding the fact that its preamble declares, "Canada is founded upon principles that recognize the supremacy of God." To achieve the total retransformation of Canada would require the amendment of the Charter, which, as part of the Constitution, would require that seven provinces having at least 50 per cent of the population of Canada must agree. That is a very high threshold. Alternatively, social conservatives could hope that, over a very long period of time, appointments to the judiciary by governments staunchly committed to reclaiming the religious moral agenda could rely upon the "supremacy of God" wording in the preamble to reinterpret the provisions of the Charter and undo the damage done by the hated secular judicial activists. But not even Harper has ventured down that highly contentious path.

Nonetheless, the stark reality is that social conservatism's call to take back Canada, to return it to the Christian democracy of the past, cannot be met with complacency. To simply label and ignore the social conservative constituency as a fringe element or to magnanimously dismiss the movement's leaders as extremists, as many suggest, is dangerously myopic. Contrary to what their own propagandists and many in the media contend, social conservatives continue to have great influence and vast resources to pursue their agenda. They have stamina, resources, and, increasingly, the infrastructure to wage their campaign over a long period of time—perhaps, as REAL Women notes, for several decades.

Most importantly, social conservatives have, at least for the time being, a fellow evangelical as prime minister and, in the Conservatives, a governing party in which evangelicals are disproportionately represented. The Harper government's election in 2006 and re-election in 2008 were undeniably historic—and reason enough for social conservatives to be optimistic about the future. Having secured the reigns of power and being determined to make the Conservatives the "natural governing party," Harper and his evangelical colleagues are well positioned to strive for the transformation of Canada that they and their crucial social conservative constituency so ardently desire. The Harper government is testament to how the holding of strong religious views is not an impediment to gaining political power. It is proof that the movement can effectively navigate Preston Manning's "faith/political interface."

Setting aside (at least for now) the issues of same-sex marriage and abortion, the legislative and policy agendas of the Harper government have confirmed the distinct possibility of using the many instruments and levers of political power to advance a radical agenda of lasting social conservatism. As Bastien stated in 2009, "One cannot ignore the fact that the Harper government has been in a minority position and, perhaps more importantly, confronted until recently with a very hostile media seeking every opportunity to make it appear extremist." Seen in that light, the "soft" response of the Harper government on some issues important to social conservatives "has been based more on tactical prudential judgment than on a lack of commitment." For Bastien and, it seems, a majority of other evangelicals, "The Conservatives remain the national party most capable of addressing the issues of particular concern to conservative-minded people." If for short-term pragmatic reasons they cannot achieve the transformation of Canada that they seek, they may very well do so once Harper and his Conservative Party achieve a majority government. Or it may fall to Harper's successor, or to that person's successor, to be the victor in social conservatism's righteous war. The prospect remains that transforming the nation is an attainable goal, perhaps even an imminent one.[72]

Resisting the many efforts by social conservatives to regain control of the moral agenda is not just an imperative for gays and lesbians, women, youth, those who are labelled as socialist, left-wing, or even for that matter liberal, or, most especially, all of those deemed to be moral transgressors. The challenge of doing so must necessarily be met by all Canadians who prefer the morality of rights and equality of treatment over the puritanical religious morality preached by evangelical Protestants and the Roman Catholic Church. This project requires confronting the social conservative groups and organizing uncompromising opposition to their disturbingly retrograde moral agenda. Because what the warriors of social conservatism really seek is not the right to practise their religion. Rather, it is entrenchment in the Constitution and the laws of the land of the presumption that religious and moral values should be imposed on everyone, and enforced by the instruments of the state.

The social conservatives may seemingly have lost control of the moral agenda, but we must all strive to make sure that they do not ever regain that control. Canadians who want to ensure the continued existence of a more secular state—to advance the continued expansion of the separation of church and state—must remain vigilant. When the need arises, they will need to respond swiftly and decisively to beat back the multitude of social conservative crusaders who are so fervently dedicated to bringing the nation back to God.

NOTES

ONE
Social Conservatism and the Canadian State

1. Stephen Harper, "Rediscovering the Right Agenda," *Citizens Centre Report*, June 2003, 72–77.
2. Brian Stiller, "Vision 2000–Evangelism (Evangelical Fellowship of Canada)" <http://www.brianstiller.com>.
3. Ken Campbell, *No Small Stir: A Spiritual Strategy for Salting and Saving Secular Society* (Burlington, Ont.: G. R. Welch Company, 1980), 20–22.
4. George Egerton, "The Rise and Fall and Return of Public Religion: Church-State Relations in Canada Since 1945," Event Record, Research Colloquium, Nov. 2, 2006 <http://www.history.ubc.ca>.
5. Paul-André Lenteau, René Durocher, Jean-Claude Robert, and François Ricard, *Quebec Since 1930*, trans. Robert Chodo and Ellen Garmaise (Toronto: James Lorimer & Company, 1991).
6. Roberto Perin, "French-Speaking Canada from 1840," in *A Concise History of Christianity in Canada,* ed. Terrence Murphy and Roberto Perin (Toronto: Oxford University Press, 1996), 190–259; John Webster Grant, *The Church in the Canadian Era* (Burlington, Ont.: Welch Publishing Company, 1980; Richard Allen, *The Social Passion: Religion and Social Reform in Canada,* 1914–28 (Toronto: University of Toronto Press, 1971); Mariana Valverde, *The Age of Light, Soap, and Water: Moral Reform in English Canada,* 1885–1925 (Toronto: McClelland & Stewart, 1991).
7. *Humanae Vitae*, Encyclical of Pope Paul VI on the Regulation of Birth, July 25, 1968.
8. William L. Portier, "Here Come the Evangelical Catholics," *Communio: International Catholic Review*, 31 (Spring 2004), 44.
9. Ibid., 56.
10. Catholic Network for Women's Equality, "History" <http://www.cnwe.org/history.com>; Catholics for Choice–Canada, "What Canadians Think about Abortion," and "Who Are We?" <http://www.catholicsforchoice.ca>.
11. Rabble.ca, "Divine Intervention: Progressive Catholics Are Taking God's Work into Their Own Hands for World Youth Day," July 24, 2002 <http://www.rabble.ca>; "Challenge the Church," CBC.CA–The National, July 24, 2002 <http://www.cbc.ca>.
12. Catholic Civil Rights League, "About the Catholic Civil Rights League" <http://www.ccrl.ca>.
13. REAL Women of Canada, "About Us," "Objectives" <http://www.realwomenca.com>.
14. Peter Vere, "Gwen Landolt–A REAL Woman for Canada," *The Interim*, May 2008 <http://www.theinterim.com/2008/may/17landolt.html>.
15. REAL Women of Canada, Position Papers, "Statement of Abortion," and "The Sham of Revised Medical Technologies Bill," *REALity*, May–June 2002 <http://www.realwomenca.com>.

16. John G. Stackhouse, Jr., "Twentieth-Century Canadian Evangelicalism in Anglo-American Context," in *Amazing Grace: Evangelicalism in Australia, Britain, Canada, and the United States*, ed. George A. Rawlyk and Mark A. Noll (Montreal and Kingston: McGill-Queen's University Press, 1994), 396, 378.

17. Renaissance International, Mission Statement, reproduced in "Metro's Moderate Majority," advertisement, *Toronto Sun*, Nov. 9, 1980, 52–53.

18. Campbell, *No Small Stir*, 30–31.

19. John G. Stackhouse, *Evangelicalism in the Twentieth Century: An Introduction to Its Character* (Toronto: University of Toronto Press, 1993), 169. Calling itself "a national forum for Evangelicals and a constructive voice for biblical principles in life and society," the EFC today has forty affiliated denominations, seventy-seven ministry organizations, thirty-five educational institutions, five observer groups, and close to one thousand local church congregations that uphold a common statement of faith. See EFC, "Mission and Vision: Our Purpose" <http://www.evangelicalfellowship.ca>.

20. Focus on the Family, "About Us: Profiles Dr. James Dobson" <http://www.focusonthefamily.com>; "President Focus on the Family," advertisement, *Globe and Mail*, Aug. 29, 1997, B20; and "Who We Are" and "Our Purpose" <http://www.fotf.ca>.

21. Canada Family Action Coalition, "About CFAC: Our Vision" <http://www.familyaction.org>.

22. Miriam Smith, *A Civil Society? Collective Actors in Canadian Political Life* (Peterborough, Ont.: Broadview Press, 2005), 48.

23. Ibid., 61.

24. Barry D. Adam, *The Rise of a Gay and Lesbian Movement* (New York: Twayne Publishers, 1995); Gary Kinsman, *The Regulation of Desire: Homo and Hetero Sexualities* (Montreal: Black Rose Books, 1996); Donald W. McLeod, *Lesbian and Gay Liberation in Canada: A Selected Annotated Chronology, 1964–1975* (Toronto: ECW Press/Homewood Books, 1996); and Tom Warner, *Never Going Back: A History of Queer Activism in Canada* (Toronto: University of Toronto Press, 2002).

25. Stiller, "Vision 2000."

26. Campbell, *No Small Stir*, 20–22.

27. Council for Secular Humanism, "Welcome to the Council for Secular Humanism's Web Site" <http://www.secularhumism.org>.

28. Council for Secular Humanism, "A Secular Humanist Declaration," 1980.

29. Gay Alliance Toward Equality (GATE), "GATE," leaflet, 1975.

30. Egerton, "Rise and Fall and Return of Public Religion."

31. Beverley McLachlin, "Unwritten Constitutional Principles: What Is Going On?" Remarks by Chief Justice Beverley McLachlin, Supreme Court of Canada, 2005 Lord Cooke Lecture, Wellington, New Zealand, Dec. 1, 2005.

32. Ibid.

33. Bruce Clemenger, "Of Church, State and the Political Engagement of Evangelicals," June 2006 <http://www.christianity.ca>.

34. Arne Bryan, Founder and President, Prayer Canada, Ken Campbell, Founder and National Director of Canada's Civilized Majority, and Ron Gray, National Leader, Christian Heritage Party of Canada, "A New *Magna Carta* for Canada," Aug. 11, 2002 <http://www.renaissancecanada.org>.

35. Kyle Janzten, "Christianity and Politics, Past and Present," *C2C: Canada's Journal of Ideas* <http://www.c2cjournal.ca>; Bishop Fred B. Henry, "Of Faith and Politics," *Globe and Mail*, Aug. 2, 2003, A17.

36. Darrel Reid, "You Better Get Used to Us," *Globe and Mail*, Jan. 23, 2002, A15.

37. Brian Rushfeldt, "How Individuals and Churches Can Make an Impact," Canada Family Action Coalition <http://www.familyaction.org>.

38. Holy See, Congregation for the Doctrine of the Faith, "The Participation of Catholics in Political Life," Nov. 24, 2002, 2.

39. Catholic Civil Rights League, "The Church and Politics" <http://www.ccrl.ca>.

40. Catholic Civil Rights League, "The Laity and Political Affairs," Position Paper No. 3, June 9, 2004, 2; emphasis added.

TWO
The Right to Life and the Right to Choice

1. Environics Research Group, "Support for Freedom of Choice on Abortion at an All-Time High," Aug. 31, 2000 <http://erg.environics.net>; Angus Reid Global Monitor, "Half of Canadians Want Abortion to Remain Legal," June 21, 2008 <http://www.angus-reid.com>. Less support is expressed for late-term abortions, those performed after twenty weeks of gestation unless they are performed in limited circumstances, such as when the fetus is fatally impaired or has serious abnormalities or the life or physical health of the mother is at risk.

2. EFC, "Abortion and Fetal Rights Issues" <http://www.evangelicalfellowship.ca>.

3. Janine Brodie, Shelley A.M. Gavigan, and Jane Jenson, *The Politics of Abortion* (Toronto: Oxford University Press, 1992).

4. Ruth Roach Pierson, Marjorie Griffin Cohon, Paula Bourne, and Philinda Masters, *Canadian Women's Issues, Volume I: Strong Voices* (Toronto: James Lorimer & Company, 1993).

5. Joyce Arthur, "Abortion in Canada: History, Law and Access," October 1999 <http://www.hackcanada.com/canadian/freedom/canadabort.html>.

6. Ibid.

7. *Badgley Report*, note ii at 68 and note 2 at 29; Council of Women in Politics and Public Policy, University of Ottawa, Presentation to the Panel on Reproductive Rights in Canada, March 2, 2006, on Senator Lucie Pépin's website <http://www.sen.parl.gc.ca>.

8. Alphonse De Valk, "The Abortion Issue in Contemporary Canadian History: The Unfinished Debate," Canadian Catholic Historical Association, CCHA Study Sessions, 41(1974), 81–99 <http://www.manitoba.ca/colleges/st_pauls/ccha/Back%20Issues/CCHA1974/DeValk.html>.

9. Government of Canada, "Abortion: Constitutional and Legal Developments," August 18, 1998 <http://dsp-psd.pwgsc.gc.ca>.

10. Brodie, Gavigan, and Jenson, *Politics of Abortion*.

11. Albert J. Menendez, *Church and State in Canada* (Amherst, N.Y.: Prometheus Books, 1996), 109.

12. Brodie, Gavigan, and Jenson, *Politics of Abortion*.

13. Michael W. Cuneo, *Catholics Against the Church: Anti-Abortion Protest in Toronto, 1969–1985*, 11, 21–22.

14. Ibid.

15. Mary Jukes, "500 in Pro Abortion Demonstration Orderly, Attentive," *Globe and Mail*, May 8, 1970, 10.

16. Judy Rebick, *Ten Thousand Roses: The Making of a Feminist Revolution* (Toronto: Penguin Canada, 2005).

17. Murray Goldblatt, "Abortion Group Holds Hill Rally," *Globe and Mail*, May 11, 1970, 11.

18. Angie Gallop, "Abortion Caravan, 1970: Ladies Close the House," *This Magazine*, July–August, 2007 < http://www.thismagazine.ca/issues/2007/07/risingup.php>;

Joyce Arthur, "Abortion in Canada: History, Law and Access," October 1999 <http://www.hackcanada.com/canadian/freedom/canadabort.html>.

19. Goldblatt, "Abortion Group Holds Hill Rally."

20. Becki L. Ross, *The House that Jill Built: A Lesbian Nation in Formation* (Toronto: University of Toronto Press, 1995).

21. Rebick, *Ten Thousand Roses*.

22. Brodie, Gavigan, and Jenson, *Politics of Abortion*.

23. Ibid.

24. Arthur, "Abortion in Canada."

25. Erin Anderssen, "'I Practically Told the Jury to Find Him Guilty,'" *Globe and Mail*, July 5, 2008, F3.

26. Lianne Laurence, *Borowski: A Canadian Paradox* (Toronto: The Interim Publishing Company, 2004).

27. Ibid., 92–93.

28. Ibid., 7.

29. Ibid.

30. "Looking Back to 1986: Borowski Appeal Heard at Last," *The Interim*, January 2003 <http://www.theinterim.com/2003/jan/19lookingback.html>.

31. *Borowski v. Canada (Attorney General)*, [1989] 1 S.C.R. 342.

32. Laurence, *Borowski*, 387.

33. Ibid.

34. Rebick, *Ten Thousand Roses*.

35. Ibid., 159.

36. Toronto Right to Life Association, "Our History" <http://righttolifetoronto.org>.

37. Laurence, *Borowski*, 185.

38. Ibid.

39. Ian Scott with Neil McCormack, *To Make a Difference: A Memoir* (Toronto: Stoddart Publishing Co., 2001), 151–152.

40. Ibid., 152–153.

41. *R. v. Morgentaler* [1988] 1 S.C.R., 32–33.

42. *Tremblay v. Daigle*, [1989] 2 S.C.R. 530.

43. Ibid.

44. Brodie, Gavigan, and Jenson, *Politics of Abortion*.

45. Toronto Right to Life Association, "Our History."

46. Kim Campbell, *Time and Chance: The Political Memoirs of Canada's First Woman Prime Minister* (Toronto: Doubleday Canada, 1996).

47. Government of Canada, "Abortion: Constitutional and Legal Developments" <http://dsp-psd.pwgsc.gc.ca>.

48. Cambell, *Time and Chance*, 166–167.

49. Brodie, Gavigan, and Jenson, *Politics of Abortion*.

50. Laurence, *Borowski*.

51. Canadian Press, "Law Must Protect Fetus, Bishops' Conference Says," *Globe and Mail*, Nov. 10, 1989, A12.

52. Cambell, *Time and Chance*, 168.

53. Ken Campbell, *5 Years Rescuing at 'the Gates of Hell'* (Toronto: Coronation Publications, 1990), 3.

54. Ibid., 66.

55. Ibid., 67.

56. Ibid., 125- 126, 137–138.

57. Ibid., 127.

58. Ibid., 147, 173.
59. Ibid.,147.
60. Brodie, Gavigan, and Jenson, *Politics of Abortion*.
61. Cambell, 5 *Years Rescuing*, 183.
62. *Ontario (Attorney General) v. Dieleman*, [1994] CanLII 7509 (ON S.C.).
63. Ibid.
64. Paul Tuns, "CLC Mounts Ontario-Wide Injunction Protest," *The Interim*, December 1998 <http://www.theinterim.com>.
65. Tim Bloedow, "Ontario Injunction May Be Here to Stay," *The Interim*, October 1998 <http://www.lifesitenews.com>.
66. Tony Gosgnach, "Pro-Life Heroine Linda Gibbons Sentenced to Only One Additional Day in Prison," LifeSiteNews.com, July 28, 2008 <http://www.lifesitenews.com>.
67. *R. v. Lewis*, [1996] CanLII 3559 (BC S.C.).
68. The primary suspect, deemed a "person of interest," identified by police is James Kopp, an American pro-life radical who is serving a life sentence, with no provision for parole, in a U.S. prison for killing a doctor who performed abortions. The Ontario Provincial Police recently announced that they would not be proceeding with charges against Kopp. "Abortion Foe Avoids Ancaster Charges," *Toronto Star*, May 27, 2009, A10.
69. *R. v. Lewis*, [1996] CanLII 3559 (BC S.C.); *R. v. Demers* [2002] BCCA 28; *R. v. Spratt*, [2004] BCCA 367; *R. v. Spratt*, [2008] BCCA 340.
70. *R. v. Spratt*, [2008] BCCA 340.
71. Catholic Civil Rights League, "Appeal Rejected in 'Bubble Zone' Case," press release, Sept. 5, 2008.
72. Don Spratt, "The Decision of BC Court of Appeal and My Reaction" <http://donspratt.org/sup_crt_appel/sca_htm>.
73. Don Spratt, "Bibliography" [sic] < http://donsprat.org/about.htm>.
74. Don Spratt, "The Appeal ... What's It All About?" <http://donspratt.org/ sup_crt_appeal/index.htm>; Don Spratt, "The Decision of BC Court of Appeal and My Reaction" <http://donspratt.org/sup_crt_appel/sca_htm>.
75. Judi McLeod, "Toronto Grandmother Languishes in Prison," Canada Free Press, January 1999 <http://www.canadafreepress.com>; "Gibbons Arrested for Pro-Life Witness," *The Interim*, June 2008 <http://www.theinterim.com>; "Linda Gibbons: Political Prisoner," Lifesite: Linda Gibbons: Arrest History <http://www.lifesitenews.com>.
76. AbortionInCanada.ca, "Where Do Canadians Obtain Abortions?" <http://www.abortionincanada.ca/facts/abortion_clinics.html>.
77. André Picard, "Choice? What Choice?" *Globe and Mail*, Jan. 24, 2008, L1.
78. Those periods range from 12 weeks in Nunavut and the Yukon, to 20 weeks in Alberta and British Columbia, to 23 and 24 weeks respectively in Quebec and Ontario.
79. Toronto Right to Life, "Our History."
80. Ken Campbell, 5 *Years Rescuing,* 221.
81. Campaign Life Coalition Ontario, "The Issues: Explanations of Some of the Ontario Life Issues Abortion Funding," 1999.
82. Vaughn Palmer, "In 1988, the Abortion Issue Went Toxic. Remember Bill Vander Zalm?" *Vancouver Sun*, Aug. 22, 2008 <http://www.canada.com>.
83. Committee to End Tax-Funded Abortions, "Backgrounder on Public Funding of Abortion," May 1996.
84. Committee to End Tax-Funded Abortions, "This Man Wants to Perform Abortions ... With Your Tax Dollars," advertisement, *Leader-Post* (Regina), Oct. 18, 1991, D5; Campaign Life Coalition Saskatchewan, "Attention Pro-Life Voters," advertisement, *Leader-Post*, Oct. 19, 1991, A19.

85. "New Brunswick Mulls Morgentaler Decision Appeal," *Calgary Herald*, Aug. 29, 2008, online; "N.B. Won't Appeal Morgentaler Ruling," *Globe and Mail*, Aug. 19, 2009, A9.

86. Campaign Life Coalition, "Pro-Life MPs & Pro-Life with Exceptions," CLC National News, January 2006 <http://www.campaignlifecoalition.com>.

87. Abortion Rights Coalition of Canada, "About Us – Why ARCC" <http://www.arcc-cdac.ca>.

88. Kady O'Malley, "Lust for Life," Macleans.ca, May 10, 2007 <http://www.macleans.ca>.

89. Hansard, Number 034, House of Commons, 37th Parliament, 1st Session, May 22, 2001, 1739.

90. Benoit is a Conservative MP from the rural Alberta riding of Vegreville-Wainwright, and Epp is a Conservative MP for Edmonton Sherwood Park in Alberta. Bill C-291, *An Act to amend the Criminal Code (injuring or causing death of a child before or during its birth while committing an offence)*, First Session, Thirty-ninth Parliament, 55 Elizabeth II, 2006; Bill C-484, *An Act to amend the Criminal Code (injuring or causing death of an unborn child while committing an offence)*, Second Session, Thirty-ninth Parliament, 56 Elizabeth II, 2007.

91. Abortion Rights Coalition of Canada, "Talking Points Against the 'Unborn Victims of Violence Act,'" Dec. 12, 2007 <http://www.arcc-cdac.ca>.

92. Ibid.

93. Campaign Life Coalition, "Two More Tragic Murders in Toronto," press release, Oct. 3, 2007; Catholic Civil Rights League, "League Welcomes Next Step in Legislation for Unborn Victims of Violence," press release, Dec. 6, 2007.

94. Paul Steckle, M.P., "Paul's Bio" <http://www.psteckle.com>; Bill C-338, *An Act to amend the Criminal Code (procuring a miscarriage after twenty weeks of gestation)*, First Session, Thirty-ninth Parliament, 55 Elizabeth II, 2006.

95. Joyce Arthur, "A Direct Attack on Abortion Rights," Abortion Rights Coalition of Canada, June 26, 2006.

96. Bill C-537, *An Act to amend the Criminal Code (protection of conscience rights in the health care profession)*, Second Session, Thirty-ninth Parliament, 56–57 Elizabeth II, 2007–2008; Douglas Cryer, "Unborn Victims of Crime Act Is Just Plan Common Sense," 2007 <http://www.christianity.ca>.

97. Susan Delacourt, "Ambrose Defends Tory Fetal Rights Bill," *Toronto Star*, June 6, 2008, A17; Allan Woods, "Tories Act to Avoid Abortion Fight," *Toronto Star*, Aug. 26, 2008, A15; Campbell Clark, "Harper Ups Ante on Election Ultimatum," *Globe and Mail*, Aug. 26, 2008, A1.

98. Peter Ryan, "LifeCanada: Standing on Guard for Life," *Life Canada News*, Vol. 1, No. 1, 2002 <http://www.lifecanada.org>.

99. "Considering the Question of Criminal Punishment for Abortion," *The Interim*, November 2007 <http://www.theinterim.com>.

THREE

Regulating Sexuality and Social Order

1. Jerry Falwell, foreword in *No Small Stir: A Spiritual Strategy for Salting and Saving Secular Society*, by Ken Campbell (Burlington: G. R. Welch Company, 1980), 13.

2. EFC, "Marriage and Family Status in Canada, A Position Paper of the Evangelical Fellowship of Canada," 1996, 1–3.

3. Holy See, *Catechism of the Catholic Church*, 2360, Oct. 11, 1992.

4. EFC, "Innocence Preserved Protecting Children from Child Pornography," May 2002, 5.

5. Mariana Valverde, *The Age of Light, Soap, and Water: Moral Reform in English Canada, 1885–1925* (Toronto: McClelland & Stewart, 1991).

6. Bruce Clemenger, "Of Church, State and the Political Engagement of Evangelicals" <http://www.christianity.ca>, 2006.

7. Dany Lacombe, *Blue Politics: Pornography and the Law in the Age of Feminism* (Toronto: University of Toronto Press, 1994), 23.

8. Brenda Cossman, Shannon Bell, Lise Gotell, and Becki L. Ross, *Bad Attitudes on Trial: Pornography, Feminism, and the Butler Decision* (Toronto: University of Toronto Press, 1997).

9. Lacombe, *Blue Politics.*

10. Gerald Hannon, "Censored," *The Body Politic*, April 1977, 1.

11. Gerald Hannon, "Pornography, Feminism and Children's Literature," *The Body Politic*, April 1978, 5.

12. Lacombe, *Blue Politics*, 1994.

13. Holy See, *Catechism of the Catholic Church.*

14. REAL Women of Canada, "Statement on Pornography," Position Papers <http://www.realwomenca.com>; EFC, "Pornography" <http://www.evangelicalfellowship.ca>; EFC, "Innocence Preserved Protecting Children from Child Pornography," May 2002, 17.

15. Lise Gotell, "Shaping Butler: The New Politics of Anti-Pornography," in *Bad Attitudes on Trial: Pornography, Feminism, and the Butler Decision,* ed. Brenda Cossman, Shannon Bell, Lise Gotell, and Becki L. Ross (Toronto: University of Toronto Press, 1997), 66.

16. Brenda Cossman and Shannon Bell, Introduction to *Bad Attitudes on Trial,* ed. Cossman, Bell, Gotell, and Ross, 19.

17. REAL Women of Canada, "Statement on Prostitution," Position Papers <http://www.realwomenca.com>.

18. Gotell, "Shaping Butler."

19. *Hansard*, Oct. 7, 1986, 166; quoted in Lacombe, *Blue Politics*, 100–1.

20. Lacombe, *Blue Politics*, 1994; Tom Warner, *Never Going Back: A History of Queer Activism in Canada* (Toronto: University of Toronto Press, 2002).

21. Lacombe, *Blue Politics*, 114.

22. *Ibid.,*109–111; REAL Women of Canada, "Statement on Pornography" <http://www.realwomenca.com>; emphasis added. The statement does not cite the "recent studies."

23. Lacombe, *Blue Politics*, 115.

24. Ibid., 118.

25. Susan G. Cole, *Pornography and the Sex Crisis* (Toronto: Second Story Press, 1992), 79–80.

26. Lacombe, *Blue Politics*, 118–123, 129–130.

27. Gotell, "Shaping Butler," 49–50.

28. Ibid., 84.

29. *R. v. Butler*, [1992] 1 S.C.R. 452; emphasis added.

30. REAL Women of Canada, "Statement on Pornography" <http://www.realwomenca.com>.

31. EFC, "Innocence Preserved Protecting Children from Child Pornography," 5–6.

32. *Hansard,* Commons Debates, June 15, 1993, 20878.

33. *Hansard*, Minutes of the Proceedings and Evidence of the Standing Committee on Justice and the Solicitor General, June 15, 1993. See also Warner, *Never Going Back.* The organization Coalition for Gay Rights in Ontario (CGRO) changed its name to Coalition for Lesbian and Gay Rights in Ontario (CLGRO) in 1987.

34. Francine Dube, "Top B.C. Court Strikes down Child-Porn Law," *National Post*, Jan. 16, 1999; Jane Armstrong, "Child-Porn Law Is Struck Down by B.C." *Globe and Mail*, Jan. 16,

1999, A1; Jane Armstrong, "Kiddie-Porn Law Headed to Top Court," *Globe and Mail*, July 1, 1999, A1; Stan Persky and John Dixon, *On Kiddie Porn: Sexual Representation, Free Speech & the Robin Sharpe Case* (Vancouver: New Star Books, 2001), 99–117.

35. Carla Yu, "See No Evil," *BC Report*, Feb. 8, 1999 <http://www.axionet.com/bcreport/web/990208f.html>; Neall Hall and Lori Culbert, "Surrey Judge Dismisses Child Porn Charges," *Vancouver Sun*, Jan. 19, 1999, A3; "Child Porn Case Judge Gets Death Threat," *Vancouver Sun*, Jan. 23, 1999, A1.

36. Sheldon Alberts, "McLellan Rejects Calls to Overturn Child Porn Ruling," *National Post*, Feb. 2, 1999, A1.

37. EFC, "Child Pornography Prayer Vigil: Event Follow-Up," media release, Jan. 20, 2000.

38. *R v. Sharpe*, [2001] 1 S.C.R. 45, 2001 SCC 2.

39. Focus on the Family, "The Sharpe Case: Child Pornography," familyfacts.ca, April 3, 2002 <http://www.fotf.ca>; Focus on the Family, "Anti-Child Pornography Press Conference," press release, April 11, 2002 <http://www.fotf.ca>; Focus on the Family, "Statement by Dr. Darrel Reid, President of Focus Canada: Child Pornography," April 11, 2002 <http://www.fotf.ca>; Focus on the Family, "Focus Calls for Immediate Action on Child Pornography," press release, Oct. 24, 2002.

40. Focus on the Family, "Pornography," issues statement, familyfacts.ca <http://ww.fotf.ca/familyfacts/issues/pornography/index.html>.

41. This account of the Roundtable is taken from a report authored by journalist Lloyd Mackey and posted on the website of *Canadian Christianity*, April 17, 2002. John Mackey, "Comment: The Roundtable Has Sharpe Corners" <http://www.canadianchristianity.com/cgi-bin/cgk?nationalupdates/040417comment>.

42. REAL Women of Canada, "Child Pornography and the Public Good," press release, Dec. 5, 2002.

43. Canada Family Action Coalition, "CFAC Election Plan 2004" <http://www.familyaction.org>; REAL Women of Canada, "2004 Federal Election: This Election Is Crucial to the Future of Our Nation! We Must All Do Our Part" <http://www.realwomenca.com>.

44. Conservative Party of Canada, "Demanding Better: Conservative Party of Canada, Platform 2004," 37.

45. Brian Laghi, "Tories Try to Connect Martin to Child Porn," *Globe and Mail*, June 19, 2004, A1.

46. United Nations, *Optional Protocol to the Convention on the Rights of the Child on the Sale of Children, Child Prostitution and Child Pornography*; emphasis added.

47. British Columbia Civil Liberties Association, "Brief of the British Columbia Civil Liberties Association re: Bill C-2," 2005.

48. Writers' Union of Canada, "Submission of The Writers' Union of Canada to the Standing Committee on Legal and Constitutional Affairs on Bill C-2," June 28, 2005.

49. *Hansard,* Standing Committee on Justice, Human Rights, Public Safety and Emergency Preparedness, Evidence, April 21, 2005, 3–4; *Hansard,* Standing Committee on Justice, Human Rights, Public Safety and Emergency Preparedness, Evidence, April 14, 2005, 7–8.

50. REAL Women of Canada, "Age of Consent—a Movable Feast for Deviants," *REALity*, November–December, 1999 <http://www.realwomenca.com>.

51. Canadian Association of Police Service Boards, "Resolutions Approved at the 1998 Canadian Association of Police Boards' Annual Meeting," Aug. 22 1998, Edmonton, Alta.; Sue Careless, "Ottawa Looks at Changing Age of Consent for Sex," *The Interim*, December 1999 <http://www.theinterim.com/1999/dec/23ottawa.html>; Beyond

Borders Inc., "Submission to the House of Commons Justice Committee on Bill C-2: Raising the Age of Consent," Norman Boudreau, Vice President, April 19, 2005.

52. Pollara Strategic Public Opinion & Market Research, "Canadian Opinions on Child Pornography Legislation and the Age of Consent," May 2002.

53. *Hansard,* Standing Committee on Justice, Human Rights, Public Safety and Emergency Preparedness, Evidence, April 21, 2005, 3–4.

54. Ibid., April 14, 2005, 8.

55. Canada Family Action Coalition, "National Campaign Launched to Raise Age of Consent for Sex," press release, Sept. 20, 2001.

56. William Walker, "Canada a Centre for Child Sex, Report Says," *Toronto Star*, Jan. 25, 2000, A1; the CCSD report, "Progress of Canada's Children into the Millennium," was published in 2000. The findings of the CCSD report echoed what was contained in the United Nations Protocol to the Convention on the Rights of the Child on the Sale of Children, Child Prostitution and Child Pornography, which the government and social conservative groups cited in their calls for tougher laws to deal with child sexual exploitation. The Protocol stated: "The elimination of the sale of children, child prostitution and child pornography will be facilitated by adopting a holistic approach, addressing the contributing factors, including underdevelopment, poverty, economic disparities, inequitable socio-economic structure, dysfunctioning families, lack of education, urban-rural migration, gender discrimination, irresponsible adult sexual behavior, harmful traditional practices, armed conflicts and trafficking of children."

57. David Thompson, "Canada's Abuser-friendly Age of Consent," Beyond Borders, Winnipeg, 2005, 2.

58. Ibid.

59. Catholic Civil Rights League, "Child-Adult Age-of-Consent Changes Needed," February 2002 <http://www.ccrl.ca>; Focus on the Family, "Reality Check: Teen Sexuality," March 2003 <http://www.fotf.ca>.

60. EFC, *Response to the Department of Justice Child Victim Consultation*, March 30, 2000, 2, 3.

61. Focus on the Family, "Reality Check."

62. Canada Family Action Coalition, "CFAC Election Plan 2004" <http://www.familyaction.org>; REAL Women of Canada, "2004 Federal Election: This Election Is Crucial to the Future of Our Nation! We Must All Do Our Part" <http://www.realwomenca.com>.

63. Conservative Party of Canada, "Stand Up For Canada: Conservative Party of Canada Federal Election Platform 2006," 24.

64. *Hansard*, Standing Committee on Justice and Human Rights, Evidence Contents, March 22, 2007, 0905.

65. Ibid., March 21, 2007, 1530.

66. Ibid., March 29, 2007, 1215.

67. Ibid., March 27, 2007, 0920, 0945.

68. Department of Justice Canada, "Report and Recommendations in Respect of Legislation, Policy and Practices Concerning Prostitution-Related Activities," December 1998 <http://canada.justice.gc/en/news/nr/1998>.

69. Sex Professionals of Canada, "Mission" <http://www.spoc.ca/>.

70. *Reference re ss. 193 and 195.(1)(c) of the Criminal Code (Man.)*, [1990] 1 S.C.R. 123. Also known as *Re: Prostitution*.

71. REAL Women of Canada, "Statement on Prostitution."

72. EFC, "Prostitution" <http://www.evangelicalfellowship.ca>.

73. House of Commons Committees, Subcommittee on Solicitation Laws, "History" <http://www2.parl.gc.ca/CommitteeBusiness>; "A Green Light for Red Light?" *Globe*

and Mail, June 4, 2005, F2. In December 2007 Pickton was convicted of second-degree murder in the killing of six women. He was also charged with the murder of twenty other women. In October 2009 the RCMP disclosed that they had evidence in hand for another six more murder charges. Robert Matas, "Robert Pickton Could Face Six New Murder Charges," *Globe and Mail*, Oct. 29, 2009.

74. EFC, "Submission to the Subcommittee on Solicitation Laws of the Standing Committee on Justice, Human Rights, Public Safety and Emergency Preparedness," February 2005, 5,1.

75. REAL Women of Canada, "Brief on Solicitation Laws," Feb. 14, 2005, 12; Focus on the Family, "MPs to Propose Decriminalizing Sex Solicitation," Oct. 19, 2005 <http://www.fotf.ca>.

76. "A Green Light for Red Light?" *Globe and Mail*, June 4, 2005, F2.

77. House of Commons of Canada, "The Challenge of Change: A Study of Canada's Criminal Prostitution Laws," Report of the Standing Committee on Justice and Human Rights, December 2006.

78. Tom Sandborn, "Platitudes, Moralism and Band-Aid Solutions," *Xtra West*, Dec. 21, 2006 <http://www.spoc.ca>.

79. Libby Davies, "Sex Work: the Charter v. the Criminal Code," June 12, 2007 <http://www.spoc.ca>.

80. "The Prostitution Law—REAL Women to Intervene in the Legal Challenge of the Law," *REALity*, January–February 2008 <http://www.realwomenca.com>.

81. Kirk Makin, "Religious Groups Seek Standing at Prostitution Challenge," *Globe and Mail*, June 20, 2009, A4.

82. Kirk Makin, "Groups Refused Standing at Prostitution Law Trial," *Globe and Mail*, July 3, 2009, A6.

83. Kirk Makin, "Groups Can Back Prostitution Laws, Court Rules," *Globe and Mail*, Sept. 23, 2009, A8.

84. Richard Blackwell, "Top Court Redefines Obscenity," *Globe and Mail*, Dec. 22, 2005, A1; Jessica Leeder, "A New Measure of Decency," *Toronto Star*, Dec. 22, 2005, A1.

85. Jessica Leeder, "New Measure of Decency"; Richard Bastien, "Canada's Supreme Court Ruling on Group Sex Abandons Fundamental Tenets of Law and Legal Reasoning," Jan. 3, 2006 <http://www.canadianvalues.ca>.

86. Gudrun Schultz, "Only Harper Says His Gov't Would Address Swingers Club Ruling," *LifeSiteNews.com*, Jan. 10, 2006 <http://www.lifesite.net>.

87. Janet Epp Buckingham, EFC, letter to the Honourable Vic Toews, P.C., M.P., Minister of Justice, June 5, 2006.

FOUR
Anti-Gay Activism in the Age of Rights

1. Focus on the Family, "Marriage and Homosexuality: A Christian Response," 2003, 7.

2. Holy See, Congregation for the Doctrine of the Faith, "Letter to the Bishops of the Catholic Church on the Pastoral Care of Homosexual Persons," Oct. 1, 1986, 3; *Catechism of the Catholic Church*, Oct. 11, 1992, 2257, 2259.

3. Focus on the Family, "Marriage and Homosexuality," 8; emphasis added.

4. REAL Women of Canada, "A Voice for Canadian Women: REAL Women of Canada Position Papers," March 1994, 44; REAL Women of Canada, "President's Message," *REALity*, September-October 2003 <http://www.realwomenca.com>.

5. In 1984 the Board of Directors of the Nebraska Psychological Association, of which Cameron had been a member, passed a resolution formally disassociating the association from the representations and interpretations of scientific literature

contained in Cameron's writings and public statements. In 1986 the American Sociological Association condemned Cameron for what it described as his consistent misrepresentation of sociological research.

6. REAL Women of Canada, "A Voice for Canadian Women," 51. The paper cites, as the source, "Paul Cameron, William J. Playfair and Stephen Wellum, 'The Homosexual Lifespan," Family Research Institute Inc., Washington, D.C., 1992."

7. Paul Cameron, *Medical Consequences of What Homosexuals Do,* Family Research Institute, Colorado Springs, 1999, 3; Cameron, *Child Molestation and Homosexuality,* Family Research Institute, Colorado Springs, 1993, 1. Other Cameron pamphlets are *Violence and Homosexuality* and *What Causes Homosexual Desire and Can It Be Cured?*

8. REAL Women of Canada, "A Voice for Canadian Women," 51. The paper cites, as the source, "P. Cameron, W. Coburn Jr. et al., "Child Molestation and Homosexuality," *Psychological Reports,* 1986, 58, pp. 327–337." For the FRC, see Timothy J. Dailey, *The Connection between Homosexuality and Child Sexual Abuse,* in *Homosexuality and Children,* Family Policy, Volume No. 15, Issue No. 5, May 23, 2002, Family Research Council, Washington, D.C., 9.

9. REAL Women of Canada, "Laws Protecting Homosexuals or 'Sexual Orientation' Legislation: How It Will Affect Canadians," leaflet, 1986; Focus on the Family, "Homosexuality" <http://www.family.org>, and "Love Won Out" <http://www.lovewonout.com>.

10. EFC, "You Were Asking about Homosexuality?" leaflet, 1993.

11. National Association for Research & Therapy of Homosexuality, "NARTH's Purpose," 2004 <http://www.narth.com>; National Association for Research & Therapy of Homosexuality, "Our Track Record," and "What We Offer," 2004 <http://www.narth.com>. In Canada the websites of Focus on the Family, REAL Women of Canada, and Canada Family Action Coalition all provide links to the NARTH website.

12. "American Psychiatric Association Rebukes Reparative Therapy," American Psychiatric Association, news release, May 9, 2001.

13. American Psychological Association, "Answers to Your Questions for a Better Understanding of Sexual Orientation and Homosexuality" <http://www.apa.org>.

14. EFC, "You Were Asking about Homosexuality?"

15. Focus on the Family, "Love Won Out in Vancouver," May 2004 <http://www.fotf.ca>.

16. Focus on the Family, "Does Homosexuality Matter to You?" announcement for Love Won Out Conference, May 1, 2004, Vancouver, B.C. <http://www.fotf.ca>.

17. Exodus International, "Policy on Homosexuality" <http://www.exodus-international.org>; Exodus International, "Exodus Healing Statement" <http://www.exodus-international.org>.

18. EFC and New Direction for Life Ministries of Canada, "Church Leaders Connection: The Church and Sexual Orientation," brochure, June 2004.

19. Homosexuals Anonymous, "About HAFS," "Statement on the Healing of Homosexuals," and "The Fourteen Steps of HA" <http://members.aol.com/HAwebpage>; for HLI, see "Human-Life Talks Spur Tight Security at Abortion Clinics," *Globe and Mail,* April 17, 1995, C5; Courage, "Welcome to Courage!" and "Frequently Asked Questions (FAQ)" <http://couragerc.net>.

20. "Lawrence Rejects Law on Homosexual Rights," *Toronto Daily Star,* Sept. 17, 1971, 37; Donald W. McLeod, *Lesbian and Gay Liberation in Canada: A Selected Annotated Chronology,* 1964–1975 (Toronto: ECW Press/Homewood Books,1996), 79.

21. "'Homos and Perverts' Running NDP: Borowoski," *Winnipeg Tribune,* June 20, 1973, 12.

22. See, for instance, "Minister Criticized by Gays," *Vancouver Province*, Dec. 20, 1972, 7, and "Labour Minister Responds," *The Body Politic*, No. 7, 1973, concerning the NDP B.C. labour minister William King.

23. Tom Warner, *Never Going Back: A History of Queer Activism in Canada* (Toronto: University of Toronto Press, 2002).

24. Ibid.

25. Ontario Human Rights Code Review Committee, *Life Together*, Toronto, 1977, 9.

26. Warner, *Never Going Back*.

27. Claire Hoy, "The Limp Wrist Lobby," *Toronto Sun*, Nov. 2, 1977, 16.

28. Hudson Hilsden, Dec. 1, 1977 letter on Scarborough Gospel Temple letterhead, reproduced in advertisement of the Coalition for Gay Rights in Ontario, *The Body Politic*, February 1978, 5.

29. Warner, *Never Going Back*. For Bryant and the U.S. religious right, see Perry Deane Young, *God's Bullies: Power Politics and Religious Tyranny* (New York: Holt, Rinehart and Winston, 1982), 37.

30. "Eggleton: Artful Dodger," *The Body Politic*, October 1980, 9.

31. Chris Bearchell, "Strange Bedfellows," *The Body Politic*, February 1981.

32. Ed Jackson, "Ontario Human Rights 'Omission': CGRO at Code Review Hearings," *The Body Politic*, July-August 1981, 13.

33. *Canadian Churchman*, "A Role for the Church," October 1976, 4.

34. REAL Women of Canada, "Laws Protecting Homosexuals or 'Sexual Orientation' Legislation: How It Will Affect Canadians," leaflet, 1986; REAL Women of Canada, "A Voice for Canadian Women," 43.

35. Social Action Commission of the Evangelical Fellowship of Canada, "Uncharted Waters: An Examination of the Federal Government's Plan to Include 'Sexual Orientation' in the Human Rights Act of Canada," EFC, December 1986, 47; Brian C. Stiller, "Homosexual Rights and the Law," EFC, fundraising letter, February 1993.

36. REAL Women of Canada, "Laws Protecting Homosexuals."

37. EFC, "Protect Family Values," "Dear Friend," letter from Brian C. Stiller, Executive Director, January 1995.

38. Focus on the Family, "Marriage and Homosexuality," 4.

39. *The Holy Bible*, King James Version, Genesis, 3:16.

40. Holy See, "The Truth and Meaning of Sexuality Guidelines for Education within the Family," The Pontifical Council for the Family, Alfonso Card. Lopez Trujillo and Most Rev. Elio Sgreccia, Vatican City, Dec. 8, 1995, para. 59.

41. Focus on the Family, "Marriage and Homosexuality," 3.

42. The Social Action Commission of the Evangelical Fellowship of Canada, "Uncharted Waters," 2–3.

43. Coalition for Family Values, "Dear fellow Ontarian" letter, Oct. 4, 1986, Hudsen T. Hilsden, Chairman.

44. Coalition for Gay Rights in Ontario, "Toward Equality: A Publication of the Coalition for Gay Rights in Ontario," 1975.

45. Social Action Commission of the Evangelical Fellowship of Canada, "Uncharted Waters," 3.

46. REAL Women of Canada, "Laws Protecting Homosexuals."

47. Coalition for Family Values, "Dear Fellow Ontarian."

48. Government of Canada, "Minister of Justice Tables Progressive Measures for Equality and Social Justice," news release, March 4, 1986; John C. Crosbie and Geoffrey Stevens, *No Holds Barred: My Life in Politics* (Toronto: McClelland and Stewart, 1997), 272.

49. Geoffrey York, "Tory Politicians Form Family Compact," *Globe and Mail*, June 3, 1992, A1.

50. Coalition for Family Values, "Dear Fellow Ontarian." Members of the CFV included the Pentecostal Assemblies of Canada, Canadian Baptist Federation, Ontario Conference of Catholic Bishops, REAL Women of Canada, Canadian Organization of Small Business, National Citizens Coalition, and Christian Farmers Federation.

51. Matt Maychak, "Homosexual Rights Amendments Will Be Supported by Liberals," *Toronto Star*, Nov. 21, 1986, A12.

52. Robert Sheppard, "Ontario Liberals Consider Permitting Rare Free Vote on Homosexual Rights Bill," *Globe and Mail*, Nov. 5, 1986, A5; Cheryl Cornacchia, "Planned Bill to Protect Gays Is in Trouble, Churchman Says," *Globe and Mail*, Nov. 3, 1986, A13.

53. Matt Maychak, "Don't Duck Homosexual Rights Vote: Tory," *Toronto Star*, Nov. 27, 1986, A12; *Hansard*, Official Report of Debates Legislative Assembly of Ontario, Nov. 27, 1986.

54. Maychak, "Homosexual Rights Amendments Will Be Supported by Liberals."

55. Coalition for Gay Rights in Ontario and The Right to Privacy Committee, "Your Rights Are at Stake! Act Now," leaflet, 1986; William Clark, "Passage Urged of Homosexual Rights Bill," *Toronto Star*, Nov. 21, 1986, A12.

56. "United Church Backs Protection for Homosexuals," *Toronto Star*, Nov. 21, 1986, A12.

57. David Peterson, letter to Tom Warner, Jan. 17, 1987.

58. David Peterson, letter to Brian Stiller, executive director of EFC, quoted in "Uncharted Waters," 2–3.

59. Lynda Hurst, "Homosexuals See Rights Bill as Key to New Benefits," *Toronto Star*, Dec. 6, 1986, A1.

60. Dorothy Lipovenko, "A New Era for Ontario," *Globe and Mail*, Dec. 6, 1986, D2.

61. For more, see Ken Popert, "Gay Rights in the Yukon," *The Body Politic*, January 1986, 21.

62. Warner, *Never Going Back*, 201; Sharon Carstairs, *Not One of the Boys: A Woman, a Fighter, a Liberal with a Cause* (Toronto: Macmillan Canada, 1993), 109–10.

63. "Homosexuals in Saskatchewan Can't Adopt Children Says Schmidt," *Prince Albert Daily Herald*, Oct. 30, 1987, 13; "Denying Gays Right to Adopt May Violate Charter: Prof," *Saskatoon StarPhoenix*, Oct. 30, 1987, A3; Earl Fowler, "Employers Entitled to Reject Gays, Schmidt Claims," *Saskatoon StarPhoenix*, Oct. 31, 1987, A1; "Schmidt At It Again," *Perceptions*, Volume 7, Issue 4, May 31, 1989, 8.

64. "Schmidt's Critics Fear Retribution," *Saskatoon StarPhoenix*, Nov. 3, 1987, A3; "CHE Revitalized," *Perceptions*, Volume 7, Issue 4, May 31, 1989, 6; "Romanow has Difficulty," *Perceptions*, Vol. 8, Issue 8, Nov. 21, 1990, 11.

65. "Morality Campaign Fails," *Perceptions*, Vol. 9, Issue 7, Nov. 6, 1991, 8.

66. Murray Mandryk, "Homosexual Debate Strikes a Chord," *Leader-Post* (Regina), May 1, 1993, A4.

67. Mark Wyatt, "NDP Caucus Backs Plan on Rights Vote," *Leader-Post*, May 1, 1993, A4; Mark Wyatt, "Bill 38 May Be Amended," *Leader-Post*, May 4, 1993.

68. "Bill 38 Looks Harmless Enough. Why All the Fuss?" advertisement, *Leader-Post*, June 5, 1993, A8.

69. "Victory Near," *Perceptions*, Vol. 11, Issue 4, June 9, 1993, 11; "Saskatchewan Rights," *Perceptions*, Vol. 11, Issue 5, July 28, 1993, 11.

70. "Saskatchewan Rights," *Perceptions*, Vol. 11, Issue 5, July 28, 1993, 11.

71. *Haig v. Canada (Minister of Justice)*, [1992] 94 D.L.R. (4th) 1 (Ont.C.A.), 24.

72. Graham Fraser, "Rights Protection Extended to Gays," *Globe and Mail*, Dec. 10, 1992, A8; "Gay-Rights Bill Blasted as Betrayal of Equality," *Toronto Star*, Dec. 11, 1992, A14; Graham Fraser, "Bill Protects Gay and Lesbian Rights," *Globe and Mail*, Dec. 11, 1992,

A4; Geoffrey York, "Human-Rights Bill Appears Doomed," *Globe and Mail*, March 18, 1993, A5.

73. Brian Stiller, "Homosexual Rights and the Law," letter addressed "Dear Prayer Partner," EFC, February 1993.
74. Marc A. Morrison, "Grits Lobbied in Ottawa," *Xtra!*, Dec. 10, 1993, 13; "Discrimination Against Gays to be Forbidden by Law," *Globe and Mail*, Dec. 23, 1993, A5; Philip Hannon, "Prime Minister's Fears Delay Changes," *Xtra!*, Dec. 23, 1994, 1.
75. On Skoke, see Tu Thanh Ha, "Dissident Liberals Fight Bills on Gays," *Globe and Mail*, Sept. 28, 1994, A1; Tom Wappel, "Sexual Orientation," *Issues to Consider*, Nov. 16, 1994.
76. Sean Durkhan, "Reform Takes Stock," *Toronto Sun*, Oct. 10, 1994, 14.
77. Anne McIlroy, "Yalden Flunks Liberals on Gay Rights," *Globe and Mail*, March 20, 1996, A1.
78. Parliament of Canada, Bill C-33, *An Act to amend the Human Rights Act*, 45 Elizabeth II, Chapter 14; Anne McIlroy, "Liberals Introduce Gay-Rights Reform," *Globe and Mail*, April 30, 1996, A4.
79. The Coalition of Concerned Canadians, "Jean Chretien & Allan Rock vs. the Canadian Family," advertisement, *Globe and Mail*, May 7, 1996, A15.
80. Evidence, Standing Committee on Human Rights and the Status of Persons with Disabilities, Meeting No. 8, May 2, 1996; Evangelical Fellowship of Canada, "Submission to the Standing Committee on Human Rights and the Status of Persons with Disabilities on Bill C-33, *An Act to Amend the Canadian Human Rights Act*," May 2, 1996; Most Reverend Francis J. Spence, "Submission to the House of Commons Standing Committee on Human Rights and the Status of Disabled Persons by the Canadian Conference of Catholic Bishops concerning Bill C-33 and the Government's Proposal to Amend the Canadian Human Rights Act so as to Include Sexual Orientation as a Prohibited Ground of Discrimination, May 2, 1996," Canadian Conference of Catholic Bishops, 1996.
81. Evidence, Standing Committee on Human Rights and the Status of Persons with Disabilities, Meeting No. 8, May 2, 1996. The term "sexual orientation" was not defined in Bill C-33.
82. Ibid.
83. King's University College, "About King's" and "Statement of Faith" <http://www.kinsu.ab>; Lynn Iding, "Alta. Community to Aid Fired Gay Professor," *Rites*, April 1991, 7.
84. Matthew Hays, "Gay Man Challenges Alberta Government," *Xtra! XS*, July 1992, 15; "Vriend Goes to Court," *Perceptions*, Vol. 10, Issue 5, July 29, 1992, 10; "Commission Picketed," *Perceptions*, Vol. 9, Issue 4, June 12, 1991, 11.
85. EFC, *Factum* submitted to the Supreme Court of Canada, in *Vriend v. Alberta*, 1997. See also Scott Feschuk, "Alberta Tories in a Bind Over Gay-Rights Decision," *Globe and Mail*, April 14, 1994, A4; Jonathan Eaton, "Top Court to Rule on Job Rights for Gays," *Globe and Mail*, June 30, 1997, C3.
86. Ibid.
87. *Vriend v. Alberta* [1998], 156 DLR (4th) 385, SCC.
88. Canada Family Action Coalition, "It's Not Too Late! If Vriend Wins ... Who Loses?" advertisement, *Calgary Herald*, April 8, 1998, B3.
89. Brock Kecham, "Both Sides in Debate See Court Decision as Milestone," *Calgary Herald*, April 2, 1998, A2.
90. Canada's Civilized Majority and Choose Life Canada, "Canada's Supreme Court Has No Business Imposing 'Bathhouse Morality' on the Churches and in the Nation's Living-Rooms," advertisement, *Globe and Mail*, April 18, 1998, A17.

91. "Forces of Gay Ruling Bombard Klein," *Globe and Mail*, April 8, 1998, A4; Brian Laghi, "Rage Finds Its Voice in Alberta," *Globe and Mail*, April 11, 1998, A1; Steve Chase, "Klein Ponders Overruling Courts on Gay Rights," *Calgary Herald*, April 7, 1998, A1; Don Martin, "Barrage of Phone Calls Has Klein Starting to Waffle," *Calgary Herald*, April 7, 1998, A14.

92. "Klein Blasts Anti-Gay Campaign," *Calgary Herald*, April 8, 1998, A1.

93. David Vienneau, "Gay Hate Law Threatening to Split Liberals," *Toronto Star*, Nov. 22, 1994, A11; Philip Hannan "Hate-Crimes Bill Goes Through," *Xtra!*, June 23, 1995, 1; Svend Robinson, "Bill C-41 Passes," *Ottawa Inside Out*, July 1995.

94. REAL Women of Canada, "Phony Statistics By Homosexuals," *REALity*, March-April 1998 <http://www.realwomenca.com>; REAL Women of Canada, "The Truth about Hate Crimes," *REALity*, November-December 2000 <http://www.realwomenca.com>.

95. Douglas Victor Janoff, *Pink Blood: Homophobic Violence in Canada* (Toronto: University of Toronto Press, 2005), 124.

96. Catholic Civil Rights League, "Bill C-415 Seeks to Incriminate Public Expression of Moral Opposition to Homosexual Conduct," *CCRL Newsletter,* October 2002, Vol. 5 No 3, 8.

97. EFC, "Hate Propaganda," Oral Submission on Bill C-250, *An Act to amend the Criminal Code,*" May 13, 2003, 2.

98. Ibid., 3.

99. Frank Stirk, "Hate Crimes Bill Passes House of Commons, Heads to Senate," *Christian Week*, Oct. 14, 2003, Volume 17, Issue 15 <http://www.christianweek.org>.

100. Antonia Zerbisias, "Anti-Gay Preacher Threatens Vision TV," *Toronto Star*, July 17, 1995, C5.

101. Canadian Broadcast Standards Council, Prairie Regional Council, "CKRD re: Focus on the Family," Decision 96/97–0155, Dec. 16, 1997, 6; Canadian Broadcast Standards Council, "Vision TV re: an episode of *Power* Today," Decision 01/02–0617, Sept. 13, 2002, 1; Paul Gallant, "Demon Seed," *Xtra!*, Nov. 28, 2002, 14.

102. REAL Women of Canada, "Action Alert—Bill C-250" <http://www.realwomen.com>; Peter Stock, "What's Wrong with the Hate Crime Legislation?" *The Interim*, Aug. 5, 2002 <http://www.lifesite.net>; "Millions for Marriage," *Globe and Mail*, advertisement, Sept. 16, 2003, 10.

103. Free Dominion, "National Liberty Day Rally, April 17, 2004" <http://www.freedominion.ca>; "Two Sides Face Off on C-250," *To Be*, Vol. 3, No. 5, May 2004, 3.

104. Frank Stirk, "Christians Brace for Fall-Out under Newly Passed Hate-Crimes Law," *Christian Week*, June 8, 2004, Volume 18, Issue 06 <http://www.christianweek.org>; Catholic Civil Rights League, "Senate Passes Bill C-250—A Chill Is in the Air," press release, April 29, 2004.

FIVE
The Defence of Family and Marriage

1. John Wilson, "On Our Own Terms?" *Rites,* September 1989, 4.

2. Coalition for Lesbian and Gay Rights in Ontario, "A Message from Svend Robinson of Importance to All Lesbians and Gay Men," leaflet, 1989.

3. Coalition for Lesbian and Gay Rights in Ontario, "A Short History: 25th Anniversary Edition," 2000, 20.

4. Kathleen A. Lahey, *Are We 'Persons' Yet? Law and Sexuality in Canada* (Toronto: University of Toronto Press, 1999), 52.

5. Bruce MacDougall, *Queer Judgments: Homosexuality, Expression, and the Courts in Canada* (Toronto: University of Toronto Press, 2000), 123–129.

6. Dana Flavelle, "Wanted: Family Status," *Toronto Star*, July 27, 1990, B1; Sean Fine, "Homosexual Couples Denied Family Status," *Globe and Mail*, July 5, 1990, A1.

7. *Canada (Attorney General) v. Mossop*, [1993] 1 SCR 554; "What Exactly Is a Canadian Family?" extracts from the Feb. 25, 1993 judgment of the Supreme Court, *Globe and Mail*, March 2, 1993, A21.

8. *Anderson v. Luoma*, [1986], 50 RFL (2d) 126 (B.C. SC); *Andrews v. Minister of Health*, [1988], 64 OR (2d) 258 (HCJ).

9. David Vienneau, "Gay Couple Lose Court Bid for Pension," *Toronto Star*, Dec. 5, 1991, A13.

10. *Egan and Nesbit v. Canada*, [1995] 2 S.C.R. 513, 4–5.

11. Rory Leishman, "Judicial Imposition of 'Gay Rights,'" Canada Family Action Coalition <http://www.familyaction.org>; Most Reverend Francis J. Spence, "Submission to the House of Commons Standing Committee on Human Rights and the Status of Disabled Persons by the Canadian Conference of Catholic Bishops Concerning Bill C-33 and the Government's Proposal to Amend the Canadian Human Rights Act so as to Include Sexual Orientation as a Prohibited Ground of Discrimination," Canadian Conference of Catholic Bishops, May 2, 1996, 2.

12. Frances Lankin, Chair, Management Board of Cabinet, letter to Tom Warner, Coalition for Lesbian and Gay Rights in Ontario, Jan. 23, 1991.

13. Paula Todd, "NDP Faces Battle over Gay Rights," *Toronto Star*, Jan. 1, 1991, A1; Dayne Ogilvie, "Getting in a Family Way," *Xtra!*, Jan. 11, 1991, 1.

14. Bob Rae, *From Protest to Power: Personal Reflections on a Life in Politics* (Toronto: Viking, 1996), 250–53.

15. "Gays Fight for Legal Reforms," *Toronto Star*, Aug. 11, 1992, A13; Anita Elash, "Gays Occupy A-G's office," *Toronto Sun*, July 29, 1991, 20.

16. *Leshner v. The Queen*, [1992] 92 CLLC 16, 329 (Ont. Bd. of Inq.).

17. Jack Kapica, "Hampton Says He Won't Fight Ruling on Same-Sex Pensions," *Globe and Mail*, Sept. 29, 1992, A17.

18. Leslie Papp, "Same-Sex Couples to Get New Rights," *Toronto Star*, March 1, 1994, A3. See also Bill 45, Human Rights Code Amendment Act (Sexual Orientation), 1993; Lois Sweet, "Pulpit Power," *Toronto Star*, June 4, 1994, B1; Ontario, *Hansard*, Legislative Assembly of Ontario, Nov. 23, 1993; David Rayside, *On the Fringe: Gays and Lesbians in Politics* (Ithaca, N.Y.: Cornell University Press, 1998), 145.

19. Campaign for Equal Families, *Fact Sheet: Family*, leaflet, 1994; Craig McInnes and James Rusk, "Gay-Couples Bill Survives Vote," *Globe and Mail*, May 20, 1994, A1; Ed Jackson, "Evangelical Crusade against Legislation," *Xtra!*, May 27, 1994, 15; D'Arcy Jenish, "A Clash of Values," *Maclean's*, June 13, 1994, 10–11; Rayside, *On the Fringe*, 155–157. Bruce DeMara and Donna Jean MacKinnon, "Priests Renew Calls to Oppose Bill," *Toronto Star*, June 6, 1994, A10.

20. Bob Rae, *From Protest to Power*, 252.

21. Heather Bird, "Making Amends," *Toronto Sun*, June 9, 1994, 2; William Walker and Leslie Papp, "NDP Alters Same-Sex Bill," *Toronto Star*, June 9, 1994, A1; "Boyd Backs Off on Gay Spouses," *Globe and Mail*, June 9, 1994, A1; Heather Bird and James Wallace, "Retreat," *Toronto Sun*, June 9, 1994, 2.

22. Craig McInnes, Martin Mittelstaedt, and James Rusk, "Ontario Bill on Gay Rights Defeated," *Globe and Mail*, June 10, 1994, A1.

23. "B.C. Now Allows Gays to Apply for Adoption," *Toronto Star*, Feb. 17, 1995, A11; Cindy Filipenko, "BC Grits Slam Adoption," *Xtra!*, May 26, 1995, 12.

24. "B.C. Tables Same-Sex Legislation," *Globe and Mail*, June 6, 1997, A6; Richard Banner, "Queer Families Okay," *Angles*, August 1997, 01; "Church Decries Gay Spouses," *Globe*

and Mail, June 24, 1997, A4; Robert Matas, "Religious Leaders out to Scuttle B.C. Spousal Law," *Globe and Mail*, July 11, 1997, A10; Wendy Cox, "B.C. Bill a Boon to Gay Couples," *Globe and Mail*, July 16, 1997, A5.

25. Réal Ménard, "Québec and Gay Rights: A Long Road Toward Tolerance and Openness," *Icon* 73, November 1996, 73–74.

26. Sean Durkan, "Feds to Outlaw Gay Bias," *Toronto Sun*, March 16, 1994, 16; David Gamble, "Rock Knocks Same-Sex Bill," *Toronto Sun*, May 27, 1994; Jenish, "Clash of Values"; David Vienneau, "Couple Status Not an Issue, Rock Suggests," *Toronto Star*, May 31, 1995, A10.

27. "Feds Vote Down Spousal Recognition," *Xtra!,* Sept. 29, 1995, 20.

28. Rayside, *On the Fringe*; Warner, *Never Going Back*.

29. Bruce MacDougall, *Queer Judgments: Homosexuality, Expression and the Courts in Canada* (Toronto: University of Toronto Press, 2000).

30. *M v. H*, [1996], 27 OR (3d) 593, Ontario Court (General Division).

31. Interfaith Coalition on Marriage and Family, "Factum of the Interfaith Coalition, The Evangelical Fellowship of Canada, the Ontario Council of Sikhs, the Islamic Society of North America and Focus on the Family," to the Supreme Court of Canada, in *M v. H*, [1998], paras. 2, 3, 6.

32. Egale Canada, "M v. H: An EGALE Backgrounder," May 20, 1999 <http://www.egale.ca>; *M. v. H.,* [1999] 2 SCR 3.

33. *M. v. H.,* [1999] 2 SCR 3.

34. Ibid.

35. "Religious Leaders Condemn Ruling," *Toronto Star*, May 21, 1999, A28.

36. Aloysius Cardinal Ambrozic, Archbishop of Toronto, "Statement of Cardinal Ambrozic Concerning the Decision of the Supreme Court of Canada in *M. v. H.*," press release, May 20, 1999.

37. Legislative Assembly of Ontario, *Hansard*, Oct. 25, 1999.

38. Rory Leishman, "The Judicial Imposition of 'Gay' Rights," articles archives, Canada Family Action Coalition <http://www.familyaction.org>; Derek Rogusky, "The Impact of Bill 5: Ontario's Response to M. v. H.," research papers, Focus on the Family <http://www.fotf.ca>; C. Gwendolyn Landolt, "The Ontario Government and the Supreme Court of Canada," *REALity*, REAL Women of Canada, November–December 1999, article 10 <http://www.realwomenca.com>.

39. Valerie Lawton, "Same-Sex Legislation Is Expected This Week," *Toronto Star*, Feb. 8, 2000, A1.

40. Egale Canada, "EGALE Submissions to the House Of Commons Standing Committee on Justice and Human Rights Bill C-23: The Modernization of Benefits and Obligations Act," March 2000.

41. Evangelical Fellowship of Canada, "EFC Submits Brief re: Bill C-23 to Standing Committee on Justice and Human Rights," press release, March 1, 2000; EFC, "Submission to the Standing Committee on Justice and Human Rights on Bill C-23," March 2, 2000, 2; Canadian Conference of Catholic Bishops, "Submission by Canadian Conference of Catholic Bishops to the House of Commons Standing Committee on Justice and Human Rights on Bill C-23: Modernization of Benefits and Obligations," 2000, 2.

42. Toronto District Muslim Education Assembly, "Muslim Objection to Bill C-23 According to Islamic Law (Shar'ah) and Its Consequences for Society," submission to the Standing Committee on Justice and Human Rights, March 21, 2000, 3–5.

43. Egale Canada, "Egale Position Statement on Equal Marriage for Same-Sex Couples," January 2003.

44. The case later became merged with challenges of same-sex couples who sought to have their marriages legally recognized—cases that became known as *Halpern v. Canada (Attorney General)*. See also ch. 5, n54.

45. Elie Schuster, "Marriage Definition in Court," *The Interim*, December 2001 <http://www.theinterim.com>.

46. The Catholic Civil Rights League, "Ontario Divisional Ruling on Gay Marriage Creates Confusion," press release, July 12, 2002.

47. Egale Canada, "Ontario Court Releases Landmark Judgment: Same-Sex Couples Have Equal Right to Marry," press release, July 12, 2002; Egale Canada, "Quebec Court Rules: Opposite-Sex Definition of Marriage Unconstitutional," press release, Sept. 6, 2002.

48. Egale Canada, "Federal Government Arguments on Marriage an 'Insult to Canadians': Egale," press release, Sept. 16, 2002.

49. Darrel Reid and James C. Dobson, "Dear Friends," letter, Focus on the Family, "Do You Believe in Marriage?" March 2003 <http://www.fotf.ca>.

50. EFC, "EFC to Defend Marriage before Justice Committee," press release, Feb. 13, 2003 <http://www.evangelicalfellowship.ca>.

51. *Hendricks v. Quebec (Attorney General)*, [2002] J.Q. NO. 3816 (S.C.), Lamelin J., para. 164; translation provided by Egale.

52. *Ligue catholique pour les droits de l'homme c. Hendricks,* Court of Appeal, Canada, Province of Quebec, Montreal Registry No. 500–09–012719–027, J.J. Michel Robert C.J.Q, Paul-Arthur Gendreau J.A., Louise Mailhot J.A., France Thibault J.A., André Rochon J.A., March 19, 2004, para. 39; unofficial English translation.

53. *Barbeau v. British Columbia (Attorney General)*, 2003, BCCA 251.

54. *Halpern v. Canada (Attorney General)*, [2003–06–10] ONCA C39172; C39174.

55. REAL Women of Canada, "The Arrogance of the Courts," press release, June 10, 2003.

56. Nick Pron, "Gay Marriage Case Attacked," *Toronto Star*, June 17, 2003, B4; Derek Rogusky, "Marriage Is Debased," *Globe and Mail*, June 11, 2003, A19.

57. Canadian Alliance Party, "Declaration of Policy," May 2002 <http://www.canadianalliance.ca>.

58. William Walker,"Church Leaders Urged to Vote for Day," *Toronto Star*, June 6, 2000, A1.

59. Lloyd Mackey, "The Pilgrimage of Stephen Harper," Christianity.ca, 2005, <http://www.christianity.ca>; Irving Hexham, "Canadian Alliance Changes Leaders," *Christianity Today*, July 8, 2002, Vol. 46, No. 8, 15 <http://www.christianitytoday.com>.

60. Kim Lunman, "Ottawa Backs Gay Marriage," *Globe and Mail*, June 18, 2003, A1.

61. Daniel LeBlanc, "Ottawa Urges Brief Opposing Gay Unions," *Globe and Mail*, July 26, 2003, A5.

62. EFC, "Government Questions to Supreme Court Are Too Limited, Says the EFC," press release, July 17, 2003; Valerie Lawton, "Draft Law Defines Marriage as Union 'of Two Persons,'" *Toronto Star*, July 17, 2003, A6; Daniel LeBlanc, "Cauchon Pushes Same-Sex-Marriage Bill," *Globe and Mail*, July 18, 2003, A7; Campbell Clark, "Liberals Fear Issue Could Curtail Gains for Martin," *Globe and Mail*, Aug. 1, 2003, A4.

63. Letter from Canadian Conference of Catholic Bishops President Bishop Jacques Berthelet, C.S.V., to Prime Minister Jean Chrétien regarding Marriage and Same-Sex Unions, June 19, 2003; "Marriage and Same-Sex Unions," statement by the Permanent Council of the Canadian Conference of Catholic Bishops, Ottawa, June 19, 2003; Janice Tibbets, "Liberals Deeply Split over Gay Marriage, MPs Say," *National Post*, July 30, 2003, A6.

64. Campbell Clark and Kim Lunman, "48 Liberals Line Up Against Same-Sex," *Globe and Mail*, Aug. 8, 2003, A4.

65. Most Reverend Jacques Berthelet, C.S.V, President, the Canadian Conference of Catholic Bishops, "Marriage in the Present Day," Sept. 10, 2003; Jane Taber, "Catholic Church Lobbies against Letting Gays Wed," *Globe and Mail*, July 16, 2003, A4; Kin Lunman, "Priests Carrying Same-Sex Attack to Pulpit," *Globe and Mail*, Aug. 2, 2003, A1.
66. Tonda MacCharles, "Gay-Marriage Foes Plan Prayer Protests," *Toronto Star*, Sept. 3, 2003, A17; "Millions for Marriage: A Campaign to Defend the Traditional Definition of Marriage," and "Rally Declaration," Sanctity of Marriage.ca, 2003 <http://www.familyaction.org/sanctityofmarriage>.
67. LeBlanc, "Cauchon Pushes Same-Sex-Marriage Bill."
68. Dennis Bueckert, "Same-Sex Could Cost Grits, Goodale Says," *Globe and Mail*, Oct. 24, 2003, A6.
69. Egale Canada, "Religious Leaders from Diverse Faiths Speak Out in Favour of Equal Marriage Bill," press release, July 18, 2003.
70. Kim Lunman, "Priest Says He Must Keep Silent or Leave," *Globe and Mail*, Aug. 26, 2003, A8; Leslie Scrivener, 'Priest Shut Out over Views," *Toronto Star*, March 5, 2004, A3.
71. Egale Canada, "Egale and Other Groups Form 'Canadians for Equal Marriage,'" press release, Sept. 12, 2003; Egale Canada, "Launch of Nation-Wide Coalition in Support of Same-Sex Marriage and Canadian Values," media advisory, Sept. 14, 2003; Canadians for Equal Marriage, "Support of Same-Sex Marriage Growing," press release, Sept. 25, 2003.
72. EKOS Research Associates, "Public Attitudes toward Same-Sex Marriage," Nov. 10, 2002; Brian Laghi, "Gay Unions Split Country, Poll Finds," *Globe and Mail*, June 14, 2003, A10; Kim Lunman and Campbell Clark, "Ottawa Considers Testing Same-Sex Marriage Definition," *Globe and Mail*, Aug. 9, 2003, A1; Tom Blackwell, "Support for Gay Marriage at 31%," *National Post*, Dec. 3, 2003, A1; Margaret Philp, "Support for Same-Sex Marriage Still Split," *Globe and Mail*, Oct. 7, 2004, A4; Tonda MacCharles, "Canadians Split over Same-Sex Marriage," *Toronto Star*, Feb. 12, 2005, A1.
73. Campbell Clark, Brian Laghi, and Steven Chase, "Leaders' Last Push for Power," *Globe and Mail*, June 26, 2004, A1.
74. Interfaith Coalition on Marriage and Family (made up of the Islamic Society of North America, Catholic Civil Rights League, EFC), Association for Marriage and the Family in Ontario (made up of Focus on the Family and REAL Women), Canadian Conference of Catholic Bishops, Ontario Conference of Catholic Bishops, Church of Jesus Christ of Latter Day Saints, and Seventh-Day Adventist Church in Canada.
75. Interfaith Coalition on Marriage and Family, *Factum of the Interverner: The Interfaith Coalition on Marriage and Family*, to the Supreme Court of Canada, May 7, 2004; Canadian Conference of Catholic Bishops, "Summary of the Factum Filed on the Marriage Reference in the Supreme Court of Canada by the Canadian Conference of Catholic Bishops," May 11, 2004 <http://www.cccb.ca>.
76. Egale Canada, Metropolitan Community Church of Toronto, Canadian Coalition of Liberal Rabbis for Same-Sex Marriage, Foundation for Equal Families, Coalition pour le mariage civil des couples de même sexe, United Church of Canada, Canadian Unitarian Council, and the human rights commissions of Canada and in Manitoba and Ontario.
77. Canadian Civil Liberties Association, "News & Events 2004–2005," "Supreme Court Hears Same-Sex Marriage Case" <http://www.ccla.org/news/winter04–05_1.html>; British Columbia Civil Liberties Association, "BCCLA Intervenes in Same-Sex Marriage Reference," *The Democratic Commitment*, July 2004, Volume 38, Number 2, 4–5.
78. *Reference re: Same-Sex Marriage*, [2004] SCC 79.
79. Ibid.
80. Enshrine Marriage Canada, "Enshrine Marriage in the Constitution," press release, Dec. 8, 2004.

81. Catholic Civil Rights League, "CCRL Denounces SCC Decision in Marriage Reference," press release, Dec. 9, 2004.

82. Canada Family Action Coalition, "CFAC Calls for National Referendum on Marriage," news release, Dec. 9, 2004.

83. Evangelical Fellowship of Canada, "The Supreme Court on Redefining Marriage," press release, Dec. 10, 2004; Focus on the Family, "Supreme Court Indicates Government Is Not Obligated to Redefine Marriage," press release, Dec. 9, 2004.

84. Egale Canada, "Supreme Court Upholds Equal Marriage Legislation," press release, Dec. 9, 2004.

85. Canada Family Action Coalition, "CFAC Calls for National Referendum on Marriage," news release, Dec. 9, 2004; Focus on the Family, "Supreme Court Indicates Government Is Not Obligated to Redefine Marriage," press release, Dec. 9, 2004; REAL Women of Canada, "The Courts Do Not Represent Canadians," press release, Dec. 9, 2004; Brian Laghi, "Klein Pushes for Same-Sex Plebiscite," *Globe and Mail*, Dec. 11, 2004, A1; Campbell Clark, "PM Rejects Same-Sex Referendum," *Globe and Mail*, Dec. 13, 2004.

86. Sean Gordon, "Churches, Groups Wade In," *Toronto Star,* Feb. 2, 2005, A7; Tonda MacCharles, "The Battle Is Joined," *Toronto Star*, Feb. 5, 2005, F1.

87. F. B. Henry, Bishop of Calgary, "Pastoral Letter," Jan. 15–16, 2005, Catholic Civil Rights League <http://www.ccrl.ca/>.

88. Michael Valpy, "Block Gay Marriage, Catholics Tell Martin," *Globe and Mail*, Jan. 19, 2005, A1; Marc Cardinal Ouellet, Archbishop of Quebec and Primate of Canada, "Marriage and Society for a Free and Enlightened Vote in Parliament," Jan. 22, 2005.

89. MacCharles, "Battle Is Joined"; Focus on the Family, "I Can Usually See Both Sides of an Issue," advertisement, *Globe and Mail,* Feb. 12, 2005, A9; Focus on the Family, "Speaking of Marriage," advertisement, *Globe and Mail*, April 23, 2005, A.14.

90. Brian Laghi and Katherine Harding, "Martin Says Harper Lacks 'Courage' on Gay Marriage," *Globe and Mail*, Dec. 17, 2004, A1.

91. Gloria Galloway, "Harper's Use of Same-Sex Ads Questioned," *Globe and Mail*, Jan. 25, 2005, A4; Brian Laghi, Anthony Reinhart, and Roy McGregor, "Harper Uses Same-Sex to Tap into Ethnic Vote," *Globe and Mail*, Feb. 12, 2005, A1.

92. House of Commons, Evidence, Legislative Committee on Bill C-38, May 12, 2005, 1410; House of Commons, Evidence, Legislative Committee on Bill C-38, June 9, 2005, 1555.

93. Douglas Farrow, "Remarks to the Parliamentary Committee on The Civil Marriage Act (C-38)," June 7, 2005, 6.

94. Roy Beyer, Submission: "Bill C-38 Special Committee Hearings Presented by Roy Beyer, Operations Director," The Defend Marriage Coalition, 5.

95. Peter Kuitenbrouwer, "Faiths Unite vs. Same-Sex," *National Post*, May 24, 2005, A1.

96. Canada Family Action Coalition, "Immediate call for PRAYER Action Alert," June 24, 2005.

97. REAL Women of Canada, "Homosexual Editorial Confirms Effectiveness of Our Efforts," Alert, July 20, 2005 <http://www.realwomenca.com>; Evangelical Fellowship of Canada, "EFC Laments the Passage of Bill C-38, the Civil Marriage Act," press release, June 29, 2005; Canadian Conference of Catholic Bishops, "Comment by the President of the Canadian Conference of Catholic Bishops on the Passing of Bill C-38 by the House of Commons," June 28, 2005; Defend Marriage Coalition, "Dear Friends of Marriage," letter from Roy Beyer, Operations Director, June 30, 2005 <http://www.defendmarriage.ca>.

98. Canadian Conference of Catholic Bishops, "Comment by the Canadian Conference of Catholic Bishops on the Approval of Bill C-38, *An Act Respecting Certain Aspects of*

Legal Capacity for Marriage for Civil Purposes," July 20, 2005 <http://www.cccb.ca>; Douglas Farrow, "Professor Urges Canadians Not to Recognize Gay 'Marriage' Even If It Is 'Law,'" press release, July 12, 2005, LifeSiteNews.com; Canada Family Action Coalition, "Marriage Bill Railroaded Through Senate," news release, July 19, 2005.

99. Catholic Civil Rights League, "CCRL Predicts Numerous Rights' Challenges under Bill C-38," press release, June 28, 2005; REAL Women of Canada, "Liberal Government Will Meet Defeat within the Year," press release, June 29, 2005. See also Focus on the Family, "Marriage Matters: Message from the President about Marriage," June 2005, <http://marriagematters.ca>.

100. Brian Laghi, "Same-Sex Marriage Bill Must Stand, Majority Say," *Globe and Mail*, July 18, 2005, A1; "PEI Will Be Ninth Province to OK Same-Sex Marriage," *Globe and Mail*, July 7, 2005, A6.

101. Dawn Walton, "Klein Signals Truce over Gay Marriage," *Globe and Mail*, July 13, 2005, A1; "Alberta Issues Gay Marriage Licence," *Toronto Star*, July 22, 2005, A4.

SIX
Conflicting Rights and Clashing Values

1. Interfaith Coalition on Marriage and Family, "Factum of the Intervenor: The Interfaith Coalition on Marriage and the Family," filed in the Supreme Court of Canada, May 7, 2004, para. 43.

2. Lois Sweet, *God in the Classroom: The Controversial Issue of Religion in Canada's Schools* (Toronto: McCelland & Stewart, 1997).

3. Focus on the Family, "School Choice in Canada: What Are the Options?" June 2003 <http://www.fotf.ca/familyfacts>; EFC, "Education," Explore Social Issues <http://www.evangelicalfellowship.ca>; EFC, "Submission to the Special Joint Committee of the House of Commons and Senate Concerning the Amendment to Section 93 of the Constitution Act, 1867," Oct. 27, 1997.

4. EFC, "Room for All Reflections on Diverse Religious and Cultural Values in Education, A Discussion Paper," March 21, 2000.

5. Sweet, *God in the Classroom*, 19–37; Rick Haliechuk, "Public School Religion Classes Banned," *Toronto Star*, Jan. 31, 1990, A1.

6. Province of Quebec, "Religion in Secular Schools: A New Perspective for Québec," 1999, v, 20.

7. Province of Quebec, "Establishment of an Ethics and Religious Culture Program: Providing Future Direction for All Québec Youth," 2008.

8. Assembly of Quebec Catholic Bishops, "Statement from the Assembly of Quebec Catholic Bishops on the Ethics and Religious Cultural Program, March 17, 2008.

9. John Carpay, "Quebec's Parents Have Lost the Freedom to Choose," *Globe and Mail*, May 11, 2009, A11. The case seems destined to end up before the Supreme Court.

10. Coalition for Gay Rights in Ontario, "Toward Equality: The Homosexual Minority in Ontario," leaflet, 1977; Coalition for Gay Rights in Ontario, "Toward Equality: Gay Equality and the Schools," leaflet, 1977.

11. REAL Women of Canada, "Public Schools Are the Next Battleground over Homo-sexuality," *REALity*, September–October 2005 <http://www.realwomenca.com>.

12. Ibid.

13. EFC, "Next Steps: The EFC Comments to Supporters on the Redefinition of Marriage," press release, July 21, 2005; Canada Family Action Coalition, "CFAC Vows to Continue Defending Traditional Marriage," press release, June 2005.

14. Focus on the Family, "Help Restore Marriage, Church Leaders Urged," Oct. 14, 2005 <http://www.foft.ca>.

15. EFC, "Defending Marriage" <http://www.evangelicalfellowship.ca>; Focus on the Family, "Our Guiding Principles" <http://fotf.ca>; Canada Family Action Coalition, "About CFAC" <http://www.familyaction.org>

16. Holy See, "Charter of the Rights of the Family," Vatican City, Oct. 22, 1983.

17. *The Holy Bible*, Colossians, 3:20.

18. Joe Woodward, "The Protestants Tackle Another Reformation," *Alberta Report/ Western Report*, Vol. 23, Sept. 16, 1996, 32 <http://home.earthlink.net>; Alanna Mitchell, "School Trustees Create Storm over Gay Rights," *Globe and Mail*, March 7, 1997, A2; Victor Dwyer with Sandra Farran, "Education: Class Action: Fighting Homophobia at School," *Maclean's*, May 19, 1997, 52; "Intolerance Banned," *Perceptions*, March 12, 1997, 10. Some news stories have given the Calgary parents' rights group different names, such Parents' Choice Association (*Globe and Mail*) and Parents Response Association (*Xtra!*). However, the name most commonly used, including in the *Calgary Herald* and the social conservative media (LifeSiteNews.com), is Parents' Rights in Education.

19. Alanna Mitchell and Brian Laghi, "Calgary Board Bans Two Books," *Globe and Mail*, Nov. 20, 1997, A14; "Gay-Friendly Book Reinstated," *Globe and Mail*, Feb. 7, 1998, A8; "School Board Furore" *Perceptions*, Volume 17, Issue 3, April 21, 1999, 13; Eva Ferguson, "CBE Bans Book Dealing with Homosexuality," *Calgary Herald*, Feb. 7, 1998 <http://www.lifesitenews.com>.

20. "Declaration of Family Rights," Citizens Research Institute <http://www.machiavelli.com/cri>; "Brave New Schools," WorldNetDaily.com, April 14, 2003 <http://www.theologyweb.com>.

21. Dwyer with Farran, "Education"; Dave Cunningham, "On the March for B.C. families," *B.C. Report*, online edition, Nov. 24, 1997 <http://www.axionet.com>; "B.C. Ed Minister Takes Stand," PlanetOut.com, May 6, 1997 <http://www.planetout.com>.

22. British Columbia Parents and Teachers for Life, "Life Views about US" <http://www.bcptl.org>.

23. British Columbia Parents and Teachers for Life, "Parents' Directive Regarding the Education of Their Children"< http://www.bcptl.org>.

24. Hoddy Allan, "The Fight for the Minds of Children," *Xtra!*, Oct. 23, 1997, 18; Paul Sullivan, "Gay/Straight Clubs on the Planet Zirconium," *Globe and Mail*, March 16, 2000, A15; Caroline Alphonso, "Some Question Need for B.C. Teachers' New Resource Book on Homosexuality," *Globe and Mail*, Sept. 7, 2000, A3.

25. "Settlement Agreement Between Murray Corren and Peter Corren (Complainants) and Her Majesty the Queen in Right of the Province of British Columbia as Represented by the Ministry of Education," April 28, 2006; Janet Steffenhagen, "Gay Guarantee for Sex-Ed," *Vancouver Sun*, June 16, 2006 <http://www.canada.com>.

26. British Columbia Parents and Teachers for Life, "The Correns Settlement Agreement: How Did We Arrive at This Point and What Should Parents of Traditional Morality and Their Supporters Do About It?" <http://www.bcptl.org>; Chantal Eustace, "Gay Couple Has Too Much Say over Lessons: Petitioners," *Vancouver Sun*, Aug. 28, 2006 <http://www.canada.com>.

27. Jim Coggins, "High School Social Justice Course 'Propaganda,' Say Critics," *Canadian Christianity*, Sept. 13, 2007 <http://www.canadianchristianity.com>.

28. Jim Enos, Hamilton-Wentworth Family Action Council, "HWDSB Equity Policy Update," newsletter, February 2007 <http://www.hamiltonfamilyaction.org>; Richard Leitner, "Board Gay Equity Initiative under Fire," *Mountain News*, May 16, 2008 <http://www.hamiltonmountainnews.com>.

29. Legislative Assembly of Alberta, *Bill 44 Human Rights, Citizenship and Multiculturalism Amendment Act,* 2009; Katherine O'Neill, "Alberta Law to Expand Parents' Rights in Classroom 'Out of Left Field,'" *Globe and Mail,* May 29, 2009, A4.
30. Craig McInnes, "B.C. Board Bans Books on Gay Parents," *Globe and Mail,* May 6, 1997, A6; Celia Sankar, "School-Board Ban on Gay Books Reaches B.C. Supreme Court," *Globe and Mail,* June 30, 1998, A4.
31. Jane Armstrong, "B.C. Board Finds New Basis to Ban Books," *Globe and Mail,* June 14, 2003, A10; *Chamberlain v. Surrey School District No. 36,* [2002] SCC 86.
32. Egale Canada, "Supreme Court of Canada to Hear Surrey Book Banning Case," press release, June 11, 2002; B.C. Civil Liberties Association, "BCCLA Applauds the Supreme Court Decision to Overturn the Surrey Book Ban," press release, Dec. 20, 2002. The appellants in the case were Egale members James Chamberlain and Murray Warren (who later changed his surname to Corren), Rosamund Elwin, the author of *Asha's Mums,* Diane Willacott, a mother of two children attending a Surrey elementary school, Blaine Cook, a student in a Surrey secondary school, and Blaine's mother, Sue Cook.
33. EFC et al., "Factum of the Intervenors: The Evangelical Fellowship of Canada, The Archdiocese of Vancouver, The Catholic Civil Rights League and The Canadian Alliance for Social Justice and Family Values Association submitted to the Supreme Court of Canada," 2002, para. 13, 18, 19, 30, 34.
34. *Chamberlain v. Surrey School District No. 36,* [2002] SCC 86.
35. Catholic Civil Rights League, "Supreme Court of Canada Trumps Views of Trustees in Assessing the Use of Gay-Positive Materials for 5 and 6 Year Old Children," press release, Dec. 20, 2002; REAL Women of Canada, "An Analysis—Chamberlain vs. Surrey School Board Supreme Court Orders Homosexual Propaganda in BC Schools," *REALity,* January-February 2003 <http://www.realwomenca.com>; Canada Family Action Coalition, "Supreme Court Decision Offensive and Discriminatory," news release, Dec. 21, 2002.
36. Kirk Makin, "Schools Can't Ban Gay Books, Court Rules," *Globe and Mail,* Dec. 21, 2002, A1; Joel Dupuis, "Ban on Gay Books 'Unreasonable,'" *Xtra!,* Dec. 26, 2002, 11; B.C. Civil Liberties Association, "BCCLA Applauds the Supreme Court Decision to Overturn the Surrey Book Ban"; Egale Canada, "'Tolerance Is Always Age-Appropriate', Supreme Court Rules. Egale Canada Delighted at Victory for Diverse Families in the Classroom," media advisory, Dec. 20, 2002.
37. Jane Armstrong, "B.C. Board Finds New Basis to Ban Books," *Globe and Mail,* June 14, 2003, A10.
38. David Roger, "Evangelical Schools Ordered to Teach Darwin," *National Post,* Oct. 24, 2006 <http://www.nationalpost.com>; Caroline Alphonso and Rhéal Séguin, "Teach Darwin, Quebec Tells Evangelicals," *Globe and Mail,* Oct. 25, 2006, A6.
39. British Columbia, Alberta, and Manitoba provide varying degrees of tax-funded financial support. Saskatchewan provides funding only to Catholic schools and to a small group of historically designated private schools. The Northwest Territories funds only Catholic schools. The Yukon does not publicly fund religious schools but does give the Roman Catholic Church the right to select Catholic teachers and provide religious instruction in the schools. New Brunswick, Nova Scotia, and Prince Edward Island do not publicly fund denominational schools. In Ontario, only Catholic religious schools are publicly funded under a Constitutional guarantee provided in 1867. Quebec provides only partial funding of private schools. In Newfoundland, public funding is provided to denominational schools where numbers warrant it.

40. Michael McAteer, "Can Values Be Taught without Reference to Religious Principles?" *Toronto Star*, Feb. 17, 1990, M23. Members of the Multi-Faith Group consisted overwhelmingly of evangelical Protestants but also included Hindus, Muslims, Sikhs, Buddhists, and Native peoples.

41. *Adler v. Ontario*, [1996] 3 S.C.R. 609.

42. United Nations Human Rights Committee, "Views of the Human Rights Committee under Article 5, Paragraph 4, of the optional protocol to the International Covenant on Civil and Political Rights—Sixty-seventh Session—concerning Communication . No. 694/1996," Nov. 3, 1999, para. 10.6; Ron Csillag, "Ontario Snubs UN Ruling on School Funding," *The Canadian Jewish News*, Nov. 11, 1999 <http://www.cjnews.com>; Ontario Multi-Faith Coalition on Equity in Education and Evangelical Fellowship of Canada, Centre for Faith and Public Life, "Fairness In Funding, Submission on Equity in Funding for Religiously-based Schools," December 1999, 2–3.

43. Ian Urquhart, "Private Schools: How They Decided," *Toronto Star*, May 12, 2001, A1; Richard Mackie, "Tax Plan Aids Intolerance, Manners Says," *Globe and Mail,* Aug. 25, 2001, A8.

44. Richard Mackie, "Tax Credits Attacked for Promoting Division," *Globe and Mail*, July 5, 2002, A13; Ron Csillag, "Tax Break Taxes Religious Tolerance," *Toronto Star*, June 9, 2001, M18.

45. Debra Black, "Extend Faith-Based Funding, Group Says," *Toronto Star*, April 17, 2007, D6.

46. Ron Csillag, "Tory Wants to Reinstate Private School Tax Credit," *The Canadian Jewish News*, June 21, 2007 <http://www.cjnews.com>; Progressive Conservative Party of Ontario, "For a Better Ontario, Leadership Matters: The PC Party Plan for Ontario's Future," 2007, 10.

47. Robert Benzie, "McGuinty Rules Out School Vote," *Toronto Star*, Sept. 18, 2007, A13; Green Party of Ontario, "The Green Plan for Better—and Better Funded—Schools," Sept. 6, 2007.

48. Coalition for Lesbian and Gay Rights in Ontario, "Queer Issues Election 2007," leaflet, 2007; Canadian Civil Liberties Association, "Fostering a More Tolerant Society," advertisement, *Toronto Star*, Sept. 21, 2007, A17; Benzie, "McGuinty Rules Out School Vote"; Karen Howlett, "Voters Reject Faith-Based Education as McGuinty on Course for Minority, Poll Finds," *Globe and Mail*, Sept. 18, 2007; A1; Prithi Yelaja, "Minorities Tune Out Tory's Gospel," *Toronto Star*, Sept. 28, 2007, A16.

49. Judgment: Ontario Superior Court, Between George Smitherman in his capacity as litigation guardian of Marc Hall, Plaintiff, and Michael Powers and the Durham Catholic District School Board, Defendants," R. MacKinnon, J., May 10, 2002, Court File No. 12-CV-227705CM3; Stan Josey, "Gay Teen Plans Fight over Prom," *Toronto Star*, April 9, 2002, B1.

50. Coalition for Marc Hall, "Legal Factum for the Coalition for Marc Hall," May 6, 2002. The members of the Coalition in Support of Marc Hall included the Canadian AIDS Society, Egale Canada, Metropolitan Community Church of Toronto, Coalition for Lesbian and Gay Rights in Ontario, Canadian Auto Workers Union, Canadian Federation of Students, Ontario Federation of Labour, Public Service Alliance of Canada, Catholics for Free Choice, Challenge the Church, and Canadian Foundation for Children, Youth and the Law.

51. Judgment: Ontario Superior Court, Between George Smitherman and Michael Powers and the Durham Catholic District School Board.

52. Ibid.

53. Leslie Scrivener, "Gay Teen's Fight Wins Praise," *Toronto Star*, May 7, 2002, A19; Estanislao Oziewicz, "Supreme Court Challenge Looms," *Globe and Mail*, May 11, 2002, A10.

54. Durham Catholic District School Board, "Durham Catholic District School Board Responds to Court Ruling," press release, May 10, 2002.

55. Catholic Civil Rights League, "Ontario Court Intrudes into an 'Authentically Catholic Position,'" press release, May 10, 2002.

56. Supreme Court of Canada, *Trinity Western University v. British Columbia College of Teachers*, [2001] SCC 31.

57. Guy Safford, "We Won't Be Slaves to Political Correctness," *Globe and Mail*, Nov. 12, 2000, A23.

58. British Columbia Civil Liberties Association, "Factum of the Intervener: The B.C. Civil Liberties Association," June 19, 2000; EFC, "Factum of the Intervener," para. 30.

59. Supreme Court of Canada, *Trinity Western University v. British Columbia College of Teachers*.

60. ECP Centre, "About Chris Kempling Biography" <http://www.ecpcentre.org>; Christian Heritage Party, "Chris Kempling, Cariboo-Prince George," biography <http://www.chpelection.ca>; Christian Heritage Party, "Biblical Principles That Guide the Christian Heritage Party of Canada" <http://www.chp.ca>; Chris Kempling, *Challenging Homophobia in Schools: A Critical Review,* Dec. 31, 2000 <http://bcptl.org>.

61. "Rod Mickleburgh, "Teacher Suspended for Antigay Letters," *Globe and Mail*, April 23, 2003, A2; *Kempling v. The British Columbia College of Teachers*, [2004] BCSC 133.

62. REAL Women of Canada, "The Tyranny of the BC College of Teachers," *REALity*, March-April 2003 <http://www.realwomenca.com>; Catholic Civil Rights League, "League Urges Support for Christian Teacher," press release, Nov. 4, 2002.

63. *Kempling v. The British Columbia College of Teachers*.

64. Chris Kempling, letter to supporters, Feb. 4, 2004, Catholic Civil Rights League website <http://www.ccrl.ca>; Catholic Civil Rights League, "Kempling: Re-stating the Obvious," press release, Feb. 12, 2004 <http://www.ccrl.ca>; Ron Gray, "Chris Kempling: Our 'Canary in a Coal Mine,'" CHPS Speaks Out <http://www.chp.ca>.

65. Canadian Religious Freedom Alliance, "Factum of the Intervenor," Court of Appeal of British Columbia, 2004, 1–2.

66. *Kempling v. British Columbia College of Teachers*, [2005] BCCA 327.

67. EFC, "Kempling Decision Very Disappointing," press release, June 13, 2005; Catholic Civil Rights League, "CCRL Disappointed with Ruling in Kempling Case," press release, June 16, 2005; Robert Jason, "Kempling Statement on Supreme Decision," *christianity.ca*, January 2006, 004 <http://www.christianity.ca>.

68. *Ontario (Human Rights Commission) v. Brillinger*, [2002] CanLII 13799 (O.N. S.C.D.C.) (2002–12–11).

69. Ibid.

70. Canadian Religious Freedom Alliance, *Factum of the Intervenor, Canadian Religious Alliance*, Aug. 10, 2001, 4, 7, 10.

71. *Ontario (Human Rights Commission) v. Brillinger*.

72. Focus on the Family, "Christians Disagree over Brockie Court Decision"; EFC, "Court Opens Door to Right of Conscience," press release, June 17, 2003.

73. Catholic Civil Rights League, "Ontario Court Forces OHRC to Respect Religious and Conscience Rights, but Fails to Recognize Toronto Printer's Conscientious Objection," press release, June 18, 2002.

74. REAL Women of Canada, "Court's Mixed Message to Christian Printer Brockie," *REALity*, July-August 2002, article 8 <http://www.realwomenca.com>.

75. REAL Women of Canada, "Saskatchewan Human Rights Tribunal Bans the Bible," *REALity*, July-August 2001, article 7 <http://www.realwomenca.com>; Charles Moore, "Bible Declared Hate Literature," *Western Catholic Reporter*, July 2, 2001 <http://www.wcr.ab.cal>.

76. *Owens v. Saskatchewan (Human Rights Commission)*, [2002] SKQB 506. *Owens v. Saskatchewan (Human Rights Commission)*, [2006] SKCA 41.

77. Jason Warick, "Addict Turns into Activist," *Saskatoon StarPhoenix*, June 2, 2002 <http://www.recomnetwork.org>.

78. Saskatchewan Human Rights Tribunal, "In the matter of the *Saskatchewan Human Rights Code* and a complaint by Brendan Wallace of Regina, Saskatchewan, a complaint by James Komar, of Saskatoon, Saskatchewan, a complaint by Guy Taylor, Saskatoon, Saskatchewan, and a complaint by Kathy Hamre, of Regina, Saskatchewan against William G. Whatcott, Regina, Saskatchewan. Decision of the Saskatchewan Human Rights Tribunal," Chair: Anil K. Pandila, May 2, 2005, 1–4.

79. Ibid., 6.

80. Rory Leishman, "Homosexual Activism Threatens Freedom of Speech," *CatholicInsight.com*, July 25, 2005 <http://catholicinsight.com>.

81. "Activist Barred from Distributing 'Hateful' Materials," May 18, 2005, < http://www.fotf.ca>.

82. Hilary White, "Catholic Activist 'Banned for life' from Publicly Criticising Homosexuality," LifeSiteNews.com <http://www.lifesitenews.com>; Canadian Constitution Foundation, "Whatcott v. Saskatchewan Human Rights Tribunal" <http:///www.canadianconstitutionfoundation.ca>.

83. Canadian Civil Liberties Association, "Factum of the Intervenor, Canadian Civil Liberties Association," Sept. 8, 2008.

84. F. B. Henry, Bishop of Calgary, "Pastoral Letter," Jan. 15–16, 2005, Catholic Civil Rights League <http://www.ccrl.ca/>. See also"Catholic League Supports Bishop Henry in Human Rights Suit over Gay 'Marriage,'" LifeSiteNews.com, April 1, 2005 <http://www.lifesite.net>.

85. Stephen Boissoin, "Homosexual Agenda Wicked—Red Dear Advocate June 17, 2002," letter posted on Stephen Boissoin's website <http://www.stephenboissoin.com>; Dawn Walton, "Hearing Begins for Alberta Pastor Who Wrote Anti-Gay Letter," *Globe and Mail*, July 17, 2007, A5; Walton, "Letter Was God's Will, Not Hate, Former Pastor Says," *Globe and Mail*, July 18, 2007, A4; Alberta Human Rights Commission, "Darren Lund v. Stephen Boissoin and the Concerned Christian Coalition Inc.," Nov. 30, 2007.

86. *Boissoin v. Lund,* 2009 ABQB 592; Karen Selick, "Albertans Can Now Speak a Little Freer Than Before," *Globe and Mail*, Dec. 14, 2009, A17.

87. Canadian Civil Liberties Association, "Freedom of Expression and Human Rights," statement posted on the CCLA website <http://www.ccla.org>.

SEVEN
Faith, Politics, and the Transformation of Canada

1. Elisabeth Gidengil, André Blais, Richard Nadeau, and Neil Nevitte, "Making Sense of the Vote: The 2000 Canadian Election," a paper prepared for presentation at the Biennial Meeting of the Association for Canadian Studies in the United States (ACSUS), San Antonio, Texas, November 2001, 10; Aileen Van Ginkel, "Evangelical Beliefs and Practices: A Summary of the 2003 Ipsos-Red Survey Results," Evangelical Fellowship of Canada, December 2003.

2. Stephen Harper, "Rediscovering the Right Agenda," *Citizens Centre Report*, June 2003, 72–77.

3. Brian Laghi, "Public Spurning Politics, Poll Finds," *Globe and Mail*, Feb. 10, 2003, A4.

4. Canada Family Action Coalition, "Politicians Discuss Role of Faith in Politics," 2002 <http://www.familyaction.org>; Stuart Laidlaw, "Faith and the Left," *Toronto Star*, April 8, 2006, L1.

5. "Faith and Politics: Party Leaders Respond," *Faith Today*, January–February, 2006 <http://www.christianity.ca>.

6. Holy See, Congregation for the Doctrine of the Faith, "The Participation of Catholics in Political Life," Nov. 24, 2002, 2.

7. Catholic Civil Rights League, "The Laity and Political Affairs Position Paper No. 3," June 9, 2004, 2, emphasis added.

8. Bruce Clemenger, "Of Church, State and the Political Engagement of Evangelicals," June 2006 <http://www.christianity.ca>; Brian Rushfeldt, "How Individuals and Churches Can Make an Impact," Canada Family Action Coalition <http://www.familyaction.org>.

9. Murray Dobbin, *Preston Manning and the Reform Party* (Halifax: Goodread Biographies, Formac Publishing Company, 1992), 144–145; Sydney Sharpe and Don Braid, *Storming Babylon* (Toronto: Key Porter Books, 1992), 81–104, 125–148.

10. Brooke Jeffrey, *Hard Right Turn: The New Face of Neo-Conservatism in Canada* (Toronto: HarperCollins Publishers, 1999), 310–311.

11. Gordon Laird, "Inside the Little Town That Nurtured a Would-Be Prime Minister—and Some of the Most Notorious Hate-Mongers in Canada," *Now*, April 13–19, 2000, 18; William Walker, "Church Leaders Urged to Vote for Day," *Toronto Star*, June 6, 2000, A1; Paul Tuns, "Assessing the Pro-Life Credentials of Alliance Leadership Candidates," *The Interim*, May 2000 <http://www.theinterim.com>.

12. Brian Langhi, "Lobby Group Targets 'Progressive Policies' of Alliance-PC party," *Globe and Mail*, Nov. 6, 2003, A9.

13. Evangelical Missionary Church, Canada West Division, "Action Item—The New Social Conservative Caucus," Dec. 11, 2003 <http://www.emcwest.ca>.

14. CBC News, "Conservative MP Calls for Repeal of Hate Law," June 6, 2004 <http://www.cbc.ca>; Canoe cnews, "Conservative MP: Abortion Same as Terrorism," June 7, 2004 <http://cnews.canoe.ca>.

15. REAL Women of Canada, "Alert!!! Don't Let the Conservative Party Drift to the Left," Dec. 2, 2004 <http://www.realwomenca.com>; Gloria Galloway and Brian Laghi, "Harper Faces Split in Party," *Globe and Mail*, Feb. 4, 2005, A1.

16. Bill Curry, "Silence a Strategy for Success, MP Says," *Globe and Mail*, Feb. 3, 2006, A5; Gloria Galloway, "Christian Activists Capturing Tory Races," *Globe and Mail*, May 27, 2005, A1; Jeffrey Simpson, "Why Stephen Harper Is Going to Lose More Sleep," *Globe and Mail*, May 27, 2005, A19.

17. Gloria Galloway and Brian Laghi, "Harper Reopens Same-Sex Debate," *Globe and Mail*, Nov. 30, 2005, A1; Brian Laghi and Daniel Leblanc, "Harper Won't Use Opt-Out Clause on Same-Sex," *Globe and Mail*, Dec. 16, 2005, A1; Bill Curry, "Silence a Strategy for Success, MP Says," *Globe and Mail*, Feb. 3, 2006, A5.

18. Conservative Party of Canada, "Stand Up for Canada," Federal Election Platform 2006 <http://www.conservative.ca>; Campbell Clark, "Harper Warned on Same-Sex," *Globe and Mail*, Dec. 12, 2005, A6.

19. André Blais, Patrick Fournier, Elisabeth Gidengil, Neil Nevette, and Joanna Everitt, "Election 2006: How Big Were the Changes ... Really?" 2006 Canadian Election Study, York University, Toronto, January 2006.

20. Michael Valpy, Caroline Alphonso, and Rhéal Séguin, "Same-Sex Vote Likely to be Tight," *Globe and Mail*, Feb. 1, 2006, A1; Catholic Civil Rights League, "League Pledges to Work with New Government on Key Issues," press release, Jan. 24, 2006; EFC, "The Evangelical Fellowship of Canada Statement on Election 2006" <http://www.evangelicalfellowship.ca>; Michael Foust, "Canadian Christians Hopeful after Conservative Election Win," *Baptist Press*, Jan. 24, 2006 <http://www.bpnews.net>; Brian Rushfeldt, "The Enemy Is Not Done with Canada— But Neither is God!" *City Lights News*, March 2006 <http://www.familyaction.org>.

21. Marci McDonald, "Stephen Harper and the Theo-cons," *The Walrus*, Nov. 4, 2006, 8 <http://www.walrusmagazine.com>; Brian Laghi, "Social Conservatives to Sell Tory Daycare Plan," *Globe and Mail*, April 19, 2006, A1.

22. REAL Women of Canada, "Statement on Child Care," position papers <http://www.realwomenca.com>.

23. REAL Women of Canada, "Conservative Government Bringing Common Sense to Public Finances," press release, Sept. 26, 2006.

24. REAL Women of Canada, "Counter-Attack by Feminists," Alerts, Aug. 7, 2006 <http://www.realwomenca.com>; "12 Status of Women Offices Set to Close," *Toronto Star*, Nov. 30, 2006, A11.

25. "Harper Government Working to Silence Women," National Association of Women and the Law, press release, Sept. 20, 2007.

26. Gens Hellquist, fundraising letter, Canadian Rainbow Health Coalition, November 2007.

27. Gloria Galloway, "Ottawa Redirects AIDS Funds for Gates Initiative," *Globe and Mail*, Nov. 29, 2007, A1; Krishna Rau, "AIDS Funding under Attack," *Xtra!*, Dec. 6, 2007, 9.

28. Carolyn Abraham, "Critics Troubled by New Fertility Panel," *Globe and Mail*, Dec. 23, 2006, A1.

29. REAL Women of Canada, "The Sham of Revised Medical Technologies Bill," *REALity*, May–June 2002 <http://www.realwomenca.com>; Campaign Life Coalition, "'Fresh' Human Embryos to be Killed for Scientific Experimentation," media release, June 27, 2006.

30. EFC, "Response to Bill C-47," April 9, 1997, 1, 2; EFC, "Oral Presentation, Bill C-56—An Act Respecting Assisted Human Reproduction, June 13, 2002, 2.

31. Kirk Makin, "PM's Pick for Bench Draws Fire," *Globe and Mail*, Sept. 21, 2006, A5.

32. REAL Women of Canada, "Taxpayers Funding of Sexually Explicit and Violent Material," *REALity*, May-June 2008 <http://www.realwomenca.com>; Charles McVety, "We Don't Want to Pay for Porn," *The Canadian Times*, April 18, 2008 <http://www.canadiantimes.ca>.

33. Susan Noakes, "Bill C-10 and Canada's Film Industry," CBCnews.ca, April 10, 2008; Gayle MacDonald, "Harper Scraps Censorship Clause in Bill C-10," *Globe and Mail*, Oct. 7, 2008 <http://theglobeandmail.com>.

34. Harper, "Rediscovering the Right Agenda."

35. Tom Flanagan, *Harper's Team: Behind the Scenes in the Conservative Rise to Power* (Montreal & Kingston: McGill–Queen's University Press, 2007), 278, 279–80, 282.

36. Ibid., 282.

37. *Catholic Insight*, "Easter, Reform and Prime Minister Stephen Harper," editorial, March 3, 2008 <http://www.catholicinsight.com>.

38. "When Lobbyists Speak in Tongues," *Ottawa Citizen*, April 12, 2008 <http://www.canada.com>; Link Byfield, "A Dangerous Crack Is Spreading across the Conservative Party Windshield," Citizens Centre for Freedom and Democracy, Nov. 6, 2008 <http://www.familyaction.org>.

39. Ted Hewlett, "Social Conservatives Should Not Depend on Politicians to Spread Their Message—But Socially Conservative Politicians Should Stop Undercutting Their Base," 2008 <http://www.socialconservatives.ca>.
40. Paul Wells, "Harper's Canadian Revolution," *Maclean's*, Sept. 18, 2008 <http://www.macleans.ca>.
41. "Maclean's Interview: Jason Kenney," April 29, 2009, *Macleans.ca* <http://www2.macleans.ca>.
42. Citizenship and Immigration Canada, "Discover Canada: Rights and Responsibilities of Citizenship," 2009.
43. Dale Smith, "Evangelicals Get Top PMO Jobs after Shuffle," *Xtra!*, Feb. 19, 2009 <http://www.xtra.ca>; Jenn Ruddy, "Harper's New Speechwriter Is a Gay Rights Opponent," *Xtra!*, Oct. 21, 2009 <http://www.xtra.ca>; Linda Diebel, "Boom Times for PMO's God Squad," *Toronto Star*, Dec. 19, 2009, INI.
44. REAL Women of Canada, "President's Message," *REALity*, July/August 2009 <http://www.realwomenca.com>; Institute for Canadian Values, "Conservatives Announce New Program to Fund Sex Parades," rightthecourse.ca <http://www.canadianvalues.ca>; Joseph Ben-Ami, "$400,000 to Toronto Gay Pride Stimulant Too Far," June 24, 2009 <http://www.proudtobecanadian.ca>; Louise Elliott, "Ablonczy Punished for Giving Pride Parade Cash: Tory MP," CBC News, July 7, 2009 <http://www.cbc.ca>; Tonda MacCharles, "Ablonczy Finds Tory Support in Pride Controversy," thestar.com, July 10, 2009 <http://www.thestar.com>.
45. REAL Women of Canada, "The Silencing of the Conservative Voice in Canada," booklet, 2004.
46. Adam Daifallah, "Building a Conservative Canada—From the Ground Up," *National Post*, July 15, 2004, A18.
47. Paul Tuns, "Social Conservatism's Canadian Barriers," *Comment Magazine*, Dec. 2005, v. 251.6 <http://www.wrf.ca>.
48. "The State of the Canadian Church—Part III: Are Christians in Danger of Becoming a Persecuted Minority?" Canadianchristianity.com, December 2007 <http://www.canadianchristianity.com>.
49. David Ben-Ami, "Endorsements," "Christian Government—Timothy Bloedow—State vs. Church" <http://christiangovernment.ca>.
50. Richard Bastien, "Social Conservatives and the Harper Government," *C2C: Canada's Journal of Ideas*, "Reclaiming Compassion," Volume 3, Issue 4, Nov. 26, 2009 <http://www.c2cjournal.ca>.
51. Preston Manning, "Navigating the Faith/Political Interface," *C2C Canada's Journal of Ideas*, June 19, 2009 <http://www.c2cjournal.ca>.
52. Social Conservatives United, "Welcome to Our Site" <http://www.socon.ca>; *C2C Canada's Journal of Ideas*, "About Us" <http://www.c2cjournal.ca>.
53. Manning Centre for Building Democracy, "Our Vision" <http://www.manningcentre.ca>; Manning Centre for Building Democracy, "Projects" and "Faith Political Interface" <http://www.manningcentre.ca>; Manning Centre for Building Democracy, "Navigating the Faith Political Interface" <http://www.manningcentre.ca>.
54. *Democracy Talk*, "A Message from Preston Manning," Manning Centre for Building Democracy, May 2007.
55. "Address of His Holiness Benedict XVI to the Bishops of the Episcopal Conference of Canada-Ontario on the 'Ad Limina' Visit," Sept. 8, 2006.
56. Institute for Canadian Values, "Welcome" <http://www.canadianvalues.ca>.

57. Institute of Marriage and Family Canada, "Welcome," brochure
<http://www.imfcanada.org>; Marci McDonald, "Stephen Harper and the Theo-cons,"
The Walrus, Nov. 4, 2006, 11, 13.

58. Institute for the Study of Marriage, Law and Culture, "About the Institute"
<http://www.marriageinstitute.ca>.

59. Canadian Constitution Foundation, "About the Canadian Constitution Foundation"
<http://www.canadianconstitutionfoundation.ca>; Canadian Constitution
Foundation, "The Future of Freedom: Law and Liberty in Canadian Jurisprudence,"
leaflet for the Inaugural Conference of the Canadian Constitution Foundation, 2007.

60. REAL Women of Canada, "A Timely Organization of Lawyers—Faith and Freedom
Alliance," *REALity*, May/June 2009 <http://www.realwomenca.com>.

61. "Laurentian Leadership Centre," Trinity Western University <http://www.twu.ca;
https://www/twu.ca>.

62. *Canadian Christianity,* "The State of the Canadian Church—Part VI:
Those Pesky Moral, Social Issues," Canadianchristianity.com, Jan. 17, 2008
<http://www.canadianchristianity.com>; Richard Bastien, "Social Conservatives and
the Harper Government," *C2C: Canada's Journal of Ideas*, "Reclaiming Compassion,"
Volume 3, Issue 4, Nov. 26, 2009.

63. EFC, "Sample Letter to Our Constituents to Send to Parliamentarians," 2009
<http://www.evangelicalfellowship.ca>.

64. Harold Albrecht, "A Non-Partisan Triumph: M388 Passes Unanimously," press release,
Nov. 19, 2009.

65. Campaign Life Coalition, "12,000 March for Life in Ottawa: 4 x the 1999 Participation"
<http://www.campaignlifecoalition.com>; Campaign Life Coalition, "Campaign Life
Coalition Petition Drive Continues Due to Overwhelming Response"
<http://www.campaignlifecoalition.com>.

66. Alliance for Life Ontario, "Media Campaign," 2009 <http://www.allianceforlife.org>.

67. Bastien, "Social Conservatives and the Harper Government"; C. Gwendolyn Landolt,
"The Tragedy of No-Fault Divorce," *REALity*, March/April 2009
<http://www.realwomenca.com>.

68. Institute of Marriage and Family Canada, "Make Divorce Easier? Make Marriages
Stronger," press release, Dec. 17, 2009; Bastien, "Social Conservatives and the Harper
Government."

69. Bastien, "Social Conservatives and the Harper Government"; EFC, "Human Trafficking:
A Report on Modern Day Slavery in Canada," April 2009.

70. REAL Women of Canada, "Report by Professor Moon to Repeal S.13 of the CHRA," media
release, Nov. 26, 2008; Canada Family Action Coalition, "IMMORALITY an Ethos of
Human Rights Activists," May 1, 2008 <http://www.familyaction.org/>.

71. Tasha Kheiriddin and Adam Daifallah, *Rescuing Canada's Right: A Blueprint for a
Conservative Revolution* (Mississauga, Ont.: John Wiley & Sons Canada, 2005), 202.

72. Bastien, "Social Conservatives and the Harper Government."

INDEX

Ablonczy, Diane, 239
abortion, 25–64, 194, 249; access to, 9, 15, 32, 34, 36, 57–59, 216; condemnation of, 8, 10, 11, 13, 25, 26, 224, 226, 236; criminalization of, 27–28; decriminalization of, 7, 12, 14–15, 25, 29, 31, 246; early years of in Canada, 26–32; public funding of, 57–59; quickening and, 26–28; recriminalization of, 32, 39, 45, 46–49, 220, 245; remedicalization of, 47–48, 59, 62. *See also* pro-choice movement; pro-life movement
Abortion Caravan, 14, 34–36
abortion clinics, 42–46
Abortion Rights Coalition of Canada (ARCC), 59–62
abstinence education, 91
ACTRA, 234
Act Respecting Offences Against the Person, An, 28
Adler, Susie, 203
Adler v. Ontario, 203
affirmative action, 224
Agarwal, Rajan, 98–99
age of consent, 13, 86–93, 221, 227, 228
"age of protection" legislation, 91–92
age of rights, 20, 115–16, 118, 139, 158, 212
AIDS programs, 231
Alberta: abortion, 58, 255n78; Committee to End Tax-Funded Abortions, 58; Human Rights, Citizenship and Multiculturalism Act, 138, 198, 215, 219; imposition of morality, 135–39; Individual Rights Protection Act (IRPA), 135–36, 138; parents' rights, 198; same-sex relationships, 177, 186
Alberta Civil Society Association, 138
Alberta Court of Queen's Bench, 219
Alberta Federation of Women United for Families, 135, 137
Alberta Human Rights Commission, 219
Albrecht, Harold, 226, 246

Alliance Against Abortion (Winnipeg), 32, 39, 40, 43
Alliance for Life, 32, 35–36, 38, 43, 246
Ambrozic, Aloysius, 161, 173, 181
American Academy of Pediatrics, 107
American Association of Social Workers, 107
American Psychiatric Association (APA), 107
American Psychological Association, 107–8
Anderson, Penny, 150
Anglican Church of Canada, 115–16, 175; *Canadian Churchman*, 115–16
anti-abortion activism. *See* pro-life movement
anti-censorship, 69, 73, 75
anti-gay activism, 5, 12, 102–45
anti-pornography, 68–75; new politics of, 71
Ashraf, Mohammad, 203
Assembly of Quebec Catholic Bishops, 191
Assisted Human Reproduction Canada, 232
assisted suicide, decriminalization of, 245–46
Association des médecins du Québec pour le respect de la vie, 38
Association for Marriage and the Family, 165, 233, 269n74
Association for Social Knowledge, 15

Barbeau v. British Columbia (Attorney General), 166
Basford, Ron, 39
Bastien, Richard, 100, 241, 245, 246, 249
bawdy house laws, 93–94, 96–97, 99, 101
B.C. Civil Liberties Association (BCCLA), 85, 92, 94, 178, 199, 201, 208
B.C. Coalition for Marriage and Family, 165
B.C. College of Teachers, 208–10
B.C. Confederation of Parents Advisory Councils, 196
B.C. Court of Appeal, 81, 167, 169, 199
B.C. Ministry of Education, 197
B.C. Parents and Teachers for Life, 196–97, 209

B.C. Teachers' Federation, 195–96;
"Challenging Homophobia in the Schools,"
196
BEAVER (Better End All Vicious Erotic
Representation), 94
Bedford, Terri Jean, 98
Bell, Derek, 99
Bell, Sharon, 72
Ben-Ami, Joseph, 239, 241
Benedict XVI, Pope, 243–44
Bennett, William, 129
Benoit, Leon, 60–61
Bergen, John, 130
Beyer, Roy, 183
Beyond Borders, 89, 91
Big Brothers, 123
Bill and Melinda Gates Foundation, 231
bills, government: Bill C-10, 233–34; Bill C-22,
91–92; Bill C-23, 163–64; Bill C-33, 132–34;
Bill C-38, 182–87; Bill C-41, 139–40; Bill
C-43, 48; Bill C-54, 74–75; Bill C-114, 73–74;
Bill C-250, 141–44, 226; Bill C-384, 245; Bill
C-415, 141
Binns, Pat, 129
Birch, Joshua, 131
Bisson, Claude, 38
Blackett, Lindsay, 198
Blais, Pierre, 79, 132
Blakeney, Allan, 129
Bloc Québécois, 224
B'nai Brith Canada, 134
Boissoin, Stephen, 219, 244
Borovoy, Alan, 79
Borowski, Joe, 39–42, 43, 110
Borowski v. Canada (Attorney General), 41
Bouchard, Lucien, 157
Bourassa, Robert, 37
Bourne, Aleck, 29
Breitkreuz, Garry, 59
Brillinger, Ray, 213
British Columbia: abortion, 53–55, 58,
2556n78; Access to Abortion Services Act,
54; Adoption Act, 157; Family Maintenance
Reinforcement Act, 157; Family Relations
Act, 157; Human Rights Code, 199; same-
sex relationships, 157, 166–67, 177; School
Act, 199; sexual-orientation discrimination,
129, 137; Supreme Court, 150, 199, 208. *See
also under* B.C.
Brockie, Scott, 213–15, 217
Brown, David, 233

Bryant, Anita, 113, 115, 122
Buchanan, John, 128
Buckingham, Janet Epp, 88, 100, 214, 228
Butler, Donald, 76–78
Byfield, Link, 236

Calgary Board of Education, 195
Cameron, Paul, 105
Campaign for Equal Families, 155
Campaign Life Coalition, 33, 48, 52–53,
57–58, 59, 60, 233, 246; Borowski case, 40;
Civil Marriage Act, 182; Daigle case, 45;
The Interim, 63; Morgentaler Clinics, 50;
politics, 226; stem cell research, 232
Campbell, Donald, 128
Campbell, Gordon, 157
Campbell, Ken, 4, 153; *5 Years Rescuing at 'the
Gates of Hell,'* 51; gay and lesbian rights, 12,
111–15, 137, 156; Morgentaler, 44, 49–50;
rescue missions, 51–52, 55, 56; secularism, 17
Campbell, Kim, 46–47, 131–32
Campbell, Margaret, 114
Canada (Attorney General) v. Mossop, 150–51
Canada Family Action Coalition (CFAC),
12–13, 23; age of consent, 88–89, 227; child
pornography, 83, 91, 227; homosexuality,
137, 142, 152; human rights commissions,
247; politics, 222, 225; same-sex
relationships, 161, 169, 172, 173, 180, 185,
193; schools, 197
Canada's Civilized Majority, 12, 22, 137–38
Canadian Abortion Rights Action League
(CARAL), 36, 37, 42, 45, 46
Canadian Advisory Council on the Status of
Women, 46, 74
Canadian AIDS Society (CAS), 92, 274n50
Canadian Alliance (Canadian Reform
Conservative Alliance), 170, 221, 225
Canadian Alliance for Social Justice and
Family Values, 197, 199, 210
Canadian Association for Repeal of the
Abortion Law (CARAL), 15, 36
Canadian Association of Police Boards, 87
Canadian Association of University Teachers,
175
Canadian Baptist Federation, 263n50
Canadian Bill of Rights, 18, 38, 40
Canadian Broadcasting Corporation (CBC), 79
Canadian Broadcast Standards Council, 143
Canadian Civil Liberties Association
(CCLA): abortion, 38, 45; Bill C-10, 234;

Homosexuals Anonymous (HA), 109

Horgan, Philip, 166, 179–80, 185, 212, 228

Hoy, Claire, 112

Hudson, Natalie, 64

Hughes, Jim, 40, 53

Humanist Fellowship of Montreal, 30

Human Life International (HLI), 109

human rights, 13, 18, 24, 118, 192; for gays and
    lesbians, 11–12, 19, 35, 148, 220; legislation,
    110–12, 116, 118–19, 121, 124–35; same-sex
    marriage and, 177–78

human rights commissions, condemnation of,
    193, 214–15, 218–19, 238, 247

identity, 14; Catholic, 6; French, 6; national, 5

Imaging Excellence, 213

immigration laws, 224

immorality, 232, 248

"inclusive-accommodation approach," 159–61

Income Tax Act, 233

incrementalism, 234–39, 240, 248

indecency, legal definition of, 100–101

indoctrination, of children, 189, 192–93, 198

Infant Life Preservation Act, 29

Institute for Canadian Values, 239, 241, 244

Institute for the Study of Marriage, Law and
    Culture, 244

Institute of Marriage and Family Canada, 244

Integrity group, 134

Interchurch Committee on Pornography, 12,
    70, 74, 75

Interfaith Coalition on Marriage and the
    Family, 151, 159, 177, 189, 269n74

Interfaith Committee on Theological
    Concerns, 107

Interim, The, 144, 166

intolerance, 5, 156

Islam, 200. *See also* Muslims

Islamic Society of North America, 159, 165,
    203, 269n74

Janoff, Douglas Victor: *Pink Blood*, 141

Jantzen, Kyle, 22

Jeffrey, Brooke, 224

John XXIII, Pope, 7

John Paul II, Pope, 9

Judaism, 157, 200

judicial activism, 233

Kempling, Chris, 209–12

Kennedy, Helen, 238

Kenney, Jason, 222, 244

Kheiriddin, Tashha, 248

King's College (Edmonton), 135–36

Klein, Ralph, 58, 136, 138, 180, 186

Kopp, James, 255n68

Lacombe, Dany: *Blue Politics*, 68

Lahey, Kathleen, 148

Lalonde, Francine, 245

Lalonde, Marc, 33

Lamer, Antonio, 95

Landolt, Gwendolyn, 10, 80, 83, 85, 88, 150,
    162

Langan, David, 207, 214

Laurence, Lianne, 41

Law Commission of Canada, 229; *Beyond
    Conjugality*, 229

Law Reform Commission, 94

Lawrence, Allan, 110

Layton, Jack, 181

LEAF. *See* Women's Legal Education and
    Action Fund

League Against Homosexuals, 114

Leibovitch, Amy, 98

Leishman, Rory, 152, 162, 217–18

lesbian and gay liberation movement. *See* gays
    and lesbians

Leshner, Michael, 154

Lévesque, René, 39, 110

LifeCanada, 63

Life Together. *See* Ontario Human Rights Code
    Review Committee

Lipovenko, Dorothy, 127

Lobby for Inclusion of Sexual Orientation in
    the Human Rights Act (LISO), 128

Lundrigan, Paul, 175

Lutheran Church, 175

MacDougall, Bruce, 159

MacKinnon, Robert, 207

Maggie's. *See* Toronto Prostitutes' Community
    Service Project

Mainse, David, 11, 111

Making Space, Giving Voice, 197

Manitoba: abortion, 39–40, 59; Human Rights
    Commission, 269n76; sexual-orientation
    discrimination, 128

Manitoba Court of Appeal, 76

Manitoba League for Life, 43

Manners, Earl, 204

Manning, Ernest, 224